Studies on Pre-Capitalist
Modes of Production

Historical Materialism Book Series

The Historical Materialism Book Series is a major publishing initiative of the radical left. The capitalist crisis of the twenty-first century has been met by a resurgence of interest in critical Marxist theory. At the same time, the publishing institutions committed to Marxism have contracted markedly since the high point of the 1970s. The Historical Materialism Book Series is dedicated to addressing this situation by making available important works of Marxist theory. The aim of the series is to publish important theoretical contributions as the basis for vigorous intellectual debate and exchange on the left.

The peer-reviewed series publishes original monographs, translated texts, and reprints of classics across the bounds of academic disciplinary agendas and across the divisions of the left. The series is particularly concerned to encourage the internationalization of Marxist debate and aims to translate significant studies from beyond the English-speaking world.

For a full list of titles in the Historical Materialism Book Series
available in paperback from Haymarket Books, visit:
www.haymarketbooks.org/category/hm-series

Studies on Pre-Capitalist Modes of Production

Edited by
Laura da Graca
Andrea Zingarelli

Haymarket Books
Chicago, IL

First published in 2015 by Brill Academic Publishers, The Netherlands
© 2015 Koninklijke Brill NV, Leiden, The Netherlands

Published in paperback in 2016 by
Haymarket Books
P.O. Box 180165
Chicago, IL 60618
773-583-7884
www.haymarketbooks.org

ISBN: 978-1-60846-687-0

Trade distribution:
In the US, Consortium Book Sales, www.cbsd.com
In Canada, Publishers Group Canada, www.pgcbooks.ca
In the UK, Turnaround Publisher Services, www.turnaround-uk.com
In all other countries, Publishers Group Worldwide, www.pgw.com

Cover design by Jamie Kerry of Belle Étoile Studios and Ragina Johnson.

This book was published with the generous support of Lannan Foundation
and the Wallace Action Fund.

Printed in Canada by union labor.

10 9 8 7 6 5 4 3 2 1

Library of Congress Cataloging-in-Publication data is available.

Contents

Preface

United by common concerns, historians from Argentina and Great Britain have come together for this work. Mindful of interpretation, and drawing from the works of classical social history by Karl Marx and Max Weber, the authors share concepts and problems: modes of production, social formations, classes and status groups are some of the categories they bring to bear in order to elucidate the functioning, practices and transitions of pre-capitalist societies.

This circumstantial grouping has its own history. Let me begin with the larger group of Argentine historians, carriers of a tradition initiated early in the twentieth century and centred on medieval history, which evolved from the institutionalist positivism of Claudio Sánchez Albornoz to the social history that began with José Luis Romero around 1950. Studies by other scholars followed suit, notably the works of Reyna Pastor on medieval Castile and León, of Tulio Halperín Donghi on the rebellion of Valencian *moriscos* in modern times, and Ernesto Laclau's essays on the markets and the agrarian economy of the transition to capitalism. The pre-eminent scholar of ancient Eastern history was Abraham Rosenvasser, an Egyptologist who directed archeological expeditions in Nubia sponsored by UNESCO. The forward progression of this knowledge of pre-capitalist societies was hindered by successive dictatorships and the exiles and proscriptions they entailed. It was only after 1983 that democracy offered a more stable environment. The authors featured in this book reflect in part this evolution.

From its inception, Argentine social history found two essential sources of inspiration in the school of the *Annales* and in English Marxist historians, among others. At present, the French influence has become somewhat diluted, while the heirs of Hobsbawm and Thompson have held on to that tradition. Indeed, that ascendancy carries significant weight for those who persevere in classic social history, that is to say, for those interested in the relationship between past and present as illuminated by the analysis of economic and political structures as well as classes, their ideologies and their conflicts. This explains the presence of Chris Wickham and John Haldon in this book, two historians who absorbed this tradition directly from Rodney Hilton at the University of Birmingham.

The issues addressed by the Argentine scholars have been inspired to a large extent by Wickham's elaborations on peasant-based societies and Haldon's studies on tributary societies. Proposing questions to be researched is important but is far from being all in view of the disqualifying juncture we confront: one cannot comfortably pursue studies on classical social history if it is repeatedly alleged that the preoccupation with modes of production and transitions is outdated. Yet such is the atmosphere that has been created by fashionable scholars, and it imposes upon us solitary navigations against the tide. It is invaluably encouraging to know that great journeys of magellanic proportions through the great problems and comparisons of history are being undertaken from other harbours with greater historiographical visibility.

I would like to add two more points that are relevant to this discussion. Firstly, in this book we espouse the straightforward language style advocated by Marxist English historians in opposition to positivist history. For them, this syntax was a weapon in a battle that French Marxist historians did not engage in: fascinated by the *Annales*, French Marxist historians submitted meekly to phenomenological descriptions that never ceased to mesmerise them. Their language became filled with circumlocutions and euphemisms in an attempt to find, like the Scholastics, the nuance that would achieve concordance in discordant propositions. By contrast, English Marxism presented history and commitment without ambiguity: if classes struggle, it is called class struggle, and if a caliph extracts surpluses by force, it is called exploitation. This direct language that represents with clarity what is revealed by the analysis has exerted a healthy influence on the authors of this book.

The second point is that the reception of the arguments put forth by Wickham and Haldon was not devoid of criticism in Argentina. The concepts were taken up, at times they were partially accepted, other times corrections and changes were suggested and in other instances they were used as springboards to venture other possible answers. Indeed, when looked at in perspective, the picture does not show a one-way flow of ideas from the centre, that is to say, from the European nucleus into the Third World. The concept of tributary mode of production – of crucial importance in the works of Haldon and Wickham – was elaborated in the periphery by Samir Amin and later updated by Turkish historian Halil Berktay. English historians took it up once again, and from there the concept made its way back to the Third World. In 2004 the tributary mode of production was discussed in the review *Anales de Historia Antigua, Medieval y Moderna*, published by the University of Buenos Aires, with contributions by some of the authors who have worked on this book. This two-way street of intellectual exchange is one of the reasons why the concept is so rich, because balanced dialogue creates thought. This book reflects that exchange. The pluralist, democratic and leftist approach, far removed from the aristocratic elitism that has striven to colonise, reminds us that scientific thought and political ideas go hand in hand. We are dealing once more with the fundamentals of the classical social analysis that Eric Hobsbawn did in England and José Luis Romero recreated in Argentina.

Carlos Astarita

List of Contributors

Carlos Astarita
University of Buenos Aires – National University of La Plata
E-mail: carlos.astarita@gmail.com

Octavio Colombo
University of Buenos Aires
E-mail: octacolombo@hotmail.com

Carlos García Mac Gaw
National University of La Plata – University of Buenos Aires
E-mail: cgmacgaw@hotmail.com

Laura da Graca
National University of La Plata – University of Buenos Aires
E-mail: lauradagraca@gmail.com

John Haldon
Princeton University
E-mail: jhaldon@princeton.edu

Chris Wickham
University of Oxford
E-mail: chris.wickham@history.ox.ac.uk

Andrea Zingarelli
National University of La Plata
E-mail: azingarelli@gmail.com

Introduction to Studies on Pre-Capitalist Modes of Production: Debates, Controversies and Lines of Argument

Laura da Graca and Andrea Zingarelli

This book analyses a variety of historical problems related to pre-capitalist societies and explores both the concept and the range of modes of production arising from the writings of Marx and Engels[1] and subsequent Marxist elaborations. There are differing assessments of the Marxist tradition on pre-capitalist modes of production, which reflects the debate within historical materialism with regard to the potential or the inconsistencies of some of the categories proposed by Marx. The critique of these categories, or the perception that they are insufficient, has led to the elaboration of new concepts such as the domestic mode of production proposed by Claude Meillassoux aimed at the analysis of agrarian lineage societies,[2] Marshall Sahlins's homonymous concept covering hunter-gatherer societies,[3] or Chris Wickham's recently proposed peasant mode of production geared to the analysis of agrarian societies without systematic surplus extraction.[4] These categories attempt a more precise structural study of different types of societies that are usually bundled into the concept of the primitive communist mode. The latter is for many the only non-exploitative mode of production proposed by Marx, whose evolutionary variations would express transitional modes such as the ancient and Germanic modes; other perspectives consider these structures independently, which widens the scope of non-exploitative modes of production; in the case of the Germanic mode, the varying interpretations of its contents highlight either the communal or the private component.[5] The revision of the *Formen* has also given rise to an

---

1 Mainly, Marx and Engels 1965; Marx 1964, 1977a, 1977b and 1979. On the evolution of the ideas held by Marx and Engels regarding pre-capitalist societies and the successive reformulations starting with *The German Ideology* and up to writings subsequent to the *Formen*, see Godelier 1970, pp. 14–142.

2 Meillassoux 1991.

3 Sahlins 1972.

4 Wickham 2005, esp. pp. 535–50. The whole issue of the review *Historical Materialism: Research in Critical Marxist Theory*, volume 19(1), from 2011 is devoted to the analysis of this work.

5 The Germanic mode has been neglected according to Moseley and Wallerstein 1978. Maurice

intense debate on the viability of the concept of the Asiatic mode of production and its substitution for the tributary mode proposed by Samir Amin[6] and later re-elaborated by John Haldon as the universal mode of pre-capitalist class societies based on the extraction of rents or tribute, of which feudalism would be an institutional variant.[7] Another perspective emphasises the singularity of the feudal mode of production, characterised by its specific form of coercion and private appropriation of rents.[8] Moreover, the study of ancient societies has posed the problem of the evolution of the ancient mode toward exploitative forms;[9] this evolution would be expressed not only in the development of slavery in those societies – systematised in the concept of the slave mode of production – but also in the development of exploitation through taxation;[10] from this perspective, the exploitative phase of the ancient mode has been understood as a subtype of the tributary mode, considering in this case the centrality of taxation in contrast to the private extraction of rents.[11]

The most important debates and arguments regarding the mode of produc-tion and pre-capitalist modes of production took place between the 1960s and the 1980s, mainly in the 1970s, which witnessed a remarkable effort of compila-tion and publication in Latin America,[12] the joint work published by Harold Wolpe,[13] the work of systematisation by Barry Hindess and Paul Hirst[14] and

---

Bloch 2004, pp. 35 ff., remarks on the lack of relevance of the Germanic mode in Marxist studies, and he attributes it to the weakness of the sources used by Marx in his elaboration of the concept. Among others, Godelier 1964 considers the Germanic mode in its own terms; Macfarlane 2002 stresses the centrality of private property in the Germanic mode; however, Wickham 1994a, pp. 29–30 stresses the communal component.

6   Amin 1976.

7   Haldon 1993, and 1995.

8   Anderson 1979, pp. 402 ff.

9   On the ancient mode of production, see Hindess and Hirst 1975, pp. 79 ff.; on its evolution toward the appearance of classes, see Padgug 1975.

10   Haldon 1993, pp. 90 ff.

11   Wickham 1994a.

12   For example, in 1978 Gebran published a volume titled *Conceito de modo de produção* compiling earlier publications; see also Sempat Assadourian et al. 1973.

13   Wolpe 1980, with the participation of Banaji, Dupré and Rey, Lublinskaya, Meillassoux, Morris and Quijano Obregón.

14   Hindess and Hirst 1975 encompasses both the general concept of mode of production and the study of the concepts of primitive-communist, ancient, slave, feudal and Asiatic modes of production, without analysing concrete social formations; it is based on Marxist theory and attempts to avoid the generalisation into a series of historical societies in the sense of Weberian ideal types: Hindess and Hirst 1975, p. 2.

the joint discussions on the Asiatic, slave and feudal modes of production that we will discuss below. Discussions on the study of non-European societies in terms of mode of production and their articulation with other systems also developed during this period, especially after the work of Pierre-Philippe Rey, Harold Wolpe and Claude Meillassoux provided a framework for their analysis.[15] In subsequent decades, Marxist historians addressed specific aspects of the modes of production present in the writings of Marx and Engels, while abandoning in part the joint discussion and to some extent the comparative discussion of the concept of mode of production. At the same time, however, new modes of production not present in the original Marxist tradition were proposed. In that regard, among the works of the last few decades worthy of note are the joint publications on the concept of the tributary mode of production[16] and the work of Jairus Banaji on pre-capitalist modes familiar to the Marxist tradition such as the Asiatic mode and recently formulated ones such as the peasant mode.[17]

The notion of Asiatic mode of production is one of the most controversial ones in Marxist historiography.[18] This is due to its scant textual presence in Marxist writings and to the fact that it was associated both with ancient nascent states and with contemporary Eastern societies (such as India), which preserved the statism of the communities and had not yet experienced capitalism. In the Soviet Union during the 1930s, the issue of Asiatic stagnation was especially discussed (particularly with regard to China but clearly with Russia in mind), giving rise to the 'feudal interpretation' and the 'slavery interpretation'.[19] At that time, the notion of Asiatic mode of production was suppressed for political and academic purposes, and the notion became anti-Marxist. In subsequent decades, there were attempts to revive the notion such as Karl Wittfogel's *Oriental Despotism*,[20] which highlights the hydraulic character of societies and analyses despotism in bureaucratic-administrative terms, thus simplifying the problem of the Asiatic mode of production. For its part, the remarkable work of Childe does not reject the notion of Asiatic mode of production, and although his study on the origin of civilisation takes into account irrigation

---

15   See, for example, Harries 1985, Freund 1985, and Geschiere 1985; about Latin America, see
      Goodman 1977, Soiffer and Howe 1982, and Scott 1976.
16   Haldon et al. 1998, and Haldon and García Mac Gaw 2003.
17   Banaji 2010. This work collects thirty years' worth of essays and critical studies.
18   Krader 1975; Sawer 1977; O'Leary 1989, among others.
19   See Sofri 1969 and Dunn 1982.
20   Wittfogel 1981.

control, he considers it to be one among a number of other factors.[21] During the 1960s the notion of Asiatic mode of production was addressed once more in a more reflexive vein.[22] The debate is acknowledged as existing in English Marxist academic circles, in France, and also in the Soviet Union. The department of Asiatic and African studies of the Centre d'etudes et de recherches marxistes developed research on said notion, and *La Pensée* published various articles and a special booklet on the concept as it applies to the early class societies.[23] Eventually, the concept of Asiatic mode of production was revisited in studies on pre-Columbian America, black Africa and China, thus exceeding the original geographic nucleus formulated by Marx, which led to the proposal of other denominations such as communal-exploitative mode or despotic village mode.[24] At the same time, although Hobsbawm's 1964 introduction to the first English edition of the *Formen* does not address the Asiatic mode of production too thoroughly, it does posit that this mode disappeared from the systematic treatments in the later work of Engels (*Anti-Dühring* and *The Origins of the Family*) because he had changed his mind on the issue of primitive communities. He also suggests that later Marx and Engels had considered a historical stage of communal disintegration in which different types of dominant classes would have emerged.[25] This type of anti-Asiatic mode of production position is based on the fact that it ceased being included in the arguments found in the later works of Marx and Engels. Quite to the contrary, Maurice Godelier[26] picks up where Marx left off in the *Formen* when acknowledging the unity of contradictory elements in the exploitation of particular communities, village communities exhibiting the ultimate form of classless society, by a minority or superior community understood as a nascent form of class society. Godelier's proposal makes this structural contradiction viable and extends it to different societies. The combination between village communities and the state described by Marx in the *Formen* as Asiatic despotism is held by Samir Amin[27] among others – although this author proposes significant nuances and calls it the tributary mode – and by Guy Dhoquois,[28] for whom there would exist different degrees in the contradictions between productive forces and social relations of produc-

---

21   Childe 1936.
22   Also to reject it, as in Shapiro 1962, p. 284.
23   Ruiz Rodríguez 1979.
24   Chesneaux 1964.
25   Marx 1964, pp. 51–2.
26   Godelier 1971, 1978b.
27   Amin 1976.
28   Dhoquois 1971, pp. 67 ff.

tion, which would allow for distinct variants: the Asiatic mode of production, the sub-Asiatic mode of production, and the para-Asiatic mode of production.

A majority of the anti-Asiatic mode of production positions (Wickham, Anderson, Hindess and Hirst, Banaji)[29] underscore that the concept is invalid, especially the coexistence of self-sufficient village communities and a state[30] that has to contain classes, and they also question the absence of private property of land in some of the societies to which the concept is applied. According to Wickham,[31] the survival of the Asiatic states is due to the persisting dominance of the tributary mode in a variety of social formations in spite of the continuous weakening effected by feudal relations. On the other hand, Banaji's characterisation of Asiatic regimes[32] places them in the tributary rather than the feudal mode, but he establishes a difference between tax and rent and between European feudalism and the Asiatic systems. Hindess and Hirst,[33] as well as Anderson, emphasise that it is impossible to conceive that a state which imposes forms of production will not give rise to classes, although they focus their critique on the tax/rent couple, which would not correspond to an exploitative system of appropriation. On the other hand, those who hold the validity of the Asiatic mode of production, like Cardoso[34] or O'Leary,[35] are attached to Marx's postulates, even when they are critical, and they question the idea that Marx and Engels abandoned the notion of Asiatic mode of production in their later works.

The discussion surrounding the slave mode of production, which Stalin dogmatically held was a necessary stage in the development of societies, is focused on the problem of establishing the role of slavery as a relation of production and whether or not it constitutes the productive foundation of the societies in which we verify the existence of slaves.[36] Thus, the publications of the period

---

29   Wickham 1994b; Anderson 1979, esp. pp. 484 ff.; Hindess and Hirst 1975, esp. pp. 198 ff.; Banaji 2010, pp. 17 ff.

30   Thus postulated from its formulation in the *Formen* and in the article Marx wrote for the *New York Daily Tribune* in 1853, Marx 1979, pp. 125–9.

31   Wickham 1994b.

32   Banaji 2010.

33   Hindess and Hirst 1975.

34   Cardoso 1990.

35   O'Leary 1989.

36   Prieto et al. 1986, with translations of articles previously published in specialised publications: Petit 1972, Vittinghoff 1960, Sereni 1973b, Parain 1963, Guenther and Schrot 1953, among others. Giardina and Schiavone 1981 gathers the contributions of a colloquy celebrated at the Gramsci Institute in Pisa.

question the idea of the slave mode as the only analytical tool for the Greco-Latin world, highlighting the problem of the coexistence of slavery with other forms of exploitation and the study of the whole based on the concept of social formation.[37] The variety of occupations held by slaves also poses a problem for considering them as a class. The work of Ste. Croix is crucial for addressing these questions, since he understands class as the collective social expression of the fact of exploitation, and the slave mode of production as the dominant mode in ancient societies in that it is the pre-eminent manner in which the proprietary class extracts surplus. This criterion, rather than the manner in which product is obtained – in the ancient world it came mainly from subsistence peasants – is for the author what determines the dominance of a mode of production in a given social formation.[38] Perry Anderson also postulates the dominance of the slave mode of production in the Classical world (specifically, for Greece in the fifth and fourth centuries BC and Rome from the second century BC to the second century AD).[39] The concept of slave mode of production has been systematised by Hindess and Hirst, who assert its independent statute based on the theoretical possibility to identify productive forces and specific relations of production and of property, whose basic traits could be summarised as the total separation of direct producers from the means of production, the effective possession by non-producers of all the factors of production, the total dependence on non-producers for the launching of the productive process, the appropriation by non-producers of the totality of what is produced by slaves and the treatment of the latter as fixed capital, which explains the need to constantly supervise them and the predominance of simple cooperation. Hindess and Hirst distinguish the slave mode from the simple possession of slaves, seeing as the former implies that slave labour is the foundation of production, which presupposes the development of private property, exchange, and a necessary connection with specific superstructural aspects such as a legal form of slave property and ideological practices adapted to the contradiction implied by the situation of the slave as both a means of production and a direct producer. Although in theory the slave mode of production does not require the existence of other modes of production, the historical rule has been its

---

37   Parain et al. 1975 gathers contributions by Parain, Kolendo, Staerman, Annequin, Clavel-Lévêque and Favory, among others. See also *Marxism and the Classics*, special issue of *Arethusa*, a collection of articles expressing a general revalorisation of the *Formen*, especially Konstan 1975 and Padgug 1975.

38   Ste. Croix 1981.

39   Anderson 1996, pp. 18–28.

coexistence with other systems, as exemplified by the ancient world and the American case.[40] The articulation of slavery with other modes of production is an essential trait for Claude Meillassoux, who addresses the problem from the perspective of the social reproduction, relying partially on the societies that slaves hail from, a circumstance that increases the benefit of slaveholders and discourages breeding.[41] Lastly, the concept of slave mode has been discussed in the context of the debate over the transition to feudalism, which at one time centred on the causes of the decline of slavery, a question that stimulated discussions on the profitability of the system and the role of class struggle.[42] Nowadays the debate over the transition to feudalism has shifted to the issues surrounding social formation, which includes other forms of exploitation such as colonate and taxation, and the emergence of non-exploitative modes,[43] the conversion of slaves into tenants being only one of the shifts to consider in the study of the transition toward the full dominance of the feudal mode of production.

The concept of feudal mode of production became widespread with the pioneering work of Maurice Dobb and Eugene A. Kosminsky, who stream-lined its contents to the extraction of rent through legal-political means.[44] The debate around this concept, however, developed later. The most significant joint publication emerged from a colloquium on classical feudalism and the pre-colonial Maghreb with the participation of, among others, Charles Parain, Pierre Vilar and Renè Gallissot, which brought forth the idea of feudalism as a social formation whose nucleus is the feudal mode of production identified with a basic social relation that does not necessarily imply the presence of a fief;[45] from the consideration of the superstructure as a secondary element

---

40   Hindess and Hirst 1975, pp. 109–77, esp. pp. 125 ff.

41   Meillassoux reiterates this argument with regard to the articulation of capitalism with the domestic economies that provide temporary labourers whose reproduction is not entirely paid by capital; he understands the problem in terms of a transference of value from one mode of production to another: Meillassoux 1992, part II.

42   Bloch, Finley et al. 1975. Dockés 1982 is still a valuable reference in what pertains to the structure of the slave *villa* and the forms assumed by class struggle; on the persistence of the slave mode of production during the Middle Ages, see Bonnassie 1985, which also summarises the debate on the decline of slavery. For a study on slavery in America that questions the argument of low profitability, see Stampp 1956, ch. 9. A review of the debate over this and other issues related to the slave mode can be found in Cardoso 1973.

43   Wickham 1994a.

44   Dobb 1946, ch. 2, and Kosminsky 1956, preface.

45   Centre d'Études et de Recherches Marxistes 1972.

emerges the tendency to extend the concept of feudalism to extra-European societies that did not experience the political configuration derived from vassalage and fiefdom.[46] Contrary to this tendency, Perry Anderson asserts that the superstructural elements, to the extent that they shape the specific type of coercion required for the extraction of surplus, constitute not only an essential component of pre-capitalist modes of production but serve to distinguish them from one another. At the same time, in Anderson's view it is of crucial importance that only Western feudalism gave rise to capitalist relations, a circumstance he attributes to the fragmentation of sovereignty, which permitted the autonomous development of cities.[47] Chris Wickham questions this perspective, proposing instead an analysis of Eastern empires as social formations in which feudal rents and tax coexist; the persistence of states that control the aristocracy of proprietors would express the strength, rather than the stagnation, of 'Asiatic' type societies, which would in turn challenge the singularity of Western dynamism. Adding nuance to earlier statements, Wickham concludes that the private or public extraction of surplus from peasant producers does not substantiate the existence of different modes of production.[48] This tallies with the proposal to limit the coercive extraction of rent or tribute to just one mode of production, allowing its denomination as feudal or tributary to be a matter of terminology.[49] However, for some authors the study of tributary societies reveals the existence of singular structural features such as, among others, a state domination that preserves the cohesion of peasant communities, as opposed to the nature of the feudal relation, which presupposes the dissolution of those communities due to the extension of personal dependence. In this regard, Eduardo Manzano Moreno has posited the need for structural studies to consider not only the nucleus of the productive relation but also the specific form in which control over people and means of production is exerted.[50] In opposition to the universality of a feudal or tributary mode, other authors have asserted that historical contextualisation is central when it comes to modes of production[51] as well as the essential character of political elements and their

---

46   For example, for feudalism in Byzantium, see Ostrogorsky et al. 1974.

47   Anderson 1979, conclusions, and 1996, pp. 147–53 and pp. 182–96.

48   Wickham 1994b. Byres and Mukhia 1986 compiles contributions to the debate on the categorisation of Eastern forms as feudal. On this debate in the *Journal of Peasant Studies* see Bernstein and Byres 2001, pp. 9–10.

49   Wickham 2008, n. 5.

50   Manzano Moreno 1998.

51   Banaji 2010, pp. 183–5 and 212–14. Also Banaji 2011, pp. 111–12.

privatisation in the feudal mode of production, which creates the possibility of autonomous processes of accumulation.[52] Beyond this debate, the place of political forms in pre-capitalist societies has been underscored by Marxist theorists whose starting point is the absence of a split between the political and the economic spheres that characterises the period before the full dominance of the capital relation: Cesare Luporini, for example, notes the absence of economic mechanisms analogous to the productive reinvestment of surplus value, a circumstance that demands the constant recreation of political forms for the reproduction of the exploitative relation;[53] Georg Lukács stresses that legal-political elements are inseparable from the relations of production, which thwarts the development of class consciousness in pre-capitalist societies.[54]

The use of the term feudalism in reference to Eastern societies has been rejected by historians specialising in Muslim studies,[55] an opinion cited by Ludolf Kuchenbuch and Bernd Michael, who systematise the concept of feudal mode of production and circumscribe it to Western Europe.[56] With regard to the dynamics of the system, these authors subscribe to the scheme proposed by Guy Bois, which is based on a concept of feudal mode of production that assigns to small peasant production analytical pre-eminence over lordship.[57]

It is worth noting the controversy surrounding the transition from feudalism to capitalism initiated in the 1940s with the studies by Rodney Hilton, Eugene A. Kosminsky and Maurice Dobb, who take up Lenin's point that the enriched sectors of the peasantry – as they liberate themselves from serfdom – tend to become simple commodity producers and later turn into capitalists.[58] During the 1950s, Marxist authors focused on determining the changes that occurred during the fourteenth and fifteenth centuries. The debate zeroed in either on the primacy of endogenous factors such as the relation of exploitation and the development of peasant social differentiation – expressing the first road proposed by Marx ('the really revolutionary way') which is centred on the trans-

---

52   Monsalvo Antón 1986; Astarita 1994, and 2003.

53   Luporini 1981.

54   Lukács 1967.

55   Cahen 1963; Rodinson 1978, ch. 3; Guichard 1984; Manzano Moreno 1998; Chalmeta 1973;
      Barceló 1994.

56   Kuchenbuch and Michael 1977 refer to Cahen and Rodinson.

57   Bois 1984.

58   Hilton 1947; Dobb 1946, ch. 2; Kosminsky 1956.

formation of the economy of direct producers[59] – or, conversely, on influences that are external to the system, such as the actions of commercial capital,[60] a factor that some consider undermining and others perceive as functional to the reproduction of feudalism.[61] The debate was renewed in the 1970s with Robert Brenner's proposal, which, although initially meant to counter the approaches centred on demography and trade, nonetheless provided a new model for interpretation that was remarkably well received in Marxist academic circles. In opposition to British Marxist historians, Brenner rejects the protagonism of direct producers and small holdings, which he considers subject to rules of reproduction directed toward subsistence rather than profit maximisation; instead, in his view the agrarian transformation can be attributed to the large-scale leases promoted by the lord, the formation of which – an English singularity – Brenner attributes to the failure of the peasantry to consolidate its property rights; the author posits that the loss of direct access to subsistence brings about an economic behavioural pattern that is functional to the requirements of capitalist development.[62] Brenner combines the methodological individualism of liberalism with the Marxist tradition according to which the increase in productivity occurs in large holdings and presupposes a process of expropriation. Brenner's thesis has been questioned within the framework of other debates, such as the studies on the productivity of small and medium holdings,[63] on the

---

59   Dobb 1946, ch. 2.

60   Sweezy 1976. The Dobb-Sweezy debate influences the discussion on modes of production in Latin America, which counts among its central points the pre-eminence of the sphere of circulation versus the pre-eminence of the sphere of production and the idea of productive stagnation as an essential trait of feudalism as opposed to the dynamism of commercial capital; regarding this, see Laclau 1973.

61   Hilton 1985b insists on the non-revolutionary character of urban sectors of the population whose income depends on the success of seigneurial exploitation; the thesis is adopted by Kuchenbuch and Michael 1977.

62   Brenner 1976. Aston and Philpin 1985 collect the debate developed in *Past and Present* in the 1970s with the participation of authors who advocate the demographic approach. In Brenner 2000 the author brings his thesis outside of England; the dispossession from means of subsistence and the change in mentality are no longer related to class struggle but are related to a natural process of deterioration of the soil. Wood 1999, and Comninel 2000 follow Brenner's general scheme, although they refer to historical conditions specific to England in order to explain the formation of large properties.

63   For example, Allen 1992 questions the premise that attributes the increase in productivity to enclosures; instead, he detects a trend toward development in medium holdings that remain in the open field and are managed by yeomen. Hoffman 1996, ch. 4 and 5 also proves the possibility to increase productivity in small holdings.

conditions of transmission and possibility to expropriate the copyhold,[64] and in general by empirical evidence, which tempers the importance of seigneurial leases and reveals the ambivalent profiles of large farmers, who had emerged from the stratum of enriched peasants.[65]

In contrast with the idea – proposed by Marx in the *Formen* and further developed with various nuances by scholars of the transition to capitalism – that the relation of capital entails the dissolution of earlier forms of property,[66] the thesis put forward by Guy Bois, albeit incorporating elements that are extraneous to Marxist analysis, restates the terms of the problem by associating the emergence of capitalist relations to the laws governing the functioning of the feudal mode of production.[67] This matrix has been developed by authors who link the origin of the capital relation with specific traits of feudalism and its dynamic, which unfold independently of regular economic and demographic features.[68]

Lastly, the debate on the transition to capitalism has spawned works of synthesis that reflect either the different interpretations – Marxist and non-Marxist ones which we have not addressed in the present work – or the discussions surrounding all the stages of the process.[69]

---

64   This line of research, whose importance for English agrarian history had already been noted by Tawney 1912, pp. 287 ff., finds further development in the debate on the land market, a problem that includes the analysis of the legal conditions for land tenancy. Among others, Whittle 2000, pp. 74–84, and Hoyle 1990 question the view that copyhold could be easily expropriated.

65   In this respect Dyer 1994 offers a sufficient approach.

66   Brenner presents the more extreme formulation of this perspective, which appears in more nuanced forms among authors who advocate the gradual development of commodity production; there are differences among these latter authors too; Kosminsky, for example, has insisted that 'capitalist relations are gradually generated *within* the feudal mode of production', Kosminsky 1956, preface, p. xiii.

67   Bois 1984.

68   Astarita 2005, ch. 5, explains the emergence of wage-earners due to a number of factors inherent to the system, such as the seigneurial appropriation of space, a phenomenon derived from the forms of property; da Graca 2009 associates the conditions of possibility for social differentiation to specific structures of coercion that imply distinct degrees of peasant autonomy and seigneurial intervention.

69   Some useful references are Kaye 1984, which includes an analysis of the period addressed by Hobsbawm and Thompson; Wood 1999, in line with Brenner, and Rigby 1995, ch. 2 and 3; the author combines a didactic formulation of the problems under analysis with a disenchantment with Marxism, which at times undermines his perspectives.

Through the study of various problems, the contributions included in this book deal with the concepts of primitive-communist, Asiatic, Germanic, domestic, peasant, ancient, slave, tributary, ancient tributary, feudal and capitalist modes of production.

In general, the concept of mode of production is understood in the present work either as the social configuration corresponding to certain relations of production more or less associated to a certain development of productive forces (an aspect deemed to be less relevant or subordinated to relations of production), or as a combination of productive forces and relations of production which express themselves by means of property relations. Some authors derive modes of production from the relation of real appropriation or non-appropriation of the means of production by direct producers – which determines the basic form of surplus extraction – thus identifying modes of production with forms of labour exploitation, as in the perspectives held by Chris Wickham and John Haldon; the link of producers with the means of production as a central element for the categorisation of a mode of production – as posited by Marx in his writings on the evolution of land rent – supplies the basis for Carlos García Mac Gaw's questioning of the concept of slave mode of production as it has been used by historians. From the perspective of some of the authors who contributed to this book, property relations encompass the specific form of surplus appropriation, which results in a wider set of modes of production derived from the private or common appropriation of the conditions of production and the surplus. This approach, which follows the *Formen* more closely, attributes a differentiated dynamic to the mode of production. For example, Andrea Zingarelli underscores the collection of peasant rents by the state as a dominant mechanism and its imposition in pharaonic history; she posits that the state or state institutions (including religious institutions) are the main recipients of the surplus production of immediate producers: land rents are collected in the form of taxes. Thus, it is the state that confronts direct producers as a landowner, which results in the convergence of rent and tax, a question posed by Marx, and differentiates the Asiatic mode from other modes of production, because most of the property is in state hands (the superior community) and private property only exists as a secondary and non-pure form, and is even subordinated to state property in certain historical periods. Laura da Graca categorises the distinctions among different forms of property and the centrality of individual property, which she assigns to the Germanic mode of production. In her view, the peasant mode of production is to be understood in terms of the Germanic mode, applied to societies with a prevalence of allodial property and emancipation from kinship. The potential for social transformation brought about by the individual appropriation of the fruits of labour – explored by Marx and

Engels in various works[70] and analysed by scholars of the transition to capitalism[71] – is the condition of possibility for multiple developments that are not found in societies with other forms of property: from this perspective, Carlos Astarita links the origin of the medieval craftsman with the individual appropriation of the conditions of production, which is the common denominator both in the free peasant household of Germanic or peasant-based societies and of the household subject to rent under the feudal mode of production. In the contribution by Octavio Colombo, the feudal mode of production and the conditions it imposes on commodity production explain the inequivalence in the exchange whose functionality to processes of accumulation is also linked to the specific structure of property that allows for individual appropriation of benefits derived from the trade practices of wealthier villagers.

In most of the contributions, the analysis of one or more modes of production presupposes or implies the concept of social formation. The authors approach this concept with different criteria that have emerged from the debate over this analytical category within Marxist thought, which touches on the epistemological question related to the construction of the universal term. This debate – which deals with the problem of how to think a social whole – starts with the work of Lenin who, in the context of his controversy with Mikhailovsky's subjectivist interpretation (*What the 'Friends of the People' Are and How They Fight the Social-Democrats*), poses the question of what an economic-social formation consists of. Lenin understands this category as the set of relations of production in their natural historical development.[72] In view of the influence it exerted on later developments, Lenin's main contribution to the concept of social formation appears in *The Development of Capitalism in Russia*,[73] where he analyses the particular Russian social formation following the reform of 1861 with a view to characterising the social structure whose degree of differentiation is crucial in the definition of policies. The prevalence of capitalist relations in the country, empirically demonstrated by Lenin, implies the advance of commodity production over pre-existing forms, but also the partial validity of the latter forms; thus, the Russian social formation is a combination of different systems (capitalist relations, serfdom, communal structures) under the dominance of commodity production, which in turn tends to subordinate the other socio-productive structures by modifying their essential contents.

---

70   Marx 1964, pp. 75 ff., Marx 1989; Engels 1989, and 1987.
71   For example Kosminsky 1956, p. 207.
72   Lenin 1963, pp. 129–332.
73   Lenin 1964.

The social formation is thus understood as a hierarchical totality rather than a simple combination. As suggested by Christine Glucksmann, the modification of persisting structures implies a theory of transition, and therein lies Lenin's main contribution.[74] This conception rising from the analysis of the Russian economic-social regime is consistent with Lenin's earlier formulation according to which a social formation was the aggregate of all the relations of production in their processes of change; therefore, the concept of social formation is especially appropriate to the study of transitional social formations featuring a diversity of relations of production and social forces in a state of struggle, while it could be identified with the mode of production when said mode has full dominance.

Lenin's perspective is partially taken up by structuralism, which understands the social formation as the combination of modes of production in a specific articulation, with the dominant mode of production providing the general guidelines of the whole. This articulation presupposes superstructural elements – given that a social formation is a system of levels of the different modes of production, which are in turn integral systems of the various spheres (political, ideological, economic) – expressing the phenomenal aspect, the singularity of real societies. In the structuralist approach, the social formation, as a historically determined real-concrete object, is analytically distinct from the mode of production, considered as an abstract-formal object that does not exist in reality.[75] This approach is questioned by Emilio Sereni, for whom the relationship between mode of production and social formation does not imply different levels of abstraction: Sereni understands the social formation as the unity of the different spheres and the conditions for their development, that is to say, as the totality of structural and superstructural elements in their historical progression; the mode of production would only express the economic aspect of the social formation, which in turn comprises all other social relations; thus, the analysis of a social formation is no less susceptible to theorisation than the mode of production, or is not confined to the purely empirical plane.[76] Lenin's statements on the category of the social formation also provide a basis for this approach in that they suggest the inclusion of superstructural

---

74   Glucksmann 1973, pp. 167–75. This volume reproduces studies published in Italy (*Critica Marxista*) and France (*La Pensée*) in which the traditions established by Althusser and Gramsci are discussed in conjunction. See Starcenbaum 2011, pp. 45–6.

75   Poulantzas 1973, pp. 13–16, and 1975, pp. 21 ff.; Hindess and Hirst 1975, pp. 9 ff., esp. p. 15, and 1977; Althusser and Balibar 1970, pp. 108 ff.

76   Sereni 1973a.

aspects and the idea of dynamism: in his review of the use of the expression in the work of Marx, Lenin refers to the social formation as a 'living thing' – therefore, a changing thing – in which the relations of production are the 'skeleton' that the analysis has to fill in with other components through the study of the superstructure and the 'actual social manifestation of class antagonism'.[77]

In line with Sereni's arguments questioning the structuralist approach, the debate on the concept of social formation involves a critique of the identification of the categories of historical materialism with different levels of abstraction. Faced with this trend, some authors enhance the role of the conceptualisation of the mode of production as an empirically identifiable structure that must be developed through analysis rather than reduced to its essence; from this point of view, the social formation considered as a combination of structures is equally susceptible to theorisation.[78] Another side of the debate suggests that the relationship between mode of production and social formation corresponds to the model and to specific historical manifestations respectively, and that the model should be understood as an elaboration for the purposes of interpretation, as Luporini puts it.[79] Thus, for example, the development of the concept of capitalist mode of production as it appears in *Capital* – which Marx refers to as an 'ideal average'[80] – should guide the study of other societies, such as the Russian social formation, where it will confront empirical variations; the confrontation is possible because the model expresses the real and develops laws that govern its functioning; in this way the variants of the case in point can contribute to a reformulation or an enrichment of the theory, as in the case of the conditions for the genesis of capitalist relations, which according to Lenin's study on Russia would not entail the total dispossession of the means of production as had been posited by Marx starting with his study on England.[81] According to Luporini, Lenin's work is an example of this approach to theory, which Lenin summed up in his statement that *Capital* cannot be regarded 'as anything more than an explanation of a particular social-economic formation', and never 'as some universally compulsory philosophical scheme of history'.[82]

77   Lenin 1963.
78   Dhoquois 1973; Herzog 1973.
79   Luporini 1973a and 1973b; Labica 1973.
80   Regarding the meaning of this expression used by Marx, see Althusser's observations interpreting the 'ideal average' as a concept of the real rather than an abstract or empirical average in Althusser and Balibar 1970, Appendix: On the 'Ideal Average' and the forms of transition.
81   Lenin 1964.
82   Lenin 1963.

To the extent that the model is conceived of or constructed as an ideal type in the Weberian sense instead of an 'ideal average' that can be identified with the deep inquiry into a particular case, it is not being confronted with eventual variants but with the complexity of the real. In this book, the above perspective is developed in John Haldon's contribution, which posits that a mode of production is an ideal type informing an essential nucleus that is common to a number of societies and constituted by a combination of relations of production and productive forces. The concept only illuminates the form of appropriating the surplus, not its specific mechanisms, which would correspond to the sphere of the social formation understood as the specific historical configuration of a specific mode of production where all the elements of the superstructure concur. This perspective affects the theory of social transformations because institutional forms determine the concrete manners of historical change, while the mode of production can only indicate the potential for this change to occur. Chris Wickham also addresses the levels of abstraction: the peasant mode, like every other mode of production, is for him an ideal type that appears in real societies in combination with other modes of production, which are understood on principle not as a set of determinations but as an essential nucleus of relations of production. In this case, he focuses on demonstrating the dominance of the peasant mode in social formations with developed aristocracies such as Norway; this dominance (as it is posited in the structuralist approach) expresses itself mainly in political practices, which, in the case analysed by the author, correspond to the basic guidelines of a peasant society. In a dissenting view, Laura da Graca systematises the concept of mode of production as a structure of reality, which allows for the consideration of a specific dynamic combining evolutionary trends derived from the form of property and social functioning; in contrast to Wickham's example, da Graca analyses a social formation dominated by feudalism; in line with Lenin's general argument, this dominance alters the contents of the other existing modes of production, which tend to become denaturalised. According to this perspective, a theory of social formation can be approached in terms of the subordination mechanisms of the dominant mode of production (as suggested by Godelier for other social formations).[83]

Carlos García Mac Gaw's contribution proves that the centrality of the concept of social formation extends beyond the analysis of transitional societies. The author provides examples of the variety of relations of production in which slaves participated in the Roman economy around the time of the Latin agro-

---

83   Godelier 1973b.

nomists; this adds nuance to the relevance of the concept of slave mode of production in the characterisation of the whole and of its main socio-productive structure, the *villa*, inasmuch as this mode subsumes unto itself different relations of production; in his view, the slave mode of production (understood as only one relation of production, that in which the slave has no control over the productive process or its reproduction) cannot exist in history but in combination with other modes of production, which entails thinking of the social formation as a combination of structures. As an element of comparison between social formations, García Mac Gaw enhances the role of the articulation between modes of production (the subordination of slavery to central capitalism in the American case, and to the ancient tributary mode of production in the Roman case).

In his first formulations of the concept of social formation, Lenin's main goal was not to define an analytic category but to restore the pre-eminence of relations of production in the analysis of the historical process. The contributions by Carlos Astarita and Octavio Colombo show that this is not just a statement. Astarita's study explains the origin of trade specialisation as deriving from the relations of production and productive forces that characterise the period before the full configuration of the feudal mode, a period that must be understood as a social formation in which various structures coexisted, some in a nascent state and others trending toward dissolution, such as slavery; the trade – initially associated to the instruction of domestic slaves – finds an environment that favours its development in the households where fugitive slaves find shelter, and later in the holdings where they settle as rent-payers; this trajectory illustrates the formation of new social relations derived from already existing ones, whose potential becomes apparent in the analysis of the whole. Colombo's study assesses the functioning of the law of value in the context of social relations and productive forces, whose hierarchy in the analysis is given by the subordination of simple commodity production to a dominant mode of production, in this case, to feudalism; the mode of production provides the conditions in which exchange occurs, hindering the adaptation of price to value.

This book analyses historical processes that involve the problems posed by the transition from one mode of production to another, and most of the contributions address the problem of social transformation. García Mac Gaw detects an early trend toward indirect exploitation in the spread of the *servus quasi colonus*; according to Astarita, the same trend contributes to the fixation and development of trades in medieval times (and it also reflects the survival of slavery). The essays by Chris Wickham and Laura da Graca attempt to explain the transformation of peasant societies and the emergence or expansion of feudal relations; Wickham attributes this process to the accumulation of lands;

da Graca relates it to the ability to dispose of property and the gradual alteration of the contents of social practice which nonetheless maintain the appearance of reciprocity. John Haldon's contribution also addresses this problem when – among other examples related to the place of ideology in social reproduction – he cites the belief systems that enable surplus extraction, which reflects the functioning of said systems as relations of production. Haldon questions the explanation that attributes structural transformation to the development of productive forces, to which he assigns a secondary role; to wit, he offers the example of Western Europe during the third and eighth centuries, where the development of techniques or patterns of consumption did not beget alterations in the relations of production. Although they do not deal explicitly with the effect of productive forces on relations of production, the contributions by Astarita and Colombo imply an approach to this problem from a different angle: Astarita stresses the qualitative aspect of the analysis of productive forces such as the creative skill of the craftsman, whose conditions for development are linked to the process of building new social relations; in Colombo's argument, the features of the productive forces determine the non-functioning of the law of value, which in turn favours the emergence of capitalist relations.

The different contributions are arranged according to an approximate chronological order and address the following periods: in the first chapter, Andrea Zingarelli focuses her argument on ancient Egypt; in the second chapter, Carlos García Mac Gaw addresses the case of the Roman late Republic and the Empire, complementing it with references to the Brazilian Northeast and the American South during the nineteenth century. In the third chapter, Carlos Astarita analyses documents of the Roman-Germanic kingdoms as well as Castile and León between the ninth and eleventh centuries, adding comparative references to nomadic pastoral societies, ancient eastern societies, primitive Germanic societies and Latin America during the eighteenth century. In the fourth chapter Chris Wickham refers to Iceland and Norway in the eleventh and twelfth centuries; in the fifth chapter Laura da Graca analyses documents from Northern Spain during the eleventh and twelfth centuries, providing also secondary references to tenth century Iceland; the sixth chapter written by John Haldon cites cases from Southern India from the fourteenth through the seventeenth centuries, and from medieval Christendom, Islam, and Byzantium during the eleventh and twelfth centuries; in the seventh chapter, Octavio Colombo works from Castilian evidence dating from the later Middle Ages.

The studies address historical problems that involve different modes of production:

In the first chapter, Andrea Zingarelli addresses the functioning of the ancient Egyptian state, whose most evident political form is the centralising monarchy, and acknowledges the persistence of the state in pharaonic history. Zingarelli analyses the manifestations of statehood that can be found in different settings, and the difficulty in finding spaces in which the state has not left its mark. Thus, the author acknowledges that in the Asiatic mode of production this all-encompassing unit appears as a superior and effective proprietor who appropriates the work of the individuals who are assigned plots in lands owned by the state and held by the individuals as tenants and/or in the lands of village communities. The greater part of surplus labour belongs to the state in the form of taxes and compulsory *corvée*. This appears as the dominant form into which the power to exploit and dominate the social whole is articulated, also allowing for its reproduction. The state supports the bureaucratic class, who in turn derives the possibility of accumulation and some prestige from its articulation with state institutions. The author concludes that the Egyptian state, considered as a redistributive state, rejects accumulation by an elite of privileged officials and craftsmen while at the same time enabling said accumulation as a side effect of its functioning. In line with the previous argument, the author verifies that private acquisition of land occurred since the earliest times of pharaonic history, although it is often juxtaposed to royal lands, temples or funerary foundations and it generally appears as a donation from the king or a village/city. It is undeniable, however, that certain individuals could manage certain properties, which indicates the presence of forms that coexisted with the extractive mechanism that prevailed especially during the New Empire. The author also detects differentiated forms of extraction in the quasi-slaves – who were acquired mainly in the course of wars of conquest – within the framework of the exploitation of lands most often linked to the temple. Zingarelli concludes that these social changes did not replace previous forms but rather created new forms of bondage. Thus, in the author's view the relations of production that correspond to other modes of production coexist with the dominant mode.

In the second chapter, Carlos García Mac Gaw addresses the question of whether it is accurate to characterise the whole of the Roman economy, its dominant class and even the form of exploitation of the *villa* as slave-based. He notes that the studies of ancient slavery have used the modern system of the plantation as a frame of reference, which leads him to establish comparisons that take into account the specific historical context of the systems under study. The slave-based character of Roman society has been grounded on the proportion of slaves with respect to the general population and the idea that slave labour provided the nucleus of the income of the dominant class; García Mac Gaw suggests that the larger portion of the product of the Roman Empire came from peasant labour, that the colonate was the more widespread form of labour exploitation in large holdings, and that we can only assert the primacy of the benefit derived from slavery in the income of the landowning class if we consider the income originated in Italy and Sicily as more important than the income originated in the rest of the provinces. With respect to the exploitation of slaves, the author posits the existence of not one but several forms of surplus appropriation, paying special attention to the situation of the *servus quasi colonus*, whom the jurists tend to equate with the *colonus* when addressing questions of their relationship with land and working tools. In disagreement with the minimalist view by which the figure of the *servus quasi colonus* would be limited to the higher stratum of more qualified slaves, García Mac Gaw suggests that the spread of the institution points to a general trend toward indirect exploitation originating in the period of the Late Republic. The sheer variety of forms of exploitation of slaves (domestic, under direct supervision, through rent, through leases by the owner, etc.) questions the concept of slave mode of production as it implies different ways of linking producers with the means of production and therefore different forms of surplus extraction, among which the plantation is the only one reflecting a singular mode. Lastly, the author considers American slave systems that were subordinated to central capitalism; it is this link – instead of the plantation system – that serves the purposes of comparison. For García Mac Gaw, the articulation with other systems is a general characteristic of slavery, and slave exploitation in the ancient world must be considered within the larger framework of the ancient tributary mode of production, whose dynamics of expansion favour the accumulation explained by the *villa*; that is to say, slavery in its varied formats was a response oriented to the exploitation of these properties while at the same time it served to reinforce the position of the dominant class with regard to the control of the state apparatus; such would be, in the author's view, the role of slavery as a feature of the dominant class.

In opposition to Adam Smith's view that the emergence of trades was a product of the natural evolution of the division of labour, in the third chapter Carlos Astarita explains the origin of the medieval craftsman based on the relations of production and productive forces. Astarita argues that craftsmanship implies a set of qualities that can only be deployed under certain conditions, and that these conditions were provided by the peasant household within the framework of the social structures that developed in the period between the dissolution of the ancient state and the widespread establishment of the banal lordship. Astarita traces the origin of trade specialisation to the consumption needs of the aristocracy of the early medieval period, who resort to the instruction of domestic slaves to compensate for the shortage of dependent labour (the case of the visigothic aristocracy is an example); this leads to the configuration of a servile segment of craft-producers (blacksmiths, carpenters, etc.) that is differentiated from the rural slaves. The weak social control favours the flight of slaves, many of whom are craftsmen who find it possible to settle in villages and boroughs by joining peasant households as dependents, and after 800 by becoming *casati* within the framework of the estates. Seigneurial policy favours this incorporation by encouraging in many cases the settlement of slaves, which stimulates the integration and social promotion of the fugitives, unlike what happens in other societies where the fugitive slave becomes marginalised. This shift of the specialised slave from the seigneurial house to the tenure implies conditions that are favourable to an increase in labour productivity, which results from the rent demands of the lord, especially for finished goods; on the other hand, being a private undertaking, the peasant household promotes concentration and the preservation of the family trade; the exploitation of labour by the family provides a model of coercion that favours learning and anticipates the authority of the master craftsman, while deploying at the same time a form of adaptation to the changing needs of the family cycle (incorporation of servants, etc.) that leads to the employment of wage earners, which in turn implies the potential for producing exchange values in the case of tenures that manufacture goods. The servile craftsman fits in with the village household, yet he is distinct from it: the teleological nature of his activity distinguishes the craftsman from the peasant, whose work blends with that of nature and is a source of social recognition that bestows on the craftsman a superior status contradicting his legal condition, cements his self-esteem and promotes the fixation and transmission of the knowledge, as opposed to slaves confined to special environments where the diffusion of the trade is limited by the lack of socialisation. Lastly, the fixation of land property and the individual exploitation in plots of land divided for petty cultivation are assumptions of the argument, which means that the centrality of the domestic unit in the development of trades is circumscribed to the modes of production and social formations based on the individual appropriation of the conditions of production (Germanic mode, peasant-based societies, feudal mode).

In the fourth chapter, Chris Wickham discusses how political power operates in peasant-based societies and the problem of its transformation. He analyses the cases of Iceland and Norway during the eleventh and twelfth centuries, as they are known through the 'family sagas' and 'the kings' sagas' of the thirteenth century. Dissenting from the tradition, reinforced by advocates of the linguistic turn, that denies the historical value of those narratives, Wickham argues for the plausibility of the picture emerging from the sagas, given that it was plausible to the audiences of the thirteenth century, whose society was not all that different from that of their predecessors who are the objects of the narrative. Both Iceland and Norway must be understood as social formations in which the peasant mode and the feudal mode coexist, with a dominance of the former. The trend toward the dominance of the feudal mode begins in Norway, where tenancy is more developed, but it is insufficient to imprint changes in political practices, which will occur at a much later time; during the thirteenth century, both societies are still dominated by the peasant mode in view of the fact that the aristocracy, despite having acquired some stability, still has to negotiate with the free people. Wickham analyses the actions of two prominent figures of eleventh century Norway whom Snorri Sturluson refers to in his *Heimskringla*. They are royal retainers who wield enormous political influence in the royal entourage and have sizeable convening power in the regions they dominate, but are nonetheless known as *bœndr*, that is to say, free peasants, and owe their position to their personal performance or their allodial bases rather than to royal favour; the examples confirm that the elites of the eleventh century, and those of the thirteenth century who described them, accepted as normal the existence of peasant leaders. The analysis of their degree of wealth reveals it was not substantial; in Iceland few of them own more than one farm, and in Norway, although aristocrats use dependants in the exploitation of their lands, they must allocate political and material resources to obtaining support among the free peasantry, and it is the success or failure of this undertaking, rather than wealth itself, that the sagas take into account when assessing the qualities of the leaders. The possessions of prominent figures are often based on the direct exploitation of domestic dependents, which indicates the presence of the slave mode under the dominance of the peasant mode, given that the wealth generated is allocated to reciprocity expenses to build clienteles; in turn, this form of labour exploitation is limited to medium-sized farms whose proprietors share living quarters with the servants they employ and are not removed from productive chores. The slave form tends to disappear as the feudal mode makes inroads in the form of tenures; lastly, the advance of this mode of production will depend on the concentration of lands by the aristocracy and on the priority its members assign to that task.

In the fifth chapter, Laura da Graca systematises Wickham's concept of peasant mode. Da Graca notes that while some traits of the productive forces and the relations of production are consistent with those of other modes proposed for 'primitive' societies, the form of property corresponds to the Germanic mode as put forth in the *Formen*, which implies that this is the aspect that gives the mode of production its singularity; she also remarks that the peasant mode combines an evolutionary trend toward inequality, which is inherent to individual appropriation, with the limitations imposed by a social functioning based on reciprocity between households. Da Graca analyses the evolution of clientelar relations between aristocrats and free peasants in a social formation dominated by feudalism (Northern Spain during the eleventh and twelfth centuries) with a view to establishing the transformation of those relations into relations of exploitation or relations of feudal vassalage, a process by which the feudal expansion over free spaces is achieved. The persistence of enclaves where the peasant mode is manifest explains why feudal aristocracy resorts to the ideology of reciprocity and the formal preservation of peasant practices as a mechanism for the construction of relations of exploitation; the condition of possibility for said relations of exploitation is the widespread existence of individual private property, which is a feature both of the Spanish villages analysed and of the society described in the Icelandic sagas that the author uses for the analysis of social practice. In that regard, da Graca discusses land endowments in exchange for military services and fosterage, the role of patrons as mediators, the election of a chief by the clients and hospitality; these practices tend to be placed at the service of the reproduction of feudal relations. This happens in two stages: one marked by the prominence of the peasant, a formal respect of customs and the ambivalence of the aristocratic role, then another stage in which the full subordination to the feudal mode has been achieved, as reflected in the transformation of voluntary donations into agrarian rents and their forceful imposition on communities, a process that is consistent with the separation of *milites* from labourers, the loss of autonomy on the part of the clients and the stabilisation of the relations between aristocrats and free people. The original contents of the primitive practice favour the mutation of functional power into the power to exploit: the practice of repaying mediation services with land becomes functional to the absorption of properties; the indissoluble quality of the fosterage bond enables the restriction of a client's ability to change allegiances, etc.; this shift is supported by a property structure that promotes the spread of transactions involving land. Da Graca shows that the peasant mode, for which she proposes the name of allodial mode of production, has its own dynamic of transformation.

In the sixth chapter, John Haldon addresses the problem of the link between agency and structure. Questioning the treatment of this problem in analytical Marxism, methodological individualism and structuralism, Haldon discusses the role of ideology in the explanation of historical change and its relationship with the conceptualisation of a mode of production, which he understands as an ideal type from which a dynamic cannot be predicated; the institutional forms are what determine the concrete manner in which historical change occurs. Given that in pre-capitalist societies there is a dominance of non-economic aspects such as politics, kinship and religion, Haldon proposes as a metaphor of the whole the idea of an organism whose skeleton (relations of production) determines a basic configuration, but in which all the elements are vital to the physiognomy and the evolution of the social body, and that they relate dialectically to one another. One of these elements is ideology, to which Haldon assigns a structuring role in social action: individuals are both agents and carriers of the structures they reproduce through social practice, whose contours are defined by the symbolic universe of which they are a part. Haldon takes W.G. Runciman's model with its categories of 'culture' and 'structure', which correspond respectively to the planes of conscience and the objective situation of the actors depending on their role; both dimensions converge in social practice. Haldon argues that ideology affects the praxis on which social reproduction depends, and this is why it has a pre-eminent role in explaining preservation or transformation in a society. This can occur through 'ritual incorporation or penetration'. Ritual penetration is apparent in cases where the belief system legitimises surplus extraction and determines its distribution (for example, India from the fourteenth to the seventeenth centuries or pre-Columbian societies), or in systems where, even without becoming assimilated with the relations of production, the belief system is inseparable from central aspects such as the transmission of property, the system of kinship, the legitimation of authority, etc. (as in the case of Christianity in the Byzantine world); another form of ritual incorporation is conversion, which functions as an instrument of domination and political integration, as in medieval Christendom or Islam. With respect to the problem of ritual incorporation, it is relevant to determine elite investments, which reveal the importance attributed to the belief system. Another example of the link of causation between economic and cultural elements is the underdevelopment of the mercantile elite in Byzantium during the eleventh and twelfth centuries – in sharp contrast with the prosperity of Italian cities – which could be explained in large part by the fact that the elites, even in the context of the period's mercantile development, consider this activity culturally irrelevant.

In the seventh chapter, Octavio Colombo analyses the functioning of the law of value in pre-capitalist markets drawing from the empirical study of local markets in Castile during the later Middle Ages. The author reviews two diverging perspectives: one supporting the idea that exchange is governed by the law of value where commodity production occurs, and another advocating that the law of value can only function fully under the capitalist mode of production. The first perspective assigns pre-eminence to the labour time embodied in the commodity as the substance of value; the second one views value largely as a social form. Colombo questions the arguments that defend the validity of the law of value in a pre-capitalist context; in his view, this law is better understood in a qualitative sense, as a mechanism for the proportional distribution

of labour in order to fulfil social needs; this presupposes a process of capital valorisation in the context of inter-capitalist competition, which objectively leads
to the tendential adaptation of prices to values. Colombo argues that the commodity as a social form is not identical to its determinations, and therefore
does not imply the functioning of the law of value. Given that simple commodity production only exists as a subordinate form within the framework
of a dominant mode of production, Colombo discusses the problem in the
context of the social relations and productive forces within which exchange
occurs. In this respect, he notes that the fluctuations in agrarian production
and labour productivity are prominent features of the peasant economy and
that these features affect both the secondary sector and prices, which indicates
that production is not adapted to social needs and that there is no economic
mechanism to regulate the social distribution of labour. These features explain
the existence of extra-economic mechanisms such as price fixing by the authorities and other forms of intervention. Confronted with the idea that the notion
of 'just price' could imply a certain perception of equivalence, the author poses
the question of whether the subjective perception of labour as abstract labour
is possible given that the peasant does not conceive of work as a productive
activity and that, in the case of the craftsman, the perception of worth attached
to the trade makes it difficult to abstract its concrete qualities. In the author's
view, the actual viability of labour mobility is relative, and with regard to haggling he argues that its widespread use evidences the existence of particular
prices for each transaction that are determined by the negotiating power of the
parties, and that in turn this negotiating power depends on factors such as taxation pressure that lead to the acceptance of disadvantageous conditions; on
the other hand, even if the approximation of price and value may sometimes
be achieved through haggling, the equivalence has to be tendential in order to
posit the full functioning of the law of value. Lastly, Colombo considers a number of speculative trade practices that further distort the adaptation to value
and enable accumulation processes on the part of wealthier peasants, indicating that the non-functioning of the law of value favours the formation of village
capital, which in turn magnifies the inequivalence of exchange as it undergoes
the process of valorisation.

In summary, although the different contributions address a variety of historical problems from distinct or even opposing theoretical and methodological
standpoints, their shared thrust is the attempt to analyse societies and the
problems posed by the historical process understood in terms of modes of production. That notion is at the heart of this work. As is apparent, we have not
aimed for a cohesive perspective but, quite to the contrary, we have attempted
to discuss a number of problems inherent to pre-capitalist modes of produc-

tion. We are grateful to the authors who have participated and expressed an interest in contributing to this goal even when they do not share some of our perspectives. It is also pertinent to state that the views expressed in this introduction are our own, and that the other authors do not necessarily share the interpretations and opinions expressed herein.

CHAPTER 1

Asiatic Mode of Production: Considerations on Ancient Egypt

Andrea Zingarelli

This chapter will inquire into the validity of Marx and Engels's elaborations on the Asiatic mode of production – with their contradictions and the modifications they went through over time[1] – in connection with the historical process of an ancient state. It will also analyse in part how these elaborations were later received and transformed by the more relevant Marxist historiography.

More precisely, our aim is to analyse the Asiatic mode of production from the particular perspective of the dominant relations of production in pharaonic Egypt.[2] The goal of our inquiry does not merely imply a recourse to the 'facts' of Egyptian history in the empirical sense so strongly criticised by Hindess and Hirst,[3] but a recourse to an abstraction of the historical process, which is not the same as the abstraction of an ideal elaboration devoid of historical meaning. We will thus focus on a certain social formation and on the economic, social, political and ideological relations that appear historically in consonance with the dominant Asiatic mode of production, and with other relations typical of other modes of production.

Tackling this inquiry is not an easy task given that Marx did not publish his theory on the Asiatic mode of production in one singular work and did not give it a definitive shape.[4] Indeed, the only textual mention of the Asiatic

---

1 It is hard to top O'Leary's chronological analysis of the works of Marx and Engels and of the interpretative problems they pose; however, it is not our intention to present a historiographical assessment. See O'Leary 1989, pp. 82–151; book review in Loone 1995.

2 An analysis based on comparative history would be more fruitful, but I lack the specific knowledge and skills to attempt it. My academic training led me to approach this problem from the perspective of the history of ancient Egypt. Or perhaps exploring the terms under which the Asiatic mode of production was conceived allows me to think of Egypt's history in Marxist terms, as part of the larger logic of historical processes and not as micro-history.

3 Hindess and Hirst 1975, pp. 1–20.

4 Krader 1975, p. xii; Bailey and Llobera 1981, p. 23. O'Leary 1989, p. 132, points out the many ideological and theoretical goals that Marx and Engels pursued in their publications on the subject.

mode of production[5] is found in the preface to *A Contribution to the Critique of Political Economy*, and the formulations associated with the Asiatic mode are found in the section of the *Formen* that Marx worked on between 1857–8 in preparation for *Capital* and *A Contribution to the Critique of Political Economy*. Due to this, the debate has often centred on the definition and characterisation of the alleged attributes of the Asiatic mode of production – such as Asiatic despotism, the existence of self-sufficient village communities and the absence of private property – or on a kind of geographical determinism associated to irrigation control.[6] There have also been attempts to chronicle the history of those attributes and trace their origins in order to reconstruct them. It has even been suggested that although Marx and Engels gave the concept a new perspective, the idea itself might not be original to the German authors,[7] and should therefore be understood as part of a Western tradition. However, if it were to be understood as part of the Western tradition, it would still be original in the sense that it explained the transformation of social relations related to productive forces.[8]

Another difficulty lies in the fact that studying the Asiatic mode of production is like trying to raise the dead[9] given that the notion was denied, declared

---

5 Also, in *Capital*, volume I, section 4, in a section on the fetishism of commodities, Marx 1965, pp. 50–1, writes '[i]n the *ancient Asiatic and other ancient modes of production*, we find that the conversion of products into commodities, and therefore the conversion of men into producers of commodities, holds a subordinate place, which, however, increases in importance as the primitive communities approach nearer and nearer to their dissolution'.

6 These two attributes are addressed in the correspondence between Marx and Engels of June 1853: Marx 1983, pp. 330 ff. and Engels 1983, pp. 335 ff.; as well as in an article Marx wrote for the *New York Daily Tribune*, also in 1853, Marx 1979, pp. 125–9; we will return to these further on in this article.

7 For example, Bartra 1983, pp. 21–34, analyses the evolution of related concepts, especially that of Oriental despotism from Plato and Aristotle to Richard Jones and Hegel. Anderson also traces the origins of concepts associated to Asiatic countries as a way of contrasting them with Europe, which would have influenced the works of Marx and Engels, Anderson 1979, pp. 462 ff.

8 Godelier 1977, p. 33. The French edition of this book was published under the title *Sur les sociétés précapitalistes* by Éditions Sociales, Paris, 1970.

9 It was Anderson 1979, p. 548, who suggested that we 'let this last notion (the Asiatic Mode of Production) be given the decent burial it deserves'. Zaccagnini 1989, p. 13, wonders ironically what other heuristic model an author like Komoróczy could propose for the interpretation of the socio-economic formations of ancient Mesopotamia once the Asiatic mode of production is dead and buried.

anti-Marxist and officially banned in the 1930s.[10] It was later misused by Wittfogel in his monumental[11] *Oriental Despotism: A Comparative Study of Total Power*
in order to emphasise the hydraulic feature of the societies where the Asiatic
mode of production came into existence,[12] and to propose that when said mode
exists in non-hydraulic societies it must have been copied or imposed by a
hydraulic society.[13] Wittfogel's critique was aimed at Marxist historiography
and to some extent at the concept of mode of production, but above all it was
a critique of the Soviet system.[14] Wittfogel kept the geographical determinism, underscoring political-administrative aspects, and eliminated the socio-
economic phenomena, which are only addressed in piecemeal descriptions.
The problem was that this idea of the hydraulic society was a vehicle for the
transmission of a crude and simplified notion of the Asiatic mode of production.[15]

---

10   Godelier 1977, p. 9. For the preceding period, see esp. Sofri 1969, pp. 81–103. In Tiflis,
     May 1930, several scholars discussed the Asiatic mode of production and the extension
     of this category to the modern East. During the Leningrad debate some months later
     (1931) – at the behest of the Association of Marxist Orientalists – the failure of the Chinese
     revolution of 1927 was ascribed to Asiatic stagnation, thus questioning that position and
     the theoretical concept behind it; participants supported the feudal or the slaveholding
     interpretation, Bailey and Llobera 1981, p. 52. For a detailed and complex analysis of the
     arguments brought to bear in that debate see Dunn 1982, esp. pp. 7–37. Some scholars
     continued to hold that it was possible to consider the Asiatic mode of production for
     Mesopotamia and ancient Egypt. See Sofri 1969, pp. 117 ff. Stalin does not mention it in his
     Dialectical and Historical Materialism (published as part of *History of the Communist Party
     of the Soviet Union*) of 1938. However, some English-speaking Marxists continue to mention
     it, such as Namboodiripad 1952. A recently published essay by the same author values the
     points Marx made in the *Formen* regarding India, Namboodiripad 2010, pp. 23–31.
11   Published in 1957 by Yale University Press, New Haven. The edition we used is by Vintage
     Books, New York, 1981. Bartra 1975, p. 28, remarks on the number of pages: 450, the number
     of chapters: 10, subchapters: 58 and subtitles: 193. Bartra 1975, pp. 21–37, devotes part of
     this book to discussing the theory of hydraulic societies and the historical cases he cites
     are from ancient Mexico; this section was originally published in the review *Tlatoani*, 21
     in 1967. For a review, see Vidal-Naquet 1964.
12   It is remarkable that, as O'Leary 1989, p. 139, notes, Wittfogel's subtitle to one of his
     chapters is 'Marx, Engels and Lenin Accept the Asiatic Concept'; given that Marx created
     the notion, the idea that he would accept it is less than generous.
13   Godelier 1977, p. 148.
14   See Sofri 1969, pp. 133–47, esp. p. 135.
15   Zamora 1997, p. 17. O'Leary 1989, p. 141, explains that it was mostly orthodox Marxists who
     agreed with Wittfogel on some issues.

Based on empirical evidence and passages in Jones and Volume I of *Capital*, Struve – a Soviet scholar who was removed from the traditional European schools – denied the existence of the Asiatic mode of production but proposed the existence of a dual exploitation related to two different social groups: the agricultural and the slaveholding exploitation.[16] The discussion on the slaveholding social order in ancient societies was central in Soviet historiography, although by the late 1940s the review *Vestnik drevnei istorii* – Journal of Ancient History – already considered that the bulk of the working population in the Near East were peasants. The latter publications were written under the influence of the *Formen*, which were available at the time in the USSR.[17]

Later, Hindess and Hirst attempted to prove that the concept of Asiatic mode of production had no place in the Marxist theory of modes of production.[18] The authors made it emphatically clear that it is a theoretical notion and that it must be constructed based on general Marxist concepts (productive forces, relations of production, etc.) and not based on the writings of Marx about Asia; that is to say, in their view one must build on what is written in *Capital* rather than taking into consideration the journalistic articles and the letters on Asia.[19] The authors assume that the basic form of pre-capitalist rent is the feudal rent as labour rent, rent in kind and rent in money, questioning Marx's postulate on the coexistence of rent and tax in Asiatic states, an issue we will address below.

For his part, Anderson found theoretical and methodological inconsistencies in the understanding of the Asiatic mode of production.[20] In particular, the author points at the notion of the self-sufficient village with its own communal property as the main empirical flaw in Marx's construction. The fundamental elements of the self-sufficient village are isolation and distance from the affairs of state. Anderson also points out that the presence of a powerful and centralised state presupposes a highly developed class stratification, while the pre-eminence of village property implies a social structure that is practically pre-classist or classless. The author insists that the autonomy and self-sufficiency of the village communities is incompatible in practice with the

---

16   Mandel 1971, p. 120.
17   Dunn 1982, p. 66. The title of Dunn's book is almost identical to the title of chapter 9 in the aforementioned *Oriental Despotism* by Wittfogel: 'The Rise and Fall of the Theory of the Asiatic Mode of Production'.
18   Hindess and Hirst 1975, p. 3.
19   Hindess and Hirst 1975, pp. 180–1.
20   Anderson 1979, pp. 487, 489.

importance of public irrigation works carried out by the state. In his view, the combination of a strong and despotic state with egalitarian village communities is intrinsically improbable.

Wickham has questioned the Asiatic mode, stating in no uncertain terms that it has no analytical validity whatsoever. He argues that it is very rare to find autarkic villages next to a state that collects taxes, owns all the land and carries out large-scale public works. Wickham also considers that the political and legal components of the concept are too specific. Thus, for this author feudalism would also encompass the East, since all class societies experiment with some form of land property and coercive extraction of rent.[21]

Similarly, Dunn[22] seems to suggest that the hypothesis of the Asiatic mode of production was abandoned by Marx in his later years and must not be considered as a 'full member' in the sequence of social orders. Moreover, in Dunn's view any revival of the concept of the Asiatic mode of production will depend on data and considerations not endorsed by Marx and Engels. This author, however, positions himself as neo-Asiatic, supporting the idea of a pre-feudal stage instead of a slaveholding social order.

For his part, Banaji[23] considers that the bi-polar model of village communities and a powerful state fails for three reasons: (1) The self-sufficiency of villages is a myth (he refers only to India); (2) The notion that the Asiatic sovereign did not confront powerful landowners and that there was no significant type of class formation is not true despite the fact that this was claimed by Richard Jones and implied by Marx; (3) The issue of the absence of private property of land is based on the repetition of the central doctrine of Orientalist tradition without any kind of in-depth analysis. In any case, Banaji proposes the characterisation of Asiatic regimes under the tributary mode rather than the feudal

---

21   Wickham 1994b, p. 49. In Asia, state taxes would have coexisted with more typical feudal relations, those in which landowners extract rent from their tenants; thus the state would always have an antagonistic relationship with said extraction.

22   Dunn 1982, pp. 85–6.

23   Banaji 2010, pp. 17–19. He makes a distinction between his perspective and that of Haldon by pointing out that the latter considers that the difference between tax and rent is purely formal since both are modes of surplus appropriation, and thus variations of a common mode of production: the tributary mode. It is worth noting that Haldon has developed the concept of tributary mode in greater depth than other scholars. As we shall see below, the name of tributary mode was also used by Amin in the sense of common mode of production, and Amin himself remarks that the term was probably used by Jiro Hoyakawa, a Japanese Marxist, in 1934.

mode, although he does establish a difference between tax and rent and between European feudalism and the Asiatic systems.[24]

So far, the perspectives against the Asiatic mode of production range from the invalidity of the concept from its very formulation to the idea that it ceased to constitute a part of the thought of Marx and Engels in their later writings. Indeed, for some Marxists the Asiatic mode of production was nothing more than a display of euro-centric arrogance on the part of Marx and Engels, a theoretical and methodological mistake based on the incorrect interpretation of Asian history that was later abandoned by the authors.[25]

The work of Childe, carried out in the 1940s and 1950s, is an exception in an era in which the Asiatic mode of production was not even mentioned.[26] Especially noteworthy is his publication of *Man Makes Himself*,[27] where he salvages some of the theses of the Asiatic mode of production, such as the transition from simple agrarian communities to states with professions and classes.[28] According to Blackledge, Childe showcases the concept of the Asiatic mode of production in contrast with the prevailing tendency since it was banned.[29]

It was Maurice Godelier who understood that this mode of production was situated in the transition from a classless into a class society.[30] Godelier recognises the unity of contradictory elements in the exploitation by a minority – a superior community exploiting particular communities – which exhibits the ultimate form of classless societies in the form of village communities together with a nascent form of class society.

---

24   Banaji 2010, p. 22.

25   Tan 2000, p. 1.

26   Harris 1994, pp. 31–2.

27   Childe 1936.

28   Bartra 1975, p. 23, considers that Wittfogel's description of the process by which the nuclei of hydraulic societies emerge is taken from Childe.

29   Blackledge 2006, p. 101, also refers to *What Happened in History*, where Childe develops the structural contradictions of Asiatic states in an attempt to explain the rise and fall of the slave mode of production associated with states such as Athens and Rome (Childe 1942). This author 2006, pp. 97–103, cites Childe's authority on the Asiatic mode when analysing modes of production and social transitions.

30   Godelier 1971, p. 7. Originally published by the Centre d'Études et de Recherches Marxistes (Paris, 1964) as *La notion de 'mode de production asiatique' et les schémas marxistes d'évolution des sociétés*. In English, see Godelier 1978. Godelier posits that Marx and Engels revisited the general hypothesis according to which human history is the transition from a classless into a class social organisation. He cites Marx's letter to Weydemeyer of 5 March 1852, in Marx 1983, p. 58. Also in this line of thought, Bartra 1975, pp. 87–8 and 110–12.

We can certainly view the Egyptian state as a pristine state[31] since it exists autonomously from the beginning, born of the transition toward political forms[32] from a classless society – labelled with the misnomer of 'primitive' – in which the surplus extraction is either absent or non-systematic and with a pre-valence of familial and communal forms of organisation.[33] The problem of this transition has been addressed in an effort to understand how the state comes to take on certain controls, in particular that of land ownership[34] and how the proto-states of Upper Egypt extended their domination over large swaths of the Egyptian territory starting from their mythical bases.

Godelier made the concept of the Asiatic mode of production extensive to Egypt in the Valley of the Nile late in the fourth millennium, as well as to different eras and societies in Europe (Etruscan or Creto-Mycenaean royalty), in black Africa (the kingdoms of Mali and Ghana, the royalty of Bamun and Cameroon), and in pre-Columbian America (Central American and Andean civilisations).[35] Indeed, starting in the 1960s, with the emphasis on the *Formen*, the West revived the concept of the Asiatic mode of production in studies on pre-Columbian America, black Africa and China, which lead to the proposal of other denominations such as communal-exploitative mode or village despotic mode.[36]

Thus, the 1960s ushered in new writings on the Asiatic mode of production, and revived the debate among English, French and Soviet Marxists. Hobsbawm

---

31   According to Zamora 1997, pp. 12–13, it is possible that Marx even gave the Asiatic mode of production a certain historical location: the Asiatic Near East of the first cities, communal water works, temples and palaces. Although that could possibly include pharaonic Egypt, it would exclude China and India, who belong to the group of early riverside civilisations, but are located further East.

32   According to Krader 1975, p. 9, this would be one of the directions pointed at by the theory of the Asiatic mode of production: the transition '[f]rom primitive economy to political economy and from primitive society to political society'.

33   According to the *Formen*, there are various alternative paths for development in the transition away from this primitive communal system: the *Oriental* way, the *ancient* way, the *Germanic* way and the *Slavic* way. He thus broadens the range of class societies: ancient slaveholding societies, feudal societies and *bourgeois* societies; the latter type is limited to Western and Central Europe and described in *The German Ideology* and the *Communist Manifesto*, Marx 1964, p. 32.

34   As Wickham 1994b, p. 62, remarks, it is hard to say how the state came to take control of all the land, but it is certainly related to the circumstances of conquest.

35   Godelier 1971, p. 43.

36   Chesneaux 1964, pp. 33–55; Zamora 1997, pp. 31–2, calls it the neo-Asiatic mode; Dunn 1982, p. 103, also assigns this denomination to anti-slaveholding arguments.

wrote the introduction to the first English edition of the *Formen*,[37] and at the same time George Lichtheim published an article analysing the Asiatic mode of production.[38] Various books and articles on the subject were published in the section of Asiatic and African studies of the Centre d'Études et de Recherches Marxistes[39] and *La Pensée*.

The arguments of Amin merit a more detailed review because, though briefly, they deal specifically with Egypt[40] and follow Marx in their treatment of state centralisation as an imposition of nature, ecology and the large-scale hydraulic works as well as for the purpose of surplus extraction from the peasantry.[41] Amin even points to the persistence of the relative autonomy of the village community and small families. With the four river valleys in mind (Egypt, Mesopotamia, the Indus Valley and the Yellow River Valley), Amin concludes that irrigation allows for more productivity and population density, which results in identical civilisations. The tributary form – that theocratic-bureaucratic class-state – emerges from the communities and imposes itself as organiser. Thus far, there are no major differences aside from the denomination of tributary form.

Amin adds to these considerations an interesting note on the rapid decline of the village community and its near disappearance, a question also addressed by Marx in the *Formen*;[42] nevertheless, the village community would persist as a family community, but ceding the legal property of the land to the superior community as the state becomes more powerful.[43]

Furthermore, Amin analyses the despotism of the class-state in terms of its 'consideration of the common interest' and 'organisation of useful works'.[44]

---

37   Marx 1964.

38   A lucid review of Marx's alleged changes with respect to the Asiatic mode of production is in Lichtheim 1963, pp. 86–112.

39   For example, Suret-Canale 1961, p. 101, posits that it is possible to find similarities between the Asiatic mode of production and the mode of production prevailing in Africa. See also Suret-Canale 1964. The Hungarian scholar Tokei gave a lecture on the Asiatic mode of production in June 1962 at the Centre d'Études et de Recherches Marxistes.

40   To a large extent, he equates Egypt to China, Amin 1976, pp. 20–1, 24 and 27.

41   For an in-depth analysis of Amin with respect to Egypt, see Campagno 2003.

42   Marx 1964, pp. 82–3. For example: 'Production itself, the advance of population (which also falls under the head of production), in time necessarily eliminates these conditions, destroying instead of reproducing them, etc., and as this occurs the community decays and dies, together with the property relations on which it was based. The Asiatic form necessarily survives the longest and most stubbornly'.

43   Amin 1976, p. 53.

44   He seems to posit the idea of a dominant class with regard to the state, Amin 1976, pp. 19–20 and 23.

Amin's benevolent view of the dominant class is remarkable, especially with respect to the peasantry. Indeed, Amin posits that this society is despotic for groups like free craftsmen and servile production, but 'not with respect to peasants'. Despotism is only verifiable when an external force (the Barbarian invaders) appropriate the state or when 'the state disappears to the benefit of feudal autonomies which then begin to resemble feudal Europe'.[45]

In a departure from Marx, Amin states that the Egyptian village community is not much more restrictive than those of medieval Europe. However, later on he establishes an ethical division between the feudal lords who oppress their peasants without control and the Oriental state which is benevolent toward peasants. Amin holds a clear position with regard to the excellence of Egypt and China as models (achieved tributary formations) and the failed attempts at imitation by other regions (peripheral capitalist formations). Feudal Europe belongs in this last category, although the lack of centralisation liberates merchant sectors and the expansion of trade coupled with the disintegration of feudal relations will give rise to capitalism. That is to say, the great, rich, resilient and benevolent tributary formation of ancient Egypt could not have given rise to a system as prejudicial as capitalism.

On another note, the field of research on the Near East undertook an attempt to revisit the notion of the Asiatic mode of production evoking the articulation of two modes of production: the palace (or temple) mode and the village mode. This bisectorial model had been previously introduced in the 1950s by the Russian scholar Diakonoff,[46] although it was published in the West at a later time. Diakonoff belonged to the so-called School of Leningrad,[47] and along with some colleagues he emphasised this two-part model based on land property rights and the notion of freedom in a legal sense.[48] In his studies on Oriental Antiquity,[49] Mario Liverani revisited the bisectorial model based on a paper

---

45   Amin 1976, p. 53.

46   Diakonoff 1974. Sometime earlier, Diakonoff had discredited the views of a slaveholding social order that prevailed in the studies of ancient Russian societies; however, as pointed out by Dunn 1982, p. 75, he departs from the fundamental notion of the Asiatic mode of production when he considers that taxation does not constitute exploitation.

47   On Struve's influence on Diakonoff, see Dunn 1982, pp. 45–62.

48   Zamora 1997, p. 23. Also see Zamora for an in-depth analysis of the postulates of the School of Leningrad and the ideas held by other scholars on Oriental societies and the Asiatic mode of production after 1930.

49   It is unfair to overlook the works of orientalists such as Zaccagnini 1989; or the publications of the *Société Jean Bodin*, but that would constitute a separate undertaking.

published in 1976 titled 'Il modo di produzione',[50] and in subsequent works he brought together different historiographical positions, which led to a more widespread acceptance for scholars of the field.[51]

The work of Ciro Flamarion S. Cardoso, who published several studies on the Asiatic mode of production,[52] is an exceptional case in the research on ancient Egypt. In his studies, Cardoso makes use of Marx and Engels's ideas and concludes that although the concept cannot be understood in the terms under which it was conceived, it is still valid in order to explain the functioning of ancient societies and constitutes 'one of the pertinent forms in which to inquire into the history of these societies'.[53] The present study subscribes to Cardoso's view on this issue.

I

Let us begin, then, by treating as valid the terms under which Marx detects in the *Formen* the presence of a unit identifiable as a state and the persistence of communal forms,[54] and by stating the pre-eminence of the relations of appropriation and exploitation, regardless of other intermediate, secondary, subordinate, subsidiary and derived forms that can be found together with that dominant mode.

When observing the functioning of the ancient Egyptian state and its persistence through pharaonic history, we perceive that statehood is manifest in the different spheres; indeed, it is hard to find spaces where the mark of the state is absent. Thus, this *all-encompassing unit* exists at the beginning of pharaonic history, and it is worth noting that it appears to be the superior and effective proprietor,[55] appropriating the labour of those individuals who own plots of

---

50   Liverani 1976.

51   Liverani 1975.

52   Cardoso 1982, pp. 14–25, 1986, 1988, ch. 1 and 3 and critical vocabulary, 1990.

53   Cardoso 1990, pp. 13–14.

54   Anderson underscores that the *Formen* present as a new and decisive element the idea that, in Asia and other parts, self-sufficient villages held communal property of the land, and that this was veiled by the official affirmation that all land was state property, which Marx would label a year later as the Asiatic mode of production. We can agree with Anderson in that this is a decisive element, however, as we shall see below, Marx wrote in 1853 about the *village system*. Anderson 1979, p. 477, himself notes that Marx never confirmed this 'new conception' in his finished and published works.

55   Marx 1966, p. 453: '[T]he owner may be an individual representing the community, as in Asia, Egypt, etc.'

land in the village communities. This dominant mode of production would define the general guidelines of the totality: the Asiatic mode of production. The largest share of surplus labour belongs to the state and the ruling elites in the form of taxes and compulsory *corvée*. This would be the dominant form in which the power to dominate and to exploit articulates itself within the social whole and what permits its reproduction.

In this way, the state is the main recipient of the surplus production of immediate producers: land rent is perceived in the form of taxes.[56] Thus, the state or state institutions confront immediate producers as landowners, and in this sense there is a convergence of tax and rent.[57] Although they doubt its existence, Hindess and Hirst[58] call this mode of appropriation tax/rent couple, considering that it corresponds to a division of labour between producers and non-producers as well as to the absence of private property and of a ruling class that is not subsumed into the state. The authors also develop a series of deductions based on the relations contained in such a mode of appropriation, although they wonder whether those elements allow for an articulated combination of productive forces and relations of production. They conclude that they do not. The authors emphasise that such a mode of appropriation would require two different types of productive forces, the ones implied in independent peasant cultivation and the ones implied in communal cultivation. In their view, such an articulation would be arbitrary and this leads them to believe that the productive forces corresponding to the tax/rent couple did not exist. Of note is the emphasis on demonstrating the determinism of productive forces and the insistent denial of a mode of appropriation other than the general form of all state taxation. This denial leads to the notion that the tax/rent couple does not imply an exploitative mode of appropriation. In agreement with Anderson, the authors consider that it is impossible for a state to impose forms of production without giving rise to classes.

It is clear that the closed articulation proposed by Hindess and Hirst leads them to erroneously propose differences with regard to the division of labour and the cooperation among members of a commune, as well as the regulation of large-scale enterprises, something that independent peasants could not undertake in the authors' view.[59] The forms of communal property may vary in

---

56   So much so that in Ramesside Egypt the term *shemw* is used to name both the harvest and the harvest tax; indeed, it is sometimes difficult to distinguish between the terms used for the different qualities of soil and the terms used for royal taxes.

57   Marx 1966, pp. 555–6.

58   Hindess and Hirst 1975, p. 192.

59   Hindess and Hirst 1975, pp. 194–6.

their historical presentation or even in their evolution, but not in their content, which is the relationship between the cultivator or direct producer and the land.[60] In the *Formen*, Marx himself points to individuals working independently in a plot of land assigned by the community as labouring in a form of communal property. Even though Marx underscores the collective nature of property for the sustenance of the communal entity, its survival is dependent on the fiscal pressure and the stronger or weaker control by the state bureaucracy, as well as on the contradictory relationships within the communities. Indeed, later (after Morgan),[61] Marx remarked on the dualism of certain communities – the so-called 'agricultural community' – which have both communal property of the land and parcellary exploitation by individual families.[62] In a letter responding to an inquiry by Zasulich written in 1881, Marx lays out the possibilities and conditions of Russian communes, and he refers to the decadence of primitive communities and to their different types, stating that they were all based on the natural kinship of their members, hence the existence of individual possession of plots of land, and that '[a]lthough arable land remains communal property, it is divided periodically between the members of the agricultural commune, so that each cultivator tills the fields assigned to him on his own account and appropriates as an individual the fruits thereof, whereas in more archaic communities production took place communally and only the yield was shared out'.[63] This primitive type of cooperative or collective and parcellary production is the contradictory expression of the development of these agricultural communities. In *Anti-Dühring*, Engels also dealt with the problem of the origin of classes and the state in the primitive community,[64] briefly

---

60   Krader 1975, pp. 127–8.

61   Krader 1972. On reviewing the book *Ancient Society* by Morgan, Marx made comments with respect to village communities and integrated other works about India and earlier civilisations. At that time there was a debate on the persistence of those Oriental communes in tsarist Russia. See O'Leary 1989, pp. 128–9. Although some authors like Dunn 1982, pp. 85–6 hold that after Morgan and the consideration of further evidence, Marx abandoned his theory on the Asiatic mode of production, others such as Melotti 1977, p. 11, hold that those same ideas are expounded in Volume III of *Capital*, published by Engels in 1894, after Marx's death.

62   See Godelier 1977, pp. 87–8.

63   Marx 1989, p. 351.

64   'The more the products of the community assumed the commodity form, that is, the less they were produced for their producers' own use and the more for the purpose of exchange, and the more the original spontaneously evolved division of labour was superseded by exchange also within the community, the more did inequality develop in

mentioning the delegation of functions on certain individuals acting under the control of the agricultural commune and to the transformations that created the conditions for the emergence of classes.[65]

To a large extent, agricultural production in ancient Egypt originated from peasant and/or village organisation,[66] which in turn had its own conditions for reproduction that were increasingly encroached upon by the state over time.[67] The perception of this encroachment is nuanced by the irregular and erratic nature of the interventions and by the fact that agricultural villages were relatively isolated in the hinterland for part of the year, which allowed for the existence of a strong local identity[68] and a self-sufficient economy.[69] Unfortunately, we know next to nothing about those villages[70] or about the peasants

---

the property owned by the individual members of the community, the more deeply was the ancient common ownership of the land undermined, and the more rapidly did the commune develop towards its dissolution and transformation into a village of smallholding peasants. For thousands of years Oriental despotism and the changing rule of conquering nomad peoples were unable to injure these old communities; the gradual destruction of their primitive home industry by the competition of products of large-scale industry brought these communities nearer and nearer to dissolution': Engels 1987, pp. 150–1.

65   In general, the notion of Oriental Despotism does not depart from arguments previously set forth by Marx, although Engels 1987, p. 168, is interested in explaining their evolution toward forms of production such as those based on slave labour.

66   Hoffman 1979, p. 17, characterises pharaonic Egypt as a 'village farming society'; Cardoso 1986, p. 16, n. 17 and 25–6, takes up Hoffman's idea, but also emphasises the principles of 'village community organisation'. For his part, Eyre 1999, p. 35, holds that 'Egypt was probably always a village society'. 'The domestic and peasant spheres probably had their own forms of organisation of productive processes and space, as well as agricultural practices and techniques that were almost assuredly different from those employed by the institutional sector, with which they maintained certain relations determined by state taxation', Moreno García 2004b, p. 30.

67   Authors such as Menu and Harari 1974, p. 125, posit the centralised administrative organisation under one royal family as a function of two forces: economic *dirigisme* and the persistence of communal structures. Also, Janssen 1979b, pp. 507–8, considers the economic structure of ancient Egypt on the basis of two spheres; a local subsistence economy: village peasants and craftsmen made most of the goods necessary for subsistence and could exchange through barter with their neighbours. A second sphere of state redistribution rests on this basis of subsistence economy.

68   Eyre 2010, p. 291.

69   Eyre 1999, p. 36.

70   Eyre 1999, p. 35; Moreno García 2001, p. 429. Cardoso 1986, p. 10, warns against some authors' view of a 'real dis-balance' and suggest it is actually a 'dis-balance of sources'.

themselves aside from the relationships (including religious relationships) they established with state institutions which demanded that they relinquish part of the production and/or perform compulsory labour. Nonetheless, there is recognisable evidence of joint forms of labour, shared properties[71] and the regulation of justice in local councils, namely, communal or clannish modes of functioning[72] that survive in relation to labour, property and the administration of norms and standards.[73]

Furthermore, considering the importance of funerary and divine cults in that social formation, it can be surmised that during the Old Kingdom the crown assigned village lands and populations for the purpose of maintaining those cults. It would indeed appear that, at least during the Old Kingdom (ca. 2686–2125 BC),[74] the royals controlled religious centres in different regions and the pharaohs participated in religious activities.[75]

Royal decrees formalised these acts. Decrees could also be used to bestow immunity on lands dedicated to the funerary cult of certain individuals with the aim of assigning all the resources obtained therein to sustaining the cult. This implied that the state gave up the tax revenue and that the affected population was released from fulfilling personal obligations. However, such exemptions were subject to revocation and the goods deposited in temple warehouses could be utilised by royal envoys on official missions.[76]

The Coptic decrees illustrate the creation of a foundation[77] and the exemp-

---

71   For example, the Berlin papyrus 10470 of the Twelfth–Thirteenth Dynasties registers a slave woman as shared property of the village, Smither 1948, pp. 31–4.

72   The organisation of work in *phyles* registered during the Old Kingdom and the Middle Kingdom, by which the labourers were divided into groups, each with a totemic name, seems to preserve ancient forms of organisation from prior times: Roth 1991, pp. 142 ff.

73   Cardoso 1986, p. 19, resorts to iconographic sources and texts from the second half of the third millennium to describe villages and their characteristic traits.

74   The artificial division between kingdoms and empires derives from a nineteenth-century convention dividing pharaonic history in empires/kingdoms – Reich – which began with Bunsen, a Prussian scholar, and was adopted in the twentieth century. Whatever the case may be, and despite the fragmentation of the sources, it is beyond discussion that state power, especially the central power, was the most visible entity in terms of organisation, bureaucratisation and appropriation of agricultural surplus during certain periods of pharaonic history.

75   Moreno García 2004b, pp. 32–4. For a different view, see Kemp 2006, pp. 60 ff.

76   Moreno García 2004b, p. 39. Moreno García 1996, pp. 161–5. See text on the tomb of Herkhuf at Qubbet el-Hawa, Strudwick 2005, p. 333; *Urk.* I, 131: 4–7.

77   Decree from Koptos (Koptos G) establishes the creation of a dominion for the mainten-ance of the cult of a royal statue. Due to the damaged condition of the papyrus, it is not

tion it received from the king.[78] Such foundations were in the orbit of the
per-shena,[79] an administrative centre of the royal dominions, or of another
dependency of the royal dominions.[80] According to Moreno García,[81] the *per-shena* was a building dedicated to agricultural tasks that housed labour[82] and
means of production and was attached to state temples or agricultural facilit-
ies. By means of these decrees, the palace made sure that the economic activity
of the temple was not affected. Thus, local temples in certain nomes became
hubs of institutional agriculture and therefore of local power.[83]

From these and other royal decrees it can be gleaned that village chiefs were
obliged to provide labourers to insure the cultivation of the crown's agrarian
exploitations,[84] the compulsory *corvée*:

> You shall divide the land of this *per-shena* together with the village
> chiefs[85] and the local councils,[86] of the fields under corvée and of *sened-
> works.*
>
> *Urk.*I, 294: 15–16

A king's advice to his son to take care of the men of influence in the village, and
his recommendation to find and earn the loyalty of a leading man among the
villagers who will protect the king's son, attests to the direct relationships that

---

possible to ascertain whether the decree was issued by Pepi II during the Sixth Dynasty or
by one of his successors, Strudwick 2005, pp. 114–15; *Urk.* I, 288–95.

78   Decree from Koptos (Koptos D), Strudwick 2005, pp. 112–13.

79   'Arbeiter': *Lexicon der Ägyptologie* (*LÄ*) I, 371, 'Arbeitshaus': *LÄ* I, 377 and 'Domänen': *LÄ* I,
1118. Faulkner translates it as 'labour establishment', Faulkner 1991, p. 90.

80   For example, the *per-djet* estates acted as its subsidiary holdings, Papazian 1999.

81   Moreno García 1994, p. 41.

82   Moreno García 1998; Allam 2004.

83   This allows us to think of the evolution from the *per-shena* of the Old Kingdom to the
per-shena of the New Kingdom in terms of an increasing organisation of economic activity
first by the palace and then by the temples. Also, the temple-based economy of the New
Kingdom may have its origins in the Old Kingdom: '[w]hen the Great Household of the
king relinquished active control of the economy in favour of the temples', Papazian 1999.

84   Moreno García 2004a, p. 17.

85   The term *heka* can mean 'governor' or 'ranking man', but it is mostly used in reference to
local leaders, Eyre 1999, p. 40; Faulkner 1991, p. 178. For a specific analysis, see Piacentini
1994.

86   *Djadjat* are local councils in a collective sense. The term has been translated as 'magis-
trates, assessors', Faulkner 1991, p. 319.

could arise between royals and village chiefs.[87] Likewise, it is also a testimony of the hierarchical differences occurring within the village through external action and of the mediation of chiefs in the relationship between the villagers and the pharaoh.

On the other hand, according to the Gebelein papyri the villagers were listed in registers[88] and could be summoned to perform a variety of tasks for the pharaoh[89] such as temple or waterway construction, military service or a mining expedition.[90] In turn, several villages could be under the control of a senior officer as is attested to in an inscription on the Metjen mastaba of the Fourth Dynasty:

> And he was promoted to govern Per-desu and the villages under its con-
> trol.

Labour demands were probably imposed on the communities rather than on individuals, although it is difficult to ascertain whether regular recruitments were established for labour in royal projects.[91]

In all probability, the relationship between state institutions and villages was not an immutable or harmonious one, and this was also true for the different institutional actors who were in charge of organising agrarian production in all its stages. Similarly, one cannot assume the existence of a monolithic, permanent and centralised efficiency. That said, can we really doubt that the state and its institutions directed the exploitative relationship over agrarian villages?

On reviewing the historical process of this economic-social formation it becomes evident that the crown and the temples advanced over village lands and that in some regions[92] they intervened in the organisation of the agricultural space.[93] Indeed, as mentioned before, the Old Kingdom witnessed

---

87   Helck 1977, p. 6.

88   Posener-Kriéger finds close to three hundred names, but it is not possible to ascertain whether they are the whole of the population, Posener-Kriéger 1975, p. 215; Eyre 1999, p. 36, n. 20.

89   A majority are agricultural labourers, although other specific occupations are mentioned, such as baker, brewer, herdsman, measurer of grain, sealer of the granaries, and 'nomads', among others, Troy 2002, p. 11.

90   Posener-Kriéger 1975, p. 212; Parra Ortiz 2011, p. 178.

91   Eyre 2010, p. 302.

92   Especially in the Delta, also in Elephantine.

93   During the Fourth Dynasty, the crown undertakes the incorporation of the Delta, and later

the establishment of royal agricultural facilities in the rural sphere.[94] Certain types of fields, the *akhet*, which were dedicated to grain cultivation, were attached to those royal facilities and were associated to taxes and compulsory *corvée*. State forms appear to extend over uncultivated lands[95] as well as over older communal forms, giving rise to an internal contradiction in the latter case.[96] Notwithstanding the internal contradiction, the global unit in these regions no longer *appears to be* the proprietor of the land; 'it has acquired real dominion even though the communities persist within it'.

We shall review this problem by analysing the historical development of the *whyt* villages.[97] This type of village was far removed from the institutional space and refers to the clan-family[98] during the Middle Kingdom (ca. 2055–1650 BC).[99] We have more data on the New Kingdom (ca. 1550–1069 BC) since this type of village is mentioned in an inscription (in Mes)[100] dealing with a dispute over lands in Southern Memphis, although the village is named after the first proprietor of the lands. Thus, some of these communities were known by proper names, and it appears that the families lived therein and the village was

of a region in Middle Egypt, as areas for the production of goods by ploughing up virgin soil and exploitation, Parra Ortiz 2011, p. 147.

94   Moreno García 2004a, p. 17. We owe this analysis to Moreno García. In Upper and Middle Egypt, the crown established the Hwt, agricultural and administrative centres that controlled land, labourers and animals, and constituted the bases for state taxation, Parra Ortiz 2011, pp. 184–5. Royal chapels were founded in different localities with land and rents at the disposal of the crown, Moreno García 1996, and 2001.

95   Eyre points out that these rural communities could be populated with war prisoners or immigrant groups, and that being royal domains they provided for the king and the royal administration or for royal officials, Eyre 1999, p. 35.

96   Zamora 1997, p. 4. For Godelier 1971, p. 45, the internal contradiction is the unity of communal and class structures.

97   On the term *whyt*, see Gardiner 1947, 205*; *Wb.* I, 346 and 258, 5.6, Erman and Grapow 1971, from now on *Wb*.

98   Redford states that 'wahyet "clan, family" was applied to those small hamlets or encampments of kin groups', Redford 1993, p. 8; see also Spiegelberg 1904, p. 150; Franke 1983, pp. 219 ff.

99   In the Execration Texts, *whyt* were referred to as clans or *aAmw* 'asiatics' from Byblos. See Helck 1971, p. 53. In Story of Sinuhe, wHyt is written in several forms, although the determinative of people or man in plural is kept in all words (Berlin Papyrus 3022, 28, 86, 94, 113, 130, 239 and 240). And for other short references, see Mazar 1990, p. 185.

100   Loret discovered the text and published it in 1901, pp. 1–10; see Moret's interpretation 1901, pp. 11–39; Gardiner 1905; Gaballa 1977; Allam 1989.

named after the first individual who owned the lands. These practices came about in the context of a process of colonisation of the Fayum region.[101]

However, a tax document from the reign of Ramesses V[102] registers almost thirty *whyt*,[103] many of them also bearing proper names or referring to the occupations held by the inhabitants.[104] The evidence allows us to infer that these villages were within temple estates or royal lands. Some of them were located in royal landholdings (*khato* lands), which are named in text B of the Wilbour Papyrus.[105] The village population[106] could be obliged to work these *khato* lands – lands belonging to the crown – and during the New Kingdom the documentation attests to an atypical occurrence related to the *nemehw*,[107] in which said *nemehw* or independent holders associated to the villages pay the state a compensation in gold.[108]

While during the Middle Kingdom the *whyt* are only associated with the village in its familial or clannish sense, later they are to be found in colonised areas or in crown and/or temple dominions. During the New Kingdom, thousands of agricultural estates and religious-administrative centres were attached to the most important temples such as the Amon and Karnak temples.

Whether the villages were based on bonds of kinship or within the domain of an institution, the state's relationship with those villages was one of taxation.[109] So much so that periods of crisis corresponded to an improvement in

---

101   The location of the Neshi village could link it to internal military colonisation of the area from the beginning of the New Kingdom. Eyre 2004, pp. 161–2, points to the colonisation cycles registered for that area during different periods of pharaonic history.

102   Gardiner 1941–52; Menu 1970; Katary 1989; Janssen 1986. Review and summary of I.A. Stuchevsky, *The Cultivators of the State Economy in Ancient Egypt during the Ramesside Period* (in Russian), Moscow: Nauka, 1982.

103   From Gardiner 1948, pp. 74–5.

104   For example, village of Sinuhe (*Wilbour* A 79, 17; 87, 31; 97, 32); village of Merek (*Wilbour* A 35, 23); village of the soldiers (*Wilbour* A 35, 45, 36, 12); village of Tamarisk (*Wilbour* A 12, 12; 15, 40; 20, 28; B 15, 20. 21), etc.

105   Village of Iryt (*Wilbour* B 11, 27; 12, 33); village of Amenmose (*Wilbour* B 20, 16); village of Nesh (*Wilbour* B 9, 22.24).

106   On population distribution by occupation in different areas as *per* the papyrus, see O'Connor 1972, pp. 692–5.

107   On the complexity of the term *nemehw*, see Zingarelli 2010b, pp. 89–90; David 2011; Moreno García 2011b.

108   We will revisit this when we analyse the property of the *nemehw*.

109   This communal fiscal responsibility that delegates functions to local magnates or middlemen is not easily visualised, according to Eyre 1999, p. 45. Nevertheless, as we have pointed

living conditions, as Moreno García points out, which could be related to the disappearance of tax-collecting palace bureaucracies leading to more freedom for peasants to organise productive activities.[110]

Since Egypt was a territorial state, we must doubtlessly consider the relationship between the central dominant class that governed in certain historical junctures and the regional and local elites that disputed that power. The history of centralisation and decentralisation of state politics reflects that struggle. On the other hand, regionalisation created a complex constellation of political-religious institutions that depended on the central government to a larger or lesser extent. Although the role of provincial temples and sanctuaries as representatives of state authority has recently been questioned,[111] the formation of regional elites is beyond doubt as evidenced by the ancient administrative divisions (nomes)[112] and the clientelar networks.

On the other hand, from the beginnings of state organisation to the Fifth Dynasty, the intervention of the royal family was felt in that its members held the highest offices, including that of visir.[113] The close relationship between the sovereign and his officials became less so as the number of officials increased and individuals unrelated to the royal family came to have access to high posts. The bonds were tightened by different types of compensation, such as the usufruct of royal lands that could later revert to the king.[114] Another mechanism used by the earlier dynasties was the marriage of princesses to senior officials in order to sustain through kinship the higher offices of the administration.[115]

The great population centres – which often belonged by right of inheritance to the king,[116] hence the term of 'royal camps'[117] that Marx used in reference to

---

out, it is the villages and not the individuals that bring offerings to the tombs of the Old Kingdom, Eyre 1999, p. 47.

110   Moreno García 2004a, p. 44.

111   Moreno García 2004b, p. 32, n. 6.

112   On the alleged reform dissolving nomes and the replacement of nomarchs for local mayors, see Franke 1991.

113   Baud 1999, pp. 170 ff.; Lupo 2011.

114   More on this topic later.

115   Parra Ortiz 2011, p. 149.

116   Throughout pharaonic history, settlements of different types and hierarchies were established by the king, and they developed as pyramid cities or were associated to them. We have opted not to develop this aspect due to its complexity and its subsidiary relationship to our argument. See Lupo 2007.

117   Letter from Marx to Engels, London, 2 June 1853, Marx 1983, pp. 330 ff.

them – became nome capitals.[118] Toward the end of the Old Kingdom, a governor could control several nomes and be acknowledged as a great potentate in the context of the emergence of local potentates and leaders of military troops.[119]

However, the state had not disappeared, rather it had become fragmented. Even on the regional level, the relationship between the villages and the nomarchs or regional leaders was maintained. The nomarchs, for example the Thebans during the First Intermediate Period (ca. 2160–2055 BC) assumed royal titles and control of local temples. In the waning years of the Old Kingdom, the provincial elites reproduced the royal style in statuary, chapels or mastabas, which were consecrated as spaces for cult and became objects of deification.[120]

In some way, this historical process had its correlate in the funerary sphere to the extent that although initially the benefits of the funerary cult applied to the king, they were later extended to the members of the royal family, state officials and priests in separate sections of the pyramids. During the First Intermediate Period, the individual pyramid disappeared and a family group belonging to the local elite could be buried in a mastaba.[121]

The rhetorical statements of those rulers emphasise their role as protectors of the people and boast of having alleviated the effects of famine. The ideological content of those statements is linked to individual action and not to being at the king's service. This legitimation before those who are dependent on him introduces a new social type in the rhetoric of the inscriptions, that of the patron, he who can change destiny and save the people from misfortune.[122]

The integration of the local elites into the state apparatus and into the culture and values of the palace, and vice versa, is reflected by the inclusion of those rhetorical statements in the written production of the Middle Kingdom.[123] This validates to a certain extent Assmann's statement regarding the

---

118 Greek name for the *spAt*, districts or administrative divisions. On the importance of nome capitals especially during the New Kingdom, see O'Connor 1972, esp. pp. 687 ff.

119 Moreno García 2011a, pp. 188–9.

120 Moreno García 2004b, pp. 34–5; Moreno García 2011a, p. 190. See, for example, Heqaib of Elephantine, Habachi 1985.

121 Seidlmayer 1990, p. 403.

122 Assmann 2005, pp. 69 and 118–32.

123 The written production refers to political and social unrest while maintaining that royalty and certain values associated to that institution are necessary. Given that the king is synonymous with order, this apparent contradiction found in literary accounts reflects political arguments disguised as fiction, Zingarelli 2010a, esp. pp. 211–15.

'rhetoric of motives'[124] to explain and justify the acts of the dominant class and governing policy to newly incorporated literate elites.

Notwithstanding the above, during the Middle Kingdom the bureaucratic structure became larger and more specialised on the basis of a tax system, which was in turn based on production estimates for land and waterways. Similarly, the system of compulsory labour organised by the state was maintained but with the mediation of chiefs and representatives from villages and towns. Those who did not comply with those obligations were severely punished, and we know that those who helped labourers to flee were sent to border fortresses like Askut in Nubia.[125]

Concomitantly with this greater bureaucratisation, the central government became more visible in the different regions and there was an increase in the obligations it was owed. Paradoxically, part of the local control was delegated to local leaders in villages and towns. Temples and pious foundations assumed the collection of grain per person in each of the plots of land in the district and in turn paid taxes to the crown, although certain institutions could be exempted from such payment.

In spite of this, some individuals emphasised their own initiatives and economic practices[126] in what can be termed private autobiographies, but at the same time the protagonists of these texts held titles associated to a religious institution, for example that of priest of Mentuhotep.[127]

The social range of characters portrayed in fictional and non-fictional texts[128] became wider, giving rise to a schematic and taxonomic view of social differentiation. Authors from the past century[129] interpreted this phenomenon as revelatory of a democratic age featuring a middle class of craftsmen and merchants, among other occupations. Later on, even the existence of a type of *bourgeoisie*[130] was suggested for the case of the society of the Middle Kingdom. The idea for the emergence of such a middle class at the beginning of the Middle Kingdom was based on funerary evidence and considered other textual and iconographical references.[131] The grave goods of the necropoleis of this

---

124   Assmann 2005, pp. 146–9, esp. 148.

125   Callender 2000, p. 161.

126   Diego Espinel 2011, p. 232.

127   Petrie 1925, pl. XXIII; Lichtheim 1988, p. 69.

128   For example, a contrast is established between small – *nedyes* – and great – *wrw*.

129   See esp. Wilson 1951, pp. 123–4; Hayes 1961, p. 45. Previously also Erman 1894, p. 101, and Hall 1924, p. 318.

130   Loprieno 1988, p. 87.

131   Richards 2005.

period show a high degree of wealth in the tombs of individuals who did not belong to the pharaonic administration, and other secondary burial sites attest to the existence of clientelar networks around local magnates.

The concepts of middle class and *bourgeoisie* are anachronisms,[132] but it is pertinent to inquire into the extent of social differentiation in this period. The incorporation of social categories that hardly fit the description of village population or high bureaucratic or state elite is understandable in a society that was becoming fairly complex. We accept that the evidence is ambiguous, and that in general the cultural texts show that the self-awareness of the middle sectors appears to have been dependent on the literate elites and sub-elites that name them and esteem their existence.[133] This does not negate the existence of a class identity defined by labour exploitation[134] and the status that invariably presents itself as a category in pre-capitalist societies.

We have already mentioned the view held by several authors (Anderson,[135] Hindess and Hirst),[136] for whom the Asiatic mode of production is unacceptable given that the existence of a state without classes is an impossibility. Notwithstanding that, Hindess and Hirst made a significant contribution to the notion that the state and the political level develop the contradiction between economic structure and ideological superstructure in the transition from a classless to a class society. However, they sidestep that contradiction and discuss the terms of class domination within the state through conquest, arguing in particular that no form can explain the existence of a state reflecting the appropriation of the surplus through tax/rent.[137]

The binary opposition between state and communities is the manner in which the dominant mode of production expresses itself, although it would be illusory to deny the differentiation and social intersections occurring not only

132   Meaning the notion of a middle class as an ascending class associated to universal processes and to modernisation, democracy, *bourgeoisie* and liberalism: Visacovsky and Garguin 2009, pp. 13 and 21–2. This approach presents problems from the point of view of interpretation, sources, and methodology, which are rooted in larger historiographical discussions pertaining to the modern world.

133   Evidence of a 'subelite', that is, people 'lying somewhere between the small ruling elite and the rest of the population' begins to emerge from the archaeological record, Parkinson 2002, pp. 64–5; Richards 2005, p. 15.

134   I want to thank Astarita for this personal observation.

135   Anderson 1979, pp. 487 ff.

136   Their argument is based on the irreconcilable class antagonism implied by the existence of the state according to Lenin in *The State and Revolution* and Engels in *The Origin of the Family, Private Property and the State*, Hindess and Hirst 1975, p. 198.

137   Hindess and Hirst 1975, pp. 198–9.

within the framework of the villages but also in the agricultural holdings of the king and the temples; the same applies to contradictions within and between the dominant classes: the royal family, nobles or palace officials, members of the temple, priests and other officials such as scribes,[138] men of arms and among provincial families.

In this regard, Haldon makes a sensible suggestion on the contradiction between the interests of the 'state' (the ruler, the bureaucratic elite, the dominant aristocratic faction in the court or in the provinces) and other factions of the dominant class in relation to the control of surplus appropriation and its distribution.[139] However, those contradictions do not directly affect the mode of labour exploitation, and above all they do not affect the forms of property, a question we shall address in the next section.

II

In a letter dated 6 June 1853, Engels posits that the absence of land property is the key to understanding all of the East.[140] One of Marx's postulates was that there was no private property of land, but he acknowledged the private possession and use of land.[141] Much later, in *The Frankish Period* published in 1882, Engels holds that the form of state power is conditioned by the form of the communities, and that therefore the Asiatic mode of production appears when the land is tilled by the communities or assigned to different families without becoming private property and the power of the state is despotic.[142]

More subtly, Marx remarks in the *Formen* that the all-encompassing or superior unit appears as superior or sole proprietor (the *unity* is the real owner)

138   De Melo Tunes 1990, p. 61.

139   Haldon 1993, p. 146, makes this point when addressing the question of the autonomy of tributary states.

140   Letter from Engels to Marx, London, 6 June 1853, Engels 1983, pp. 335 ff.

141   Sofri 1969, p. 28, argues that Marx had some uncertainty about this postulate. Also in Marx 1966, p. 555: '[N]o private ownership of land exists, although there is both private and common possession and use of land'.

142   In 1884, when writing *The Origin of the Family, Private Property and the State*, Engels focused on the evolution of Western societies in particular, because he linked the emergence of the state to private property and the monogamous family. Furthermore, Engels himself stated that he wanted to verify Morgan's theory for pre-history and for Europe's ancient history. For another explanation of Engels's abandonment of this idea, see Godelier 1971, pp. 27–35.

in most of the fundamental Asiatic forms. 'The real communities only as *hereditary* possessors' and 'the individual is then in fact propertyless or property – i.e., the relationship of the individual to the natural conditions of labour and reproduction, the inorganic nature which he finds and makes his own, the objective body of his subjectivity – appears to be mediated by means of a grant [*Ablassen*] from the total unity to the individual through the intermediary of the particular community'.[143]

The empirical solution to the problem of the property of land in terms of the Asiatic mode of production became a matter or establishing whether the documents of a given economic-social formation registered private forms of property. The oversimplified argument that 'there is private property, therefore there is no Asiatic mode of production' permeated published papers and discussions on this topic without categorial complexity and theoretical rigour.

It is possible to state that dominant relations and means of production may correspond to political and institutional forms and to forms of property within a certain mode of production. In the Asiatic mode, surplus labour is extracted in the name of a god or the king from the labourers of the communities or from the labourers of state lands. These features, which may be common to different social formations, are present as constitutional structural features in ancient Egypt from the very origins of the state.

Can we explain within the same mode of production the extraction of surplus labour in a productive unit based on personal bonds and the same extraction in funerary communities or domains belonging to a temple or to the crown?

Everything seems to indicate that the exploitation and dependency of peasants under the Asiatic mode of production is different from the forms of submission and exploitation of peasants in, say, the feudal mode. Egyptian cultivators could possess plots of land in the communities or even in lands attached to institutions, and they had to deal with officials or middlemen from their community or village, all in the name of the pharaoh. These relationships were impersonal, and mediated by violence at the time of tax collection,[144] by

---

143   Marx 1964, p. 69. Also Marx 1966, p. 555: 'The state is then the supreme lord. Sovereignty here consists in the ownership of land concentrated on a national scale'.

144   The *Satire of the Trades*, a literary text from the Middle Kingdom, Lichtheim 1975, pp. 184–93, highlights the advantages of being a scribe as opposed to the difficulties of having any other trade and/or activity; it sings the praises of being a scribe; the adversities that peasants face in their agricultural labour are exaggerated, as well as the actions of the state as represented by the scribe and his assistants who arrive with 'clubs and sticks' to collect the grain. The source reflects institutionalised violence toward the peasant in the first place,

cooperation or by paying tribute to the god. Even so, it is a matter not just of the mode of appropriation (personal or impersonal), but also of the specific form that exploitation takes in the different forms of property, which evidently lead to differentiated social and economic practices.

But let us return to the issue of private property and the mystical determination of its presence or absence in the so-called Asiatic societies, especially in ancient Egypt. In our view, Marx suggests in the *Formen* that private property did not develop in the so-called Asiatic societies because the proprietor of the land was the state and the state and religious institutions belonging to what he called the superior community. In pharaonic Egypt there are documents attesting to the existence of communal lands, personal holdings of the pharaoh, lands belonging to the crown, lands belonging to royal foundations, lands belonging to the treasury and other divisions of the central government and lands belonging to temples, all forming a complex and juxtaposed network of properties, with a prevalence of one type of property or another according to the period.[145]

Notwithstanding the above, the acquisition of 'private' fields existed from the very beginnings of pharaonic history although (1) it was often juxtaposed to lands belonging to the crown, to temples or to funerary foundations, and (2) it was generally a donation from the king or the village/town. It is undeniable that some individuals could manage certain properties, which attests to the existence of forms that coexisted with the dominant mechanism for extraction. So much so that in land transactions (some carried out with equivalents during the New Kingdom)[146] the value of the plots of land is very low, a situation derived from the dominant mode of production that supported direct subsistence.

Let us analyse then the forms under which those individual properties present themselves and the relations of production established around them. The lands are granted to high-ranking officials as a reward for their performance and they could be royal donations for the purpose of funerary cults.

---

then toward his family. In spite of the document's bias, the dominant mechanism seems to be the collection of peasant rent by state officials. The New Kingdom version in Blackman and Peet 1925, pp. 284–98; Lichtheim 1976, pp. 168–75. Moreno García 2004a, pp. 42 and 54, warns that using this type of document presents a complex challenge due to its rhetorical and didactic nature, and resorts to using administrative sources.

145   Menu's arguments that the pharaoh's property was the only one that could be disposed of is based on legal aspects, Menu 1982, p. 1.

146   Land transactions with equivalents, see Baer 1962, pp. 25–45; Zingarelli 2010b, pp. 94–6.

The lands are granted by the landlord (the crown) to a class of lords that is indistinguishable from the state or its institutions. Those who own the lands are at the same time state officials or depend on the state's religious or funerary institutions. In other words, during the Old Kingdom and the Middle Kingdom there is a supreme landlord, that is to say, the sovereignty over land is concentrated on a 'national' scale. During the New Kingdom, the great temples (an adjunct of the state in Kemp's view)[147] fulfil the same function of supreme landlords.

As stated above, a type of land possession was granted to royal officials as a reward for their services. These types of estates are known to us through the biographies of the officials themselves, which underscore the fact that they received a reward from the king.[148] Metjen's biography, dating to the Fourth Dynasty, states that he received from the king fields of different sizes as rewards for his work as ruler of various centres in Lower Egypt, and that he inherited from his mother 50 arouras, acquiring besides 200 arouras with people from the king. The same document registers the founding of domains under his control, especially the fourth/fifth nome and the second nome in Lower Egypt. In any case, lands related to funerary cults were transmitted, granted and inherited, creating foundations devoted to providing offerings and maintaining the cult.[149]

Confronted with this evidence, let us consider two questions related to the creation of private holdings. The first question relates to the inheritability of land. We note that in general the land had to remain undivided, it was only transmissible from parents to children, and according to the available information it could not be ceded to a third party, probably because essentially it continued to be the property of the pharaoh.

The second question, related to this last statement, is that the king assigned the lands based on an individual's functions. Did the lands revert to the crown when the beneficiary of a reward was replaced by another in the same post?

A disposition found in the decree of pharaoh Neferirkare of the Fifth Dynasty allows us to partially answer this question:

---

147   Kemp 1972, p. 676.

148   *Urk.* I, 1–5; Goedicke 1970, pp. 5–20; Strudwick 2005, pp. 192–4.

149   Another example of a donation: a certain Sabni of Elephantine (Sixth Dynasty) received 11 hectares of land after carrying out a mission in Nubia, *Urk.* I, 140; Strudwick 2005, p. 338; and Ibi of Deir el-Gabrawy (Sixth Dynasty) received a field of about fifty hectares linked to a *hwt*, *Urk.* I, 145; Strudwick 2005, pp. 364–5.

(And with regard to) any noble, royal acquaintance, or person concerned with reversionary offerings (28) who shall act counter to this decree of my majesty (29a) which has been registered in the Great Mansion. (29b) (his) house, land, people, and everything he owns shall be taken away and he shall be put into compulsory labour.[150]

Even granting that this is a royal law, it establishes that individuals who receive properties do not have sovereignty. There are no large holdings that give rise to large rents. The historiographical tendency is to think of great concentrations of land coupled with an increase in servile relationships linked to feudal property. Similarly, there is a tendency to confuse feudalism with aristocracy; in Egypt, it is possible to identify an aristocracy that is essentially a state aristocracy.[151]

The epistolary sources related to Hekanakhte,[152] a funerary priest[153] linked to a pious foundation devoted to the cult of the statue of a senior state official[154] as well as the head of a large family[155] pose a series of questions related to property and land leases. Described by Wente[156] as a gentleman farmer, according to Eyre it could be considered that he belonged to a class of notable rural middlemen[157] who begin to show up in the sources during the first period of state fragmentation. In some ways, these documents provide information on

---

150   *Urk.* I, 170–2; Strudwick 2005, pp. 98–101.

151   Moreno García 2008, p. 108, rightly points to the absence of a true hereditary landed aristocracy whose interests might collide with those of the state. The nobility is what it is by virtue of its functions, it is created, maintained and brought down by the state, which does not confront any counterpower standing between the state itself and the village communities that could take over certain fiscal, military or ideological sovereign functions and hold on to them over time.

152   James 1962; Baer 1963; Allen 2002. Other references in the footnotes below.

153   *hem-ka*, 'servant of the ka'. On one occasion he refers to himself as *bak n per djet*, 'servant of the funerary domain', Cardoso 1993, p. 107.

154   It was found in Meseh's tomb in the Theban necropolis, one of the four small tombs in the northernmost section of Deir el Bahari in Thebes, Winlock 1922. The owner was probably a dependent of Ipi, the visir of Nebhepetre-Mentuhotep, Goedicke 1984, p. 3. Perhaps of the visir of Thebes named Ipi, Diego Espinel 2011, p. 231. However, Goedicke 1984, p. 12, doubts he was *hem-ka*, 'servant of the ka' of the funerary cult of the visir, since the source does not explicitly say so.

155   Moreno García 2004a, pp. 86 ff., notes the importance of the extended family in social organisation, see also Moreno García 2004a, pp. 191–7. For a different view, see Cardoso 2009, p. 90.

156   Wente 1990, p. 58.

157   Eyre 1999, p. 48.

the household and the large family as the basic unit of rural organisation.[158]
Certainly, it can be said that the centre of this extended domestic system mentioned in the documents would be what Hekanakhte calls 'my property', which
included the adjacent fields tilled by him, his family and other labourers. Other
fields attached to his property were leased out to peasants in exchange for
monthly rations in grain and clothing. He probably received these fields as
a perpetual endowment in return for his duties.[159] There are remarkable references to costs, seed reserves, maximising the extension of cultivated land,
household weaving, clothing sold, and so on.

There is no evident relationship between the properties mentioned by Hek-
hanakhte and the foundation where he serves as priest, nor is it readily apparent whether the rents obtained from production allow for something more
than the mere subsistence of the family and its dependents. The documents do
mention, perhaps with some exaggeration, situations of extreme poverty; the
family and their dependants go hungry during a bad year.[160] However, these
households of the sub-elite were linked to state organisation in a manner that
is difficult to define. In fact, this type of funerary domain (*per-djet*) functioned
as subsidiary holdings[161] of the *per-shena* or administrative centre mentioned
above, and of the royal domains in times of political centralisation. In his letters, Hekanakhte refers to himself once as *bak n per djet*, 'servant of the funerary
domain',[162] and in ledgers the *per-shena* appears mentioned among the places
where supplies are available.

Nevertheless, Hekanakhte appears as administrator of his own holdings,
laying down guidelines, giving orders on how to care for people and crops,
handling parental and economic relationships. The ledgers register supplies
that were available in different households, villages and in the *per-shena* itself.
Therefore, these forms of individual property could be juxtaposed with the

---

158   Eyre 1999, p. 49.

159   Allen 2002, pp. 149 and 178. Receiving a modest stipend for his services, the farmer would
      have remained dependent on his own land and upon the land he administered for the
      mortuary cult, Grajetzki 2009, p. 151; Allen 2002, pp. 105–6.

160   The metaphor of hunger appears in the biographies that are contemporary to these
      sources. See, for example, the inscription of Ankhtifi at Moalla: Vandier 1950; Lichtheim
      1975, pp. 3–12, 83, 85–6; Serrano Delgado 1993, pp. 85–9.

161   See, for example, the *djadjat nt per djet*, 'council of *per-djet*', which functioned as both an
      administrative organisation and a tribunal in the large areas of the Old Kingdom, Menu
      2004b, p. 180.

162   According to Goedicke, *per djet* must not be interpreted as the domain thus identified, but
      as *per* 'house' and *djet* 'eternally', Goedicke 1984, p. 81.

production of villages and local associations, linking people with bonds of patronage and dependency.[163]

However, this type of patronage does not give rise to a hereditary landed aristocracy whose interests, although they could conflict with those of the crown, could hardly be expected to dispute the primacy of the central state.[164] That is to say, the appearance of this type of property did not transform the dominant forms of exploitation of the communities and the royal domains. Indeed, according to sources of the period, by the New Kingdom most (two thirds) of the lands belonging to smaller temples, funerary holdings and even entire villages had been brought under the aegis of the great temples. In summary, the major institutional landowners were the temples,[165] who received income from the product of large holdings, rents from leaseholders of temple land and rents for services hired from other institutions. The relationship between the crown and religious institutions is evident in the fact that the latter were led by senior officials who were often palace dignitaries or officials of the crown. In turn, the latter could own small fields within the jurisdiction of the temples or of the crown.

Other plots of equal size (between two and three arouras) could be associated to a local entity or to different professional categories (soldiers, stable grooms, women), and such plots were hereditary and generally inalienable.[166] However, they could be sub-leased. Evidently there was a strong link between land division and taxes on crops.

Based on Herodotus, Menu notes that such land divisions and the adjudication of temple lands to private individuals was the work of Ramesses II, who established a system of rewards for officials that replaced previous systems. Later sources mention annual income received by the Theban temples, their treasuries, warehouses and storehouses.[167]

---

163 Eyre 2010, p. 302.

164 Moreno García 2008, p. 108. Nevertheless, Moreno García finds that considering the state as a distant institution without influence in local affairs is problematic; he highlights a model that contains within itself the notions of decentralisation, delegation of power and clientelism. In other words, he points out the risk of falling into what he deems to be an old historiographic tradition that opposes the fragility of Oriental state formations with the persistence of villages and rural conservatism. For further reading on the theoretical questions and historiographical positions, see Moreno García 2008, esp. pp. 99–106.

165 Papyrus Harris and the above mentioned Wilbour papyrus supply information on the administration of temples and their properties, Grandet 1994.

166 About the zone prevalence of different categories, see O'Connor 1972, pp. 693–5.

167 Papyrus Harris records temple endowments of ca. 2680 sq. km, Grandet 1994, pp. 91–101.

In summary, in contrast with earlier periods, this era presents more evidence of land owned by private individuals, whose origins were in royal grants or family inheritance. Let us first consider the types of royal donation or transference. The evidence on donations allows us to state that senior officers of the crown or military men were rewarded with lands since the Eighteenth Dynasty. It must be considered that the fields varied in size and were located in different regions:[168] there is a categorical difference between the 154 arouras granted to an official (Chief of the Royal Harem)[169] specifically stating that those lands belong to a temple in Giza and the 16 arouras in a village and waterway close to Qantir granted to reward a military man.[170]

This latter type of grant given to military men can also be found in biographical inscriptions[171] in which the beneficiary underscores that he was granted 'people, livestock and fields' in his own village or town. In Middle Egypt we find landowners who are mentioned as military men in the Wilbour papyrus,[172] although this may be related to the above-mentioned process of colonisation of said region.[173]

In general, lands were granted to the gods,[174] or the king granted lands dedicated to the cult of a royal statue.[175] A priest could manage the land, and he was obliged to make a ritual offer of one ox per year to the statue. The holding consisted of a certain number of arouras managed by the same priest, and other persons could be hired to manage the remaining fields.

We previously referred to independent holders (*nemehw*) in lands belonging to the crown (*khato*), who paid a compensation directly to the treasury toward the end of the Ramesside period. The connection between independ-

---

This represents more than half of the arable land of Upper Egypt, Eyre 2010, p. 303: 'Papyrus Harris also records donations of 3,000,000 *khar* of grain to the temple of Karnak, and 309,950 *khar* to Medinet Habu and the minor temples of, Haring 1997, pp. 412–4'.

168   Thebes, Nubia, Giza, Qantir and Memphis.

169   Stela Cairo JE 28019. Zivie 1976, pp. 177–82, 273–4, pl. 13; Meeks 1979, p. 663, from Ay reign. Also Berlin Stela 14994, from Thutmose I's reign, records the 150 arouras given to a military man, Nekry, Schulman 1964, p. 98, no. 80; Meeks 1979, pp. 661–2.

170   Stela Cairo JE 88879, from Ramesses III, Meeks 1979, p. 664; Schulman 1988, pp. 22–4.

171   *Urk.* IV, 1–10; Loret 1901; Lichtheim 1976, pp. 12–15.

172   Katary 1989, p. 69.

173   Eyre 2004, p. 161.

174   Montu, Amon-Ra, Mnevis, Horakhty, Amon and one to the sphinx's temple in Giza.

175   An inscription of Pennut's tomb in Aniba, dated in Ramesses VI's realm, Steindorff 1935, pl. 101 shows regulations taken by this pharaoh in favour of his own statue: Inscription on Stela Stuttgart, Menu 1998, p. 140.

ent holders (*nemehw*) and villages must be considered in the light of the forced labour in lands belonging to the crown to which villagers were subject, and the sources underscore that independent holders were exempt from such labour in exchange for a payment in gold. In addition, however, the Stela of Israel[176] explicitly remarks on a certain contrast: 'He (the king) has let *nemehw* return to villages' and 'he has let officials/nobles – *srw* – retain their possessions'.[177]

It seems therefore that the *nemehw* owned small plots of land in the context of villages, and that, in some manner undisclosed by the sources, they were able to obtain gold to pay the tax in order to be exempted from the *corvée*. They have been identified[178] with the parcel holders found in the papyrus Wilbour and in other sources of the period,[179] but it does not appear possible to subscribe to such an identification based on the available information.

Secondly, family inheritance is acknowledged in legal documents or wills that were unknown in earlier periods. The will of a woman who calls herself *nemehyt*, 'of the pharaoh's land',[180] enables the conclusion that the fields belonging to this category of individual could be inherited[181] by the individual's children. This right to decide over the property she inherited from her father, from her first husband and a part of what her second husband accumulated seems to support the hypothesis that the inheritance remained in the nucleus of the family. Incidentally, this was a family of the elite and linked to the necropolis.

It is worth noting that local councils such as the *kenebet*[182] intervened in these events, attending to questions related to rights and property disputes as

---

176   Stela of Israel, line 16 = Cairo 34025 vs.: Spiegelberg 1897, pp. 1–25, pls. 13–4; Lacau 1926, pp. 52–9, pls. 17–19; Kitchen 1981, pp. 12–19; Lichtheim 1976, pp. 73–8.

177   See Römer 1994, pp. 412–51, regarding this contrast.

178   Gardiner 1948, p. 206; Janssen 1986, p. 363; Menu 1970, p. 30.

179   Janssen 1986, p. 363, called those little owners: 'virtual proprietors' or 'private owners', whose rights over the land may have been the same as that of private proprietors, even when the land belonged theoretically to the pharaoh.

180   Naunakhte's will (Papyrus Ashmolean Museum 1945.97) from Ramesses V, Černý 1945, pp. 29–53; Théodoridès 1966, pp. 31–70; Allam 1973, pp. 268–74, no. 262; Kitchen 1983, pp. 236–40; Mc Dowell 1999, pp. 38–40, no. 14.

181   *imyt-per*, literally, 'what is at home'. Ein Testament machen, *Wb*. I, p. 73; see Seidl 1939, p. 58; Théodoridès 1970.

182   During the New Kingdom, the disputes on property rights were under the jurisdiction of *kenebet* which, although mainly judicial, also had administrative functions and dealt with the countless cases of rights and disputes over property. Also, there were central councils (*Great kenebet*), in the New Kingdom, whose functions were both judicial and administrative.

well as fulfilling administrative functions. There is also an increase in the number of references in written documents, land registers and cadastres, personal lawsuits and often in decisions of the oracle pertaining to lawsuits involving fields.

Did this type of economic-social practice reinforce the private nature of property? We believe that the nature of the sources needs to be analysed in order to distinguish the type of property and the aspects involved in its transference. In general, what we find is a system of family tenure, and although there is no explicit specification regarding how the families came to own the fields, it can be inferred that they originated as royal favours or rewards in view of the titles held by the men in those families: a male nurse of the royal son, in favour of his wife and children,[183] or the scribe of the royal offering table who went to court with documents to prove his and his brothers' rights on some arouras.[184] It must be taken into account that such fields could be part of the tenure system of the temples and that a payment had to be made for priestly rituals. Other examples refer to the practice of adopting the wife as a daughter or the adoption of slaves in order to keep the property within the family.[185]

Based on this evidence, Eyre posits the creation of 'certain types of disposable (i.e. private) property in land, as a vital feudal device'.[186] This author considers that 'entail provides security of tenure, but then complex social tensions over property rights come into play'. Documents allow us to recognise social tensions resulting from property rights of different families and descendants.[187]

In summary, we encounter forms of individual property, which could be deemed private property, during the New Kingdom, but this type of property does not develop; it does not engender proper feudal forms. Godelier's idea that

183   This case is laid out in a monument – on a stelophorous statue – given the subject's link to royalty. = Stela Cairo 34016, *Urk.* IV, 1065–1070; also Théodoridès 1970; Spalinger 1984, esp. p. 633.

184   Papyrus Berlin 3047, year 46 of Ramesses II, Helck 1963, pp. 65–73; Baer 1962, pp. 36–9; Kitchen 1979, pp. 803–6; Katary 1989, pp. 223–5.

185   Papyrus Ashmolean Museum 1945.96, known as Adoption Papyrus. Gardiner 1940, pp. 23–9; Théodoridès 1965, pp. 79–142; Allam 1973, pp. 258–67, no. 261; Cruz-Uribe 1988; Allam 1990, pp. 189–91; Eyre 1992.

186   This kind of land property might have been close to private property, resulting in certain types of availability of the land, Eyre 1994, pp. 112–13.

187   Ibid.

certain forms of the Asiatic mode of production could lead to certain forms of feudalism[188] cannot be corroborated in this process of transformation of property relations in this economic-social formation.

In other words, we do not encounter a landed monopolist class, and we do not encounter great landowners exercising non-economic coercive powers in order to impose control, neither in an informal manner nor through the public or private system of justice. Indeed, it could be argued that we encounter the opposite of what would constitute a feudal system as defined by Hindess and Hirst[189] and even Wickham.[190] Even though we do find forms of rent, a majority of those rents appear in juxtaposition with state (or temple) forms of property, or with the village or town forms of property. During the New Kingdom, it is possible to refer to individual forms of property that contradict the dominant forms.

III

In the *Formen*, Marx states:

> [C]ities in the proper sense arise by the side of these villages only where the location is particularly favourable to external trade, or where the head of the state and his satraps exchange their revenue (the surplus product) against labour, which they expend as labour-funds.

This thesis becomes irrefutable in the face of the compelling evidence available for social formations such as the one analysed herein. In particular, it can be legitimately argued that the availability of surpluses and the accumulation that allowed the class of officials to obtain goods – for example, funerary goods – above and beyond what was granted by the king arose from the state sphere itself and became evident in the 'metropolitan' centres where the elites resided.[191] In Thebes during the New Kingdom, for example, the craftsmen of the necropoleis were the ones who generated resources and amplified

---

188   Godelier 1971, p. 47.

189   Hindess and Hirst 1975, pp. 18–19.

190   Wickham 1994a, p. 10.

191   However, exceptions can be found in cemeteries such as Abydos, Riqqa and Haraga, which present us with '[b]urial practices of the population outside of royalty and the highest elite, specifically in the twelfth dynasty', according to Richards 2005, esp. p. 174.

the circulation of goods, but what allowed them to do so was their dependency and the rations they received from the state. It is possible that the very possibility of economic accumulation, as well as a certain prestige, derived from their articulation with state institutions. Thus we arrive at the conclusion that the Egyptian state as distributive state (among the dominant class and high-ranking officials) negates accumulation on the part of an elite of officials, but at the same time enables such accumulation as a side-effect of its functioning. Furthermore, the observation of the interstitial circulation mechanisms of this period shows merchants operating with surpluses derived from the dominant classes. In the words of Marx, this type of private accumulation would be found in the 'pores of the ancient world'.[192]

An analysis of the circulation of funerary goods, especially during the New Kingdom, shows that most of the goods and the access to luxurious burials were within the orbit of the state, a matter of no small importance in a culture with such a developed culture of death as pharaonic Egypt. Nevertheless, the demands of the elites are recognisable in the different periods of pharaonic history. During the New Kingdom, however, there was an increase in the circulation of goods and people, which gave rise to processes of appropriation of the circulation and the exchanges with metallic equivalents in cities like Thebes and around Deir el-Medina.[193]

The sources from the New Kingdom present economic agents such as merchants or *shutyw* that offer alternatives to the dominant mechanism. These economic-social relationships cannot always be included in the state distributive circuit. Such merchants were often agents of the temple, but they could also act on behalf of military leaders, singers of Amon and other officials. These situations seem to have been functional to a complex system of economic relations in which the state had the monopoly of control mechanisms, but these did not operate in only one direction.

How to explain the appearance of these forms of economic circulation?

In the field of Egyptology, the answers to this question are rooted in theory, either economic anthropology theory or economic theory. In the first case, the Egyptian economy is understood as a complete otherness; in the second case, it is viewed as a primitive version of a modern economy. The principle

---

192 Marx 1964, p. 40.
193 The village of the labourers, *set maat*: 'place of truth'.

of redistribution that Karl Polanyi[194] proposed as an integration mechanism has been the template for understanding the economy of pharaonic Egypt. The problem is that the scope of this principle is limited to the possibility of describing the economy, but it does not allow for an analytical understanding of said economy, confusing forms of production with forms of circulation. The principle's validity, however, resides in the fact that it permits us to understand that in ancient societies the economy *appears* to be subjected to a political unit and not to atomised individual decisions.[195]

Some explanations, such as Kemp's in *Ancient Egypt: Anatomy of a Civilization*,[196] suggest the combination of an institutional redistributive aspect with individual or private demand. However, in our view the power of private demand would not come from 'individual' power but rather from accumulation processes generated by state surpluses.

To explore how those processes arise, we must look into the state economy, especially that of the temples located in the area of Thebes. Those temples had control of the main resources; the productivity of the lands under their administration was remarkable, as well as the volume of storage[197] and transport.[198] Certainly, as stated above, the temples had a significant role in the administration of land and tax collection. For example, we know that the temples of the western shore were responsible for paying out rations for various types of labourers and specialised craftsmen. Sources of the period reflect a certain amount of conflict between sectors that are expressed in the historical phenomenon of discontent due to lack of payment of the rations.[199] This unusual procedure is remarkable in that it includes economic demands as well as a challenge to the bureaucratic order.

Paradoxically, besides making a living with the rations handed out by the temples, craftsmen developed pseudo-private practices in the sphere of domestic and craft production that are manifested in transactions with productive animals (oxen), pack animals (donkeys) and funerary objects (sarcophagi,

---

194   Polanyi 1957, pp. 250–6.

195   Godelier 1989, pp. 224–5.

196   Kemp 2006, p. 304.

197   P. Turin 1895 + 2006 = Turin Taxation Papyrus, Gardiner 1948, pp. xiii–xiv, 35–44; 1941, pp. 19–73; 127–85; Pleyte and Rossi 1869–76, pls. 65, 100, 155; 156; 157; vs. pl. 96; Katary 1989, pp. 169–82.

198   Amiens Papyrus, Gardiner 1948, pp. vi–vii, 1–13; 1941, pp. 37–56, pl. 7; Katary 1989, pp. 184–92. Other sources related to transport of grains in Katary 1989, pp. 192 ff.

199   Edgerton 1951, pp. 137–45; Eyre 1979, pp. 80–91; Janssen 1979a, pp. 301–8; Frandsen 1990; Janssen 1992.

steles, statues) or objects of daily use (furniture) that are registered in ostraca.[200] It can be gleaned that specialised villagers obtained individual benefits
from these exchanges.[201] This is not due to the action of the subjects, nor to the
aggregate of their actions, but to the logic of social functioning.[202]

It cannot be overlooked that the basis of the surplus was the supply of goods
by the state. Commercial growth in Deir el-Medina depended on the state
infrastructure for its development, thus inhibiting an entirely free production.
The internal market arose from the surpluses of households and craftsmen.
Indeed, the testimonies from Deir el-Medina suggest the existence of commercial growth in which goods derived from household and craft production were
added to rations. Unfortunately, there is no comparable quantitative information to assess the amounts of such exchanges, although individual officials
could acquire various goods at the same time. The individual appropriation of
goods is reflected in purchases with equivalents, though they are not universal
equivalents. Officials could probably dispose of goods received as royal rewards
or even goods derived from accumulation in their properties.

In any case, in metropolitan centres we detect a process of circulation of
goods that exceeds domestic production, as well as social and economic relations derived from the availability of surpluses. Although preceding eras presented some isolated forms of this type, most of the exchanges were barter
exchanges, i.e. goods were exchanged for other goods, and those goods were
recognisable extensions of domestic activities and/or close to village/town
activities, activities of officials and/or linked to religious or funerary institutions like temples.

Although value patterns had been used since the Old Kingdom, it is worth
considering that there was an increase in the movement of goods during the
Ramesside period and metal value patterns were applied, as in Deir el-Medina.

---

200   Janssen 1975; Cooney 2007; Zingarelli 2010b, pp. 53–67.
201   These incomes could be even higher than wages, Lesko 1994, p. 21. Cooney 2006 proposes
      that Deir el-Medina artisans worked in 'informal workshops', where they produced an
      income in the private sector. She affirms on p. 44 that they could have worked within
      formal hierarchical specialisations, using their reputation to gain customers and to have
      access to materials. She bases her thesis on what she calls internal workshop records. Thus,
      according to Cooney, contextual and circumstantial evidence of work organisation points
      to work in a given place rather than individual work. However, numerous transactions
      allow us to recognise individual goods exchange making reference to partial work (paint-
      ing, decoration, pigment purchase).
202   Astarita 2000a, p. 22.

Let us consider then that these measure units were proto-money[203] and, even though there was no coin corresponding to a currency form, in some exchanges general equivalents were used but not universally.

The metal circulation first implied the introduction of these metals by the state and secondly their subsequent use in the internal circuit as equivalents, even though they were not always physically present in the transactions. One of the possible ways by which officials and military men could obtain metals, especially gold and silver, was through rewards since the Eighteenth Dynasty.

In addition, the robbed precious metals were gold and silver and the main goal was to exchange them for productive goods such as grain and animals. This circulation process was in agreement with the exchange practice in equivalents carried out in Deir el-Medina. The greed for gold, silver and even copper and bronze should not only be considered as a way of getting luxury goods, but it should also be taken into account in the general economic process at the end of the Ramesside period.

In summary, centralised administrative intervention did not prevent individual appropriation of goods in the circulation circuit, nor did it avoid certain accumulation mechanisms. However, these occurred in the metropolitan centres where the elites resided. The fact that this circulation arose from the availability of surpluses in the spheres in which the dominant groups operated is not exceptional. The monarchy's economic *dirigisme* was compatible with processes of private accumulation and exchange. As stated before, the state negates private accumulation, but enables it as a side-effect of its functioning, which is dominant.

The historical existence of money and trade cannot be linked to a modern phenomenon. The resulting force in a commercial society cannot be assigned to the markets of the dominant classes in a society whose mode of production was based on the primary appropriation by the so-called superior community. Still, during the New Kingdom it is possible to detect commercial development that implies the use of proto-money. Marx referred to these as antediluvian capital categories. They appear to reflect certain social and economic relations corresponding to other modes of production, but they are false expressions of private accumulation given that their origin derives from state property or from incomplete forms of individual property.

On the other hand, land exploitations linked to the temple during New Kingdom presented differentiated extractive forms related to slaves, most of

203   Janssen 1975, p. 546, considered that in some respects units like *seniw, deben* and *khAr* were in fact money.

whom were appropriated in the course of wars of conquest. Although these social changes did not replace previous forms, they did create new forms of bondage. The exploitation of slave labour could not become the dominant relation of production due to the absence of fully-fledged private property of land and the permanent availability of farm labourers through the *corvée*. Slave labour filled interstitial gaps in Egyptian labour and agrarian exploitation without becoming the sustaining base of the dominant classes.

The sources reveal forms of property of slave labourers in the villages/towns, especially in relation to conflicts between town leaders and other state officials, as in the case of a foreman demanding slave girls from a town mayor. The sources also describe[204] transactions involving the rent of slaves for some days at very high prices in metal equivalents, and even transactions for a period of ten years.[205] Although the labourers probably belonged to the village/town or to individuals,[206] members of institutions participated in the transactions, for example, the shepherd of a temple (literally, 'house'). We agree with Navailles and Neveu,[207] who suggest that the institutions (the pharaoh, the temples, the village) owned the slaves and assigned them nominally to certain individuals. Thus, the slaves could work successively for a number of days for one or another temporary owner; the concession could be renewed monthly, annually, or even for a period of ten years, which would justify the high values stipulated in the transactions. It is also possible to detect the inheritability of the rights over the labour days of certain families.[208]

The exchange of slaves and plots of land is a phenomenon especially related to circulation, and it is significant that it is only recorded for metropolitan areas such as Thebes, Kahun, Gurob and other important cities. This process of incorporating labour into the circulation process is limited and secondary with respect to the sphere of production and appropriation of surplus human labour by the dominant classes.

---

204   Kahun papyri of the Eighteenth Dynasty, Griffith 1898; Gardiner 1906.
205   Ostracon Gardiner 123, Allam 1973, p. 177, no. 174; Černý and Gardiner 1957, p. 16, pls. 54–54a, no. 1; Kitchen 1981, pp. 219–20.
206   See Théodoridès 1968.
207   Navailles and Neveu 1989.
208   See Hieratic Ostracon 51, 2; also known as Ostracon Gardiner 90 and Ashmolean Museum 90, from Ramesses II, Allam 1973, pp. 68–9, no. 165; McDowell 1993, pp. 23–5.

IV

For Marx, the Asiatic state was despotic.[209] He did not state this without empirical knowledge or evidence, as has been suggested, but was influenced as a man of his time by concepts of state government.[210] The category of the despotic or despotism is rooted in the values of the Enlightenment[211] for or against the absolute monarchies of Europe.[212] Hence the denomination of despotic for monarchies based on royal power that did not accept other types of power. Moreover, the development of the concept of despotism coincides with its extension to Eastern monarchies as a whole.[213] In the East, the despot as a person also becomes fused with the superior community, and he receives concessions as father of many communities, for his glory and that of the god.[214] In the case of Egyptian royalty, the despot's dominion over territories, property, people and even villages is based on mythical foundations. The most evident political form of this mode is the centralised monarchy that Westerners perceive as despotic. The Egyptian king, whom the Greeks called pharaoh or 'greatest house', is himself a god or the son of the sun god Ra, and his power encompasses earthly and divine territories. This mythical discourse is not devoid of the violence of the state represented by the figure of the king who is depicted slaughtering or crushing the enemy, but also infusing his sub-

---

209   It has been noted that he refers to the state and to the despot as an individual, that is, he equates both terms, Zamora 1997, p. 12, n. 1.

210   O'Leary 1989, p. 83, points to the differences Marx established between Asiatic despotism and modern states, as well as to his criticism of Hegel.

211   Nonetheless, Marx questions Montesquieu's theory of despotism, arguing that it is not possible to distinguish between monarchy, despotism and tyranny, O'Leary 1989, p. 84.

212   Hobbes is the first one to recommend despotic power as a normal and adequate form of sovereignty. Based on Anderson 1979, p. 463.

213   Anderson 1979, pp. 463 ff., carries out a remarkable analysis of the origins of the notion of despotism associated with Asia, starting with Aristotle. Later, spurred by the proximity of Turkish power, the notion appeared with the rebirth of political theory during the Renaissance, and the voyages of the Enlightenment allowed for a more systematic formulation. Sawer 1977, pp. 5 ff., also analyses how this idea of Oriental despotism was already present among the Greeks. In his *Politics*, Aristotle states that 'For Barbarians being more servile in character than Hellenes, and Asiatics than Europeans, do not rebel against a despotic government'.

214   'Part of its surplus labour belongs to the higher community, which ultimately appears as a *person*. This surplus labour is rendered both as tribute and as common labour for the glory of the unity, in part that of the despot, in part that of the imagined tribal entity of the god', Marx 1964, p. 70.

jects with life if he deemed it convenient. This political form corresponds to the dominant relations of production and persisted over millennia, although the expressions of legitimacy varied[215] and new myths to support the divine power of the king were developed.[216]

Marx did not develop the political and social forms of despotism;[217] rather he referred to 'Asiatic despotism' or 'Oriental despotism' when describing India under English domination.[218] He barely uses the term in the *Formen* because he focuses on Asiatic forms of property, but he describes and ascribes these forms to what he terms Oriental despotism. That is to say, certain political, extra-economical forms characterised as despotic correspond to certain relations of production and property.

Returning to 1853, a time when Marx contributed to the Republican periodical *New York Daily Tribune*[219] in the US,[220] he stated that in Asia there were three departments of government: of finance, or the plunder of the interior; of war, or the plunder of the exterior; and the department of public works. And although in view of climate and territorial conditions he does mention that Oriental agriculture is based on artificial irrigation through waterways and water-works, he also notes that 'As in Egypt and India, inundations are used for fertilising the soil in Mesopotamia, Persia, &c.; advantage is taken of a high level for feeding irrigative canals'.[221] When comparing with the Occident, he finds that oriental governments were in charge of organising public works. Note that this circumstance coupled with the concentration in small centres that brought

---

215　We have already mentioned the importance of political literature during the Middle Kingdom. On the relationship between literature and politics during the Egyptian Middle Kingdom, see Posener 1956. On the discussion over the use of the term 'propaganda' in relation to these written documents with political content, see Baines 1996, esp. p. 354. Also Assmann 1999, pp. 1–15.

216　See, for example, the theogamies of the New Kingdom, Campbell 1912 and Naville 1896.

217　He was interested in describing the economic and social features, rather than the political system, O'Leary 1989, p. 132.

218　However, O'Leary 1989, pp. 83–4, points out that the early works of Marx 1843–4 present the notion of despotism in a rather polemical sense, without differentiating between feudal monarchy and Oriental despotism. Sofri 1969, pp. 19–20, for his part, considers that at the time Marx had a Hegelian view of Asia.

219　Until the mid-1850s this was a leftist *whig* newspaper. Later it became an organ of the Republican Party.

220　These articles were written over several years and focused esp. on the political, military and social impact of British imperialism in India and China. 'The British Rule in India', published in June of 1853, is particularly relevant, Marx 1979, pp. 125–9.

221　Marx 1979, p. 127.

together agriculture and crafts gave birth to the social system called the *village system*. This system gave each of the small groups its own autonomous organisation and distinct way of life, and was destroyed by the steam engine and English trade. This is what Marx wanted to stress and assess with respect to India under British domination: the contradiction between these rural units/communities which he considers 'industrious, patriarchal, harmless and idyllic' but featuring static, vegetative life lacking dignity which in turn provided a solid base for oriental despotism, biased by superstition and deprived of all historic change.[222] Marx justifies the change that comes through England, and although he acknowledges her miserly interests, he concludes that '[w]hatever may have been the crimes of England she was the unconscious tool of history in bringing about that revolution'.[223] The idea of England's double mission, both destructive and regenerative, is present in this article by Marx. Nevertheless, there is not just one way of dissolution for 'primitive' communal property, as Marx himself said regarding India.[224]

At the same time, in their correspondence, Marx and Engels exchanged ideas on the East. In the letter dated 2 June 1853 – based on the description of the military system of Eastern cities written by François Bernier in *Voyages contenant la description des états du Grand Mogol* – Marx underscores that the army has to follow the king, who is the sole proprietor of all the land. He also emphasises that the basic form of all Eastern phenomena – in Turkey, Persia and the Indostan according to Bernier – must be found in the absence of private property of land, as analysed above.[225] On 6 June 1853, Engels writes back saying that indeed the absence of private property of land is the key to understanding all the East,[226] and he proposes ecological and climatic motives to explain

---

222   For an in-depth development of this topic, see Sofri 1969, pp. 25–39. Sofri explains the reasons for Marx's interest in India at the time, and the lesser amount of space devoted to the history of, for example, China. Sofri 1969, pp. 76–7, believes, and we agree, that it would be a mistake to think that 'Marx saw the China and India of his time as concrete examples of the "Asiatic mode of production"', even if they had some of its distinctive traits. In the chapter on the historical considerations of commercial capital in Volume III of *Capital*, he refers to communal property in China and India.

223   Marx 1979, p. 132. According to Sofri 1969, p. 70, thirty years later, Marx thought it possible that the revolution and autonomous progress would come at the hand of Russian village communes. In the 1850s, Marx believed in the Industrial Revolution and capitalism destroying the communes of India, while in the 1880s he had arrived at the conviction that capitalism could be skipped.

224   Marx 1965, p. 56, n. 31.

225   Marx 1983, pp. 330 ff.

226   Engels 1983, pp. 335 ff.

such an absence.[227] Artificial irrigation is the primary condition of agriculture, and it is the concern of the communes, of the provinces and the central government. Here he points out – and Marx reproduced the statement a few days later in his article for the *New York Daily Tribune* – that there are three departments of government: of finance, or the plunder of the interior; of war, or the plunder of the exterior; and the department of public works. In his response dated 14 June 1853, Marx explains Asia's stagnation as due to the public works of the central government and the division of the empire in villages with their own separate organisation, although he also counts on the existence of a few large cities. Marx was searching for an explanation of the fundamental reason for British domination and the arrival of industry to the East, and he found it in the stagnation of Asiatic despotism. With regard to the first condition, Marx underscores the stagnation deriving from the public works of the central government, but he omits Engels's suggestion regarding the role of communes and provinces in artificial irrigation. Regarding the second condition, the presence of self-sufficient communities based on the unification of agriculture and manufacturing in the household will be developed in the *Formen* and become a central notion of his discourse. Moreover, in the *Formen* Marx will revisit the absence of legal property in Oriental despotism (that Engels had mentioned in his letter of 6 June 1853) and the existence of communal property containing conditions for reproduction and surplus production.[228] Perhaps the difference, not a small one, with the content of the *Formen* is that in his correspondence and in his journalistic article Marx was interested less in explaining certain features of the Eastern societies, and more in the dialectical definition of forms preceding the development of capitalism.[229]

In *Capital*,[230] Marx revisits the importance of regulating the Nile floods and the need for observation and astronomical calculations, an activity in the hands of the priests, who were in turn the administrators of agriculture.[231]

---

227   Godelier 1977, p. 36.

228   As I understand it, Hobsbawm posits that scholars who did not know the *Formen* pointed to the Oriental system as characterised by the absence of private property derived from excessive centralisation, public works and irrigation based on Marx's letters and articles on India. Hobsbawm notes that in the *Formen* Marx posits the idea of manufacturing and agricultural unity in the villages, Marx 1964, pp. 33–4. A different view can be found in Soriano Llopis 2007, p. 25.

229   O'Leary 1989, p. 102.

230   Marx 1965, p. 357.

231   Marx 1965, p. 360, n. 6.

There is a certain tension in Marx's postulates of 1853 regarding the conditions and the organisation of production in the villages[232] and the organisation attributed to the state in what pertained to great irrigation works. This could be explained up to a point, especially if we focus on the *Formen*, where Marx remarks on the presentation of government public works with respect to the 'water conduction sustained by nature appropriation through collective conditions'.[233] Evidently, in the *Formen* Marx understands the importance of, for example, aqueducts built by the state in that they imply the appropriation of village work: 'communal conditions for real appropriation through labour, such as irrigation systems (very important among the Asian peoples), means of communication, etc., will then appear as the work of the higher unity – the despotic government which is poised above the lesser communities'.

With regard to this, if we think only of ancient Egypt, the Nile's natural irrigation of arable land over several weeks created natural basins along the river and allowed for the planting of wheat, barley and flax around the month of October. This implies that peasant communities had the ability to maintain the waterways in working condition and regulate the opening and closing of the levees that allowed for water circulation.[234]

Having said that, state control over the Nile's floods and the flooded areas seems to have been crucial for the calculation of taxes.[235] This is perhaps the reason why the texts note in detail the different types of land and yields, attesting to a rich and complex lexicography related to types of soil, especially in the land surveys used for establishing taxes.[236] Likewise, scribes and priests developed certain types of knowledge, astronomical calculations and measurements that contributed to those surveys.

However, the state intervened in the conditioning of fields[237] and local communities supplied the necessary labour to carry it out. The increase in the area of arable land through artificial irrigation[238] seems to have been an option

---

232   Recall that he avoids Engels's proposition on the role of communes and provinces in the matter of irrigation.

233   Based on O'Leary 1989, pp. 97–8.

234   Moreno García 2004a, p. 46.

235   Moreno García 2004a, pp. 45–6.

236   Moreno García 2004a, p. 51.

237   Reflected ritually in a very early depiction of a king opening an irrigation waterway, i.e. a ritual of inauguration: Scorpion macehead, ca. 3000 BC.

238   It has been suggested that Sesostris II planned to convert an area of marshlands into arable land, and that the project included a levee and waterways connecting the area with Bahr Yusef. This correlates with the funerary monuments built in the region. See

from the beginning of the pharaonic dynasties,[239] although it did not entail the construction of massive water-works or complex waterway systems allowing for permanent rather than a seasonal irrigation,[240] a type of work that only becomes identifiable in the Greco-Roman period and the nineteenth and twentieth centuries.[241] As Eyre points out, 'the conversion of this wild landscape into a disciplined artificial irrigation regime was the work of the nineteenth and twentieth centuries'.[242] Some officials note in their biographies having carried out the construction of waterways, and during the first period of state fragmentation local men underscore their intervention in the construction of waterways,[243] irrigation canals[244] and cisterns[245] as well as in the use of water to enclose fields and higher ground.[246] It is not possible to establish a relationship of direct causation between 'hydraulic agriculture' and the logic of politics and social relations,[247] but neither is it possible to overlook the productivity and agricultural organisation in relation to the state, especially in areas with less propitious natural conditions.

Quite differently, Karl Wittfogel's thesis is based on Oriental/hydraulic despotism[248] as a system requiring *managerial* control. Thus, the state apparatus derives its power from the need for continuous administration and control of the waterworks.[249] Discussing in depth the problem of hydraulic despotism in the terms proposed by Wittfogel would exceed the purposes of the present chapter, but suffice it to say that, as Krader points out, it focuses on despotism, i.e. the political aspect of the problem.[250]

Callender 2000, p. 152, who accepts that the works were done but is not sure about the role of Sesostris II. Anyway, there is no firm evidence that such irrigation works were carried out, Diego Espinel 2011, p. 236.

239   Butzer 1976, p. 20.

240   Cardoso 1986, p. 13.

241   Moreno García 2004a, p. 47; Eyre 1999, p. 34 and 2004, pp. 157–76.

242   Eyre 2010, p. 292.

243   Griffith 1889, p. 11, pl. xv.

244   Griffith 1889, pl. xv.

245   Berlin Stela 14334, Andreu 1991, pl. 2, fig. 1; Roeder 1913, p. 122. Florence Stele 6365, Varille 1935–8, pp. 554–5; Bosticco 1959, pp. 24–5, pl. 18.

246   Moreno García 2004a, p. 48. Also Eyre 1999, p. 34.

247   Butzer 1976, p. 110.

248   On the flaws of the hypothesis of hydraulic causation and an analysis of ancient Egypt, see Cardoso 1982, pp. 14–25.

249   Hindess and Hirst 1975, p. 217; O'Leary 1989, p. 140.

250   According to Krader 1975, p. 115, n. 53, Wittfogel takes the issue one step further, converting the categories of despotism and totalitarianism into economic structures, as parts of

For his part, Godelier proposes a mode of production in which the aristocracy has state power at its disposal and insures the bases of class exploitation by appropriating a part of the product of the communities, although he insists on the existence of large-scale works which in turn condition the presence of a bureaucracy and an absolute, centralised power bearing the vague and antiquated name of despotism.[251] Notwithstanding the above, Godelier elaborates a typology of the various forms of the Asiatic mode of production with or without large-scale works, with or without agriculture, stressing the emergence of a primary class structure of ill-defined contours and the regular appropriation of the labour of the communities, as well as the development of productive forces in these civilisations, as attested to by the domination of man over nature through the use of metal, new forms of architecture, calculus, writing, etc.[252]

The importance of supervision and intervention in irrigation seems to be due to the accumulation the state derived from it and tax policies. Large works such as great architectural projects can be carried out to the extent that the state can provide resources obtained through surplus appropriation and its administration, and above all by the state's ability to marshal human labour, which is especially remarkable in times of political centralisation.[253] As Bard said, starting with the first dynasties of pharaonic Egypt, the monument was 'a symbol of the enormous control exercised by the crown'.[254] When the state became fragmented in times of decentralisation known as 'intermediate',[255] the great works and building projects disappeared and it seems as if the resources were managed at a local and regional level.

---

managerial and semi-managerial systems. See Bartra 1975, p. 23. See Sofri 1969, pp. 133–47, for a discussion of Wittfogel's book and criticism of his thesis.

251   Godelier 1971, pp. 43–4.

252   Godelier 1977, p. 152; 1971, pp. 44–5.

253   As Jones explains, 'in moving the colossal statues and vast masses, of which the transport creates wonder, human labour almost alone was prodigally used. The power to direct those masses is the origin of those titanic works'. Jones 1852, pp. 77–8. Marx 1965, pp. 228–9, cites this paragraph to explain the efficacy of simple cooperation.

254   Bard 2000, p. 81.

255   General bibliography on intermediate periods: First Intermediate Period ca. 2160–2055 BC: Seidlmayer 2000, pp. 108–36; Franke 2000, pp. 526–32; Moreno García 2011a; Willems 2010, pp. 81–100. Second Intermediate Period ca. 1650–1550 BC: von Beckerath 1965; Bourriau 2000, pp. 185–217; Ryholt 1997.

V

The most complex aspect to revisit is the qualifier of 'Asiatic', perhaps because Asia evokes an abstraction linked to certain negative traits, such as despotic, closed and stagnant, to express the singularity of Eastern processes as distinct from those of the West.

Nevertheless, as Said remarked, Orientalism is 'not an airy European fantasy about the Orient but a created body of theory and practice in which for many generations there has been a considerable material investment'.[256] Academic discourse included Egypt in that Orient because its history was more linked to urban and state development in the Ancient Middle East than to the African substrate of which it is also part.[257] Born in Europe, the historic construction of 'Ancient Near East' includes diverse regions and societies, and quite often the joint and global vision has let its particularities fall by the wayside. Paradoxically, it is through linguistic studies and archaeological explorations carried out in large part by Europeans, especially during the past century, that we have a body of academic knowledge called the 'Orient'. In any case, it is not a matter of stating, like Said, that for Marx it was easier to illustrate his theory using the collectivist Orient as a prophetic statement, or to reduce the attention he gave the Orient to the requirements of Western redemption.[258] There is, however, a problem in the Asiatic category due to the weight it gives to geographical factors in historical development[259] and because it is the only notion of a mode of production that is linked to a certain space.[260]

Godelier proposed abandoning the denomination of Asiatic since the phenomenon of the transition from a classless to a class society is recognisable in different historical times and spaces.[261] However, the works of Marx and Engels refer to Asia in general, although at times they mention Turkey, Persia, Afghanistan, Tartary, Arabia, Malaysia, the Isle of Java, China, India, the Hindustan, Mesopotamia and Egypt, but also the American civilisations of Mexico and Peru.[262] The criticism based on the geographical restriction[263] does not appear

---

256 Said 1977, p. 6.

257 Cervelló Autuori 1996, pp. 33 ff.

258 For a critique of Said's position, see Ahmad 1992, pp. 221–42.

259 On Hegel's influence and a critique of the notion of the Western spirit as inclined to change and development, see Hindess and Hirst 1975, pp. 203–6.

260 Sawer 1977, p. 2.

261 Godelier 1971, pp. 41–2.

262 Marx 1964, p. 70.

263 Chesneaux 1983, p. 110; Godelier 1971, pp. 41–2; Hindess and Hirst 1975, pp. 185–7.

justified given that Marx himself in the *Formen* did not limit the Asiatic form to certain spaces and pointed out the complexity of the transformation and dissolution processes of the ancient relations according to the different historical and geographical circumstances, indicating that the notion was not as limited as has been suggested.[264]

On the other hand, the emergence of feudalism has been historically associated with Europe and in this sense there is an acknowledgement of the singularity of the West with respect to the development of capitalism.[265] As Goody points out, the idea of the singularity of the West appears in relation to the 'curse' of capitalism. This author questions the perspectives that address the issue citing Western rationality, Western trade and the links between such phenomena as 'modernisation', 'industrialisation' and 'capitalism' itself. Goody admits that binarism is a presence in worldviews, but he resists the creation of false comparative assessments of the East and the West.[266]

Neither can we solve the problem by acknowledging in the Orient a feudal mode of production coexisting with other modes; in this case it could not claim for itself any kind of singularity and would still be on a level of development prior to that of the 'West'. As we have noted for the case of pharaonic Egypt, one of the spaces that Marx counted as part of the orient, it is viable to analyse that ancient state in terms of the Asiatic mode of production. The extension of this mode to historical spaces understood as Oriental is a matter that has to be understood in terms of a certain Western tradition. Nevertheless, the geographic restriction was absent in Marx's own interpretation; when Marx thought of the transition from 'primitive' or classless societies with a primitive or communal mode of production into class societies, into pristine states, he located the phenomenon in the orient because in fact the first states emerge in Egypt, Mesopotamia, China and India, although later they also emerged in America. Thus, the Asiatic form was closest to the primitive community; it was an early form related to the ancient form and the Germanic form. However, Marx notes that the Asiatic form has undergone historical and geographical variations.[267] This leads to the proposition that Marx's elaborations on the Asiatic mode in the *Formen* deal with a complex process of relations between the superior community and village communities that is associated with the early 'Oriental' states, hence its name, notwithstanding the fact that those relations can be found in other geographical spaces and historical times.

---

264   Marx 1964; Sofri 1969, pp. 46–8.

265   Goody 1996, p. 3.

266   Goody 1996, p. 10.

267   Sofri 1969, pp. 43–54.

VI

As argued above, in the Asiatic mode of production the logic of the state is pre-eminent and the relationship with the villages features extractive and exploitative forms. This first relation of appropriation defines the mode of production, whose constitutive elements are related to forms of property. Thus, the *Formen* highlight the fact that the state appears as the superior or sole proprietor to whom the surplus of the villages is due (although each peasant family can cultivate its own plot of land), and who benefits from the common labour carried out to exalt the despot or the divinity.

The analysis of this economic-social form detects village forms of property tied to the strong local identity and the self-sufficiency of the economy, as well as in consequence of shared property, the requirements of direct labour and the surrender of surplus labour for state institutions. However, there is an increasing encroachment on the part of the state through the creation of agricultural facilities in different regions of the Old Kingdom and the rising pre-eminence of the temples until they become the largest landowners during the New Kingdom, especially of holdings located in political and administrative centres. The implied or apparent property of the state becomes real and effective property. Thus, in some regions village property ends up being juxtaposed with those institutional holdings.

The transformation of these bonds with the communities does not affect their essential features based on agricultural production and manufacturing, although there is a visible differentiation and hierarchisation of village leaders, local elites and funerary institutions, each with its own functioning logic but somewhat limited by the state.

There is a visible continuity in the state, which maintains a political form and mechanisms of exploitation and domination that correspond to the dominant mode of production. The non-collapse of the pharaonic state and the persistence of its functioning forms over millennia have led to the characterisation of these societies as stagnant, unmoving. Indeed, there is identifiable political, economic and social change, but it does not undermine the dominant mode of appropriation and exploitative mechanisms of the state.

The so-called intermediate or transitional periods bring to the fore the conflicts among regional elites and allow for the identification of intermediate social categories and class contradictions, as well as expressions of status manifested during political crises that reflect a certain fragmentation of the state. Such crises do not undermine the dominant relations of production. As mentioned before, clientelar relations and the logic of the patron are to be understood as practices coexisting with the logic imposed by the state itself.

Thus, according to the *Formen*, the individual is then in fact propertyless or property appears to be mediated by means of a grant [*Ablassen*] from the total unity. In fact, sources of pharaonic Egypt document the granting of lands from the king to senior officers in retribution for their functions and services from the Old Kingdom onward. Familial forms of property appear in different periods of pharaonic history, juxtaposed with funerary and religious foundations. The emergence of a type of individual property indicates the coexistence of relations adjacent to the dominant forms of property but they do not give rise to a landed hereditary aristocracy that can challenge the dominance of the centralised state. That is to say, the appearance of this type of property did not transform the dominant forms of exploitation over the communities and the dominions of the crown. The fundamental explanations for royalty and the king's function as integrator of nature and the cosmos emanate from mythical-political contents corresponding to said forms.

The postulates of 1853 are in line with the above, alluding to the village system as a feature of Asiatic societies and also to the absence of private property. However, the references to the village system and to the absence of private property have a reduced analytical exposition as compared with the *Formen* due to the type of publication for which they were meant (*The New York Daily Tribune* and *Letters*) and because they treat India or the Orient as a whole, stressing the survival of those features in contemporary societies. The only aspect that is mentioned exclusively in the writings of 1853 is the question of artificial irrigation as a condition of agriculture and a certain geographical determinism in the explanation of the absence of private property due to ecological and climatic reasons. This feature has been overestimated, leading to an identification of hydraulic despotism with the Asiatic mode of production, when in reality the *Formen* emphasise the communal conditions for real appropriation through labour, such as aqueducts among other works like means of communication, etc., which appear as works of the superior entity above the communities. The sources of pharaonic Egypt note the existence of irrigation works on a local and state level, but above all they reflect state supervision and intervention in the irrigation works linked to its fiscal policies. Moreover, village dwellers could be summoned to carry out different kinds of labour for the pharaoh, such as temple or waterway construction, military service or a mining expedition.

In order to explain the emergence of forms of exchange derived from individual accumulation and from circulation processes that can even allow for transactions in proto-money, one must note the availability of surplus among the dominant classes, especially in cities of administrative or religious importance. Marx's argument in the *Formen* highlights that the royals and their senior officials exchanged their revenue – surplus product – in the cities. These processes occur in Egypt during the New Kingdom, especially in Thebes and Deir el-Medina, the village of craftsmen that manufactured funerary goods for the elite. Also during this period we witness the exchange of small plots of land and slaves for equivalents at a low value; senior officials intervene in these transactions, although through intricate relationships with temples or households. The revenues of the empire routed to temples and donated to senior officials gave rise to a larger availability of surpluses within the dominant classes.

CHAPTER 2

The Slave Roman Economy and the Plantation System

Carlos García Mac Gaw

In this chapter, we will analyse the scope of some historiographical concepts and assumptions that prevail in studies on Roman slavery, focusing especially on the concept of 'slave-based system' and its relationship with the productive unit of the plantation. We will consider the appropriateness of using these elements as a basis for characterising the whole of Roman economy.

Most historians would agree with Schiavone's assertion that 'it is difficult to doubt that Roman society between the Punic wars and the century of the Antonini was a slave-based society'.[1] However, the simplicity of the statement obscures the fact that what is understood by a 'slave-based society' is not altogether obvious. Citing Finley, Schiavone points out that the ideology of modern historians tried to disguise that unquestionable evidence to prevent this kind of blemish from tarnishing the classical world. One may wonder if we should still be keeping the same historiographical assumptions nowadays, more than fifty years after these forms of critical thinking reorganised historians' approaches to the Greco-Roman world. In truth, slavery has not been ignored by current historiography. Quite to the contrary, it has been placed at the centre of studies on classical ancient economy, which for some historians has meant 'an overdose of slavery'.[2]

Slavery as an institution has occurred in an important number of societies and is a privileged study field for comparative history.[3] As Patterson has observed, there are sociological aspects that often appear in different societies that practice slavery and these aspects allow for the development of some criteria of unified approach for its study.[4] But it is not evident, or at the very least one should exercise caution before stating, that the economic aspects of slavery repeat themselves as much as the sociological aspects of slavery, especially

---

1   Schiavone 2000, p. 112.
2   Starr 1958.
3   See, for instance, Biezunska-Malowist and Malowist 1989.
4   Patterson 1982.

when comparing societies whose productive development is not equivalent. Generally, it is a historiographical topos to state that there are societies with slaves and slave-based societies. The latter are societies where the 'slave-based system' has been established, according to Schiavone they are 'slave-based', for Finley, they are 'genuine slave societies'.[5] The former are recurrent in human history, the latter are few. Within this last group we find the Greco-Roman world and the American South, the Caribbean and Brazil from the seventeenth to the nineteenth centuries, areas of the ancient and modern worlds that have been comparatively well-studied, especially from the economic point of view.[6]

Clearly, interest in ancient slavery increased due to the centrality that the social-economic issues of modern slavery acquired by virtue of their relation to the development of European capitalism and the Industrial Revolution. Since then, both fields of study have evolved hand in hand.[7] Moses Finley has traced the journey followed by the history of ancient slavery, linking it with the advance of abolitionist ideas. He distinguishes two approaches in the studies on slavery: a moral approach and a sociological one.[8] The latter was carried out by authors he qualifies as 'economists', who since the mid-eighteenth century 'examined wealth, labour, production, trade, in what we should now call "economic" terms, and often with a historical dimension or perspective'. The outstanding point made in those studies was the relative inefficiency of slave labour compared to free labour due to its higher costs.[9] It could be proposed that most studies on modern slavery were mainly underpinned by economic perspectives that analysed it as a production factor of the enterprise, that is to say, the labour factor, validated to a large extent by the perspectives of a free market economy. This opened the way for the application of a type of reasoning more typical of economic rather than historical discourse to the analysis of slavery which, together with the humanistic criteria supported by abolitionist positions, brought on the advance of a body of thought for and against the efficiency of slave labour, especially in the United States of America.

---

5   Dal Lago and Katsari 2008, p. 3; Turley 2000, pp. 62 ff.: 'Societies with Slaves and Slave Societies'; Patterson 1982, p. vii; Vera 1989, p. 33: 'l'esclavitud com a fonament d'un sistema econòmic'.

6   According to Patterson 1982, pp. vii ff.; the list is much larger.

7   See a brief treatment of the advance of abolitionism in Nippel 2005, pp. 31–5.

8   Finley 1998, pp. 79, 95–6. See in Phillips 1985 the evolution of slavery in the West from Antiquity to the modern world.

9   Finley 1998, pp. 95–6.

The American slavery issue had its turning point with the development of the Civil Rights movement in the 1960s. Carandini points out that that movement ended the historical invisibility of Afro-Americans, and since then, the studies have multiplied.[10] A main aspect of the debate was triggered by Fogel and Engerman in their book *Time on the Cross*, where the aforementioned assumption about the productive superiority of free labour over slave labour was questioned.[11] The studies on ancient slavery are dependent on these approaches centred on the economic aspect constructed from the context of a capitalist economy. The bond linking the historiography on ancient slavery to the perspectives on modern slavery has been, unconsciously or explicitly, the plantation system.[12] Among other things, these studies were sustained by the fragmentary quality of our sources, the temptation to 'reconstruct' ancient slavery complementing it with the more achieved social-economic data provided by modern slavery, the development of comparative studies and, finally, the very nature of the most complete corpus available to historians of the ancient world: Latin agronomists. The slave plantation is the model on which the exploitation of forced labour in modern America was organised, and this model has also been applied to the ancient world, to the Romans in particular. Thus, Roman slavery has been identified with the slave *villa*, whose productive system would be practically identical to that of the modern plantation. That is to say, the prevailing historiographical perception of the Roman slave system is built from the main economic role played by the modern 'plantation'. *Mutatis mutandis*, in Rome the slave mode of production is identified with the *villa*.[13]

---

10   Carandini 1985, p. 187.

11   Fogel and Engerman 1989. On the efficiency of slave labour versus free labour in the American South, see Carandini 1985, pp. 194–200.

12   'Modern scholars, impressed by the agricultural Negro slavery of the United States, have, on looking back into the ancient world, naturally seen first the Roman side; and here they have found what seems to be exactly the same system, an economy of large plantations run by slave gangs', Starr 1958, p. 25; Carandini 1985, p. 187: 'I luoghi delle piantagioni'.

13   Whittaker 1993, p. 90; says: 'It has, however, come to be regarded as a useful designation (slave mode of production) for a new method of exploiting slaves during a period in the Later Roman Republic and early Empire, when there developed in Italy the systematic organisation of gangs on the farms attached to the residential villas of the rich, under the direction of an agent, whether or not his master was present ... Hence it is sometimes misleadingly called the "villa-system", although we know that other farming villas could and did exist in Italy and in the provinces in all periods without ever employing such gangs'. This model is taken by Weber, as indicated by Nippel 2005, p. 47.

This perception is based, generally, on the application of the comparative historical method, especially when our data about Rome are fragmented. Most of us would immediately note that precautions are in order when comparing these slave-based societies considering the time gap of close to two thousand years between them. Nonetheless, it is in fact very common to find at least some references to the organisation of agricultural slave labour of American plantations in texts about the classical ancient world. Surely, a comparison of ancient and modern wage labour equating both historical situations would elicit more caution.[14] However, the idea of a trans-historical slave mode of production – or a slave-based system – does not seem problematic, even when it is evident that it crosses the border of the pre-capitalist economic systems towards the capitalist ones. This way of approaching studies on slavery leaves aside the analysis of the development of productive forces whose role would be minimised or just ignored.[15]

Recognising the evidence of the complex relationship linking both historical periods does not imply leaving behind the possibility of establishing comparisons between them. Making this bond explicit, that is to say, establishing bridges between ancient and modern societies in relation to slavery, inevitably forces us to practice extreme care by refining comparative methodology. Davis proposes two ways of looking at slavery from broader perspectives:

> [T]he first method I have in mind is the comparative approach in which two or more examples of human bondage are compared, analysed, and contrasted, as in the pioneering works by Frank Tannenbaum and Stanley

---

14   Marx 1965 elaborated a general criticism of such theories based on the analytical method used therein. However, as Nippel remarks in 2005, p. 40, 'a closer look on Marx's scattered remarks on ancient slavery reveals that they are almost all by-products of his interest in the American slave debate', and further down he argues that 'he [Marx] was remarkably reluctant to draw inferences from the modern evidence (as he understood it) with respect to the ancient world', p. 43.

15   It is noteworthy that most Marxist analyses of ancient slavery have been constructed from these views. See Lekas 1988, on classical studies in Marx for an important criticism of the use of the concept of the development of productive forces. According to Nippel 2005, p. 35, 'the great problem with many later attempts to construe a Marxist theory of antiquity is that they do so by combining paragraphs, or single sentences even, from different times and with diverse intentions, often quoted without considering the respective contexts, or even selected in such a way that the original line of reasoning is deliberately obscured'. The author points out how Engels integrates slavery into a development based on economic needs, which would imply a necessary 'stage', p. 38.

Elkins. The second method is to take a global or multinational view of the origins, development, and abolition of racial slavery in the New World, which can be thought as a way of gaining broader insight into world history and the human costs of 'modernization'.

The author underscores this further on:

[B]ut while careful, empirical comparison is indispensable, especially in alerting us to the importance of such matters as the demography and sex ratios of slave societies, the differences in slave communities, and the social implications of resident as opposed to absentee planters, much recent research has also underscored the importance of 'the Big Picture' – the interrelationships that constituted an Atlantic Slave System as well as the place of such racial slavery in the evolution of the Western and modern worlds.[16]

These considerations are not focused on comparative studies between the ancient and modern worlds but specifically focus on the latter. However, they are useful in order to draw some conclusions. Davis's approach is reintroduced by Dal Lago and Katsari, who point out the possibility of establishing global or comparative historical studies for the research of 'slave systems'.[17] On the one hand, the authors affirm the relevance of carrying out comparative approaches of the 'rigorous' type, citing Peter Kolchin, who reintroduced the criteria established by Marc Bloch in his pioneering article about the comparative history of European societies published in 1928. On the other hand, they propose 'employing a "soft" approach to historical comparison, for the reason that, rather than developing into full-blown comparative analyses, they either simply hint at the possibility of doing so or provide brief comparative treatments of significant themes they treat'.

According to these methodological criteria, the comparative approach implies a more limited type of analysis that compares a limited group of examples. The global approach assumes a kind of analysis where the view is broadened

---

16   Davis 2000, pp. 452, 454.

17   Dal Lago and Katsari 2008, p. 7. Several of the chapters in this book were presented in an early form at the international conference on 'Slave Systems, Ancient and Modern' at the Moore Institute for Research in the Humanities and Social Studies, National University of Ireland, Galway, 24–6 November 2004, whose main objective was to establish comparative studies between the ancient Mediterranean and the modern Atlantic forms of slavery.

not so much by the established comparison but by taking into account the inner logics that structure the object of the study according to the dynamics of its functioning, what Davis calls 'the Big Picture'. The first method of study analysed by this author is better understood from a rather sociological perspective, resulting as it does from a limited comparison that may be useful for the construction of 'sociological types'. This comparison appears to be mostly limited to the verification of the existence of phenomena in different contexts.[18] However, the entity of the objects under comparison may complicate a task that seemed easy at first glance. Going back to Davis's quotation, we could note the difficulty in comparing demographic variables and sex ratios in slave societies. These 'objects' are not 'things' but relationships that are explained by their articulation with other kinds of elements such as the characteristics of the slave trade, the insertion of the slave product (commodity) in a specific sort of market, the existence of a regional 'domestic' supply for the demand of labour, and other equally complex aspects that pull us out of the purely comparative method and lead us into the second type of methodology identified by Davis. Such aspects include, for instance, issues that relate to slavery as an answer to the dynamics characteristic of the European capitalist market and the American and African integration in that economic framework. The notion of labour market in this case may explain the development of slave exploitation as a response to the lack of labour force in a space where it is not feasible to control the labour force due to the availability of alternative means of production (free lands).[19] If one were to study the sex ratio of Roman slaves through the work of Latin agronomists, when it came to establish comparisons between ancient Mediterranean and modern Atlantic plantations one could not avoid including the kind of global framework mentioned above. The range of such studies will depend on the approach chosen to carry them out, and will vary according to their method and scope. That said, the criterion that organises the analysis of the relationships established among the elements of the social structure immediately reaches a different level that is linked with the political economy.

Accordingly, the application of the comparative method should be extremely cautious insofar as it affects the underlying logic that explains the dynamics

---

18   Ibid.

19   Engemann 2006, p. 49, transcribes the opinion of a great plantation owner: 'De igual modo, o Barão do Paty do Alferes considerava a escravidão como um cancro, mas um cancro necessário, se é que se pode imaginar algum. Segundo o barão, o que tornava a escravidão imprescindível era a fronteira agrícola aberta. A oferta de terras aos imigrantes fazia como que estes se evadissem antes mesmo de saldar sua dívidas de viagem'.

of the social structures. All these precautions will not be present if the model of modern slavery works as a non-explicit assumption for the study of ancient slavery, and the model of the capitalist plantation imposes its logic on the functioning of the Roman *villa*. In this sense, the use of the economicist[20] perspective to organise the view on ancient slavery appears as the most persistent epistemological obstacle to guard against.

The Income Composition of the Landowning Class

Bradley remarks that, according to some historians who support the quantitative criterion, Roman society may have become a slave-based one c. 225 BC, when the proportion of slaves with respect to the total population of Italy can be estimated around one third.[21] But he argues that much earlier 'Rome had made what might be termed institutional responses to a servile presence, in its legal and religious life', and from that qualitative point of view it can be certainly called a slave-based society from earlier times. Indeed, this implies admitting that the characterisation of 'slave-based' that can be applied to a society depends on different perspectives. In this case, Bradley asserts that it is possible to refer to Roman society as a slave-based society before the moment marked by prevailing historiography on the issue as a turning point: the end of the second Punic war. I highlight the paradox in order to consider that the issue is historiographically constructed and that an author who, some paragraphs above, assumes the prevailing guidelines of that historiography also notes this inconsistency: the existence of a slave-based society before it really came to be 'a genuine slave society'. It is not my intention to criticise the perspective suggested by Bradley but to revalue some of its elements, especially what the author considers 'institutional responses to a servile presence in its legal and religious life', as an aspect to be taken into account apart from the economic factors, normally considered central when organising the analysis.

In the opening paragraphs of this chapter, we have cast doubt on the simplification implied in the statement that Roman society 'was' a slave-based society. We shall therefore analyse the grounds on which this remark is based, namely, what elements allow us to consider one society as 'slave-based' while others are not.

---

20   A view supporting the use of the criterion of production factor of the enterprise, or 'labour factor', as it relates to the approaches of the free market economy to which we referred at the beginning.

21   Bradley 1998, p. 19.

For this purpose, historians have put forward different explanations. Hopkins assumes for the Roman case that slaves have an important role in production and reach a percentage threshold that the author sets arbitrarily at 20 percent.[22] He considers Brunt and Beloch's data that range from 15 to 35 percent, taking the dates 225 and 31 BC, respectively.[23] Finley takes up some of these figures but only to criticise what he calls the 'numbers game',[24] as he understands that 'the evidence does not permit genuine quantification'. In both cases, there is a reference to the percentages of American slavery.[25] It is interesting to observe that the numeric issue is not naïve. The ratio of slaves to free men suggests the scale of the institution, which will have significant consequences in the whole of society, be it from the cultural point of view or in relation to the family structure, the economy, etc. Although the qualification of a society as slave-based or not in relation to the number of slaves is not centred on the economic aspects, it takes them into account while avoiding the complex discussion about the place that slaves occupy in the social relations of production. The trouble is that the numbers for the ancient world are speculative at best.

Another way of finding out whether or not a society is slave-based relates to the aspects pointed out in the previous paragraph. Again, Finley summarises the idea when he indicates that the place of slaves in a society is not in relation to their total number but rather to two aspects of their situation: who their owners are, and what role they play in the economy.[26] Dal Lago and Katsari's definitions are very close to Finley's approach. For them slavery defines a 'slave-based system' because it sustains the basis of an economy in which: (a) elite wealth and slave ownership were two notions inextricably connected to each other; (b) a large part of the trade revolved around buying and selling slaves; (c) a high percentage of the workers were enslaved labourers; and/or (d) states and other types of institutions relied on the profits made with slavery for their prosperity.[27]

---

22   Hopkins 1978, p. 99. See Patterson 1982, pp. 353–64, with comparative tables of different societies. To Patterson, the large-scale slave-based systems were those in which the social structure was decisively dependent on the institution of slavery, a dependence that was frequently, but not necessarily, economic, p. 353.

23   Hopkins 1978, p. 101.

24   Finley 1998, pp. 147–8.

25   See criticism by Scheidel 2005, p. 65, regarding the use of relative numbers of modern slaves applied to ancient times.

26   Finley 1998, pp. 148–9.

27   Dal Lago and Katsari 2008, pp. 4–5.

Stating that slavery defines the slave-based system may seem tautological. However, we should take into account that the authors are in search of an abstraction for the concept of 'slave-based system'. For them, slavery defines the slave-based system because it sustains the basis of the economy. It is worthwhile to consider this statement more closely since it allows us to state without hesitation that when we talk about Roman society from the second century BC to the second century AD, we are indeed talking of a 'slave-based' society. This implies analysing the scope of such a 'slave-based system', as well as the concept of a 'basis of the economy'. I understand this to mean that we have to think of what provides the basis, what structures and organises the performance of the economy in a given society. To Dal Lago and Katsari, the use of the term 'slave system' refers explicitly to the spread of the institution of slavery ('an institution based on the "slave mode of production" and system of labour') in the economy and in the society of those regions, countries and states that were interconnected parts of a unified market area. They also remark that

> In some respects, then, the concept of 'slave system' relies on the defini-
> tion of 'slave society' first advanced by Moses Finley and then utilised by
> K. Hopkins and I. Berlin. According to this definition, unlike in a 'society
> with slaves', in a 'slave society' slavery was at the heart of the economic
> and social life of a particular culture and it influenced it in such a way
> to create a large class of slaveholders, who effectively held a great deal of
> power and exercised it over the non-slaveholding population.[28]

This last statement links the slave system with the slave mode of production and the labour system, which is a frequent occurrence.[29] The slave-based production mode, identified with the labour system, appears as the basis of the economy. Let us put aside the impressionistic imagery ('the heart of the economic and social life') used to explain the basis of the economic system, and concentrate on ideas that appear more powerful. Finley states that

> [F]ree men dominated small-scale farming, much of it subsistence farm-
> ing, as well as petty commodity production and small-scale trading in the
> cities; slaves dominated, and virtually monopolized, large-scale produc-
> tion in both the countryside and the urban sector. It follows that slaves

---

28   Dal Lago and Katsari 2008, p. 5.
29   See Patterson 1979, pp. 47–52.

provided the bulk of the immediate income of property ... of the élites, economic, social and political.[30]

This agrees with point (c) of Dal Lago and Katsari. However, the grounds of this explanation, surprisingly, are not numeric. Finley indicates that in all productive units larger than the domestic one, the constant labour was made up by slaves. If the units had tenants, then the scheme would be reproduced: they either copied the peasant domestic unit or the large tenant units employed slaves.[31] Ste. Croix states that the owner class extracted most of its surplus from the working population by means of unfree labour, one of them being chattel slavery, which always played a very significant role – though not always the most important one – in the sphere of real production. However, the author remarks that we can refer to the ancient world as a 'slave economy', and to a certain extent he agrees with Finley while not being so restrictive in his statement.[32]

As we advance further in our analysis, it becomes clear that the 'qualitative approach' that should support the characterisation of the slave-based society takes us back to quantitative aspects. If we assert that 'slaves provided the bulk of the immediate income of property of the elites', then it is necessary to know: (1) what percentage of the total agricultural production corresponds to slave labour power in relation to free peasant labour power in the Roman Empire; (2) what percentage corresponds to *coloni* rent in relation to the slaves in large estates; and (3) what percentage of landowners comprising the elite obtain the largest part of their income from slave labour in relation with the rent provided by the *coloni*.[33] These three points are sufficient in order to organise an analysis of the quantitative aspects of a slave-based Roman society. Regarding point 1, many historians agree that the bulk of the product of the Roman Empire was obtained from the labour of peasants with smallholdings.[34]

---

30   Finley 1998, p. 150.

31   Finley 1998, p. 149.

32   Ste. Croix 1981, pp. 53, 133. See criticism by Wood 1988, pp. 42–80.

33   I refer to the economic, social and political elite as defined by Finley 1998, p. 150, since the author properly remarks the importance of knowing who the slave owners were (p. 148). I use the concept of 'labour rent' in the sense that Marx uses it for the pre-capitalist modes of production in Marx 1966, ch. 47, II.

34   Garnsey 1998a, pp. 94–6. Ste. Croix 1981, p. 133, 'the combined production of free peasants and artisans must have exceeded that of unfree agricultural and industrial producers in most places at all times'. Finley 1998, p. 145, points out the infrequency of slavery as

In this regard, it would be important to know the number of slaves working in domestic units or in small workshops whose product was added to that of small owners, since there is a percentage of the slave rent added to the product of free labour outside the slave-based plantation. We could apply to Rome the model that Jameson developed for Athens, which implies a different accountancy and puts in question the idea of the plantation labour system as a basic economic element for the slave-based society.[35] Point 2 illustrates the impossibility of reaching a calculation that enables us to estimate the percentage of slave rent in the whole agrarian income for large domains.[36] The *coloni* or tenants were a central component of the estate organisation and it was probably the most widespread form of labour exploitation in the territory of the Empire.[37] The slaves of the *coloni* contributed to the tenants' labour in an uncertain amount.[38] If these *coloni* exploited small plots, then that slave

---

involuntary labour and its coexistence with free labour. On this issue cf. Rathbone 1981, pp. 13–15, who refers to the interdependence of both types of labour to guarantee the profitability of the slave-based *villa*. Also see Kehoe 2007, p. 555.

35   Jameson 1977–8.

36   It is worth clarifying that if we take the *villa* as a model for the plantation, other types of large properties will be overlooked: see García Mac Gaw 2006, pp. 32–7; Evans 1980, p. 24.

37   Read further for a thorough development of the issue.

38   Plin., *Ep.* 3.19.6–7, decries that the owner of the farm he wants to buy has sold the *coloni's* slaves in order to recover overdue debts owed by the *coloni* (*reliqua colonorum*) as said slaves were subjects under guarantee (*pignora*). Since there were no labourers (*sed haec terrae imbecillis cultoribus fatigatur*), that is, *coloni* able to take over from the existing ones, Plinius himself had to cover the cost of re-equipping them. That meant Plinius had to buy those slaves (*sunt ergo instruendi eo pluris*), who had to be good (*frugi mancipiis*), therefore expensive, as it was not his habit to employ chained slaves (*vincti*). It must be observed that the functioning of this estate seems to imply either a mixed exploitation – part at the expense of the owner and part in tenancy – or a property that was wholly tenanted, but with the peculiarity that the owner would supply the slaves – instruments – to the tenants. These tenants characterised as *coloni* are evidently small tenants who rent a plot according to their economic possibilities which, as inferred from the letter, are hardscrabble enough that they are unable to come up with the instruments necessary for farming. On the other hand, the farms worked by free *coloni* could also be managed by slaves, as noted in Plin., 3.19.2. However, in this case the statute of *procuratores* and *actores* may be doubtful. Gonzalès 2003, p. 296, in the 'Index thématique des références à l'esclavage et la dependence' he elaborated for Plinius's work, considers their statute uncertain. About *actores*, see also Andreau 2001, pp. 126–7, though especially oriented to the world of business and banking. Martin 1974, p. 273, n. 1, in general characterises them as free men. Veyne 1981, p. 22, n. 82, indicates that the *vincti* form a particular slave class,

labour was organised outside the logic of the large plantation and reproduced the domestic structure. If they were great *coloni* that only used slave labour, then it was a typical case of slave-based plantation. But if these great *coloni* combined the centralised slave labour exploitation with the sub-tenancy to small *coloni* of the estate's lands, then the previous structure was repeated.[39] Most probably, certain areas of an estate were exploited directly through slave labour, whereas others were indirectly exploited through tenants.[40] Point 3 leads us to posit the problem in relation to the landowning class. For the sake of argument, let us ignore the objections stated in point 2 and consider Finley and Ste. Croix's criteria to be valid, which allows us to characterise Roman society as slave-based since the bulk of the production from the properties belonging to the landowner class derived from slave labour.[41] These profits were obtained from lands traditionally considered to be the slavery core of the Empire, Italy and Sicily,[42] that is to say, the areas where the 'slave-based system' should have been more fully developed. Immediately we are faced with a problem: according to the definition of slave-owning class proposed by our authors, we must assume that this class obtained most of the income produced by slaves from properties located in such regions. Several hypotheses arise from this: (a) if the elite owned lands throughout all the territories of the Empire, then the rent extracted from free labour in around 80 percent of those lands (a rough estimate) could not equate the agrarian slave profit produced by the 20 percent represented by Italy and Sicily, and the profit from slavery would be higher than the rent produced by tenants for landowners.[43] This is patently false, even without considering aspects related to the different productive efficiency of both labour systems; (b) conversely, if the elite owned lands only in Italy and Sicily, i.e. in 20 percent of the total lands of the Empire, then we should wonder who owned the lands distributed in the rest of the provinces. This would lead us to the proposition that there was another landowning elite equally or more powerful than the Italic-Sicilian slave-holding elite, based on the extension

---

who could be bought or not as such, and they were not punished slaves. This implies a particular form of organising slaves and not the proper standard suited to the plantation, especially in one of the regions considered central for the slave-based system.

39   These were the *coloni urbani* stigmatised by Col. 1.7. See Finley 1976, p. 105.

40   Finley 1976, pp. 105–6; Veyne 1981, pp. 7–9. Also see García Mac Gaw 2007, pp. 103–10.

41   Finley 1998, p. 150; Ste. Croix 1981, p. 133.

42   Finley 1998, p. 147.

43   Increase in property holdings by the Roman aristocracy in the provinces: Ste. Croix 1981, p. 241.

of the lands at their disposal.[44] Such an idea is nonsensical.[45] The obvious conclusion is that besides owning land in Italy the landowning elite had land possessions by *coloni* and to a lesser extent by slaves.[46]

When characterising the dominant class, I do not find any satisfactory reason for prioritising the profit resulting from slave labour force in properties located in Italy and Sicily as opposed to the rent resulting from exploitation of free labour (*coloni*) in the rest of the lands of the Roman Empire. And it is worth bearing in mind that, returning to point 2, we should question the component of the slave rent in the slave production units from Italy and Sicily.

Free Peasants and *Coloni*

The composition of the landowning class income is one of the factors, but not the only one, that questions the prevailing historiographical view on Roman

---

44 With some nuances, this evokes the analysis by Staerman 1957, pp. 153–5, where the end of the slave period comes about as the result of the confrontation between the slave-owning class represented by the government of the Principate, and the owners of large estates represented by the triumphant government of the Dominate. See Mckeown 2007, pp. 52–76.

45 The composition of the senate class indicates on the one hand that the members of the elite hailed from different areas of the Empire, especially from the Principate onwards. On the other hand, Roman aristocrats owned lands throughout all the Empire. Thus, we can only speak of one landowning aristocracy, and not two or more. At most, we can point out the existence of a central aristocracy (whose origin varies through time) linked to the system of the Republican or Imperial state, and other provincial aristocracies tied to the central aristocracy by complex mechanisms of co-optation. The government of the Empire results from the articulation of these two levels of the dominant class and not from a competition between them.

46 See especially Rawson 1976, pp. 85–102; although it highlights the legal limitations for senators to own properties outside Italy that can be inferred from Cic., *Verr.* 2.5.45, the author says that 'the position was of course entirely different under the Principate; by Seneca's time the typical rich senator had estates all over the Mediterranean world, though he still needed permission to leave Italy. In the Republican era there was naturally no restriction on travel or ownership abroad for *equites* or humbler persons', pp. 90–1. Hopkins's statements are in agreement, Hopkins 1978, pp. 47–8, and n. 65. This continued and became more widespread during the Principate. The appropriation was done directly as well as through loans extended by Roman aristocrats to the provincials for the latter to pay taxes by mortgaging their lands, which, in most cases, later passed to the hands of Roman aristocrats. The lack of coin circulation was one of the elements that facilitated this mechanism. Now see Bang 2008, pp. 100–1; Howgego 1994, pp. 5–21.

slavery. According to this historiography, the development of the slave-based society is explained by the depopulation of the central area of Italy and the crisis of the small owner peasant sector.[47] However, Garnsey has underlined the persistence of active policies carried out by the Roman state to support the reproduction of the small owner peasant class. A study on these policies can be found in Frank's work for the case of Italy.[48] Harris remarks that some regions in Etruria were punished through land confiscation for their opposition to Sulla and the beneficiaries could have been around 120,000 men (23 legions).[49] The author refers to the survival of these land plots until the period of Cæsar's decline, though exceptions can be found. Then, there are references to the foundation of colonies in these areas in the harmonious period of the Triumvirate between Antonius and Octavianus, but this can only be confirmed in the case of Florence.[50] This does not suggest the idea of a uniform landscape regarding the kind of property existing in these areas. The *praedium Arretinum* of Atticus and the properties of Domitius Ahenobarbus in Cosa and Igilium, where he organised recruitment for his troops in 49 BC, may have also been acquisitions obtained during the Sulla period, which indicates the elasticity of the phenomenon and the necessity of precaution before making categorical assertions.[51] Etruria and Campania seem to have been two of the areas most affected by triumviral and Augustan colonisation, perhaps due to the existence of coveted lands in those areas.[52] In Campania, possibly the richest region in Italy, the areas around Capua were intensively worked by small peas-

---

47   Hopkins 1978, pp. 2–3; De Neeve 1984a, pp. 9, 30, 34, 39–41; Kolendo 1991, pp. 239–44; Sirago 1971, pp. 17–29.

48   Garnsey 1998a, pp. 95–6; also see Garnsey 1998b, pp. 136–7; in this article the author points out the impossibility of clearly differentiating owners, labourers and farmers as these lines are usually blurred, pp. 139–41. Frank 1975, I, pp. 218–21, for the foundation of colonies during the Gracchan period (150–80 BC); also see Frank 1975, V, pp. 174–5, for an analysis of the inscriptions of Veleia and Beneventum during Trajan's reign. According to the author, we should conclude that the concentration of lands stated by some satirical authors did not occur in the same way everywhere, and that in the central valleys of the Apenines many small farmers were still working their own plots. Even in the lands suitable for wine and olive production, such as Pompei, the properties could have a moderate size. On free peasant survival, see also Evans 1980.

49   Harris 1971, p. 259. This probably refers to *ager publicus*, under the terms of the *foedera* confiscated in part from the cities as punishment for their military opposition.

50   Harris 1971, pp. 268–9; 282–3, 302–3.

51   Harris 1971, p. 295.

52   A catalogue of the possible colonisations and distributions by triumviri and Augustus is in Harris 1971, pp. 306–13.

ants, while the *ager Falernus* and the Sorrento peninsula were probably mostly in the hands of rich absentee owners.[53] Carrington's classical work on the *villae rusticae* of Campania clearly illustrates this coexistence.[54] In other regions like Lucania, a type of migratory extensive cattle breeding activity with a large amount of slaves seems to have taken hold as can be deduced from some information by Tacitus.[55] Both Potter and Vera indicate that in central and southern Italy there was a significant diversity in the agricultural forms adopted.[56] In his research, Dyson points out the similarities in certain problems that arose in both the Republican *ager Cosanus* and the *ager Veientanus*, especially with regard to the fluctuations in population related to the decline of small farmers and the emergence of large properties during the late Republic, which in both cases led him to consider that the decline of republican farmers had been exaggerated.[57] Liverani highlights a process of reduction in the number of archaeological sites from the third to the second centuries BC in this same region, which does not appear to have had selective criteria in favour of large properties and against small ones. Therefore, the process known as crisis of the small agrarian property and birth of the *villa* system is not observed.[58] The Augustan age marks a rebirth for the *ager Veientanus*, probably for all the Tiber valley of Etruria, with an intensive occupation that will last until about the end of the second century AD, which is in agreement with the information found in sources written between Cæsar and Augustus.[59] Liverani states that according to compiled data, this region witnesses the triumph of the agricultural system

---

53   White 1970, p. 72. Cic., *De Leg. Agr.* 2.84: *Totus enim ager campanus colitur et possidetur a plebe, et a plebe optima et modestissim*, a situation that, according to Cicero, had been ongoing since the end of the war with Hannibal, 2.89.

54   Carrington 1931, pp. 110–30. See also Frederiksen 1984, pp. 307, 309.

55   *Ann.* 12.65. White 1970, p. 74.

56   Potter 1987, p. 98; Vera 1992–3, p. 296.

57   Dyson 2003, pp. 27, 40–1. However, the author presents the different opinions reached by diverse archaeological research groups, which, according to the author's view, are due both to methodological issues and to ideological preconceptions. The most influential archaeological project was started by the British School at Rome (http://www.bsr.ac.uk) under the direction of J. Ward-Perkins after the Second World War, in the most ancient area of Veii.

58   Liverani 1984, p. 42. This article systematises the information from the archaeological excavations of the British School at Rome in the *ager veientanus*.

59   Distributions carried out by Cæsar in *Veii* lands: Cic., *Fam.* 9.17.2. Transformation of Veii into municipium by Augustus: Harris 1971, pp. 310–11. These elements correspond to similar ones which took place in Capena, Sutrium and Lucus Feroniae during the same period: Harris 1971, pp. 307–10.

of the *villa* during the Principate. However, while this implies a greater use of slave labour in the southern area of *ager veientanus*, it also implies a greater use of colonate in the northern regions. According to this author, there are no grounds for the claim that the disappearance of the small peasant property can be attributed to the consolidation of the *villa* or, even more inaccurately for this period, to the system of large estates.[60]

Finally, it is important to remember Rathbone's warning:

> We might wonder, for example, whether the average peasant could afford sufficient imported fine-wares to make them a reliable indicator to us of his settlement, in which case the decline of the 'small sites' may reflect the fortunes of a 'kulak' class, not necessarily analogous to those of the average peasant.

These peasants probably left very few archaeological traces.[61] We could broadly state that the advance of archaeological prospection in these regions is slowly asserting evidence of a resistance from the small peasant properties and puts in question the assumed depopulation of the region. The research has brought to light the great number of small farms that once existed in the Roman landscape, which has forced important revisions to our picture of their countryside.[62] The

---

60   Liverani 1984, pp. 47–8.

61   Rathbone 1981, p. 21.

62   See especially Witcher's summary work, 2006, pp. 88–123, using the results of over thirty surveys to explore the settlement and society of Etruria (*regio VII*) during the early imperial period. According to the author, in the area of *suburbium*, a wide geographic region surrounding Rome, '[o]verall site density was very high ... Most of these sites are best characterised as farms, although "residential" villas, or villas with an elaborate *pars urbana*, constitute a third or more of the settlement hierarchy across large areas', p. 102. On the coast of Etruria 'there was a sharp fall in site numbers, particularly farms, during the transition between the late republican and the early imperial periods. Villas subsequently dominated the settlement hierarchy with a much higher ratio than found in other areas', p. 103, but the existence of farms is observed during the late republican period according to the author's information. Finally, in Inland Etruria, '[t]he settlement hierarchy comprised farms, villas, and villages in varying ratios. Villas were generally modest, although there are some well-appointed sites. Overall, they formed a small percentage of the settlement hierarchy, being concentrated in areas close to towns. Farms were more numerous, though this was the category most affected by the early imperial decline', p. 105. The general tendency of the results is sustained despite some questions regarding methodological issues, pp. 114–18. Also see Dyson 2003, pp. 39–40. An inverse position can be found in Morel 1989, p. 496.

development of this knowledge indicates to us the impossibility of centring our perceptions in the existence of something resembling a uniform 'model' for the whole province of Italy that may have been the 'core' of the slave-based system from which the paradigm of slave-based *villa* is constructed. The evidence shows a coexistence of diverse forms even in the different regions of Italy, depending on their geography and their historical evolution.

As has been pointed out, the colonate was probably the more widespread form of labour exploitation in the territory of the Empire and its origin certainly dates back to the last century of the Republic, although there are references to it during the previous century.[63] Caesar and Sallustius indicate the presence of *coloni* in the ranks of Domitius Ahenobarbus and Catilina.[64] Free tenants figure in the works of Latin agronomists, though not so relevantly due to the emphasis on the role of slaves. Cato suggests, if possible, *operariorum copia* when choosing the location of a domain and recommends being a good neighbour with a view to hire employees easily (*opera facilius locabis*).[65] He indicates the treatment that the *vilicus* must give to the *mercenarii* and to *politores*, none of them slaves.[66] Varro (*RR* 1.16.4) also states that some functions performed by slaves could be fulfilled by free men. When he refers to the forms of working the land, he raises the alternative of doing it with slaves or free men (1.17.2), these latter being either *mercenarii* or *obaerarii*, and in his exploitation model this free labour appears as complementary to slave labour.[67] In Columella's first book, the whole of chapter 7 is devoted to the *coloni*. He starts with a statement identical to that of Varro, saying that men for working the land *vel coloni*

---

63 Though indirect, the first reference that we could quote, which places us squarely in the second century BC, is Ter. *Adelphoe*, 953–4: *Agelli est hic sub urbe paulum quod locitas foras: huic demus qui fruatur*; also De Neeve 1984b, pp. 73–5, analyses the fragment. Also see Cat. *De Agr.* 1.3, 6, 136 (the reference to the *politores* further on); Var. *RR* 1.16.4, 1.17.2; Col. *RR* 1.7; Plin. *Ep.* 3.19.6; 7.30.2–3; 9.15.1, 36.6 and 37. For the origin of tenant farming, see Rosafio 1993, pp. 164–76; and De Ligt 2000, pp. 377–91, who indicates that even dating back to the period of the Twelve Tables, any type of thing could be rented, including land. Also see Kehoe 1997, pp. 3–5; Garnsey 1998a, pp. 94–6; Garnsey 1998b, pp. 139–41; Witcher 2006, pp. 115–18; Finley 1976; and especially De Neeve 1984b.

64 Sallust. *B. Cat.* 59.3, Caes. *B. Civ.* 1.34.2, 56.3. Also Hor. *Ep.* 1.14; *Carm.* 2.14.12; *Sat.* 2.115.

65 1.3, and 6, respectively.

66 136: *Politionem quo pacto dari oporteat*. It is not clear from the text whether he refers to a share-cropping tenant (*partiarius*) or to a contract for labour service. The reference to the land yield (*in loco bono parti octaua corbi diuidat, satis bono septima, tertio loco sexta*) suggests the first option. The magnitude of the owed part, the second. See Finley 1976, p. 106; De Neeve 1984b, pp. 15–18.

67 On the *obaerarii*, see Finley 1981.

vel servi sunt. He recommends that the *vilicus* should pay foremost attention to the labour carried out by the *coloni* rather than to the rent payment (*avarius opus exigat quam pensiones*),[68] and to look for men who were locally born (*felicissimum fundum esse, qui colonos indigenas habesse, et tanquam in paterna possessione natos*). He also suggests it is convenient that the master or *vilicus* supervise the domain himself rather than lease it to tenants, and indicates that lands far removed from supervision by the master are better off remaining in free *coloni* hands (*Propter quod operam dandam esse, ut et rusticos et eosdem assiduos colonos retineamus, cum aut nobismet ipsis non licuerit, aut per domesticos colere non expedierint*). Capogrossi Colognesi believes that modern historians allowed themselves to be too influenced by the concern that Latin agronomists show for the absenteeism of great landowners of the Late Republic and the Imperial Age, seeing as these great landowners represented the effectively progressive element in the history of Roman agriculture. This implies a certain contradiction between the negative connotation given by agronomists and other Latin writers, and the role that absentee landowners effectively played in Roman agricultural history. The catonian *villa* is the product of transactions consciously performed by an urban nobility class, and the management system based on *vilici* and slaves complies with the double objective of reinforcing and widening the agrarian grounds of its own social supremacy and, at the same time, keeping and reinforcing the citizen role. Therefore, landowner absenteeism, regretted since Saserna's time, is not a degenerative phenomenon or a crisis, but arises at the very genesis and develops along with this agrarian model that draws the agronomists' attention almost exclusively. This feature is already present in Cato and will not be modified in the successive periods except for the increase in opulence of all Roman society.[69] If, as stated by Colognesi, the standard was absenteeism, should we not infer from these fragments of Columella that the leasing of land to free tenants was at least as widespread as the exploitation by the master himself or his slave in charge?

There are also references to the *coloni* in other letters by Plinius apart from that in 3.19 already cited, as in 5.14.7 and in 7.30.2–3.[70] In the latter, our author laments having to listen to *querellae rusticorum*, or complaints by peasants who, within their rights, take unfair advantage of his ears after a long absence; and he regrets not being able to detach himself from what he calls 'urban matters' (*urbana negotia*) since some people turn to him to act as arbitrator.

---

68   See Finley 1976, pp. 119–21, for explanations of this passage.

69   Capogrossi Colognesi 1982, pp. 332–3.

70   See n. 37 for the *Ep.* 3.19.

It is interesting to highlight that Plinius admits to a long absence, and due to this he has to bring himself up to date with the duties involved in his hierarchy as patron, which means solving the problems occurring among the different peasants who lease his lands.[71] The senator assumes here the role of the absentee owner to which Capogrossi Colognesi refers above.

Forms of Slave Rent

So far we have accepted as a fact that there is a characteristic form of exploitation of the slave labour force that is assimilated to the plantation system. However, evidence shows that there is not a standard or a model by which the master could appropriate the surplus produced by the slave. Unlike what happens in gang slavery, there were also slaves that were exploited as if they were free tenant farm workers, who were given a plot of land to work in exchange for a rent payment: the *servi quasi coloni*.[72] Legally, the lot is not assimilated to a peculium ceded by the master to the slave, but it functions as goods and the *servus quasi colonus* pays a rent, the *merces*, to his master for its usufruct, in the same conditions as the *locatio conductio* is performed. Nevertheless, the slave obtains the fruits of the exploitation as *res peculiares* even though technically the plot of land is not considered a *peculium*.[73] The tenancy relationship, though assimilated to the *locatio conductio*, cannot be understood as a contract as it involves a master with his own slave. Traditionally, this form of exploitation

---

71   Plinius's case is particular because in general he is characterised as an owner highly interested in the course of his agricultural enterprises. See an opposite opinion in Martin 1974, p. 271, where he is characterised as 'propriétaire hyper-absentéiste'. A similar situation surfaces in the *Ep.* 9.15.1, where repose eludes our author even in his lands in Tuscany, where the peasants pester him with notes and complaints, and also in 9.36.6, where he recognises that the time he allots to listen to peasants' complaints is, according to them, short. It is likely that both cases also refer to initiatives from neighbours, small landowners and *coloni*, who approached him for patronage. In *Ep.* 7.30.2–3 he indicates the necessity of coming to his lands to renew contracts that finish, presumably, after five years; see Finley 1976, p. 106; De Neeve 1984b, pp. 10–12.

72   About the use of the formula *quasi* + noun in the legal sources, see now Giliberti 1988, pp. 100–4, with literature on the topic.

73   See Giliberti 1988, pp. 37–51, for a detailed analysis on the scope of the slaves' *peculium* disposal according to jurists. However, according to Veyne 1981, pp. 4 and 6–7, the plot of land can be assimilated to the *peculium*. In fact, it is a legally controversial issue due to the ambiguity of the 'contract' between the master and the slave.

was perceived as a late phenomenon that would represent the 'missing link' between chattel slavery and the colonate of late antiquity.[74] Paul Veyne, one of the few historians to have devoted a specific work to this phenomenon by organising a collection of related texts, states rather paradoxically that

> Le dossier des *servi quasi coloni* est mince et pauvre, aussi pauvre ... que les autres dossiers relatifs à la main-d'œuvre rurale, qu'elle ait été servile ou libre. On croit entrevoir, dans cette pénombre, deux ou même trois silhouettes différentes d'esclaves-colons: un esclave riche et important, semblable à Tityre; un *vilicus* à qui le domaine a été affermé; enfin un pauvre homme, un simple *inquilinus*, de naissance servile. Les deux premières silhouettes illustrent un aspect de l'économie esclavagiste, où les esclaves n'étaient pas utilisés comme esclaves, mais comme hommes de confiance, ayant tous les talents et soumis à leur maître comme aucun client ne l'avait été;[75]

The 'slaves who were not used as slaves' is an expression that brings to mind Bradley's statement that Roman society was already slave-based before becoming slave-based. Finley and Veyne have been in favour of a minimalist interpretation of the phenomenon. The latter says that the slave-tenants were few, as he understands that, in fact, this form was a rather frequent one for the *vilici*, that is, for the qualified staff and not for the rank and file.[76] He also wonders whether it can be inferred that in the period between Marcus Aurelius and Constantinus, slave labour in gangs may have been replaced for slave labour in individual plots; while Capogrossi Colognesi understands that legal testimonies reflect the 'diffusion and normality' of this relationship in rural areas between the first and the third centuries.[77]

This form of slavery that usually appears as a late occurrence and related to the crisis of the *villa* system is in fact mentioned already by Alfenus, in the

---

74   For a statement of the issue, see Giliberti 1988, pp. 9–28; Vera 1989, p. 34.

75   Veyne 1981, p. 23. Also see Ste. Croix 1981, pp. 237–8.

76   Var. *Agr.* 1.17.5 suggests giving a land plot to the foreman in order to encourage his good predisposition: *Praefectos alacriores faciendum praemiis dandaque opera ut habeant peculium et coniunctas conservas, e quibus habeant filios*. It also appears in 1.2.17: *Agrius, Tu, inquit, tibicen non solum adimis domino pecus, sed etiam servis peculium, quibus domini dant ut pascant*. Anyway, I think that there is a difference between this *peculium* ceded to the *vilicus* and the land rented to the *servus quasi colonus*, as in the case of Varro it is clearly suggested to cede, not to rent a land plot to improve the foreman's condition.

77   Finley 1976, p. 113; Veyne 1981, p. 24; Capogrossi Colognesi 1982, pp. 344–8; esp. p. 345.

transition from the Republic to the Principate.[78] According to the content of the first law where this phenomenon appears, a person had leased land to his slave and had given him oxen.[79] As these oxen were not suitable, the master told the slave to sell them and buy others with the money obtained. The slave sold the oxen and bought others without actually paying the seller and later he went bankrupt. The slave's creditor demanded that the master pay him for the *actio de peculio aut de in rem verso*.[80] The jurist did not think that this was a question over *peculium*, unless some of this *peculium* remained after the deduction of debts that the slave owed his master.[81] The *actio de in rem verso* was not applicable in this case. It was true that the second oxen had become part of the master's patrimony (as eminent proprietor of all his slave's *peculium*), but according to Alfenus's text, the master had paid for the first oxen, so he did not benefit, therefore it was inappropriate to sentence him to pay unless there was a supplementary difference in the value of the second oxen.[82] From a legal standpoint, this slave is legally responsible because he acts independently managing his *peculium*. According to Giliberti, in Alfenus's view, the split between two different actions, *locare* in relation with the land and *dare* for the oxen, expresses the complex use of a slave labourer who does not work the land under direct dependence to the master but does so on his own as a *colonus*. Alfenus may have held the archaic view that animals were

---

78   *Dig.* 15.3.16 and 40.7.14; also abridged by Paulus in 40.1.40.5.

79   Alf. 2 *Dig.* 15.3.16: *Quidam fundum colendum servo suo locavit et boves ei dederat: cum hi boves non essent idonei, iusserat eos venire et his nummis qui recepti essent alios reparari: servus boves vendiderat, alios redemerat, nummos venditori non solverat, postea contur- baverat: qui boves vendiderat nummos a domino petebat actione de peculio aut quod in rem domini versum esset, cum boves pro quibus pecunia peteretur penes dominum essen- tentiarum respondit non videri peculii quicquam esse, nisi si quid deducto eo, quod servus domino debuisset, reliquum fieret: illud sibi videri boves quidem in rem domini versos esse, sed pro ea re solvisse tantum, quanti priores boves venissent: si quo amplioris pecuniae pos- teriores boves essent, eius oportere dominum condemnari.*

80   This action allowed for suing a slave owner whose slave had not complied with a contract in the case that the slave could not freely dispose of his *peculium*. The action was only applicable if the master had increased his fortune through his slave's behaviour. See Veyne 1981, p. 11, n. 39.

81   The slave could be debtor or creditor of his own master. If the slave had creditors, the master was responsible for his slave's debts up to the amount of the *peculium* he had given him, and he, himself, would be the first among the creditors. That is to say, he would recover the debt his slave had with him and then the rest of the creditors would have a claim if there was something left. See Veyne 1981, p. 11.

82   Ibid. Also see Giliberti 1988, pp. 30–1, for the *actio de in rem verso*.

not included within the wide concept of *fundus instructus*, and according to
the jurist's opinion in this fragment, the oxen seller cannot demand satisfaction
over the land as this has been given in location and not in *peculium*.[83]

Something similar can be observed in *Dig.* 18.1.40, where Alfenus understands that the *dolia* of a land for sale should be ceded to the buyer, as well
as those purchased by the slave who cultivated the land with his *peculium*.
Obviously, these *dolia pecularia* were a fruit of the slave's actions and not the
master's, therefore this is a case of a *servus quasi colonus*. Alfenus's opinion
rests on the idea that in this case the slave had improved the master's property (the land) with the purchase of the *dolia*, and they should be transferred
in the sale.[84]

In the following example, the occurrence of the phenomenon is used only for
the sake of a comparison which, in my opinion, leads to its reappraisal. A slave,
by his master's will, would be released by his heir when he paid ten thousand
sesterces. The slave usually delivered the salary for his labour to the heir, and
when the heir received for salaries more than 10,000 sesterces, the slave claimed
he was free. The jurist said he did not consider the slave to be free, as in fact he
had given that money not as payment for his freedom but for his labour (as
salary: *pro operis*). By reason of this, he was not free, in the same way that he
would not be free if he were to lease land from his master and gave him money
for its profit.[85] In this case, the slave works independently and renders his salary
for those *operae* to his master, a situation the jurist compares to that of the slave
who cultivates his master's land and also pays a *merces*.[86] It is noteworthy that
Alfenus uses the case of *servus quasi colonus* who owes a rent for the tenancy
of his master's land as an incontestable argument to show that the slave owes
a *merces pro operis*.[87] The example, used to clarify the doubts of this legal case,
indicates that the rent for land use by a master's slave is something natural and

---

83   Giliberti 1988, pp. 34–6.

84   *Dig.* 18.1.40.5: *Dolia, quae in fundo domini essent, accessura dixit: etiam ea, quae servus qui
      fundum coluerat emisset peculiaria, emptori cessura respondit.* See Veyne 1981, p. 12.

85   *Dig.* 40.7.14 pr.: *Servus, qui testamento domini, cum decem heredi dedisset, liber esse iussus
      erat, heredi mercedem referre pro operis suis solebat: cum ex mercede heres amplius decem
      recepisset, servus liberum esse aiebat: de ea re consulebatur. Respondit non videri liberum
      esse: non enim pro libertate, sed pro operis eam pecuniam dedisse nec magis ob eam rem
      liberum esse, quam si fundum a domino conduxisset et pro fructu fundi pecuniam dedisset.*

86   Slave independent labour was a practice already known by the Greeks: see Perotti 1974,
      47–56.

87   See De Neeve 1984b, pp. 4–5, 11–12, about the contract of *locatio-conductio operis faciendi*
      and *locatio-conductio operarum*.

frequent. In both cases the *merces* is a product of slave labour, though in the first case it is salary for the *operae*, while in the other it is rent for land usufruct. Giliberti emphasises that the jurist's opinion is based on the fact that not all payments by the slave must be interpreted as the purchase of manumission, and hence in this case the normality of the relationship between master and slave is reinforced as a relationship sustained in monetary rent as a product of the services (*operae*) performed by the latter. The author also points out the fact that Servius and Alfenus, in a certain way, are incorporating to their legal views the consequences of the development of slavery in a society where trade relationships lead to a more complex interpretation of the simple legal division between free men and slaves.[88] But this evolution not only affects such relationships but also the uses that involve the means of production: the observation of contracts that involve different social actors, as in the case of the *locatio conductio*, places the double legal morphology of the slave as *res* and *persona* at the centre of the analysis. The nature of the legal source does not allow us to estimate the actual scope of the *servus quasi colonus* phenomenon midway through the last century of the Republic, but it obviously points to its presence, which probably relates to an evolution in which land was placed into production through the system of *locatio conductio* with *coloni* of free origin.[89]

Both Giliberti and Veyne have highlighted the parallels between these legal analyses and the case of Tityrus, the character in Virgilius who, besides being in charge of breeding his master's cattle, had a plot where he worked an orchard and a vineyard and also sold cheese in the city, an activity with which the slave hoped to be able to increase his *peculium* in order to buy his freedom.[90] As a result of the civil wars, the territory where his lands were located was subject to expropriation for the settlement of veterans, and Tityrus, along with other slaves, went to Rome to ask Octavianus for an exemption from expropriation. Although it is impossible to label Tityrus as *servis peculiatus* or *conductor*, as the text does not allow for such a statement, the literary example confirms the case outside the codes.

The term appears in the exact sense in which we have been using it in a text by Ulpianus that collects the opinions of Labeo and Pegasus at the beginning

---

88   Giliberti 1988, pp. 39–40, 43–4.

89   This disputes suppositions by Giliberti 1988, pp. 1–7, who suggests that this system may have resulted from the crisis of the 'slave-based economy', which may have in turn modified the condition of free men, preparing the consolidation of the colonate during the late Roman Empire.

90   Virg. *Ecl.* 1.27 ff.; Giliberti 1988, pp. 54–7; Veyne 1981, pp. 6–7. Also see Virg. *Georg.* 4.127.

of the Principate. In it the question is whether a slave who was in the field as a *quasi colonus* should be included in the instrument of a bequeathed land.[91] The jurists answered negatively because he was not in the property as instrument, even if he usually commanded the *familia*.[92] Here a difference is established between the relevant elements to be included, the *instrumenta*, and those which remain outside the *fundus instructus* in the will. This issue resurfaces in the Digest: both Scævola and Paulus try to define the difference that exists between the land ceded to a slave by a voluntary act of the master for it to be worked (*fide dominica*) and the one ceded for being worked in exchange for a rent payment (*merces*).[93] The jurists' opinion denies the possibility of considering the *servus quasi colonus*, who fits the latter case, as part of the instruments of an equipped plot ceded in a will.[94] Scævola's text (*Dig.* 33.7.20.1), from Marcus Aurelius's time, is quite interesting in that it states that the slave Stichus, who cultivated one of the plots bequeathed to the freedman Seius, should not form part of the trust if he cultivated the land in exchange for a rent payment as outside tenant farmers usually did (*ut extranei coloni solent*) and not those working *fide dominica*. Here the notion of externality is applied to differentiate the slaves who work in similar conditions as those of free men coming from elsewhere. Veyne considers that this case is about a *vilicus* in charge of the land in block, and he understands that Paulus's interpretation (*Dig.* 33.7.18.4) of Scævola's opinion of this passage agrees with that notion.[95] Personally, I understand that it is not a question of leaning toward one or another type of slave,

---

91   A *fundus instructus* is one that is equipped with the pertinent elements (*instrumentum*) to exercise the *possessio* on it: *Dig.* 33.7.12 pr. The jurists' discussions are about what type of slave was part of a bequeathed *fundus instructus* and what type of slave would belong to the heir.

92   *Dig.* 33.7.12.3: *Quaeritur, an servus, qui quasi colonus in agro erat, instrumento legato contineatur. Et Labeo et Pegasus recte negaverunt, quia non pro instrumento in fundo fuerat, etiamsi solitus fuerat et familiae imperare.*

93   About the scope of the expression *fide dominica*, see Giliberti 1988, pp. 134–9.

94   Scaev. *3 resp. Dig.* 33.7.20.1: *Liberto suo quidam praedia legavit his verbis: 'Seio liberto meo fundos illum et illum do lego ita ut instructi sunt cum dotibus et reliquis colonorum et saltuariis cum contubernalibus suis et filiis et filiabus'. Quaesitum est, an Stichus servus, qui praedium unum ex his coluit et reliquatus est amplam summam, ex causa fideicommissi Seio debeatur. Respondit, si non fide dominica, sed mercede, ut extranei coloni solent, fundum coluisset, non deberi.*

      Paul. *2 ad Vitell. Dig.* 33.7.18.4: *Cum de vilico quaereretur et an instrumento inesset et dubitaretur, Scævola consultus respondit, si non pensionis certa quantitate, sed fide dominica coleretur, deberi.*

95   Veyne 1981, pp. 19–20; also Giliberti 1988, pp. 23 and 115–25.

vilicus or *servus quasi colonus*, but to establish the legal difference that results from the way in which labour force exploitation is organised. In the case of the *vilicus*, the slave should be included in the legacy as it is understood that he belongs to the *familia* and therefore is part of the land equipment. In fact the title under which we find the comment is *De instructo vel instrumento legato*. In the case of the *servus quasi colonus* the situation is the opposite since the slave is compared with the *coloni* from outside the *fundus* who are not part of its equipment. Paulus restricts the scope of Scævola's observation, paying attention only to the *vilicus* case.

Among the lists of names contained in Pola's tablets, which date back to the second century and whose aims remain uncertain, we find two characters, probably slaves of an imperial domain, a *Viator colonus* and his servant *Lucifer adiutor coloni*. According to the editor of these inscriptions, it would also be a case of *servus quasi colonus*.[96]

The credit record in *Dig.* 15.1.58, under Marcus Aurelius, shows slaves in debt due to various reasons.[97] Although there is no explicit reference as to why the slaves incurred such debts, a delay in the rent payment on the part of those slaves seems to be the most likely explanation.[98]

Sometime later, under Gordianus (a. 243), a law of the *CI* points out that a slave who cultivated a property was deprived of the *peculium* when he was manumitted by his female master, although he was still in debt. As can be inferred from the text, the debts were due to the obligations the slave had for cultivating the land he was deprived of when he was manumitted.[99] Even

---

96   Veyne 1981, pp. 14–15; Giliberti 1988, pp. 90–2.

97   *Uni ex heredibus praedia legavit ut instructa erant cum servis et ceteris rebus et quidquid ibi esset: hi servi domino debitores fuerunt tam ex aliis causis quam ex ratione kalendarii: quaesitum est, an ceteris heredibus adversus eum pecuniae ab his debitae actio de peculio competit. Respondit non competere.* See Veyne 1981, p. 21, n. 77; and Giliberti 1988, p. 89; about the *kalendarium* that apparently registered deadlines, the record of credits and the bag containing the credits as well as sums of money that the master allotted to loans with interest.

98   Also in *Dig.* 33.7.24 Paulus understands that the instruments belonging to a *colonus* are not included in the bequest of a property *cum instrumento*. This case refers to a slave, since the possibility of including the property of a free tenant in a will could not be discussed. In *Pauli Sent.* 3.6.40 there is a reference to the wives of those slaves who pay a rent: *uxores eorum qui mercedes praestare consueverunt*, also see Giliberti 1988, p. 149.

99   *CI* 4.14.5: *Si, ut adlegas, antequam a domina manumittereris, fundos eius coluisti posteaque adempto peculio libertate donatus es, ob reliqua, si qua pridem contracta sunt, res bonorum, quas postea propriis laboribus quaesisti, inquietari minime possunt.* Veyne 1981, pp. 6–7, interprets that the *peculium* he is deprived of is the land itself.

later is the text of *CI* 7.16.18 (a. 293), where the emperors Diocletianus and
Maximianus deny that the condition of land tenant by itself is sufficient proof
of free birth.[100]

To Giliberti all this proves 'una quanto meno discreta diffusione del feno-
meno', whereas Capogrossi Colognesi, more generally, understands that its
presence in the legal testimonies reflects the fact that this relationship was
widespread and normal in rural areas in the period between the first and the
third centuries.[101] Although the references are scarce and the extension of the
phenomenon is open to discussion, what is noteworthy is the plasticity allowed
in order to obtain the surplus produced by slaves rather than the rigidity that
suits a model.

We have already seen that when talking about a 'slave based system' we refer
to the mechanism by which a particular mode of surplus is extracted in the
productive process which, as many historians would propose, implies a 'slave
mode of production' and system of labour. In fact, when Ste. Croix and Finley
classify Roman society as slave-based, they infer this proposition from the
alleged evidence that the greater part of the income of Roman aristocrats came
from the exploitation of a slave labour force. However, there is not a particular
mode of appropriation of the surplus of slave labour defining this mode of
production. When analysing the different forms in which slaves are exploited,
either in different slave societies or within one of them, it becomes evident
that there is no single form of doing so. Slaves can be exploited individually
in the frame of the *domus* at the domestic scale; they can form gangs (gang
slavery) and work shackled as prisoners, or free from chains supervised by
monitors in the plantations while living in common *ergastula* or individual
rooms; they can have a house and cultivate a small plot for their subsistence
while working in the master's land; they can work a plot belonging to the master
in exchange for a rent payment as if they were tenants (*servi quasi coloni*)
and that payment can be a percentage or fixed; they can work as independent
traders in charge of a business (*peculium*) directly supervised by their master
or not – paying a fixed rent in this case; they can be rented by the master if
they have any skill or they can lease themselves – self-managing themselves –
owing a rent to their master, etc. All forms previously listed are historical
manifestations of slave exploitation and many of them co-existed in time and

---

100   *Ad probationem ingenuitatis ab eo, contra cuius successores postulas, facta tibi locatio non
       sufficit, nec tamen hoc solum ad servitutis vinculum argumentum est idoneum.*
101   Capogrossi Colognesi 1982, p. 345; also see pp. 344–8. Giliberti 1988, p. 158 and also
       p. 162.

space.[102] Notwithstanding this, from among all of these forms, the so-called 'gang slavery' of the shackled slaves that live in the *ergastulum* is chosen as the 'model' or prototype of slave exploitation. In my opinion, this happens because the studies on ancient slavery have been constructed through the framework of modern slavery, and the paradigm of the plantation based on gang slavery has been adopted for the latter. It is worth noting that American slavery does not fit this model either, but that it presents numerous particularities according to the different places and periods in which it takes place.[103]

Let us observe the composition of the slave owner's income in different situations, leaving aside the domestic slavery around which many of the studied cases could be framed.[104] In the 'plantation system' the slave profit is expressed as labour. It is not distinguished from the cost of labour power reproduction which the master is in charge of, i.e. the surplus value arises from the difference between rent and reproduction cost.[105] When the slaves receive an orchard for reproducing their labour force (*servi casati*) and work the rest of the time in the master's land, the *dominium*, the surplus value appears equally expressed as a labour rent, but in this case the master is not in charge of the reproduction of the slave force, therefore all the slave activity in the proprietor's land is equivalent to the surplus value. In the case of the slave whose master rents him for a *merces*, we could find variations: if the leaseholder is in charge of the reproduction of the labour force, the rent – as long as it is expressed in money – is equivalent to the surplus value generated by the slave, but if the master is in charge of the reproduction of the slave labour power then he has to deduct that cost from the surplus value. In the case that the slave acts independently by renting himself out, the master's surplus value will be equivalent to the money the slave pays him, and the slave is in charge of the reproduction of his own slave labour power. This last example is identical to the case of the *servus quasi colonus*: in this case the slave pays his master a money-rent or a rent in kind that is identical to the surplus value and the master is not involved in the

---

102   Cf. Giliberti 1988, pp. 44–5.

103   For instance, see the following works on slavery in Brazil highlighting the central role of family relations in the plantations: Florentino and Goes 1997; Miranda Rocha 2004; Engemann 2006.

104   In this situation, both the slaves of free tenants and of small owners are included.

105   We will not take into account the question of the cost of amortisation for the slave purchase. We think that in all the cases we analyse, the repayment is already done and the income received by the master is the expression of the absolute surplus value. Otherwise the cost of repayment would have to be deducted from the surplus the master obtains.

reproduction of the slave labour power.[106] The relationship with the means of production varies in each case. A sharp difference can be established between the plantation system on the one hand, and the *quasi coloni* (or slave tenant) and *servi casati* systems on the other, since in the latter two cases it is the slave who controls the land totally or partially while in the former it is the master.

Generally, the slave system has been associated to the plantation system, probably because from a theoretical point of view we can easily observe the difference between the mode of slave surplus appropriation and the feudal rent or the capitalist surplus value.[107] On the other hand, this taxonomy of labour exploitation easily fits the Stalinist evolutionist criteria by which societies develop historically through the five basic economic stages: primitive communism, slavery, feudalism, capitalism and socialism, each stage being linked to a particular form of labour exploitation. Due to its simplicity, it is impossible to apply such a theoretical construction to a hypothetical society in which, for instance, most direct producers are, from the legal standpoint, slaves settled in their masters' land paying a rent for its usufruct.

It is clear that in this analysis there is an overlap of two different types of criteria, an economic and a legal one. If we consider that the concept 'slave' refers to a particular mode of labour exploitation limited to the classical model of the 'plantation system', then there are slaves who are not exploited as slaves but as free men, which is a paradox without solution. In such a case, the slave mode of production is identified with the 'plantation system' and all the other modes in which slaves are exploited do not correspond to that mode of production.

Conversely, we can assume that slavery is a legal status without a direct economic consequence. Therefore, the slaves would be exploited in different ways, and as a result there would not be a single slave mode of production but several, among which we could find, obviously, the slave mode of production of the plantation. I tend to agree with this second notion.

---

106 According to Giliberti 1988, pp. 45–6, '[l]a *merces*, dato anche il carattere unitario del concetto di *locatio-conductio*, sovente non può essere scissa nella sua diversa natura di salario, reddito da lavoro autonomo, rendita agraria'. According to Gaius, *Dig.* 7.7.3: *In hominis usu fructu operae sunt et ob operas mercedes.*

107 The term 'feudal rent' has been used generally to mean the appropriation of the surplus over the medieval serfs. But, in fact, it should be called 'servile rent', a term not used in the English language, in order to strip from it the connotations associating the concept to a specific social relation typical of medieval society. See the distinction made by Ste. Croix 1981, pp. 267–9.

If we assume that, as Finley and Veyne proposed, the spread of the *servi quasi coloni* phenomenon began especially among the slave sectors linked to the hierarchy of the *villa*, the *vilici*, we should analyse this question further.[108] The authors presume a minimalist diffusion since they understand that this would be a form of personal reward for slaves charged with managing agricultural functions, as suggested by Varro.[109] However, we could also assume that this would be a way to allow the landowner to withdraw from the direct management of his patrimony while perceiving a rent produced by the independent administration by the *vilicus*. In this case it could happen that, depending on the size of the property, the *vilicus* became himself a *conductor* of one of his masters' plots, or that the *vilicus* exploited a set of plots belonging to the *villa* by leasing them to *coloni* or to *servi quasi coloni*. In other cases, a land exploitation could be organised wholly or in part around gang slavery under the direct supervision of the *vilicus*. *Dig.* 20.1.32 analyses the situation of a debtor who placed as collateral all the things that were taken, transported, introduced, born or prepared in a plot. In that land there was a part without *coloni*, given for cultivation to its *actor* who in turn had had slaves assigned for work in the fields. The question for the jurist is whether this *vilicus* and the slaves assigned to him should be included in the warranty, apart from the *vicarii* of the *vilicus*.[110] The relevant point here is not the legal question, but to observe that this mode of land exploitation was feasible. In fact, there is an added layer of complexity in the example as it involves both the master's slaves (*ceteri servi ad culturam missi*) and foreman's slaves (*Stichi vicarii*).[111]

---

108   See *Supra*.

109   *Var. Agr.* 1.17.5.

110   *Dig.* 20.1.32: *Debitor pactus est, ut quaecumque in praedia pignori data inducta invecta importata ibi nata paratave essent, pignori essent: eorum praediorum pars sine colonis fuit eaque actori suo colenda debitor ita tradidit adsignatis et servis culturae necessariis: quaeritur, an et Stichus vilicus et ceteri servi ad culturam missi et Stichi vicarii obligati essententiarum respondit eos dumtaxat, qui hoc animo a domino inducti essent, ut ibi perpetuo essent, non temporis causa accomodarentur, obligatos.*

111   In *Dig.* 32.91 (*reliquis actorum et colonorum*) and 32.97 (*reliqua tam sua quam colonorum*) *actores*' debts appear included in legacies. Also in *Dig.* 33.7.20.3 (*reliqua colonorum et vilicorum*).

Scope of the System and Dominant Class

In order to deepen the analysis of the elements that have been observed so far, I will present a case study from a different period and place. Engerman and Genovese review a study by Martins-Filho and Martins on the development of the slave-based economy in the region of Minas Gerais, Brazil, around 1870.[112] At the time, this region was divided into two areas, one directly linked to the production of export products, coffee being chief among them, and another larger area where the slaves worked in a diversified economy that produced little for the overseas markets. The authors compare this case with the economy of Virginia in 1860, where there were a few food products suitable for export including wheat and also slaves to supply the South. Anyone observing Virginia in isolation, as well as Kentucky and North Carolina, would have been perplexed by the role of slavery and the reasons of its long persistence and survival. In fact, anyone could have wondered whether Virginia could have held on to slavery had it not depended on the export of basic goods produced by slaves for its integration in a wider exportation economy. The authors propose that there is nothing in this article rebutting the accepted thesis that the existence of plantations oriented to exportation constituted the *sine qua non* for the possibility of slavery and its survival as a labour system. Engerman and Genovese suggest that the system of the African slave trade shows that the economy of Minas Gerais, though autarkic, should be analysed in the context of the Brazilian society as a whole. The slave supply that the authors recognise as vital for the provincial economy would be unthinkable without the plantation system of other provinces oriented to the export trade. Engerman and Genovese wonder what might have been, for instance, the price of slaves if Brazilian slavery as a whole had had the features of the Minas Gerais economy. And they also wonder whether the Minas Gerais slave drivers could have paid for the imported slaves if they had not depended on the returns of the exporting sector. Although it is certain that the foreign exchange need not have resulted from external exports in order to allow Minas slave drivers to buy slaves and various goods, the funds for that may have been obtained either through sales in Brazil itself or to local residents who could have been linked to wider markets. Otherwise, there should have been a previous wealth accumulation by the slave-owner masters. Thus, the issue of the sources of funding and their possible international implications persists. And, insofar as Brazilian slave prices

---

112   Engerman and Genovese 1983.

remained high until 1880, the question of knowing which goods were produced by slaves and if they were sold (and where) also remains.

Engerman and Genovese, based on Marx, suggest that a total collapse of the market may have pushed the slave owners of the New World to some form of natural economy and, probably, towards more suitable means of labour organisation and coercion.[113] In that vital sense, slavery and also slave-based societies such as those of the Southern states of the North American Union, always remained enmeshed in the capitalist mode of production and were unable to generate an alternate slave mode of production reminiscent of that of the ancient world. According to Engerman and Genovese, what the study they review shows is not that the slave-based system can exist without the world market, but that the slave-based system – in this case the Brazilian one as a whole, which was dependent on the world market – could expel and support economic subsystems based on slavery, though isolated from the market sector. If the survival of slavery in Minas Gerais depended on the survival of slavery in the exporting sector of the wider Brazilian plantation economy and if it could be expected that the specific conditions of the provincial economy created non-slave forms of labour coercion, what must be really questioned is why slavery persisted instead of giving rise to more attractive alternatives for both masters and workers in other historical periods and in other parts of the world. In the sugar-producing areas of the northeast, slave and feudal relationships had coexisted for a long time, thus the transition from a forced labour mode to another did not directly threaten the power of the sugar refinery lords. The authors immediately think of forms in which slavery would have been transformed in order to give rise to serfdom.

As can be observed, some elements present in the discussion have strong points of contact with Roman slavery. The first one is what I have defined in the subtitle as 'scope of the system'. Engerman and Genovese's approach criticises the idea of a slave-based system independent from capitalist trade relationships and from the exporting circuit of Brazil's economy. The authors indicate that the Southern states of the Union 'always remained enmeshed in the capitalist mode of production and could not generate an alternate slave mode of production reminiscent of that of the ancient world'.[114] I understand this to mean that in the ancient world the slave-based system did not depend on its insertion in a greater economic system. I think this view is wrong. At least in the case of Rome, the different manifestations of slave exploitation are inscribed

---

113   Engerman and Genovese 1983, p. 588.
114   Engerman and Genovese 1983, p. 589.

within the greater context of the ancient tributary mode of production. The articulation of slave labour exploitation in its various manifestations with free tenant labour (the *coloni*) and seasonal labour (the *mercenarii*) in the *villa* is a product of the huge capacity of economic accumulation due to the fast expansion throughout the Mediterranean (in this sense it is comparable to what Engerman and Genovese point out: a previous wealth accumulation on the part of the slave-owner masters, though I would prefer to call them simply the landowning class). This slave-based system, which has been considered as the 'basis' of the Roman economy, is in fact a consequence of exceptional situations among which we can mention the increase in trade relations resulting from the integration of several Mediterranean areas through taxation. It would be foolish to deny this fact, but it is worth observing that the exploitation of slave labour power is not necessary for the elaboration of commodities as shown by the production of olive oil in northern Africa. However, the slave plantation system provides a quick response for the direct exploitation of an estate as long as the supply of labour force is cheap and stable. On the other hand, trade circulation is up to a point dependent on tax accumulation, as Hopkins, Wickham and Bang have pointed out.[115] The articulation between the mechanisms for collecting (the extraction) and distributing the tax, and their relationship with the slave-based and non-slave-based economic spaces (either inside or outside Italy-Sicily) should be analysed for understanding the wider functioning logic of the system in its economic aspects.

The second aspect to consider relates to the characterisation of the dominant class as a 'slave-holding class'. Engerman and Genovese point out the case of the producing areas of north eastern Brazil, where slave and seigneurial relationships coexisted, stating that the transition from one labour mode to another did not imply a threat to the power of the sugar refinery lords. In the Roman world, according to what we have previously analysed, the rents of the landowners' properties were not based on slave labour but were formed by surplus appropriated mainly from free labourers and to a lesser extent from slaves.[116] The differentiation between a bourgeois class suitable for the full functioning of capitalist relationships as opposed to a peripheral slave-holding class linked to the economy through raw material exportation makes sense, for

---

115   Hopkins 1980, and 2002, pp. 190–230; Wickham 1988, pp. 183–93, and 2005; Bang 2008. See García Mac Gaw 2008, pp. 259–67, where trade relations are analysed within the framework of the city-state.

116   To this we must add the product of the resources appropriated through the state's tax system that reached landowners through several mechanisms.

instance, in the pre-war American South. However, the differentiation between a slave-holding class of landowners versus another non-slave-holding class of landowners does not hold in the case of Rome because in both cases we are dealing with the same social group, as in the example given by Engerman and Genovese for some areas in Brazil. Indeed, whether a Roman landowner exploited slaves or tenants did not affect his social position. The real difference between the landowning classes was given by their larger or smaller control of the state apparatus and that becomes essential when characterising the Roman dominant class. This explains why it is pointless to state that a 'crisis' of the slave system, meaning a transition to another labour system, resulted in a disaster that dragged the dominant class with it. If we had to think of a transition, we should look to Engerman and Genovese's suggestion on the change from a slave to a serfdom system in which the latter coexisted with the former during its 'dominant phase'. However, I would propose that the emerging phenomenon closest to what is understood by such transition would be related to the increasing progress toward indirect exploitation, which was already the norm in great domains, and with a withdrawal or abandonment of direct exploitation through gang slavery – which may have been important only in some limited regions of Italy and Sicily. This alteration in the use of slave labour power assumes the increase in the use of forms that were developed together with the 'slave plantation system', like the *servi quasi coloni* and the *servi casati* (hutted slaves), but they are not examples of late modes of slavery in any case.[117] Historians cannot agree on the moment when the crisis of the slave system took place, while at the same time this slave system is thought to be the basic economic structure of the Roman Empire. Perhaps, the answer lies in the fact that such a 'basis' for the economy did not exist and we have been searching in the wrong place.

If the 'slave-based system' is a mode among others of organising slave exploitation, then slavery cannot be reduced to one or another 'labour system'. Most likely, the progressive disappearance of the plantation system should be seen simply in relation to the supply for the trade circuit linked to the functioning of the rent originated from tribute.

---

117   The transition towards slave modes similar to serfdom is a main aspect of the discussion about slave-based societies and it is linked especially to the relative efficiency of slave labour in relation to free labour. I have left this topic out of this analysis deliberately, since the available space does not allow for its proper treatment. Some aspects are mentioned in Scheidel 2008; Fenoaltea 1984; Findlay 1975; Engerman 1973, pp. 43–65. The term *servus casatus* is rare in the documents, see Ste. Croix 1981, p. 238.

If the 'slave system' is a form among others of exploiting slaves, the modification of such forms does not make the class that appropriates slave labour more or less of a slave-holding class. Otherwise we would fall into the paradox of labelling the landowners who organised their land exploitation under the plantation system as 'slave-holding'; but these same landowners would not be 'slave-holding' if their slaves were exploited in a manner similar to that of free tenant farmers.

Final Considerations

In societies where the institution of slavery has developed deeply, it has been dependent on other dominant social-economic modes existing in those societies. Whether or not it acquired the form of the plantation labour system is irrelevant. As an institution it reinforced the social-economic structures prevailing in different societies. According to the cases analysed herein, we can show as examples of this the peripheral American slave systems which depended on the central capitalist mode of production and the case of Roman slavery, which developed from the economic dynamics allowed by the resource accumulation of the ancient tributary mode of production.[118] Thus, slavery contributed to consolidating the power of the dominant social classes. In the modern world, that reinforcement has been mainly economic, insofar as it is through the functioning of the economic system that the surplus appropriation is organised by the dominant class. The constitution of the American capitalist classes needed the complement of slave labour power to organise a labour market that did not function according to the requirements of the capitalist system, because the working class had easy access to the means of production due to land availability, and this sharply increased salaries.

In pre-capitalist societies, the mechanisms on which surplus appropriation is organised by the dominant classes are of an extra-economic nature. In Roman society, slavery only reinforces the position held by the class of great landowners in relation to the control of the state apparatus. The slave labour

---

118   On the role of institutions as modes of reproduction, see Meillassoux 1992. Blackburn 1996, p. 162: 'Slavery often seemed to function like a social false limb, extending the reach or capacity of a social formation – usually of its ruling group – but not fundamentally altering the principles of social organization. It was probably more often a conservative than an innovatory institution'. On the concept of tributary mode of production, see Haldon 1993, and 1998; Haldon and García Mac Gaw 2003.

system of the plantation is not a determining factor, aside from its economic consequences, but the control over the lands is a determining factor, as it reinforces the mainly political role of the Roman landowning class in relation to the city-state structures through the *villa* system.[119] In the productive units, the rent appropriation varies according to the different regions and periods, therefore there coexist heterogeneous forms of slave exploitation, together with free workers – proprietors and non-proprietors – with different levels of dependence.

The comparison between ancient and modern slavery usually results in the presentation of slavery as a transhistorical category, in which the wide range of social relationships prevailing in the economic system as a whole take second place, exposing slave relationships to the observers' view. However, it is necessary to emphasise that these relationships do not have economic substance in and of themselves, but that their role is defined in relation to the wider social-economic context where they are inserted. Likewise, it would be pointless to study wage labour independently from the historical conditions of the time, ignoring that the central role of labour as a commodity in capitalism is due to the previous alienation of workers from the means of production, something that does not occur in other social systems. Slavery, as equated to the category of factor of production, acquires that role in relation to capital in the modern market economy. We should not apply the same parameters in order to understand its functioning in Roman society. The dominance of the system of tribute in Roman economy should lead us necessarily to consider the role of slavery in that larger context. This implies further research to advance on that issue. In any case, the characterisation of Roman society as slave-based is relevant to the extent that it developed 'institutional answers to the servile presence', according to Bradley.[120] However, we consider that it is incorrect to suggest that there was a period of domination for slave social relationships, or a period in which the slave mode of production determined the whole of Roman economy. Thus, the characterisation of the Roman society as slave-based acquires a different meaning and cannot be equated to modern slave societies.

---

119   The analysis has to take into account the fact that owning slaves increased one's status: De Neeve 1984b, p. 101.

120   Bradley 1998, p. 19.

CHAPTER 3

Origins of the Medieval Craftsman

Carlos Astarita

Preliminary Issues

Historians often explain the appearance of the craftsman in the Middle Ages with the Smithian concept of the social division of labour and of trade. This matrix has been employed in different works: Henri Pirenne's thesis regarding foreign trade and economic development since the beginning of the eleventh century, and the more current works on endogenous growth.[1] This criterion explains through linear evolution the development which led certain producers to specialise in specific trades.

However, the productive abilities of the worker, as Adam Smith puts it,[2] could not have resulted merely from the division of labour, nor was the division of labour the principle chosen to increase that productive capacity the way a lever is chosen from a toolbox. Far from being a spontaneous phenomenon, being a craftsman required the complex acquisition of an unmistakable skill, which in turn presupposed its transmission from one generation to the next. The contracts of the later Middle Ages show that learning was difficult and that it took time to pass on practical working skills from one generation to the next.[3]

This is not the only question that arises when studying the origins of the medieval trade. This type of study also has to uncover a process by which we can explain why this skill was not developed by individuals confined to special environments, as happened with palace or temple craftsmen in other

---

1   Pirenne 1978; Britnell 1993, and 2001.

2   'The greatest improvement in the productive powers of labour, and the greater part of the skill, dexterity, and judgment with which it is anywhere directed, or applied, seem to have been the effects of the division of labour' (Smith 1910, p. 4); '[t]he division of labour, however, so far as it can be introduced, occasions, in every art, a proportionable increase of the productive powers of labour. The separation of different trades and employments from one another seems to have taken place in consequence of this advantage' (Smith 1910, pp. 5–6). Epstein 1998, p. 688, points out that Adam Smith has underestimated the issue of learning, acquisition and transfer of a specific expertise for a craft.

3   Sombart 1919, vol. I, pp. 197 ff.; Collantes de Terán Sánchez 1983, pp. 165–74; Córdoba de la Llave 1984; Ruiz Tejado 1988, pp. 363–74; Bermejo Borosoain 1988, pp. 329–40.

societies, but by small household workers, that is to say, workers belonging to the most basic cell which peasants shared. Our aim is to shed light on this process. In order to achieve this end, we must remove the division of labour from its preeminent position in the standard explanations and replace it with the productive forces and social relationships which are both reflected and driven by the division of labour. This change of viewpoint was already suggested by Marx when he began to turn Classical Political Economy into a Critique of Political Economy.[4]

The documents analysed are from León and Castile, and particularly from Sahagún, a monastic domain that included the burg of the same name.[5] But the scope of this interpretation goes beyond those limits as evidenced by comparisons with other regions. These parallels are not arbitrary; they reflect the dynamics of feudalism as a system which united the North of the Iberian Peninsula with France, Flanders, Southeastern England, Western Germany and North-Central Italy in a sense that is both chronological and related to the problems those regions had in common. All of these regions underwent a similar evolution starting at the very beginning of the Middle Ages in the early fifth century, until the crisis of the fourteenth century. If we take into account that this region was a system, it follows that the examination of the particular will illuminate the whole. This Aristotelian principle justifies concentrating on the case, which does not in itself mean that nuances should be overlooked. However, our main concern is with the substantive traits of this system.

---

4   Holton 1981, pp. 834 ff., rightly remarks that Marx, in *Die deutsche Ideologie*, points to classical economy as the framework for interpreting the advent of capitalism. It is an undeniable influence, as shown by the importance that Marx and Engels give to the division of labour in the general historical sketches they draw. However, they differ from Adam Smith in that their explanation rests more heavily on the development of productive forces, of which the division of labour is a symptom rather than a cause. They claim that the degree of development of productive forces can be gauged by the degree of development of the division of labour, adding that any new productive force that is not a simple quantitative expansion of existing productive forces, results in a new division of labour. See Marx and Engels 1969, pp. 21–2: 'Wie weit die Produktionskräfte einer Nation entwickelt sind, zeigt am augenscheinlichsten der Grad, bis zu dem die Teilung der Arbeit entwickelt ist. Jede neue Produktivkraft, sofern sie nicht eine bloß quantitative Ausdehnung der bisher schon bekannten Produktivkräfte ist (z.B. Urbarmachung von Ländereien), hat eine neue Ausbildung der Teilung der Arbeit zur Folge'.

5   This article is based on research done of the following documents: Mínguez Fernández 1976; Herrero de la Fuente 1988a, and 1988b; Fernández Flórez 1991, and 1994; Fernández Catón et al. 1999. Also, Puyol y Alonso 1920.

In this sense, not only is it pertinent to compare cases from the same mode of production, but it is also helpful to compare different modes of production or social formations.

Historical Development and the Craftsman

The starting point for explaining the appearance of manufacturing is in the peasant-based society that came into being between the years 400 and 800 approximately.[6] The concept refers to the existence of different peasant units in various forms of subordination to aristocratic groups. An important feature of that organisation was the *vicos*, or homesteads.[7]

In this society the relations of exploitation were markedly weak, which meant that the aristocracy was poor or, to be more precise, that there was a social stratum that had not succeeded in becoming a dominant class. Its ascent took place very slowly, since the practices of reciprocity and exchange of gifts governing social relationships imposed a foundation of non-accumulation. This was reflected in the long survival of that rank society.

The first steps leading to the appearance of the craftsman took place in the context of this framework, when the minor local aristocrats sought to resolve the contradiction between their need of consumption on the one hand, and their lack of dependent labour force on the other, with slaves who lived in their households.

This choice may likely have been influenced by an ideal dating back to Classical Antiquity; the knowledge of trades could also be a legacy from Antiquity.[8] But aside from these legacies, the need of consumption on the part of the *potentiores* must have been a factor pressuring them to provide instruction to craftsmen. In the Visigothic documents, for example, certain specific terms allude to their technical skills (*utilitas*, *meritum*). Also, the craftsmen as a whole were considered *idonei* and they were differentiated from the *inferiores*, *rusticani* or *vilissimi servi*. Due to their expertise they merited special care; crimes committed against them were punished more severely than those committed

---

6 We owe the general concept and its demonstration to Wickham 2005.

7 Aside from the quoted work by Wickham, many other studies on the subject can be mentioned. Among them, those who postulated the lack of continuity of agricultural structures, those inscribed in the thesis of the feudal revolution, and those that incorporated archeology. See Duby 1978; Fourquin 1975; Poly 1998; Gutiérrez Lloret 1998; Chavarría Arnau 2004; Carr 2002.

8 Verhulst 1989, p. 18, asserts the continuity of the craft activities from Roman times.

against the *rustici*, and corporal punishment, was reserved, in general, for the latter.[9] These practices show that a special segment of workers was already taking shape, which must have been decisive for the preservation of 'all known basic late Roman technologies for producing everyday goods in large quantities', as is shown by the Merovingian archaelogical sites.[10]

This continued through the ninth and tenth centuries, when the predominance of the feudal mode of production had already begun. During this period, the domestic slaves (*servi*), and therefore '*familiares*' of the lordly household, satisfied various needs of their owners: they were millers (*pistores*), blacksmiths (*ferrarios*), bakers (*fumarii*), coopers (*cuparii*) tanners (*pelitarios*), carpenters (*carpentarios*), tailors (*sutores*) and weavers (*textores*).[11] This explains why the lords acquired slaves, and why the capture of slaves played a role in the Spanish *Reconquista*.[12]

This violent appropriation of manual labour highlights the slow advance of the exploitation of the dependent peasant, and especially the difficulties

---

9   Verlinden 1955, pp. 81 ff.

10   Henning 2007, p. 11, and p. 10: 'it is clear that post-Roman craft production started at a considerably higher level than has commonly been assumed'; p. 14: 'not one of the advanced production technologies so often attributed to the positive influence of Carolingian monastery workshops needed to be rediscovered in the eighth century'.

11   Verlinden 1955, pp. 116 ff., esp. pp. 125 and 145; Toubert 2006, pp. 94; 122 ff.; Sánchez Albornoz 1977; García de Valdeavellano 1969, pp. 54, 96–7, and 1952, p. 78; Calleja Puerta 2001, p. 341.

12   *España Sagrada*, Vol. XVII, Crónica silense, mentions the victory of Alfonso II over Mahamud, in Galicia, year 840, and that the king returns to Oviedo with many captives, p. 280: *Rex autem cum magno captivorum pecuniarumque numero vetum revertitur*; *España Sagrada*, vol. XIII, Crónica del obispo de Salamanca: in the year 860 Ordoño I marches to Talamanca, kills the defeated Arab warriors, and sells the rest of the captives as slaves, p. 492: *multas & alias civitates ... praeliando cepit ... aliam quoque consimilem ejus Civitatem Talamancam cum Rege suo, nomine Morezo, & uxore sua cepit: bellatores eorum omnes interfecit, reliquum vero vulgus cum uxoribus, & filiis sub corona vendidit*; Crónica silense: Alfonso III obtained captives in the course of his campaigns, p. 285: *caldeorum interfecit; spoliisque direptis, captivorumque magnus adductus est numerus*; *España Sagrada*, Vol. XL, Apéndice XIX: in 897, Alfonso III donated *mancipia* to the church of Lugo, of whom he says *ex Hismaelitarum terra captiva duximus quinquaginta*; *España Sagrada*, vol. XIV, Crónica de Sampiro: during the first year of his reign (911), King García of León campaigned against the Muslims and captured many slaves, p. 461: *Garseas ... primo anno Regni sui maximum agmen aggegavit, & ad persequendum Arabes properavit. Dedit illi Dominus victoriam, praedavit, ustulavit, & multa mancipia secum attraxit*; Ibid., p. 466, Ramiro II after his victory over the Muslims, *multa millia captivorum secum adduxit*; similar notes in pp. 468 and 469; Mínguez Fernández 1976, doc. 114, year 949.

encountered in order for it to become a reliably recurrent relationship.[13] This is reflected by the fact that between the ninth and the eleventh centuries, barring some exceptions, rents were not fixed, and they depended on specific conditions occurring at the time of their extraction, a situation that justified the constant vigilance over the district by the count and his agents. Only after the years 1050–1100 were rents declared, which coincided with the organisation of the community, the settlement of tax-paying craftsmen and with the lords devoting themselves to their occupations of status.[14] Although we will come back to this, for now let us just note that these acts of plunder, intended as a compensation for the lack of workers, in fact prolonged the unreliability in the supply of work for the lord in other areas. At any rate, if the high numbers of captives quoted in the testimonies are anywhere near reality, then we are probably looking at a situation in which the cost of labour was likely lower than the cost of a slave's upbringing. But even while the lords may not have made that calculation (surely they did not think in accounting terms), the sight of a single crowd of captives driven to forced labour after a triumphant campaign must have encouraged them to return to the frontiers again and again.

Thus originated the servile families of craftsmen, which means that their biological reproduction was supported, and that the knowledge of the trade was passed on through their family lines.[15] It is not irrelevant to point out that they were given names according to their specific work skills, which sets them

---

13   Differences notwithstanding, this situation evokes that of Latin America during the colonial period, when the decrease in the native labour force was compensated with imported African slaves.

14   I partially studied this in Astarita 2003–6.

15   Mínguez Fernández 1976, doc. 39 (930): *mancipia ... Anastasium cum filiis suis et Hildosindum.* Verlinden 1955, p. 122, n. 55. Also p. 123, n. 56, charters from the monastery of Sobrado, in Galicia, from which some interesting notes can be extracted that mention the trades, craftsmen's wives and their descendants: *Genealogia sarracenorum Sancte Maria Superaddi. Frater Pelagius Ribeira duxit de Portugalia Ali petrarium; et ipse maurus habuit uxorem nomine Zamoranam, et genuerunt filios et filias ... De Marina Suarii et de Adan natus est Petrus Adan, ferarius. De alio marito Johanne Petri, dictus Galafri, qui fuit filius de Mafumate, quem duxit abbas Martinus, furnario, natus est Iohannes Iohannis et Fernandus Iohannis, et ambo ferrari ... De Petro Gil pelitario natus est Iohannes Petri ferrarius ... De Thoma pelitario nata est Maria Thomas, uxor de dominico teixilano. De Iohanne Gateira pelitario nata est Marina Iohannis dicta Gateira et alia filia ... Ista est generatio de Alii petrario et de uxore sua Zamorana. Frater Menendus Velasquit emit Ali Muogu textor ... de isto et de uxore sua Stephania natus est Iohannes Laurentii textor et Vitalis Laurenti textor ... Dominus Didacus Velasquit duxit Pedruchi petrarium et iste genuit Martinum Porra ... De Maria Martini Cipriani natus est Iohannes teixilanus et Maria Petri uxor Petri Ioannis furnarius.*

apart from common designations (*homines*, *laboratores*), and directs us once again towards a relatively distinctive segment among the lord's vassals.

This is important because different situations are often bundled together into one concept without taking into account that those craftsmen were not like servants. The latter had non-productive functions, and they came to be, from the later Middle Ages onward, particles of the non-verbal language which the higher estates used to show themselves in public. The mental processes of these two types of slaves must have been sharply different: creatively dynamic in one case and passively contemplative in the other; not to mention the pride that can be derived from the creation of an object as opposed to the blind compliance of a servant.

Neither can that craftsman be equated to the agricultural slave. A non-intense workload was a precondition for the almost artistic skill that was required of some master craftsmen such as the blacksmith, or at least a less intense workload than the one imposed in establishments where the exhaustion of human energy led to the extinction of labourers. Inevitably, the craftsman watched out for the quality of what he did, and this requirement is in stark contrast to the requirements of mass-scale production in which only the quantitative aspect matters.

But between the fifth and the eighth centuries, slaves ran away constantly, and the *servi* occupied the roads, thus contributing to the weakening and final disappearance of the *villae* of Antiquity.[16] Testimonies suggest that those slaves resisted work, which helps explain some questions regarding the productive forces and the end of slavery in the long term. Through convictions and at times through the resignation of the slaveholders, many laws reflect the existence of an indocile labour force inclined to daily acts of sabotage and ill-disposed for work.[17] As for the freedmen, a segment of emancipated slaves at the lord's service, they were as rebellious as the slaves, and they left behind many traces of their zeal to free themselves completely.[18]

---

16   Daily sabotages by slaves in Beyerle and Buchner 1954, 30, 31; Boretius 1883, pp. 3–6. Runaway slaves in Zeumer 1902, IX, 1, 5, 6, 9, 14, 21. De Salis 1892, Liber Constitutionum VI; Azzara and Gasparri 2004, Edicto de Rotario, tit. 267, 269, 270, 271, 273, 276. At the beginning of the eight century, Ibid., Leyes de Liutprando, 44, 88; Azzara and Moro 1998, n° 10, t. 8 year 801; n° 12, t. 20, year 806–10. On archaeological studies, see Chavarría Arnau 2004, pp. 67–102.

17   Beyerle and Buchner 1954, 30: *si servus fecerit furtum*; 31: *si servus fecerit incendium*.

18   Campos and Roca Meliá 1971, IX Council of Toledo, year 655, c. XIII, pp. 308–9; Council of Mérida year 666, c. XX, p. 339. Insistence on the fact that they should remain at the service of the church: I Council of Sevilla, year 590, c. I., IV Council of Toledo, year 633, c. LXVIII,

After the year 800, slaves continued to flee, and the documents of the aristocratic establishments show that the domestic servant resisted the condition imposed upon him. Significantly, at times the slaves fled after robbing goods from the pantry.[19]

Those who escaped settled in towns and villages, as reflected in the *fueros*, which shows that it was impossible in general to retain them.[20] As a consequence, the *servi* of the lordly residences or courts proceeded to settle as dependants in villages or boroughs, many times under the label of unfree and *casati*.[21] Undoubtedly, the whole range of domestic workers who had gone from

LXX. A case of a freedman who tried to poison the bishop: II Council of Sevilla, year 619, c. VIII, p. 168, canon suggesting that it was not an isolated event. Gossip against the dead bishop: Council of Mérida, year 666, c. XV; priests who fell ill and tortured their slaves for having presumably put a curse on them: Council of Mérida, year 666, c. XV.

19   Loscertales de García de Valdeavellano 1976, doc. 21: *Fugiuit itaque filius noster et sacauit de uestro ligamine unum latronem nomine Tadoy qui habebat uobis a peitare IIIes kauallos de furto, et alium uestrum seruum nomine Maurelo.* Ibid., doc. 24: *Ego Miru et uxor mea Froisenda uobis Hermegildo et uxori uestre Paterne. Non est enim dubium ... quod peccato impediente fecit furtum filius noster nomine Fafila cum illo uestro seruo nomine Gaton*; Del Ser Quijano 1994, doc. 115 year 1022: *sua ancilla, nomini Todildi, et furtauit de sua casa quartarios VIIII de ceuaria per suasione de Emlo.* Ibid., docs. 116, 118, 120.

20   Later, this issue will surface in the *fuero* of León. The town charter of Cardona of the year 986 can be taken as an example, in Verlinden 1955, p. 138, *servi* and *ancillae* are taken in among the population of that town. Ibid., p. 138; Muñoz y Romero 1847, Fuero de Villavicencio, p. 171: *In primis de illis qui ad habitandum venerint alvendarii, cuparii, servi sint ingenui et absoluti*; Fuero de Lara, p. 518.

21   Del Ser Quijano 1981, doc. 52, year 864; doc. 53. Mínguez Fernández 1976, doc. 328, year 985, Jimena gives the *villa* of Salorio with *servos ibidem servientes et ancilla mea nomine Tinonia cum filiis et nepotibus suis vel omnia cognatione sua.* Serrano 1906b, p. 19, year 978: *in rio de Lazeto XX kasatos.* De Hinojosa 1919, p. 19, year 1041, grant of land *cum totis nostris mancipiis ibidem habitantibus.* Serrano 1910, p. 316, year 981, in Poza de la Sal, *XV homines kasatos.* Serrano 1930, p. 81, year 1006, *in Ventosa undecim casatos et in Riuulosicco octo casatos.* Del Álamo 1950, doc. 8, when the count of Castile founded the monastery in the year 1011 *casati* were mentioned: *in Uientreta septem casatos. In Cantabrana septem casatos. In Ferrera duodecim casatos* (etc.). Also Rodríguez Fernández, 1984, doc. 18, tit. 19. Also Migne 1854, col. 992–3: *in Salceta, unum servitialem cum sua haereditate; in Amunio, alium servitialem cum sua hereditate; in Decia, villam de Vellegio cum sua creatione.* De Ayala Martínez 1994, p. 195, suggests that in Leonese documentation, unlike that of Castile, the use of the term *casati* is uncommon; *homines populatos* being more frequent. He adds that the contrast between *casati* or 'settled' and free men is not systematic. We will address this last issue in the present study. For other areas, see Bois 1989, pp. 31 ff.; in the village of Lournand, Bois detected *servi casati* in the tenth century, and he speculates that they would not exceed 15

slavery to servitude (although they were legally free), did not tolerate their condition, and they had opportunities to show it. This explains the scarcity of slaves offered on the market, with regard to which the hypothesis that they were unable to reproduce by themselves should be discarded.[22] The settlement of craftsmen in towns and villages was already fully achieved by the second half of the eleventh century, those who remained in the aristocratic establishments being relatively few.[23] This had its counterpart in the banal lordship, that is to say, in the second version of the feudal mode of production, whose main distinguishing feature with respect to the first form may be this type of settlement.

Conditions for Slave Flight

The absence of the state was the most serious hurdle for *optimates* who wanted to prevent the slaves from fleeing their households. Inasmuch as slavery requires a coordinated vigilance over the whole of the territory, it was very difficult or impossible to capture the fugitives without a state organisation.

This was due to two situations connected to each other in a temporal sequence. The first was the fall of the administrative machinery of Antiquity (based on *curiales*), which devolved into a vacuum of secular power due to the slow formation of the new dominant class.[24] But when power was finally reconstituted, it was shaped into lordships, and the fragmentation of sovereignty made difficult or precluded altogether a balanced control of the social whole.

---

percent of the total population, and that they would farm, at most, twenty or twenty-five percent of the land.

22 Sánchez Albornoz 1977, p. 47, proposes that the settlements of slaves can be explained in light of the difficulties owners experienced when buying slaves on the market and the lack of manpower due to the reconquest and repopulation. The assumption is that slavery was reproduced only by purchase or by conquest because the unmarried, without legitimate wife (*uxor*), had no children. Such prejudice (shared by Weber) has been challenged by historians of American slavery. See Stampp 1956.

23 Fernández Flórez 1994, doc. 1752, year 1255, mentions a bloodletter, a carpenter and a blacksmith, all belonging to the convent; there was also a shoemaker, a furrier and a carpenter of the chamber; and the *obra* had a foreman, a carpenter, a blacksmith and a master.

24 The general concept and the issue of the fall of the state can be found in Wickham 2005. On the question of whether the systemic crisis was precipitated by the crisis of the *curiales*, Astarita 2000b and 2007a.

This second situation was further complicated by the persistence of free areas. Consequently, the decline of the traditional *servus* was due, to a large extent, to the existence of slavery without a political organisation for slavery.

The flight of slaves can also be understood with regard to certain structural features. The runaway *servus*, unlike the fleeing slaves of other times and places, aimed for inclusion, because he took refuge in the domestic units awaiting him in the villages, a feature that became more pronounced with the growth of boroughs around the year 1000. This *servus* did not replicate the hardly useful heroism of Spartacus, who overcame armies without overcoming Rome, neither does he evoke the fugitive American slave, to whom we will refer when highlighting the road to non-society. The *servus*, like a hidden subversive, set out cautiously towards another mode of production. This meant that, thanks to this context, a resource common to the slaves of all times had a formative character which imprinted itself on the new social relationships, and was not merely destructive. The act of fleeing did not just imply the non-reproduction of slavery, but the genesis of another system.

On the other hand, this development coincided with the initial take-off of the European economy, between the ninth and the eleventh centuries, brought on by an expansive demographic and agricultural cycle involving reduction of the demesnes, the formation of peasant holdings, land clearing, etc.[25] This allowed the peasant-based society to overcome its very low levels of production, although the development that would be achieved later, between the eleventh and the thirteenth centuries, had not yet occurred.

The Runaway Slave and the Agricultural Household Unit

Considering that a good proportion of the slaves were craftsmen, their flight gave rise to manufacturing in villages and boroughs. Here the social base played a role, therefore peasant society was not only an antecedent but also the framework for the new activity. Such an articulation between the peasant household and manufacturing activity implies the assumption of a craftsman who fitted the ideal and the practice of an economy that tended toward self-sufficiency. In other words, he satisfied from the very beginning this desire to make everything at home. Let's explore this in some detail.

The settlement of craftsmen strengthened the basic economic cell of the village from the ninth to the eleventh centuries. This cell consisted of a nuclear

---

25   Toubert 1990.

family that lived surrounded by various buildings (houses, kitchen, oven, yards, mill) and lands (orchard, grain fields, vineyards, fruit-trees), and also participated in the use of common lands.[26] Significantly, these were the same attributes of the *domus* of the proto-urban borough in the period in which the borough had already become the characteristic sphere of the craftsman.[27] This composite unit, which German historians call *ganz Haus*, was in tune with the ideal of rural subsistence, and in it manufacturing was one more branch of the whole unit. This must have facilitated the upkeep of the new incoming workforce, since the craftsman did not withdraw from the production of his own food supply. In short, such a household, like an assemblage of parts that could be taken apart or enlarged, was not only structurally and functionally prepared to incorporate another activity, but it also offered a solution for the existence of the people who devoted themselves to secondary activities, even in a situation in which the regular transfer of food from the countryside to the city had not happened.

As for the lords, they strengthened the structure insofar as they controlled villages or incorporated them into their patrimony. As they converted the domestic unit into a source of rent collection, they favoured the nuclear fam-

---

26　Examples in Mínguez Fernández 1976, doc. 11, year 910: *villa cum domos, ortos, molinos, cum suis productibus aquis, pratis, palidibus vel ubicumque noster terminus devenerit ab integro omnia vobis vendimus*; doc 34, year 930: *Et ego Gudesteo una cum uxore mea et filiis vendimus vobis villan nostram propriam … ubi habuimus casa et molino*; doc. 303, year 980, donation to Sahagún of *villa nostra propria quam dicunt Castellanos ab omni integritate per suos terminos*; doc. 100, year 945, Diego and his wife sold to the monastery a *villa* in *Villa de Foracasas* (Melgar de Foracasas) with seven houses with their *solares*, *cortes* and *huerto*; Herrero de la Fuente 1988a, doc. 374, year 1001, a donation mentions *corte cum suos solares et suo orto et suo pumare*; doc. 510, year 1048: *cortes conclusas cun suas casas cupertas*; doc. 511 year 1048, donation of a *corte* from the presbiter Pedro to Sahagún: *corte cum suas casas et suos exitos et regressus, cum terris et uineis, pratis et pascuis, palidibus, uel cum quantum ad ipsa cortet pertinet*; located in Villalobos, in the Palazuelo valley; doc. 559, year 1053, this text demonstrates the polysemic value of the word *villa* as a production unit and as village; doc. 523, year 1049, here the *villa* is a unit of peasant production which includes a court, fields and vineyards: Zomar Díaz gave to the monastery half *de nostro habere et de nostra hereditate et de nostra corte, cum terris et vineis. Et est ipsa uilla, quam uocant Uilla Sancte, iuxta ecclesiam Sancti Saluatoris.* On small landholding on a regional level, see, among other studies, Salrach 1977, esp. pp. 33 ff.

27　Herrero de la Fuente 1988b, doc. 866, year 1090: *una corte integra, cum suas kasas, que habeo in Sancti Facundi cum suo exitu … et uno horto, integro, qui est in Sancti Facundi.* In later documents it appears that the craftsman of the *burgo* had grain fields and vineyards in the surroundings.

ilies, since a larger number of domestic units meant a larger volume of rents collected.[28] The Christian model of marriage adapted to that interest.[29]

Also favourable to the integration of the fugitive in the village was the absence of a marked difference in social rank, as shown by independent communities of the early Middle Ages where slaves lived alongside free men.[30] A similar manifestation is suggested in a law of the early eighth century, in which the Visigoth king Egica denounces that there is almost no place left (*civitas, castellum, vicum, aut villa*) in which runaway slaves cannot count on help from the local inhabitants.[31] Also there was confusion regarding unfree and intermediate status, and at times no difference was made between them. For example, one version of the *Crónica de Alfonso III* (who reigned between 866 and 910) states that the freedmen rebelled, while another version states that the rebellion was carried out by slaves.[32] That chronicle, which makes reference to the only great movement occurring in the North of Spain until the beginning of the twelfth century, appears to reflect the notion that the heterogeneous mass of rebels became a block in the course of the struggle. Also contributing to integration was the fact that a family of *servi* could live in a land that was legally free, as well as the existence of free peasants farming servile land.[33] The statutes regarding people and land were becoming mixed, thus breaking barriers, a situation reflected since the early Middle Ages in the appearance of intermediate figures such as that of the *seruus quasi colonus*.

These circumstances, in their substantial features, were to be reproduced centuries later in Latin America during colonial times, where the slaves had two main strategies of resistance. On the one hand, they appealed to legal resources, threats (of flight, suicide or sabotage), neglect of tools, laziness, malingering

---

28 Herrero de la Fuente 1988b, doc. 823, fuero of 1085: *de singulos solos dabuntur singulis solidis ... uero, si in ipso anno non populauerit illum, perdet. Post mortem parentis, quando filii solum parcierint, quanti fuerint, tantos solidos dabunt.* See also Toubert 1990.

29 Brundage 1987. The defence of the Christian model of marriage – monogamic, indissoluble and exogamic – is found in Del Ser Quijano 1994, reflecting situations characteristic of the region of León: there the counts repressed any transgression of this rule which they did not have to uphold for themselves.

30 Campos and Roca Meliá 1971, Regla Común, c. I, siglo VII.

31 Zeumer 1902, *Lex Visigothorum*, IX, 1, 21.

32 Bonnaz 1987, Crónica de Alfonso III, states in one version that *seruilis origo contra proprios dominos surrexerunt*; in another, *libertini contra proprios dominos arma sumentes tyrannice surrexerunt.*

33 For example Del Ser Quijano 1981, doc. 52 and 53, already quoted, as well as many others on *casati.*

and other behaviours of the sort that did not imply a complete break from daily life. On the other hand, they resorted to flight or rebellion.[34] It was also true of American society that emancipation did not lead to an improvement in social standing, since the freed slave remained oppressed by his former owner.[35] Finally, toward the end of colonial times, in places such as the mining regions of Nueva Granada, freedmen and slaves who had bought their freedom lived alongside many former slaves who had fled.[36]

The Behaviour of the Lords

The continuity of medieval slaves working in aristocratic establishments, which points to the slow pace of the transformations, was due not only to the general social conditions, but also to the varying behaviour of the lords.

From the year 800 onwards, the lords did not choose the same paths nor did they act corporatively as a social subject that modified social conditions. The runaway slaves must have had these differences in mind when seeking refuge, in a non-mercantile play of supply and demand, in the jurisdiction of the lord who imposed less severe conditions. As a consequence, the different strategies of the lords must have been solicitously matched by the strategies of the subordinates. Let us begin with those who desired to keep their household servants.

This sector prolonged practices dating back to the Roman-Germanic kingdoms regarding slave craftsmen, and it is possible that among them were those who encouraged campaigns of capture. Their attitude is reflected not only in the texts of the seigneurial estates, but also in the rules ordering that fugitives be returned. For example, the *fuero* of León from the beginning of the eleventh century established that a slave who was recognised by trustworthy men, whether Christian or pagan, had to be handed over to his owner.[37] Some lords, for their part, sued to reclaim their property over slaves who denied being

---

34 Leal 2003.
35 Pita Rico 2003.
36 West 1972.
37 Pérez Prendes y Muñoz de Arraco 1988, pp. 495–545: Fuero de León (O) which corresponds to the Codex of the Cathedral of Oviedo and is different from the Fuero de León (B) corresponding to the Church of Braga. See Fuero de León (O) title XXIII: *Seruus uero qui per ueridicos homines seruus probatus fuerit, tam de christianis quam de agarenis sine aliqua contemptione detur domino suo.*

such.[38] This negates the thesis of comparative profitability which has been proposed to explain the appearance of the *servi casati*. According to this thesis, after some cost and benefit calculations, the lords would have realised that it was more profitable to settle the slaves. But this looks like a case of mistaken reasoning on the part of modern historians rather than the lords.[39] In all likelihood, the lords disregarded economic calculations because even the most onerous slavery in monetary terms is 'profitable' in terms of the aristocratic lifestyle. Domestic slaves were convenient for conspicuous consumption, and their upkeep became part of the cost of status, a premium paid for the reproduction of rank. Some ways of life of Antiquity may have had some influence in this behaviour. In this respect, let us not forget that the bishops were descended from a class of impoverished senators who hoped to restore their pre-eminence by way of an ecclesiastical career, and we cannot rule out the possible persistence of this legacy in the year 1000.[40] The least we can say is that for a long time the hierarchy of the church was torn between having slaves and the religious belief (or the metaphysical fear) which led them to set them free.[41]

Other lords accepted the inevitable, that is to say, they became resigned to the burdens imposed by flights and resistance, and they ended up favouring the settlement of slaves. Besides the social struggle, another factor pushing them in that direction was the growth in agricultural activity which was better suited for having labourers living in the fields, and it is not surprising that even cavalry

---

38   Fernández del Pozo 1984, doc. x, year 1025.

39   The assumption is that, at some point, the class of power discovered that feudalism was more profitable than the slave system, and decided to change the mode of production. Dockés 1982 criticised this point of view; slavery did not end due to profit margins, and the classes of the past did not reason the way modern economic agents do. But we must consider another issue. According to this thesis, an owner could reduce costs by having settled slaves because he did not have to take care of the slave's upkeep. However, here the form of exploitation deceives the historian, because, as Marx said, it appears that all of the work belongs to the owner, obscuring the fact that the slave produces himself. In other words, the owner does not have 'outlays' related to the slave's upkeep; but still a part of what the slave produces is assigned to the personal consumption of the same slave, even though it appears as if the owner is giving the slave an allowance of supplies for his subsistence. This situation corresponds to a productive slave. An unproductive slave, who was a part of conspicuous consumption, did not feed himself and was therefore a cost of status. But this latter form of domestic slavery was compatible with feudalism, and was especially important during late feudalism.

40   Arndt and Krusch 1885, *passim*. Pietri 1986.

41   This was reflected in the Councils of Agde of the year 506 and Yenne of the year 517, and was reiterated in subsequent councils.

commanders settled their captives. Even without considering this assumption, there is no doubt that a part of those in power carried out a deliberate strategy to push things in this direction. This is reflected in one document about the settlement of Lugo in the mid-eighth century, carried out under the direction of bishop Odoario, who attended *cum nostris multis familis, et cum ceteris populis tam nobiles quam inobiles*.[42] Once the site had been reestablished, he converted those slaves into landholders for them to till the fields with oxen: *fecimus de nostra familia possessores ... et dedimus illis boves ad laborandum*. The bishop's actions were not much different from those of other proprietors who turned their slaves into freedmen with lands.[43]

Among those slaves who were finding it easier to settle in towns and villages were the craftsmen. This is reflected in the *fuero* of León, which stipulates that no *iunior*, cooper or weaver who had settled in the town, could be expelled.[44] The following chapter appears to extend this rule: 'we also stipulate', state the lawmakers, that he who is unfree of an unknown owner (*seruus incognitus*) cannot be expelled or handed over.[45]

The acquiescence shown toward settlements is also expressed by the material support given by the lord so that a destitute man might start over in a borough (although the slave could have his own *peculium*). To make sure that the newcomer found favourable conditions in order to build his house and clear the land, the lord granted temporary tax exemptions to lighten the burden of those initial works, a fact that indirectly demonstrates that, due to its relative complexity, a unit of production required significant investment in terms of labour.[46] It is possible that, for example, the initial period at the borough for a newly arrived craftsman could be made somewhat easier if the newcomer was

42   Floriano 1949–51, p. 62.

43   Loscertales de García de Valdeavellano 1976, year 1000, doc. 131, charter of freedom given by a nun: *libertis meis qui estis habitantes in comitatu Presarense*.

44   Pérez Prendes y Muñoz de Arraco 1988, Fuero de León (O), XXI: *Mandamus igitur ut nullus iunior, cuparius, aluendarius adveniens Legionem ad morandum, non inde extrahatur*. This rule is the first of the series of local rules in the charter, placed after the first 28 rules which are territorial in nature. See Martínez Díez 1988, p. 304.

45   Pérez Prendes y Muñoz de Arraco 1988, Fuero de León (O), XXII: *Item precipimus ut seruus incognitus, similiter inde non extrahatur nec alicui detur*.

46   Serrano 1906a, Fuero de Palenzuela, pp. 19–20: *Homnis homo qui adventicius fuerit in Palenciola, non dabit efforcionem nec faciet sernam in primo anno*. Ibid., p. 20: *Homo de Palenciola in primo anno quo duxerit uxorem, non faciat sernam neque facenderam aliquam*. Rodríguez Fernández 1984, year 1165, doc. 28, Fuero de Santa Eugenia given by the abbot of San Isidoro, 3: *Et si quibus ad populandum uenerit in uno anno non faciat forum*.

allowed to cook in the central oven of the Sahagún Monastery. No document reflects this, but the hypothesis can be put forward in view of the obligatory nature of this *banalité*.[47] In any case, and given the importance of this borough, there is no doubt that the monks were favourably disposed toward the settlement of craftsmen, a circumstance that the *fuero* would legalise in 1085.

This duality in the behaviour of the power class is reflected, as we have seen, in the contradictory clauses of the *fuero* of León. The same ambivalence can be found in other instances.[48] This indicates that one section of the aristocracy remained tied to the ancient forms and another supported the settlement of the *servi*. But the unequal sway of tradition over the different lords was not the only factor; their adaptation to the new conditions also mattered, since the type of lordship must have been a consideration: the king was probably more inclined to accept the settlement of a slave, even though he was himself a slaveholder, because this suited the large extension of his jurisdiction.[49] It is also possible that there existed an overlapping of issues related to domestic power.

The slave required constant vigilance, and many lords, who were in the process of consolidating their position, may have been unable to enforce such vigilance. For others, the need to attend to the tasks of their estate, which became essential as feudal competition increased, must have played a role, leading to a decrease in the attention they could pay to their domestic tasks. What is certain is that, either by force or voluntarily, the lords withdrew from tasks such as overseeing their slaves, and although in the early eleventh century they still performed daily policing activities in their domains, by 1050–1100 they had entrusted those functions to urban or rural councils. Henceforth they occupied their time in military campaigns or attending the courts of their own overlords.

The part of the aristocracy which favoured the settlement of the *servi* must have influenced this process inasmuch as they legitimised the fugitives. These fugitives not only had somewhere to go, but they could also envision possibilities of success, for this success no longer depended just on the protection

---

47   Herrero de la Fuente 1988b, doc. 823, Fuero of 1085.

48   Díaz Canseco 1924, p. 375: *Item precipio ut servus incognitus similiter non inde extrahatur, nec alicui detur. Servus vero qui per veridicos homines servus probatus fuerit, tam de Chri- stianis quam de Agarenis, sine aliqua contentione detur domino suo.* Also, in the Fuero of Villavicencio, where we saw that the unfree who had settled in the village were granted freedom, an exception is made for Muslim slaves: Muñoz y Romero 1847, p. 171: *sed si fuerit Mauros comparatos aut filios Mauri vadat cum suo seniore.*

49   Mínguez Fernández 1976, doc. 9, year 909, Alfonso III refers to his villa of Alcamín pointing out that *de squalido de gente barbarica manu propria cum pueris nostris adprehendimus.*

of the neighbours, as reflected in the previously quoted Visigoth decree of the early eighth century. Now a section of those in power, which could include the monarch, was helping them, and they could settle in places as pivotal as León, the political capital of the kingdom. The act of fleeing became a decisive step toward resocialisation. A comparison will allow us to appreciate this process.

Comparison with Another Social Formation

Let us move to the past of another world, eighteenth-century Latin America, in order to broaden our views through the life of one *zambo*. In 1776, Félix Fernando Martínez stole a monstrance and the consecrated communion bread from a church in Cartagena.[50] The subsequent trial, with its many inquiries due to the seriousness of a theft that was also a sin, allows the historian to get to know this man. In the course of these inquiries it transpires that Martínez was a fugitive slave who had been on the run for many years. He had been forced to move over a wide area, living on a peripheral grey area between legality and crime.

This story, which is similar to any other *Biografía de un cimarrón*, contrasts with that of a man who left behind his condition as medieval slave without becoming a fugitive living at the margins of society (and many *cimarrones* spent more time outside society than inside of it). A runaway European *servus* could benefit in a time of history when the settling of slaves was not infrequent. In this context, the slave's physical mobility could translate into rising social mobility, because the most destitute of the *servi* acquired a different condition by being '*casatus*' in a double sense: having his own dwelling and having a wife (*uxor*), even when his status as unfree remained unchanged. That fugitive, who found himself within society, mingling with the other villagers, could start a new life by using to his own advantage the skills he had been taught. Thus, the formation of the feudal mode of production, by which slavery was relegated to a supplementary economic form, favoured him.

This favourable environment comes into sharper focus when contrasted with the American experience, in which the flight of slaves meant an increase in social marginalisation, i.e. people who lived off menial work or petty crime without ever becoming economic agents or full-fledged members of society. The American runaways could not possibly accomplish such integration in the presence of a state apparatus of vigilance that would capture them at any

---

50   Anrup and Chaves 2005, pp. 101 ff.

misstep. In Western Europe, even though runaway household servants were captured on occasion, the chances of success were significant. But beyond that, the fundamental difference was that in America a successful escape meant social exclusion or, in certain areas toward the end of the Colonial Era, a precarious situation of poverty and exploitation. In medieval Europe, it could be a stepping-stone toward social advancement even though the runaway did not gain freedom from economic dependence. We will return to this last notion.

Settlement, Quality and Intensity of Labour

In principle, there was no reason for the craftsman to lose the skills he had acquired in the aristocratic household when moving to the town or village. On the contrary, he would hold on to those skills, and the settlement gave him the chance to develop them insofar as they helped him become established in his trade. Let us clarify this with a comparison.

In general, an unsettled person is an unskilled labourer. This type is observed in the later Middle Ages, when there was an increase in travelling labourers hired per day who, having few skills, changed from one activity to another. In the texts they are mentioned in generic terms such as *obreros y obreras*, *peones*, *jornaleros* and *omes menesteriales*, a lexicon pointing to a mass of people who sold their labour force for a variety of simple activities.[51] This differs sharply from the statements of the *Crónicas de Sahagún*, where the emphasis is placed on the professional diversity of those who lived in the village.[52]

The servile work done at the lord's house was without doubt a key factor in the origins of this specialisation, which would not arise spontaneously from the undifferentiated work routines of the peasants. This consideration should not

---

51 Real Academia de la Historia 1863, *Cortes* of Valladolid of 1351: *mando que todos los carpenteros et albannies et tapiadores et peones et obreros et obreras, jornaleros et los otros omes menesteriales que sse suelen alogar, que ssalgan a las plaças de cada un lugar do sson moradores et que an acostumbrado de sse alquilar de cada día en quebrando el alva, com ssus fferramientas et ssu vianda, en manera que ssalgan dela villa o del lugar en ssaliendo el ssol para ffazer las labores ... que lleguen ala villa o lugar do fueren alquilados en poniendo sse el ssol*, pp. 92–3.

52 Puyol y Alonso 1920, *Crónicas de Sahagún*, ch. 13: *como el sobredicho rrei ordenase e estableçiese que ai se fiçiese villa, ayuntaronse de todas las partes del vniberso burgueses de muchos e diuersos ofiçios, conbiene a sauer, herreros, carpinteros, xastres, pelliteros, çapateros, escutarios e omes enseñados en muchas e dibersas artes e ofiçios.*

be understood to mean that all craftsmen acquired skills while serving their lords, but that this instruction created the original conditions that would allow for the trades to spread throughout towns and villages.

Another comparison reinforces the thesis that the skills were maintained in the shift from the lordly house to the village. As previously stated, the domestic *servus* was probably ill suited for craftsmanship. His lack of motivation, a difficulty of slavery regimes in general, would become acutely apparent in a type of manufacturing that did not employ machinery and opposed mechanisation. A chore that had to be performed without technical mediation depended on manual dexterity, and manual dexterity could not exist without the ability to concentrate on the task at hand. This is why servitude, especially in the absence of incentives, did not lend itself to activities that were relatively sophisticated and required manual skill. This last quality was in fact the exact opposite of the simple cooperation typical of slavery, which entailed turning the collective into a dehumanised mechanism for aggregating unskilled labour.

In the workshop where he lived, the craftsman engaged in work that was not only of higher quality, but also more intense because besides having to support his own consumption he had to pay the tributes levied by the lord. This probably obliged him not to disregard any technical improvement, even though manual skill was still dominant. Such improvements could involve the adoption of a tool destined to be fine-tuned in the long term, the kind of tool with which slaves usually had a negative relationship.[53] The craftsman must also have optimised the use of his time. The most achieved expression of this optimisation – which would also serve to increase yields – was the fact that the craftsman combined his trade with farming or raising livestock, taking advantage of the down times in farm chores to engage in his craft.[54]

---

53 Marx 1976b, pp. 210–11, n. 17. Marx offers an explanation for this technical blockage based on the profound logic of the social relationship. He writes that the slaves of Antiquity were only distinguished as *instrumentum vocale* from the *instrumentum semivocale* and the *instrumentum mutum*. But the slave mistreated the animals and the tools to show them that he was human. In consequence, Marx concludes that an economic principle (*Prinzip ökonomisches*) of this mode of production mandates the use of crude and heavy instruments. About technical changes in the craftsman's workshop, see Endrei 1971; Turnau 1988.

54 Sivéry 1990, p. 81. References to landholding craftsmen abound in the documents of the twelfth century and later, Herrero de la Fuente 1988b, doc. 1479 (1193); Fernández Flórez 1991, doc. 1459 (1191); doc. 1274 (1140); Fernández Flórez 1994, doc. 1663 (1231); doc. 1621 (1219); doc. 1627 (1222); doc. 1651 (1229); doc. 1663 (1231); doc. 1684 (1236); doc. 1696 (1244); doc. 1708 (1247); Ubieto Arteta 1961, docs. 59, 137 and 160; Martín 2005, p. 70, n. 15; pp. 88–9. Represa 1973, pp. 528 and 535. Ubieto Arteta 1961, docs. 59, 137 and 160.

The demands of the lord were a condition for this principle of *carpe diem* to appear in the feudal mode of production. The lord imposed on the craftsman the need for a surplus, i.e. labour embodied in a manufactured product. With this an old postulate of medievalism becomes critically illuminated, because we allude to the notion that the *servus* did not flee to freedom (unless he made his way to inhospitable places such as the dangerous Iberian frontiers), but indeed he went from one form of coercion to another. It is only the pressure exerted by the lord, motivated by the need of diversified revenues, which allows us to understand the increase in productivity and the fixing of the acquired skills through their systematic application. Had the system been more lax, that mastery of a skill would have been forgotten for lack of use.

In this respect, it must be pointed out that in some societies studied by anthropologists which could be equated to the peasant-based societies of the early Middle Ages, scholars have found 'an untapped potential surplus' derived from the decision not to work more hours per day even while there is the possibility to do so, simply because there are no social reasons for working longer.[55] When feudal exploitation appeared, so did the need to stretch physical and intellectual energies in order to satisfy the lord. This is why medieval craftsmanship did not come into being as the work of free men, but of semi-free men subjected to the lord's logic, or, in other words, the concrete labour of the specialised craftsman did not arise from the simple inertia of having to work for a living in a free village, but from the pressure of living for work, a process reflected in special rents such as the textiles which the lords demanded from some of their peasants in the eleventh and thirteenth centuries.[56] At any rate, that pressure had its limit in the need to preserve the semi-artistic nature of the products.

These reflections suggest that the lord's role in the construction of the system should be revised.

---

55   See Godelier 1981; Herskovits 1952.
56   Rodríguez Fernández 1984, doc. 17, year 1149, the *fuero* given to Noceda de Cabrera by Abbot Pedro de Montes established, among other obligations, that of a robe. Ibid., doc. 71, year 1255, Fuero de Ribas de Sil, p. 211: *debent dare pro iantare de rege de cada fogo duos cubitos de panno stopazo, de dar et de tomar annuatim in festo de Sancti Martini.* See also that the issue was unresolved both under slavery and under the system of free peasantry, two categories that fluctuate in the analysis by Bois 1989. Verhulst 1991, see p. 199; Bois proposes that the economic growth of the ninth and tenth centuries was due to the preponderance of free peasantry; Verhulst did not miss the opportunity to point out that Bois had placed the slave relationship at the centre of the social landscape of the period, and points his criticism at this contradiction.

Historians have assigned to the lord's initiative a preponderant role in the birth of the peasant production unit. They have stated, for example, that the lords established the tenancy of the medieval peasant when they divided the ancient *mansi* into smaller units with nuclear families in order to multiply their revenues, or when they ruled that one single heir of the stem family would inherit undivided possession, thus precluding subdivisions that would reduce the size of the holdings, and simplifying collections.[57] It is possible that these explanations are valid for those structures. At any rate, although the lords may not have done a fair distribution of *sortes*, as historians once supposed, it is definitely possible that they acted based on assumptions that derived from ancient agricultural practices, and with that they may have obtained a unity of production and taxation adapted to their needs. It was a question, therefore, of changing the received structures in a way that would preserve the traditional mode of labour and the ancestral logic of the family. This is precisely the reason why this situation cannot be equated to the one we are concerned with in this study. For the craftsman to come into being it was not enough to act on a given evolution in the same sense in which said evolution was unfolding; quite to the contrary, it was necessary to lean on this secular agricultural development in order to partially move away from its principles of undifferentiated production to incorporate a specialisation whose purpose was to fulfil demands beyond the family. In order to deviate from the ancestral path, one single act was not enough; this is why the lord's contribution is an indirect one in a heterogeneous framework of objective and personal forces.

Apprenticeship and Reproduction of the System

The craftsman could not exist without reproducing himself, and one factor in this reproduction, besides the material support provided by the domestic unit, was the preservation and transmission of a know-how across the generations for which methodical instruction was a prerequisite. This is expressed in the *Crónicas de Sahagún* and constitutes one of the distinctive features of this document: '*omes enseñados en muchas e dibersas artes e ofiçios*'.[58]

Although information is scarce, there is no doubt that the father-son bond inside the productive household was one link in the chain of instruction. This instruction was most likely acquired by observation and experimentation,

---

57   Toubert 1990; Terradas i Saborit 1980; To Figueras 1993.
58   Puyol y Alonso 1920, Crónicas de Sahagún, ch. 13.

that is, by making the object, rather than by oral communication. Thus the apprentice would eventually become a master of the craft, replicating the chief craftsman of the household.

Such apprenticeship could not have differed in its fundamental aspects from the one the young man underwent in order to immerse himself in the culture that surrounded him, that is, the process of learning what he needed to learn in order to move around in a social context. In this respect, anthropologists have observed that in societies without schools a large number of practical skills (such as washing one's body or clothing) are acquired daily by means of imitation and participation. A similar phenomenon occurs with the teaching of crafts: among the weavers from Ghana, language plays a small role in learning, and the same has been reported for Liberian tailors.[59]

The way in which the medieval young man assimilated his teacher, who was his social father, probably resembled the type of instruction observed in West Africa in what pertains to tasks requiring non-linguistic learning. However, there is an additional nuance. Even if this education reflected the general pedagogical formula that society offered for the new generations, it must also have been specific.[60] Here there was no room for simple learning by inertia, that is, the type of learning that does not externalise the fact that the apprentice is incorporating behaviours. The activity of the craftsman implied a higher level of physical and mental concentration than the activities performed by other members of the household probably required, and this in itself must have defined for him a separate status. It is possible that in this departure from the spontaneous, in the knowledge of a skill whose significance was not merely learning to take part in generic social interactions, lay the urgency to exert some coercion on the apprentice, hence, this paternal instruction, in tune with the hierarchical family, must have involved no small amount of authoritarianism. This probably pushed the youth to devote himself to the routines of labour, to apply all his energy to it; in short, it helped bind him to the trade.

The typical contract of apprenticeship found in the craft corporations of later times by which the figure of the master was assimilated to that of the father

---

59   Bloch 1991, for the concept of culture. Maurice Bloch summarises studies on the subject.

60   To Figueras 1993, p. 61, for children who did not inherit: 'El aprendizaje de un oficio puede convertirse en una compensación equivalente. En 1196, Ramón de Riera al desplazar a su sobrino del manso familiar que había ocupado su hermano se compromete a enseñarle su oficio como si se tratara de una forma de resolver su futuro fuera del manso. En otro caso similar la indemnización prevista para un hijo excluido del patrimonio paterno incluía el aprendizaje del oficio de zapatero'.

with the same despotic prerogatives could then be explained as deriving from this first form of reproduction; conversely, this contract sheds some light on what the ancient customs may have been like. It is not inappropriate then to attribute to that original relationship a certain degree of labour exploitation by the family, which anticipated the abuse perpetrated by the master of later times on the young apprentice (for example, by paying him wages lower than those of the adult worker).

The above situation must have linked the economic cycle of those early craftsmen to the biological cycle of the family. The moment in which the young man was incorporated into his 'apprenticeship/work' meant the family could begin to recover from a difficult phase marked by the support of future workers. Once the young man became a full participant in the household labour, there was a phase of relative ease, which would be followed by another difficult stage with the appearance of mouths to feed that did not contribute work. Those periodic ups and downs could be overcome or mitigated by hiring other young men for a salary, which made the production unit independent from the children born to the family. This last course of action was definitely implemented from the twelfth century onwards, but it is possible that there was already some form of hired work going on in the previous century, and it is also possible that the adoption of children fulfilled some functions meant to stabilise the supply of workers. In this respect, the rationale of the peasant surfaces once again in the inner workings of early craftsmanship.

These features, while confirming the importance of the domestic unit, add another shade of meaning. In manufacturing, this primary cell was being trans-formed by bringing together a sophisticated range of sexually and generation-ally differentiated tasks, a transformation that reached greater depth when incorporating members from outside the family. In this case we are faced with a more complex form of production and reproduction than that of the ori-ginal household, a form that pushed the old biological limits and potentially transcended its aims of subsistence: the evolutionary possibility was being restated in terms of class and exchange values. As a result, this exploration of 'the world we have lost' does not bring up a picture of immobile patriarchal nuclei, because in them subsistence, which constituted their primary uniform reason for being, was also a source of inequality to the extent in which the social labour contained within those units became differentiated.[61] This inequality

---

61   These conclusions lead to the rethinking of the immutability of the European nuclear
       family in medieval and modern times as proposed by Laslett 1965. Criticism of this model

was enough to redefine the small unit, which would no longer be a derivation of kinship but an institution subjected to the need to produce goods.

This endogenous form of transmission of knowledge meant that a strong concentration on the productive unit was imprinted on the young man by the time he reached adulthood. This unit was organised as a cell folded into itself to a degree unknown by farmworkers who were much more open to communal labour, and this is at the root of the possibility that the craftsman had to guard the secrets of his labour. Simultaneously with the 'secret of the house' sprang the awareness of belonging to a distinct social group.

The structure of the peasant household, which was well suited to the incorporation of crafts, was a factor in the improvement of labour quality and its yield. This is why the craftsman's activity, which was originally rooted in the logic of self-sustenance by way of aggregation, that is to say, as a quantitative variation, had the potential to bring about qualitative change. In other words, to the extent that the domestic economy allowed for manufacturing, a transformative premise was being introduced. When the village began to recognise this capability in the craftsman's labour, the need to fix this skill in order to make use of it as a social utility also arose, a community interest that would be added to the already-mentioned private interest of the lord.

Once these features were present, there is yet another feature of the towns and villages from which the trades benefited, and that is the fact that these residential units, and not just the household, were places for the transmission of learning. If the *Crónicas de Sahagún* tell us that, besides a variety of trades, the town concentrated *personas de diuersas e estrañas prouinçias e rreinos*, providing a list of their nationalities (in the medieval sense of the word), to whom were added merchants who came from many places, we can conclude that learning was nurtured by a plurality of habits and customs.[62]

Skilled Labour and Status

These circumstances separated the craftsman's activity from that of the village as a whole, a difference that was grounded on the peculiarity of labour

---

by Laslett and his group at Cambridge has been founded on the economic changes in the household. See Seccombe 1995; also Spike, Harrington et al. 2007.

62   Puyol y Alonso 1920, Crónicas de Sahagún, ch. 13: *gascones, bretones, alemanes, yngleses, borgoñones, normandos, tolosanos, prouinçiales, lonbardos, e muchos otros negoçiadores de diuersas naçiones e estrannas lenguas.*

that is strictly human as opposed to the peasant's labour that was commingled with the work of nature. In other words, the difference was due to the teleological character of the craftsman's work, in which a mental representation of the object precedes its embodiment.[63] It is precisely this need to transfer an idea into matter, that is, the need for the hand to succeed in carrying out the design inside the craftsman's head, which made mental concentration an indispensable condition, and this in turn required a reasoned and specific mastery instead of generic automated action.

With this 'take-off' of the craftsman arose the conditions for the social recognition of his skill, and even for that to be transformed into his prerogative, so that the product might be sublimated into an article that conferred prestige, thus allowing the concrete labour to achieve a higher expression that erased all traces of abstract and undifferentiated labour, and the special worker to end up as a select type with defined monopolies over practical knowledge. These capabilities, which were only fully achieved in core regions of Flanders and Italy, are mentioned here in order to shed light on the transformation which, on a smaller scale, took place in the village or borough between the ninth and eleventh centuries. In that setting, the skill to perform a complex task meant there was a creator whom other people admired without being able to imitate him. The more the craft stood out from the regular routine of the majority, even in its use of raw materials that were not accessible to everybody (since the craftsman worked on products of nature and not on nature itself), the larger the gap in status between him and the rest of the villagers.

This development, which meant a change in the conditions of existence for one segment of the subordinates, transformed the real status of this group in spite of the lordship that bundled all vassals into a compact whose common feature was legal inequality. Indeed, there was a double divergence. On the one hand, there was a gap between the statute of the settled slave and his material reality, which no longer resembled that of the traditional *mancipia* although the legal statute had not changed. But there was also a gap between the legal label attached to an individual and his real condition with respect to the perceptions of the villagers. The *servus*, in the classical sense of the word, was fading away; he was becoming a 'servile' village neighbour with limited but real rights (in this respect, we should now begin to give the term

---

63   Interpretative questions about this appear in Gurevich 1985. About the teleological nature of labour, see Lukács 2004. The non-separation between subject and object in the work of peasants has been reflected in propitiatory rites expressing the superiority of nature. On this topic, see Gurevich 1990, and Giordano 1983.

a social interpretation, rather than remain attached to strict readings of the formal denominations found in the document).[64] This transformation was an unwritten statute.

Besides valuing the labour skills, the social context of the village facilitated an assessment of the trade itself and of the person who performed it, thus enhancing the craftsman's social and self-esteem as shown by many later examples of craftsmen holding office in town councils, which captures the premises of the subjectivity of a rebel who would play a leading role in the 'bourgeois revolutions' of the twelfth century and later. This elevation of the person was linked to a long tradition of struggle for social advancement, a struggle that in itself enhances a person's dignity. The very decision to escape ennobled the person, and this example could be imitated until it became a lesson in respectability for the masses. It is not impossible to presume the existence of channels through which the popular memory recorded the deeds of the oppressed, perhaps even adding some epic elements. There are indications of an intergenerational narrative about ancestors who had broken free from slavery, pointing to the existence of an oral history of the oppressed.[65] At the very least, we know for sure that the working classes had a sense of their own history, even when it may have been presented in the style of family history.[66]

These issues were constructing the psychosocial profile of the craftsman who had been a slave. When he arrived in a town like León, he did not gain freedom but vigilant dependence on a lord; however, his defiance of the mighty was embedded in his character, and there was nothing about him to remind us of the submissive personality which is sometimes attributed to the slave. Even though he had once been subject to the discipline of the *vilicus*, now he could stand up to breathe in what he had earned, even though the city air might not

---

64   The concept used in this analysis differs from that used by Bois 1989, pp. 31 ff. Bois, following the approach of Finley, says that the *servi casati* were slaves.

65   López Ferreiro 1898, doc. XXXIV, pp. 74–5, year 912, Ordoño I *dudum quidem temporibus diue memorie patris nostri dni. adefonsi principis accidit ut causeret lupella et muzurri uel cum sua casada ut debiti essent illi seruit; ad hec respondit muzurri et dixit: hodie nonaginta annos seu et amplius steterunt aui et parentes mei siue et ego et omnis mea casada ingenua in facie de lupella cuius uocem intendit samzote et de omni sua casada, nulli umquam seruicium aut patrocinium reddentes.*

66   Fernández del Pozo 1984, doc. X, year 1025 (already mentioned), trial presided over by Alfonso V between the bishop of Lugo and residents of the surroundings of Braga. The bishop said they were slaves; the representative of the villagers replied that they were free. He claimed that his ancestors emigrated from Oviedo as free, seized the land (*presura*) and did military service for kings and counts: *fecerunt fosato de rex nostros auolos et de comites.*

redeem him. He was not planting the tree of freedom, but he was beginning to sow the seeds from which freedom would blossom in the coming centuries.

Comparing Modes of Production

Craftsmanship coupled with settlement in a domestic unit is not a prerequisite of every social evolution, and the conditions which fostered its development within feudalism are better understood when they are compared to those of other modes of production that inhibit it. In this respect, the case of societies based on nomadic pastoral production offer what is perhaps the most revealing comparison.

By sheer contrast it becomes apparent that a decisive element in the advent of residence-based craftsmanship was the general fixing of land tenure, with differentiated reproductive activities (agricultural and pastoral), and pre-urban nuclei or villages with craftsmen subject at first to the demands of rank and later to those of class. Nomadic peoples, who lacked those attributes, also lacked a social division of labour, or at best they only possessed an under-developed version of it. That does not mean that they could do without urban societies, and this was a consequence of their productive exclusiveness: insofar as they devoted themselves solely to tending their flocks, they were economically (and also culturally) dependent on the sedentary world, on its agriculture and its manufactured goods, and historically they tended to resolve that dependence by means of political and military domination of the sedentary world thanks to their superiority as warriors. The lives of those pastoral nomads therefore remained subject to their changing relationships with the 'outside world'.[67] The assumption arising from that economic dependence is that it is not possible to live solely off livestock.[68] It is not difficult to detect at the heart of this issue the centrality of land tenure.

While in the peasant-based society the peasant established a bond of appropriation with the land under the guise of an organic integration of the individual with the inorganic conditions that surrounded him, in the nomadic structures property was not fixed because land was merely a transitory possession, a communal encampment.[69] As a result, every possibility of home-based specialisation for craftsmen was cancelled *ab ovo* by an inescapable law of the

---

67   Khazanov 1994; Anderson 1996, pp. 217 ff.

68   Wickham 1983.

69   Gurevich 1972; Anderson 1996.

same structure, and it is no coincidence that these societies presented low levels of technological innovation.

This feature of nomadic societies underscores the important role of settlement in feudalism, because it allowed the craftsman to develop as a specialised labourer. In one case, that of societies with pastoral mobility, the non-appropriation of land (the true wealth were the heads of cattle) caused the division of labour to be an external component, something culturally foreign with which only a political bond of domination could be established. In the other case, peasant property divided into parcels fostered an enrichment of the qualities of this kind of land tenure by allowing some room for the incorporation of specialised labour. This incorporation carried out in many towns and villages speaks to us of a process which was different from that of the craftsmen confined to special premises, such as those of other societies who, as a caste, i.e. as a segment which does not communicate with regular people, devoted themselves to the work of the palace or the temple, and could not be considered slaves even though they were.[70] In this last example the transmission of the trade in an extensive manner was blocked. In contrast, the craftsmen scattered all over the territories of the Western Middle Ages were a reflection of the multiplicity of trades placed at the service of a power class fragmented into many lordships.

In a different sense, we can cite at least two cases of craftsmen settled in their own dwellings and subjected to coercion. The first was in ancient Athens, where there were slaves who worked as independent craftsmen, a situation reflecting the existence of slavery as a 'legal institution' but not as a 'labour process'.[71] This form, in which the slave craftsman related to his owner as a tenant, had its parallel in the Germanic mode of production, which is the

---

70   Zingarelli 2010b, p. 102: '[I]n the given socio-economic relationships involving the temple, there were differential situations. This may have depended on the skill and previous training of prisoners. Possibly, artisans enjoyed better conditions and had more rights than agricultural workmen. Certainly, individuals assigned to temple work could not be strictly considered slaves'. Rostovtzeff 1962, p. 322: the industrial *collegia* of Asia Minor during the Roman Empire were formed by individuals hereditarily devoted to a specialty, probably descended from priestly families who knew the secrets of a craft. Another case is that of the slave woman in medieval Muslim society; see Guichard 1973, pp. 141 ff., these women, who charmed aristocrats with their cultural refinement, were agents of Arabisation and Orientalisation. Again, those qualities implied that the person enjoyed a special status, and as stated by Guichard 1973, p. 168, these slaves had far more 'freedom' than women who were legally free.

71   Hindess and Hirst 1975, pp. 138; 333, n. 38.

second example. According to Tacitus, the Germans had slaves but not in a framework comparable to the Roman one (*non in nostrum morem*), since they were divided by families (*per familiam*) and placed in their own domestic units (*suam quisque sedem*) which each governed (*regit*) in an independent manner.[72] From this form of production, which Tacitus likened to that of the colonate insofar as on principle everyone worked for himself, the master demanded rents in the form of grain, livestock or clothing.[73] Possibly because they were needed for making clothes, even if only the simple tunics worn by the Germans according to Tacitus, these subordinates were not subjected to an extreme regime of coercion, nor to intense workloads.[74]

Conclusions

Our study has led us decidedly away from Pirenne. The first craftsman was not a dispossessed small-time merchant who settled next to a lordly house in the late tenth century and then developed his skill into an art from nothing, like a self-made man. Quite to the contrary, the first craftsmen were people who lacked possessions but had a capital of working knowledge that allowed them to create an object with their hands in a domestic unit. In this cell, the general foundation of a peasant society, they found a favourable environment for the development of their skill, a development that was in no small degree demanded by the lord.

After 1050, with feudalism fully established, there was a definite predominance of craftsmen working from domestic workshops, either urban or village-based. There also arose the prosperous or middle peasant who migrated to the city to start a shop. But the roots of every medieval craftsman are found in the process we analysed. In summary, the specialisation and division of labour, the articulation between manufacturing and agrarian production, the teleological activity of the craftsman, his social recognition, the reproduction of the

---

72   Tacito, *Germania*, xxv.

73   Ibid.: *Frumenti modum dominus aut pecoris aut vestis ut colono iniungit, et servus hactenus paret.*

74   Ibid. He makes clear that slaves were not punished or coerced to work hard; if they were killed, it was due to a fit of rage: *Verberare servum ac vinculis et opere coercere rarum: occidere solent, non disciplina et severitate, sed impetu et ira, ut inimicum, nisi quod impune est.*

trade by means of instruction within the domestic unit, a labour that fulfilled consumption needs, and the potential to bring about a logic of profit, are features that appeared during the period examined.

CHAPTER 4

Passages to Feudalism in Medieval Scandinavia

*Chris Wickham**

In this article, I want to look briefly at the issue of the slow introduction of economic exploitation and stable hierarchies into peasant-dominated societies, on the basis of two such societies, Iceland and Norway, focussing on the early eleventh century. We know about these two societies because of an unusually rich set of narratives, which allow us to recognise an unusually nuanced array of criteria for economic wealth and exploitation, social status, and political power. These criteria were, furthermore, often contradictory or changeable, which shows us further nuances in the way Scandinavian writers understood socio-economic relations, which we often do not find in contemporary societies further south in Europe, even though these are better documented in most other respects. We can thus see, better than in many places, some of the ways in which a peasant-dominated social formation could develop into a social formation dominated by landed aristocrats.

This sort of data might seem too good to be true, and in a literal sense this is indeed the case, for our narratives are mostly written down in the late twelfth or thirteenth centuries, and many of them have in the last half century and more been regarded as fiction. The *Íslendingasögur* or 'family sagas', which describe the feuds and other relationships of relatively rich but essentially peasant families in Iceland around the year 1000, have in particular been seen in this light; the kings' sagas for Norway were seen for longer as reliable, although they are equally late (and also in large part written by Icelanders, not Norwegians). Much ink has been spilt on the issue of how 'true' these sagas are, in fact, with a strong tradition in both historical and literary studies which regards them as bookish texts, with no 'historical' value, except as guides as to how people in the thirteenth century constructed their past.[1] This tradition, which goes back to the 1940s and earlier in Iceland, has had a new lease of life thanks to

---

* I am grateful to Chris Callow, Laura da Graca, Richard Holt and Shami Ghosh for their critiques of this text.

1 See Nordal 1957 for a classic 'bookprose' view. For the early historiography, see Andersson 1964. For a more recent version, Clover 1982; but the bibliography here is endless. Bagge 1991 comes at it from a different tradition, and partly fits in the next note as well.

the linguistic turn, which regards the truth content of all texts as contested, and inextricable from the constraints of literary genre. By now, it would seem nothing short of naïve to attempt faithful historical reconstructions of the eleventh-century past on the basis of sources like this, which are, furthermore, apart from some much thinner narratives for Iceland from the early twelfth century, and law codes which in both countries also seem to go back to the early twelfth century, the only independent written sources we have for the period at all. The concentration of narratives on the decades around 1000 in both countries is, furthermore, largely the result of the importance of those decades for the Christianisation of Iceland and Norway, lending to the period an extra symbolic importance in later centuries which should add to our distrust.

There is an alternative historiography, however, especially strong in US work of the last generation, which regards the Icelandic narratives, in particular (but the same arguments can be made for those of Norway), as so dense and naturalistic that they can indeed be regarded as guides to some sort of social reality, even if it is only the reality of the period immediately preceding the thirteenth century: a recently-lost world, that is to say, in place just before the rather more hierarchical political system of the early thirteenth. The possibility of at least some realist construction of a past society and its values thus comes back into focus.[2] When one adds that much saga narrative in both countries is structured by and often based on poetry, associated with named poets contemporary to the events described, of a particularly complex type – one which has to be remembered exactly, or else its internal rhyme and alliteration will break up[3] – and also structured by detailed genealogies which are often the same across unrelated texts, then we can posit some quite detailed earlier accounts underlying the thirteenth-century narratives we have, which adds plausibility to the idea that at least some of the narratives about the early eleventh century have their roots in the period they recount. This does not make them 'truer', but at least it makes them more immediate.

---

2   Miller 1990 tends to locate the material in the twelfth century (e.g. p. 51); Byock 2001 is keener to see the saga narratives as describing an earlier society; Steblin-Kamenskij 1973 is more romantic but remains stimulating; Callow 2001 is a sensible and nuanced new departure. For Norway, some of this approach is adopted by Orning 2008 (see pp. 28–34 for methodological and historiographical points), but the book is focussed on a later period than ours.

3   See, for example, O'Donoghue 2005. I discussed some of the implications in Wickham 1999, pp. 165–79. This is not to say that all skaldic verse is necessarily original, just that it is harder to play with than many other literary genres. The potential malleability of skaldic verse, notwithstanding that, is a point well made in Ghosh 2011, which is a critical account of the problems of using the Norwegian material in particular.

I find both of these arguments compelling. This is certainly not the place to try to attempt a detailed characterisation of how to reconcile them; but it does seem that they can be reconciled, with some care. At the very least, one can invoke 'saga Iceland' and 'saga Norway' as partially invented realities which can serve as significant anthropological parallels to the more soberly documented societies further south in Europe. But for the purposes of this article, the very way that the eleventh century is described in our later sources has enough peculiarities to make the issues I want to confront in this article worth studying. Both Iceland and Norway were fairly hierarchical in the thirteenth century, at least in political and social terms. Furthermore, our narratives come out of an aristocratic milieu. The longest narrative of the kings of Norway, *Heimskringla*, which is also the most useful Norwegian source for our purpose, was written around 1230 by Snorri Sturluson (d. 1241), one of the most powerful aristocrats in Iceland;[4] all the *Íslendingasögur*, which are anonymous, are focussed on the activities of early Icelandic élites, and seem most probably to have been written for their descendants. Neither type of source has much sympathy for the poor, or of people of low status: no more than has any other medieval narrative. Yet the eleventh-century society each characterises is very far indeed from the totalising aristocrat-dominated social formations which a historian of the rest of medieval Europe is used to. Peasant protagonism, in particular, is far greater in each, and described more positively, than in any other type of medieval text; and aristocratic power is represented in terms which show that the authors concerned did not take its dominance for granted. Although Norway is depicted as rather more hierarchical than Iceland – something which Icelanders regarded as axiomatic, for it was part of their founding myth that they had emigrated from Norway because of the 'tyranny' of the Norwegian kings – the incompleteness of aristocratic dominance appears here as well. Our authors evidently regarded that incompleteness as normal. And when we move from the structures of political power and interaction (something to which our authors paid conscious attention) to the economic resources available to the powerful (something that was more of a backdrop in their accounts), we also see that the élites of each country were far from as rich as was normal in the rest of Europe, which has considerable implications for the counterpositions I wish to set out. What we have are only the representations of Snorri and his contemporaries, but the authors of our texts took for granted, and regarded as

---

4 Snorri Sturluson 1941–51 (*Heimskringla*). The royal lives used here are *Hákona saga goða, Óláfs saga Tryggvasonar* (vol. 1, pp. 150–97, 225–372, henceforth *Hák., OT*), *Óláfs saga ins Helga* (vol. 2, henceforth *OH*), and *Haralds saga Sigurðarsonar* (vol. 3, pp. 68–202, henceforth *HS*).

acceptable, that in the past peasant individuals and communities had a certain economic and political autonomy. Those representations are worth studying for their own sake. In what follows, when I discuss 'the society of the eleventh century', I will mean at each moment the rather more cumbersome concept 'the society of the eleventh century as represented in the thirteenth'. But, as will be proposed at the end of this article, there are considerable similarities between these two apparently distinct concepts.

Elsewhere, I have sought to counterpose two modes of production in medieval northern Europe, the peasant and the feudal modes. The feudal mode of production is taken here as being based on the economic control over land and its inhabitants by rich landowning élites, whom we call aristocrats (a term which does not have an exact translation in most medieval societies); they derived their wealth above all from the extraction of surplus from the peasants living on that land, in the form of rent and, sometimes, labour services. It dominated most medieval societies, and is in broad terms well known to historians, even those who do not use the terminology of modes of production. The peasant mode needs more detailed characterisation, which I reproduce from my earlier discussion of it.

> First, its basic production unit is the individual household; only very seldom do whole villages control agricultural production. The household works the land it controls directly ... Households are seldom egalitarian units; gender inequalities may make women work the land as well as inside the home (as in parts of Africa), or, conversely, exclude them from agricultural work altogether (as in parts of Europe); in addition, there may be (often unfree) non-family members in the household, as, in our period, in England or Scandinavia, acting as domestic help and farm labourers. But all able-bodied people in peasant households are expected to work, for at least part of the time ... The household generally contains internal inequalities, as already noted, and so can the community ... [H]ousehold surplus is generally distributed around other households, but this comes at a price. Gifts and the underwriting of collective festivities are acts of power ... people negotiate socially through reciprocity, aiming to increase their local position. Basically, people who give more than they receive gain status, social rank; they have more ritual importance, or more of a leadership role in decision-making in the community; they can get poorer people to respond to their gifts by doing things for them. People who aim at that local status may indeed choose to work harder, or to develop their productive technology, for the rewards of status are sufficient for them to do so, even if the surplus they produce is eaten or otherwise consumed

by others almost at once. But, in the ideal-type peasant mode, ranking is not structurally permanent. People have to work for their practical power, by their generosity, by their charisma, or by a capacity to negotiate for others; if they fail at these, or if they over-reach themselves and become oppressive, others will withdraw their support. They cannot take power for granted. These societies are, then, at least *relatively* egalitarian. The possibility that social support might be withdrawn keeps both wealth and power from accumulating; it is quite a leap for social differentiation to become permanent, and no longer dependent on the reciprocity, and the choices, of others. When it does, élites will characteristically come to give out less goods, and expect to receive them instead, in return for less tangible forms of service, such as protection: one can then speak of class differentiation rather than ranking, and the feudal rather than the peasant mode.[5]

This ideal-typical characterisation contains within it, as can be seen, one important way in which a society (or social formation) dominated by the peasant mode can turn into one dominated by the feudal mode, by richer peasants slowly separating themselves from their obligations to their poorer neighbours and, by gaining economic control over the latter, ceasing to be peasants. It is possible to see the two modes as existing side by side in many societies as well, with élite figures operating both as feudal-mode landowners and as less permanent patrons in the style of the peasant mode, depending on the situation. Which of the two modes dominated the basic structures of any given society would depend on individual circumstances. The trend was, certainly, towards the victory of feudal relations in medieval European societies. It is exactly this development, in fact, which in my view (and in that of others) occurred in Iceland, at different stages according to which region of the island we are dealing with, in a period often seen as focussed on the later twelfth century, though starting earlier and ending much later.[6] But that trend towards feudal dominance was neither consistent nor inevitable; it depended on empirical conditions. So what I should like to do here is to contrast Iceland in and after 1000, where this development had not really started, with Norway in the same period, where it certainly had, to see how each worked in practice as social systems. This will give us a better perspective from which to approach the quite well studied period of the growth of aristocratic power on the former island.

---

5 Wickham 2005, pp. 536–9.
6 Important points of reference are Gunnar Karlsson 1972, pp. 5–57; Jón Viðar Sigurðsson 1999.

Iceland was settled from Norway in the late ninth and early tenth century. The founding myth of Norwegian royal oppression cannot be accepted at face value, for the simple reason that Norwegian kings were not powerful enough to oppress more than unsystematically for a long time, but the Icelanders must have held kingship – a norm in Norway, however weak and localised, as in most medieval societies – in very considerable suspicion, for they carefully excluded it from their new polity. Iceland had no ruler; instead, it had one central assembly, the Althing, which met yearly and decided both court cases and issues of general significance for Icelanders. The island had numerous chieftains, *goðar* (singular *goði*), who were the main players at the Althing; canonically, there are supposed to have been 39 of these, but the narratives make it more likely that there were a variable number, in our period maybe up to as many as 80.[7] The title and power of these chieftains, called *goðorð* in Old Norse, was heritable, but also variable. It consisted in legal terms of the right to take dependants to the Althing and other local assemblies, also called *thing* (each *goði* had an assembly of his own), and to represent them in court cases; only *goðar* could deliberate in the central council of the Althing, the *lögrétta*, too. Every free man in Iceland was supposed to be subject to a *goði*, in fact, and to be his *thingmaðr*. This sounds very hierarchical, and at one level it was; it may also be that some poorer peasants were not influential enough even to be *thingmenn*. But it was mediated by the fact that *thingmenn* could transfer their allegiance from one *goði* to another, every year; our narratives take it for granted that this was a right at least occasionally exercised, at least by more influential and bolder *thingmenn* (weaker ones doubtless had less choice). In the stories contained in the *Íslendingasögur*, the commonest reasons for such transference were the political incompetence of a weak *goði*, and the overbearingness of a strong one. The second of these was more risky, for an overbearing *goði* might well take revenge on such ex-dependants, in a society where killing was common and socially acceptable within limits; but *thingmenn* did it, not only in the early eleventh century, when *goðar* were relatively modest, but even in the thirteenth, when the greatest chieftains could control large regions of Iceland and hundreds of men, as our by-then contemporary narratives make clear.[8]

---

7   Jón Viðar Sigurðsson 1999, pp. 39–54, though Gunnar Karlsson 2004, pp. 63–146 and Orri Vésteinsson 2007 doubt this and reinstate the traditional figure; the latter article is a revisionist reading, arguing for hierarchy, which deserves both attention and critique. Note that I will use the Old Norse letter *ð* in what follows, but will transliterate the letter *þ* as (unvoiced) *th*.

8   See below, n. 37.

The ability of some peasants (*bœndr*, singular *bóndi*) to choose their lord in this way is an important marker of the impermanence of hierarchies, and puts eleventh-century Iceland as a social system firmly inside the framework of my ideal-type peasant mode. In economic terms, the same can be said. Very few Icelanders, rich or poor, had more than one farm in the *Íslendingasögur*; wealth came from the relative size of those farms (plus, more rarely, rights over coasts or specialised resources), rather than from their accumulation. *Thing-menn* had to pay court dues to *goðar*, and gifts for successful court advocacy; after 1097 they also paid tithe to the owners of churches, who were usually (even if not universally) the same chieftains; but these were small outgoings, and did not make up much by way of surplus extraction by the powerful.[9] Only slowly did *goðar* begin to accumulate farms and lease them out to tenants – something which was normal in the thirteenth century, according to contemporary narratives, but rare in the accounts of earlier periods. Even someone as influential as Hvamm-Sturla (d. 1183), Snorri Sturluson's father, and in fact father of three hugely rich and powerful political players of the early thirteenth century, seems to have left at his death, according to his own saga, only 120 'hundreds', the value of two big farms or some six medium-size ones, to his sons.[10] A thirteenth-century writer, that is to say, felt no need to claim more wealth for Snorri's father than that. And his predecessors some 150 years earlier in the same area, Dalir in western Iceland, Snorri *goði* and the various descendants of Óláfr Pái, are not ascribed in our sources permanent control over more than one or two farms each.[11] Furthermore, such *goðar* are routinely in our sources represented as attending to farming themselves, even if always with the help of servants both free and unfree (see below). So, for example, Arnkell Thórólfsson in *Eyrbyggja saga*, a *goði* slightly further west from Dalir, Snorri *goði*'s enemy and victim, is depicted collecting his own hay and repairing the door of his house. There are any number of equivalent examples.[12]

These men thus achieved power and influence less from the exercise of wealth than from their success as dealers, on behalf of their *thingmenn* and in conflict with the other *goðar* and more influential *bœndr* who were their neighbours. Snorri *goði*'s well-attested influence was because he was the cleverest

---

9   Byock 2001, pp. 253–62; Jón Viðar Sigurðsson 1999, pp. 101–19; Orri Vésteinsson 2000, pp. 67–92, for tithe.

10   *Sturlunga saga* (henceforth ss), I, pp. 234, 237 (*Íslendinga saga*, cc. 6, 10); cf. Jón Viðar Sigurðsson 1999, pp. 104–5.

11   Callow 2001, pp. 131–47.

12   *Eyrbyggja saga*, cc. 36, 37; a short list of other examples is in Karras 1988, pp. 80–1.

dealer of his age, knowing when to be generous, when to be conciliatory, when to push for a win rather than a compromise at court, and when to kill with least comeback;[13] others in the sagas, such as Víga-Glúmr Eyjólfsson in northern Iceland, gained influence by successful dealing (often connected with the powerful image of *gipta*, 'luck') and then lost it again, quite abruptly, because of overbearingness and political miscalculation.[14] They were not lords in any feudal sense, but rather what anthropologists call 'big men', leaders of ranked societies who have to work for their dominance, again as in the ideal-type peasant mode characterised above.

Let us leave Iceland for a moment, and move to Norway, here too as depicted in the late twelfth- and thirteenth-century narratives. In Norway there were, of course, kings; but, more important, there was a regional aristocracy by 1000, most often called *hersar* or *lendir menn*. These were both words meaning 'royal retainer', but the men who gained this position were usually powerful already in their localities, each of which had a *thing*, an assembly, just as in Iceland, as the focus of local power. Let us take two examples as illustrative of what sort of power could be constructed in the early eleventh century. First, the case of Erlingr Skjálgsson (d. circa 1028). We know about Erlingr in most detail from Snorri Sturluson's *Heimskringla*, though some of his key sections about Erlingr rely on and develop praise poetry by Sighvatr *skáld*, a contemporary of Erlingr. Erlingr in Snorri's account was by far the most influential man in western Norway. He was from an old family there, but gained considerable prominence when King Óláfr Tryggvason (d. 1005) married his sister Ástríðr to him and gave him all the royal revenues or *veizlur* of a large tract of the west. He submitted to the later Norwegian king Óláfr Haraldsson (d. 1030) only with difficulty and tension, perhaps in 1016, and acted very much as a classic over-mighty subject until the second Óláfr surprised him in a sea-battle and had him killed after a famously brave defence, celebrated by Sighvatr.[15] There was no one richer and more powerful than Erlingr in his wide area of control, and the king could make no political headway there unless he was physically present. He had extensive lands, and always had, according to Snorri, 90 retainers at his court (see below). He was called 'king' of the Rogalanders in one story, and Snorri has him openly state to the king of Norway that he resents having to defer to royal bailiffs of servile descent, one of whom indeed was killed by one of his relatives.[16] He was

---

13   As depicted in, above all, *Eyrbyggja saga*; *Laxdœla saga*; *Brennu-Njáls saga*.

14   *Víga-Glúms saga*.

15   *OT*, cc. 54, 56–8; *OH*, cc. 22–3, 51, 53, 60, 116–21, 174–7.

16   *OH*, cc. 22 (retainers), 117 ('king'), 116 (resentment), 118 (killing).

a snob, to be blunt, an attitude with which Snorri is likely to have sympathised. But Erlingr also refused the title of *jarl* or any high royal rank/honour (*tígn*), for, as he told Óláfr Tryggvason, none of his kin had ever been more than *hersar*, so he did not want to go beyond them. He just wanted to be recognised as the greatest *hersir*, or its synonym *lendr maðr*, in Norway, which indeed he became. However, this meant that, as a rank-less man (*útiginn maðr*), Erlingr could be categorised as a *bóndi*: Sighvatr *skald* uses a synonym for *bóndi*, *búthegn*, to describe Erlingr in a contemporary verse.[17] If you did not have a royal office, a *bóndi* is what you were, even if you controlled a fifth of Norway.

Erlingr was not unique here, either. Equally indicative is Einarr Thambars-kelfir (d. circa 1060), slightly younger, who had a career lasting more than fifty years under rival kings: he was Óláfr Tryggvason's bowman at his last battle, but then brother-in-law of Óláfr's supplanter Jarl Eiríkr; opponent of Óláfr Haraldsson, like Erlingr, but clever enough to avoid being at the battle which brought the second Óláfr down at Stiklarstaðir in 1030; then, in another reversal, one of the founders of the latter's cult as a saint and patron of his son Magnús (d. 1047), although in the end, in old age, rival of Magnús's successor Haraldr Harðráði (d. 1066), who eventually had him killed. Einarr was a major player thoughout, *ættstórr ok auðigr*, 'of a great family and rich', and got many *veizlur* from Jarl Eiríkr which he mostly kept under later kings (except the second Óláfr), in his home territory of Þrœndalög in northern Norway, which he dom-inated almost as much as Erlingr did in the west. Einarr was a *lendr maðr*; when he went over to Knútr of Denmark and England against Óláfr Haraldsson, the Danish king offered him the title of *jarl* in the future, the title Erlingr had refused, and *Heimskringla* says that this marked the revival of Einarr's *höfðing-skapr*, 'lordliness' or 'authority', even if Knútr subsequently reneged on the offer.[18] But despite this highly political role, without the earldom, Einarr was still linked most closely to the *bœndr*; he appears as 'the strongest leader of the *bœndr* all around Þrándheimr [Trondheim]', and at the Trondheim *thing* he had choreographed *bóndi* opposition to Danish rule in the 1030s before he asked Magnús to take the throne.[19] So: like Erlingr, Einarr's power, though great, was unofficial, with the result that, like Erlingr, he could be effectively thought of as a *bóndi*.

There are obvious paradoxes here for anyone interested in élite identity. As Sverre Bagge has remarked, it would be wrong to see Erlingr as showing that one

---

17   *OT*, cc. 58 (refusal), 56 (*útiginn*); *OH*, c. 22 (*búthegn*).

18   *OH*, cc. 21 (*ættstórr*), 51, 144, 171 (*höfðingskapr*), 194.

19   *HS*, c. 43; *Fagrskinna*, c. 42.

could normally be powerful in Norway around 1000 without royal support.[20] He was highly exceptional, and brought down by the king in the end; and anyway he owed his unusual position to earlier royal favour. Snorri's Erlingr is regularly resentful at having to recognise the king's authority; this we can plausibly take as Snorri's viewpoint, rather than eleventh-century reportage – and it was probably regarded ambiguously by Snorri too, aware as he was of Iceland's historic rejection of kings, while himself being for a long time a keen follower of King Hákon, his contemporary. But Erlingr's wealth came from family land, not royal favour; and he came to the attention of Óláfr Tryggvason in the first place because of his good birth and his personal qualities (Bagge calls this charisma; it has some parallels with Icelandic 'luck').[21] Einarr, similarly, had *stórmiklar eignir*, 'immense properties', and lived well, even when in the 1020s he did not have royal *veizlur*, before the revival of his 'authority', and clearly remained a major player.[22] Land, birth and charisma were crucial, and they were independent of the king, who could indeed only grant one of the three even in theory. It is interesting that the commonest word for royal retainer, *lendr maðr*, literally meant 'landed man', which does indeed imply that kings granted land – as we would expect – but still, most land was inherited, *óðal*, land;[23] and Norwegian political players, both magnates and peasants, valued *óðal* very highly and rebelled against kings who threatened it. These were all structural elements which preserved large sectors of Norwegian social hierarchy and practical politics as separate from the actions of any but the most determined king. But all the same, if you did not want to be *útiginn*, rank-less, and categorised with the *bœndr*, you had to have royal patronage. *Bœndr* could be very rich, but they could also be poor and highly unprepossessing, and the word *bóndi* is sometimes used as an insult by the powerful.[24] Most powerful people clearly wanted a *tígn*; it would mark them out as special; Erlingr was again unusual in refusing one, and Einarr more normal. But Norwegian society clearly also saw no problem in having one, perhaps two, of the major leaders of the country classified as a peasant.

A combined peasant and aristocratic uprising (together with Danish support) destroyed Óláfr Haraldsson in the end in 1030. Their fighting force was called the *lið bónda* and other synonyms, the '*bóndi* army', in *Heimskringla* and

---

20   Bagge 1991, p. 128.

21   *OT*, c. 56; Bagge 1991, pp. 124–8.

22   *OH*, c. 144.

23   *Óðal* land: see *Norges gamle lov indtil 1387*, I: *Gulathingslov*, cc. 265–94, *Frostathingslov*, XII.4–8.

24   *OH*, c. 117.

the slightly earlier *Fagrskinna*.[25] It was led by *lendir menn*, but was still associated with the *bœndr*: both *ríkir* ('powerful') and *thorparar ok verkmenn* ('cottagers and labourers').[26] Conversely, when Einarr Thambarskelfir was killed, in the middle of his home territory of the Thrœndalög, the *bœndr* did not revenge themselves on King Harald, as they had no *lendr maðr* to lead the '*bóndi* army'.[27] Snorri Sturluson clearly saw *bœndr* as leaderless unless aristocrats were available. But their political protagonism is, conversely, not in doubt. There is no hint that this was an inappropriate thing for *bœndr* to be doing, both poor and rich ones, even though all our prose authors wrote after Óláfr Haraldsson was recognised as a saint; it was the *lendir menn* who are criticised by Snorri for their selfishness, not the *bœndr* with which they were allied.[28]

This is where the incompleteness of aristocratic power is crucial to our understanding of Norway. Snorri had no real sympathy for *bóndi* protagonism, but it was a normal part of his world. It was most common when it involved people like Erlingr who were in economic terms aristocrats while remaining classified as *bœndr*, but lesser people – i.e. people whom we would call peasants in an economic sense, such as the *thorparar* of 1030 – could make legitimate political choices too. This protagonism was focussed on assemblies, which *lendir menn* could dominate but never control directly; here Snorri will also have drawn on his Icelandic experience, for it was always so there, but he could see its logic even in a more aristocratic Norwegian environment.[29] This is close to unique in medieval European narratives, which otherwise so exclude peasant protagonism that it was incomprehensible to writers even when – as with fourteenth-century peasant revolts – it was impossible to deny.

What made Scandinavia so different here? I have already commented that in Iceland, before the late twelfth century, the richest and most powerful dealers had a relatively restricted economic base: only a couple of farms each. Their *thingmenn* were their political followers, but seldom economically dependent on them, and peasant landownership remained normal for centuries. In Norway, aristocrats were clearly richer. Aristocratic land was often cultivated by unfree labourers and tenants, but sometimes also by free *bœndr*, as the laws make clear.[30] That was certainly a feudal economic relationship. But it is inter-

---

25 See in general *OH*, cc. 215–35. For the *bóndi* army, e.g. *OH*, c. 226; *Fagrskinna*, c. 34; cf. for one of the contemporary poems by Sighvat, *OH*, c. 235.

26 *OH*, c. 216.

27 *HS*, c. 44.

28 *OH*, c. 181, contrast c. 205.

29 Bagge 1991, pp. 136–40.

30 For free tenure, *Norges gamle lov: Gulathingslov*, c. 72, *Frostathingslov*, XIII.1–2.

esting that our narratives, when they want to stress aristocratic power, talk about their political support much more than their actual wealth. Snorri on Erlingr Skjálgsson is typical here. Erlingr is portrayed as having with him 90 free retainers at all times, and 240 when he had to fit out an army; this is the measure of his power. But when Snorri discusses his economic activities, he depicts him simply as having a dwelling (*heimr*) with 30 farm slaves (*thrælar*), whom he treated with admirable generosity and helped to freedom. Snorri is not giving us an economic analysis of Erlingr's wealth, of course, but rather characterising his excellent character.[31] All the same, he leaves us with the clear sense that Erlingr's power is based on his entourage, not his economic dependants, and his entourage, though drinking limitlessly according to Snorri's account, could well have been independently supported, at least in part. Aristocratic wealth was certainly based on surplus extraction from dependants, but they were surrounded by many independent peasants as well, whom they needed to persuade to gain political support; they could not simply take dominance for granted.[32] Aristocrats could not claim any economic dues from landowning *bœndr*, and peasants ceded their land to aristocrats only very slowly; a third of Norwegian land (particularly away from the coast) was peasant-owned as late as the sixteenth century – more, by then, than in Iceland, where only five percent of the land was peasant-owned by 1703.[33]

This peasant autonomy was subject, of course, to royal power; the forcible Christianisation of the country is seen in the narratives as being accomplished by the kings *thing* by *thing*, against the resistance or with the sullen acquiescence of the local *bœndr, thegn ok thræl*, 'free and unfree'.[34] Kings, at least, could take dues (*veizlur, landsskyldir*) from *bœndr*, and the king could sometimes assign the dues they were owed by free men to aristocrats acting as his local officials.[35] But even this was not unconditional: angry or rebellious peas-

---

31   *OH*, cc. 22–3.

32   Saunders 1995, in a stimulating article, develops some of the archaeological implications of this.

33   Karras 1988, p. 77; Myking and Rasmussen 2010, pp. 290–1; for Iceland, see e.g. Gunnar Karlsson 2000, p. 165. The secure figures for the sixteenth century (which also include a very high proportion for church land, over forty percent) are read back into the late and central middle ages respectively by Bjørkvik 1970, pp. 70–105, and Bagge 2010, pp. 111–21. They differ in the implications they draw for landed power and social change, but the figure for peasant land will inevitably have been higher in a period when the church as yet had no properties, the situation of the early eleventh century.

34   *Hák.*, c. 15, *OT*, cc. 55, 65 (quote), 66–9, *OH*, cc. 40, 121.

35   E.g. *OT*, c. 15, *OH*, c. 22 for dues assigned to aristocrats. See Gurevič 1982, pp. 42–7, 70–4,

ant communities could withhold tribute, and kings had to negotiate with them if they did so. Overall, given a landowning peasantry in Norway, the relationship between power and the distribution of property led directly to a relatively diffuse power structure, and to kings having to negotiate, not just with aristocrats, but with peasant leaders; aristocrats had to negotiate with the peasantry too. That the peasantry was also hierarchically organised, and commonly aristocrat-led, does not subtract from its protagonism. If aristocrats had begun to gain land at the expense of the peasantry so consistently that the feudal mode was becoming dominant, it is hardly visible to the authors of our twelfth- and thirteenth-century sources.

This Norwegian reality makes some of the limits to the power of thirteenth-century *goðar* (often also called *höfðingjar*, 'lords' – a word used in the narratives about the eleventh century too) less paradoxical in Iceland as well. Modern authors are often keen to stress the unmediated dominion (they use the term *ríki*, a 'staty' word) of six *goði* families in thirteenth-century Iceland, of which the Sturlusons were one. These families by now had several *goðorð* each, could muster armies, and certainly had numerous tenant farmers on by now much more extensive sets of properties. But all the same they were getting their wider political support from, for the most part, *bœndr* who remained independent landowners just as in Norway, or more so, and who are seldom attested as giving economic dues to their leaders, apart from tithe. Jón Viðar Sigurðsson, one of the modern authors who has done most to stress thirteenth-century aristocratic power, nevertheless estimates that under a quarter of the farms on the island were as yet held in tenancy; the others were still owned by *bœndr*.[36] This is why the transactional power of *höfðingjar* remained incomplete, with more powerful *thingmenn/bœndr* in some areas still capable of moving from one lord to another if circumstances were right, and political dealing necessary to avoid such developments.[37] A real development towards state-formation was difficult under these circumstances, because, for all the ambition, violence and lack of conscience of the *höfðingjar*, they could not dominate the peasantry in any way that would have been normal further south in Europe.

---

though he interprets the development of *veizlur* (which I would see as parallel to Anglo-Saxon *foster*, not to bookland) as a stronger marker of feudal relations than I would.

36 For all this, Jón Viðar Sigurðsson 1999, p. 116, for tenancy, accepted by Gunnar Karlsson 2004, pp. 316–33.

37 E.g. ss, I, p. 240 (*Íslendinga saga*, c. 15); Jón Viðar Sigurðsson 1999, pp. 120–4; Byock 2001, pp. 128–32, 341–9; Gunnar Karlsson 2004, pp. 186–99; note that Orri Vésteinsson 2007 doubts the power of *thingmenn* to change lords.

And this, above all for the purposes of my argument here, marks the limits of the feudal mode of production, in both our societies. I have been here counter-posing political power and economic exploitation; mode of production analysis of course most clearly focusses on the second of these. But, as I have also argued elsewhere, it seems to me clear from the history of several medieval European societies that full state-formation is almost impossible if the dominance of the feudal mode is incomplete.[38] Without a proper economic base for the power not only of kings (easier to achieve, through tribute, although this tends to be small-scale in these societies) but also, above all, of the aristocratic class (based on the direct control of land and its people), power tends to remain much more diffuse, and normally locally restricted as well. This is the key point here. Essentially, feudal-mode economic control was not, in the eleventh century, more than a very small part of the economy of either Iceland or even Norway. Most peasants even in the latter remained economically independent, and always had to be persuaded, by dealing and ad hoc coercion, to support the political aims of aristocrats (or indeed kings). In Iceland, this was more acute still; the economy arguably only began to move in a Norwegian direction after 1200, and this movement was slow for some time (though, as we have seen, feudal dominance was certainly complete by 1700). The feudal mode in Iceland in our period was, in a structural sense, dominated by a still-hegemonic peasant mode, which determined the basic structures of the economy, made accumulation difficult, and forced a substantial measure of reciprocity on the powerful, even though the basic lines of hierarchies remained relatively stable. I would argue that this was, in the eleventh century, true of Norway as well, even though kings were ever more effective protagonists (just as it had still been in the stable hierarchies of the kingdoms of eighth-century England).[39] Even in the thirteenth century in Norway, in fact, there remained a strong element of peasant protagonism, as the struggles for the kingship in that period demonstrate, though the latter take us too far from the subject of this article to develop further here. Norway, like Iceland, went feudal in the end; the size of estates and the number of tenants steadily increased; aristocratic and ecclesiastical landowning became dominant by the end of the Middle Ages. But the focus of our sources for the eleventh century on kings and *lendir menn* like Erlingr and Einarr must not mislead us. That process was by no means complete yet in our period, as Snorri knew well.

---

38   Wickham 2005, pp. 303–34.

39   Wickham 2005, pp. 344–51.

Before the development of tenancy, the basis for the wealth of Scandinavian aristocrats was in effect the control of single farms. We have seen, however, that some of these could be extremely big, such as Erlingr Skjálgsson's *heimr*, with its 30 slaves. In Iceland too it was standard for the *goðar* and richer *bœndr* to have large farms with many free and unfree servants, and even quite poor peasants could have one or two slaves.[40] Although slavery seems to have dropped out in the twelfth century, and although, as we have seen, tenant farms became commoner, a certain number of large central farms continued to characterise the aristocracy. In 1237, for example, the ideal farm proposed by Sighvatr Sturluson to his son Sturla had 11 senior managers, many of them themselves aristocrats, and this is thus certainly an incomplete listing of the farm servants there.[41] Farm servants were by now legally free, but they were normally given wages in lump sums and at the end of their service, and were fed and lodged beforehand in return for their work, much as slaves had been. The end of unfree status and the weakening of the autonomy of the free peasantry are customarily linked, in Scandinavia as elsewhere,[42] though it seems to me that slavery was ending some time before the end of the relative autonomy of the free, in Iceland at least. But the existence of these foci of wealth based on the direct exploitation of household dependants, of whatever status, brings to our analysis the slave mode of production as well as the feudal mode, for the exploitation intrinsic to these large farms was indeed that of the slave mode. The extensive dominance that householders had over even free servants allows us to use some elements of slave-mode structural analysis for the great households of the thirteenth century as well. We must not neglect the reality of this domination, which was at the core of the prosperity of every aristocratic family in Scandinavia, at least at the start. But this mode, even more than tenancy, was dominated by the hegemonic structures and economic logic of the peasant mode. There were not many really big farms. Furthermore, the wealth derived from this form of exploitation was spent on display and reciprocity, to create the clienteles of free neighbours which we see so extensively in our narrative sources, in both countries. Nor was the slave mode ever used to create larger-scale economic structures; it was always intrinsic to the domination characteristic of the single

---

40   Karras 1988, pp. 80–3; cf. Wickham 2005, pp. 543–4, more cautious about the slave mode than I am here.

41   *SS*, I, pp. 407–8 (Íslendinga saga, c. 125); Jón Viðar Sigurðsson 1999, p. 110. Árni Daníel Júlíusson 2010 gives a useful analysis of such large central farms in the late Middle Ages, although his macro-economic framing is flawed, and he unhelpfully calls them 'manors'.

42   Karras 1988, pp. 134–63.

farm, and indeed in many cases everyone – masters and dependants alike – lived in a single building. The peasant mode remained dominant, and when it lost its dominance in the Scandinavian social formations, it was feudalism which would take over, as everywhere else in Europe.

Historians tend to study élites, and to analyse their activities in similar ways in every society. They were not similar, however, in their economic base, and this constrained their activities in different ways in different societies. Aristocracy and kingship were stable in our period, with no more (even if also no fewer) 'new men' in Norway than in any other western medieval society; hierarchies were generally solid. But this does not mean that they were automatically strong. Their existence was not in doubt, but their potency depended on personal ability in transactions, with successful 'big men' making it to power, at least for a time, and unsuccessful ones maintaining their inherited social status, but in obscurity. Otherwise put: social status was stable, but political power was not. I would firmly associate the economic independence of the majority of the peasantry in the eleventh century with the need to transact with them; they had to be persuaded, bought, coerced, and this took skill and resources. This is how political power in a social formation dominated by the peasant mode had to work. Aristocrats were not rich enough to dominate without having to deal. Only the extension of tenancy would produce that, and this was some way away.

Our sources are thirteenth-century, and I have been focussing on the eleventh. But however much Snorri Sturluson and his anonymous contemporaries romanticised the past, their characterisations still seem to me reliable in this sector at least. They may have invented a world of individual and consistent courage, or a world of men who could die bravely with a clever phrase on their lips, or a world of heroic Christianising kings; indeed, I do not doubt they did. This is where the fiction, or the constraints of genre, lies. But the fact that our authors also understood that political figures had to deal, at the local level, often in sordid and underhand ways, both in Iceland and in Norway, derived from their understanding of a political practice which had not gone away yet, for all the scale of thirteenth-century *höfðingi* power, and was still eminently comprehensible to a dealer as intelligent as Snorri. The great *goðar* of the latter period, and their Norwegian equivalents, still lived in a world where tenancy was in a minority, and where *bœndr*, however biddable, had to be persuaded, not directed. The economic structure had not changed enough for political practice to be able to change fully. Aristocrats would have to concentrate on the accumulation of land rather than the accumulation of political influence for this to shift substantially, and *bœndr* might resist that shift even more carefully than they resisted the oppressions of an Óláfr Haraldsson. It is clear how feudalism would come to dominate at the level of the social formation in both countries, given the sort of social practices and domineering activities of political players in each, which we have already seen. But it is nonetheless striking that it took centuries to become irreversible. The peasant mode of production is more resistant, even to the ambition of powerful aristocrats who coexist with it, than might initially be thought.

CHAPTER 5

Peasant Mode of Production and the Evolution of Clientelar Relations

Laura da Graca

In order to characterise the relatively autonomous peasant societies that predominated in the early Middle Ages after the collapse of the state, Chris Wickham has proposed the concept of 'peasant mode of production'.[1] This concept refines his earlier category of 'peasant-based society', which the author presented as 'deliberately anodyne', better than the notions of 'tribal', 'primitive communal' or 'kin-based' societies, less naïve and restricted than that of 'Germanic society' inspired in Tacitus, and close to that of 'rank society' by reason of its distinctness from societies with class antagonism, which it shares with the former types, and its clearer recognition of internal hierarchies.[2] This perspective has furnished a paradigm for the analysis of the early Middle Ages societies as parts of a coherent whole, which justifies a reworking of the category of peasant-based society in terms of mode of production, a task undertaken by Wickham in *Framing the Early Middle Ages* (a peasant-based society would be a social formation dominated by the peasant mode of production). However, the author's theoretical approach has had less of an impact than his achievements in the field of comparative studies and empirical research.

Although he proposes a new mode of production, Wickham does not go to great lengths in order to formulate its contents in the language of historical materialism and the traditions he admittedly draws from (mainly economic anthropology). The way the issue is presented – coupled with the mistrust with which a new mode of production is regarded – undoubtedly have had some bearing on the adoption of the concept by Marxist historians, who prefer the less precise but broader concept of peasant-based society. In order to contribute to an assessment of Wickham's proposal, the first section of this analysis will

---

1 Wickham 2005, pp. 535–50. For a summarised account of Wickham's concept of the peasant mode of production, see 'Passages to Feudalism in Medieval Scandinavia' in this book. I would like to express my gratitude to Chris Wickham, Carlos Astarita and Octavio Colombo for their comments on this text.

2 Wickham 1994d, pp. 216–17.

attempt a systematisation of the concept of the peasant mode of production. Given that the peasant mode, considered in isolation, corresponds to classless societies, we will follow Godelier's guidelines on the components of a mode of production in 'primitive' societies, i.e. the elements that must be encompassed in the concept, or else the aspects to be studied when determining the mode or modes of production in a given society. Some traits of the peasant mode not explicitly stated by Wickham have been gleaned through deduction; others are inferred from the development of empirical cases, Malling's imaginary village among others, where the author exemplifies the proposed concept and his general paradigm for analysis.[3] In this sense, since we will refer to empirical examples, Wickham's methodological perspective on the peasant mode as an ideal type will be replaced by another one in which the concept shall be reconstructed as a real abstraction, that is to say, not as a model but as a structure of reality.[4] This reconstruction, though based on Wickham's data, is still interpretive; indeed, the analysis yields elements not taken for granted (or even rejected) by the author, for example, the centrality of the Germanic mode of the *Formen* as property type.

We will then address the problem of clientelar relations between members of the feudal aristocracy and the peasantry, which in Wickham's proposal constitutes the main articulation mechanism between modes of production and a vehicle for the transformation of peasant societies. We will avail ourselves of the *benefactoria*, a documented form of patronage found in the North of Spain during the eleventh and twelfth centuries, in order to examine how clientelar bonds underwent a transformation into relations of exploitation.[5] We will posit that these bonds express social practices derived from the peasant mode, and that while they preserve their original appearance, their content tends to become subordinate to the dominant feudal logic of the area. Our analysis suggests that this transformation, which goes through different stages,

---

3 Wickham 2005, pp. 428–34.

4 These criteria are in Dhoquois 1973, among others. The use of ideal types has been criticised in da Graca 2008, where it is argued that the manner in which the universal term is elaborated may condition the exploration of phenomena and the conclusions drawn from the analysis. This is apparent, for instance, in Wickham's assessment of aristocratic wealth levels in Northern France based on an ideal type of 'aristocracy', which leads him to emphasise nominal landowning over effective exploitation of lands.

5 The *benefactoria* has been considered as a lax social relation, in general terms, by Sánchez Albornoz 1976a and Estepa Díez 2003, pp. 39–80; a different approach appears in Martínez Sopena 1987, pp. 50 ff., and Martínez García 2008, who equates *servitium* with serfdom. On the ambivalent meaning of the word *servitium* in the early Middle Ages, see Davis 1996, pp. 227–8.

is one of the mechanisms for feudal expansion over free spaces, and that the slow pace of change and its concrete manifestations result from the relative validity of the functioning principles of the peasant mode.

Some critics of the concept of the peasant mode of production have found it lacking in its ability to explain the change toward the dominance of another mode of production, and they have alleged that Wickham has not proved in a satisfactory manner how this transformation occurs.[6] Notwithstanding that opinion, it will be demonstrated herein that the implied dynamic of the peasant mode can explain structural change and the manners in which it occurs, and that the process can be documented.

In order to further our analysis of social practice, we will resort to the information about peasant societies contained in 'family sagas'.[7]

Wickham's Concept of the Peasant Mode of Production

According to Godelier's synthesis, the analysis of a society in terms of its mode of production must account for the productive forces that converge into the productive process and for the relations of production implicit in such process.[8] In the *Formen*, this criterion is subordinated to a specific form of property:

> Now this unity, which in one sense appears as the particular form of property, has its living reality in a specific *mode of production* itself, and this appears equally as the relationship of the individuals to one another and as their specific daily behaviour towards inorganic nature, their specific mode of labour (which is always family labour and often communal labour).[9]

6　Davidson 2011; Harman 2011.

7　On the historical value of Icelandic sagas, see Chris Wickham's chapter in this book.

8　Godelier 1974c.

9　Marx 1964, p. 94. Hindess and Hirst 1975, p. 125, follow these criteria: 'mode of production = an articulated combination of specific mode of appropriation of the social product and a specific mode of appropriation of nature. A mode of production is a complex unity of relations and forces of production: the mode of appropriation of the product is determined by the relations of production, that is, by the social distribution of the means of production, and by the distribution of the agents to definite positions (labourers, non-labourers) as a function of the former distribution'.

In keeping with Godelier's approach, the study of a mode of production must be grounded in the analysis of the production process of the dominant branch of production, which in turn necessitates establishing the features of the unit of production and the domestic group, the social forms of labour (cooperation and division of labour), the technical development of the means of labour, and an estimation of productivity and intensity of labour, considering an untapped productive potential, the conditions for its mobilisation and the demography associated with the development of productive forces; the examination must identify the mode of appropriation of the conditions of production and the social product, which is expressed in a specific form of property, as well as the form of circulation of products, which is a result of the social relations.[10] Lastly, the structural analysis must uncover the internal logic of the mode of production, that is to say, the laws that govern its functioning, and the historical conditions of its genesis, reproduction and transformation (in the case of 'primitive' societies, the emergence of relations of exploitation).[11] For the study of societies presenting more than one mode of production, Godelier resorts to the concept of social formation, which in his view calls for ascertaining both the manner of articulation among modes of production and which is the dominant one.[12]

Let us proceed to explore the features of the peasant mode of production based on this analytical scheme. In the peasant mode, the main productive activity is agriculture and that is its starting point, as opposed to other analog-

---

10   Godelier 1974c. Demography is included in the analysis of a mode of production in Marx 1965, p. 438: 'The labouring population therefore produces, along with the accumulation of capital produced by it, the means by which it itself is made relatively superfluous, is turned into a relative surplus population; and it does this to an always increasing extent. This is a law of population peculiar to the capitalist mode of production; and in fact every special historic mode of production has its own laws of population, historically valid within its limits alone'.

11   Godelier 1974a. Kuchenbuch and Michael 1977 offer a similar scheme for the analysis of a mode of production, with the variations inherent to a class society. The analysis begins with an examination of the productive forces which are applied in the production process; the form in which producers are combined with the means of production determines the form of surplus appropriation; this is expressed in specific property relations, which in turn shape a particular class structure [ständische Klassen] because of the role played by political coercion in social reproduction; exchange is considered as logically derived from social relations; finally, the analysis of the feudal mode of production accounts for its transformation (the arising of capitalist social relations).

12   Godelier 1974c. For further development of this approach to the notion of social formation, see Glucksmann 1973.

ous concepts which do not exclude pastoral-nomad or hunter-gatherer societies, such as Sahlins's domestic mode of production.[13] Land is the most important means of production and the labour force comes mainly from the members of the family. The unit of production is the individual household, which controls the conditions of production. The prevailing division of labour is that which is established naturally by gender and generation within the household, and there exist forms of simple cooperation whose development depends on the settlement patterns. Complex forms of cooperation are limited, as well as craft specialisation. The household consists basically of one nuclear family, and it includes non-family members (free or unfree servants) who fulfil auxiliary functions or collaborate in agricultural tasks without implying a withdrawal from productive work for the other members of the household.[14] This circumstance precludes from positing a situation of class-exploitation within the household.

In the peasant mode, agricultural technology is relatively simple and the intensity of labour is low because there are no social reasons for the intensive use of the productive forces.[15] Sahlins's principles with regard to the low productive intensity of the domestic mode of production apply, and these are in turn based on Chayanov's premise that the labour force of the peasant household is not fully tapped.[16] This issue has been addressed by Ester Boserup, who associates agricultural intensification with demographic growth. Boserup observes that primitive cultivators (a) work fewer hours and less regularly than their counterparts in densely populated regions; (b) do not consider agricultural work as pleasant, limiting it to the minimum necessary; (c) are generally not unaware of the existence of more sophisticated tools and alternative cultivation methods whose application would imply an intensification of labour

---

13   Sahlins 1972.

14   This situation is verified in medieval Iceland, which is the main reference used in the construction of the concept of the peasant mode. See Karras 1988, p. 81.

15   Both Davidson 2011, p. 91, and Harman 2011, p. 104 suggest a parallel between the functioning of the peasant mode and Brenner's conception of feudal peasantry, according to which the predominance of rules of economic behaviour that are contrary to innovation determines the impossibility of an internal transformational dynamic. Davidson infers that the concept of the peasant mode (as well as Brenner's notion of feudalism) cannot explain the change toward another mode of production. For Harman, even classless societies present developments in their productive forces that may precipitate structural change, and in his view the level of productive forces in the peasant mode resembles more that of the class societies with which it coexists.

16   Sahlins 1972, pp. 87–92.

they deem inconvenient; (d) prefer to forgo those options unless population growth threatens subsistence. In conclusion, there is a margin for intensifying production in response to population growth (or the introduction of relations of exploitation).[17] These premises lead to a demography that is specific to the peasant mode which implies an untapped surplus that can be mobilised in situations of demographic pressure, something that peasant populations attempt to preclude through birth control strategies (mainly late marriage); contrary to Malthus's assertion, this demographic regulation would be put to use in order to prevent labour intensification rather than to mitigate the effects of the imbalance between population and resources. These reproductive patterns result in low demographic density and a tendency toward population decline due to the decrease in birth rate, which is confirmed for the historical period of dominance of the peasant mode.[18]

In the peasant mode, the household produces autonomously and the product of labour remains at its disposal. This essential feature distinguishes the peasant mode from the concept of peasant economy derived from Chayanov's arguments, to which some authors have conferred the status of mode of production,[19] and whose functioning is independent from the eventual subjection of peasants to relations of exploitation. It is also distinct from the peasant mode of production referred to by Kautsky and other authors, who point to a form of production that is articulated to other systems rather than to specific relations of production.[20]

Since producers do not have to relinquish the surplus to an exploitative class, the most important social relations in the peasant mode are those established within the household (which do not imply class-exploitation) and between the independent households. These bonds determine a specific form of property that is not subordinated to kinship relations nor mediated through the community, and whose continuity is guaranteed mainly through systems of partible inheritance.[21] Given that for the most part the access to the means

---

17 Boserup 1993, p. 43, defines agricultural intensification as 'the gradual change towards patterns of land use which make it possible to crop a given area of land more frequently than before'.

18 Wickham 2005, pp. 551 ff.

19 According to Harrison 1977, Chayanov's theory involves social relations of production (self-exploitation of labour power), mechanisms for reproduction (the family), and a specific dynamic derived from the contradiction between consumption needs and forces of production.

20 Kautsky 1970, p. 320. On this notion, see Banaji 2010, pp. 94–5.

21 Wickham 2005, pp. 551 ff., p. 432 (the case of Malling) and p. 324 (England).

of production does not depend on membership in a community, the peasant mode is distinct from concepts based on kinship societies such as Meillassoux's domestic mode of production.[22]

Basically, the form of property in the peasant mode corresponds to that of the Germanic mode of the *Formen* due to the following considerations: (a) the individual household is an independent economic unit; (b) from the point of view of real appropriation of the conditions of production and its results, the direct producers are private proprietors; (c) the community does not exist as a state; (d) communal property is only a complement of individual property; (e) kinship has a secondary role; (f) exploitation is parcelled out and does not require communal labour for its valorisation; and (g) it develops feudal relations of production.[23]

The forms of production and the fact that the households dispose of the product determine the characteristics of exchange, which is based on reciprocity: the productive units exchange goods in order to create or maintain social bonds and to obtain what they do not produce.[24] Commercial exchange is marginal. Sahlins's criterion applies, according to which: (a) in 'primitive' societies, the households are not self-sufficient and must resort to exchange; (b) systems based on domestic production, sexual division of labour, an orientation toward consumption and product access tend toward reciprocity; and (c) transactions have an instrumental function.[25]

In the peasant mode, the exchange signifies cooperation, alliance and competition among households, and the quality of the exchange depends on the social distance (the closer to the household, the more disinterested or less 'economic' the exchange).[26] The surplus is also consumed in collective celebrations. Generosity is a mechanism for constructing hierarchies, since it imposes a debt on the recipients and creates a social relationship which on principle is to last until the gift is returned. Differences of rank in the peasant mode derive from this operative principle by which the gift-giver has a position of power: those who give more have more recognition and subordinate others by means of the obligation to repay the gift. This takes up Marcel Mauss's criterion, according to which the act of giving more than others – the essence of *potlatch* – is a mechanism to express superiority and legitimise or conquer a social posi-

22   Meillassoux 1991, pp. 34 ff.

23   Marx 1964, pp. 77–80.

24   According to Sahlins 1972, ch. 5, 'generalized reciprocity' and 'balanced reciprocity', respectively.

25   Sahlins 1972, p. 83 and ch. 5.

26   Sahlins 1972, ch. 5; Bourdieu 1990, p. 115.

tion before others,[27] and Bourdieu's proposition that due to social disapproval of open violence, gift-giving is the only means to assure domination in primitive societies.[28] As Sahlins summarises it, 'the economic relation of giver-receiver is the political relation of leader-follower'.[29]

This form of distribution of the surplus defines the features of the social structure: peasant mode societies are not egalitarian because they have mechanisms to construct hierarchy. However, dependent as they are on generosity, charisma, public performance, etc., these hierarchies are not permanent, and in consequence this mode of production is correlated to unstable political forms. Inequality is also manifested by the presence of unfree individuals in the more hierarchical units.

The peasant mode implies functioning principles that work against the accumulation of wealth and power inasmuch as the construction and preservation of a position of authority depend on munificence, which leads to a constant draining of resources, and on the effective support of followers, which inhibits the deployment of oppressive practices. This problem has been formulated in different ways: the contradiction between a leader's power aspirations and his dependence on his subordinates, which is inherent to primitive leaderships, neutralises the possible development of said power (Sahlins);[30] the accumulation of symbolic capital, the only recognised form of power, demands costly strategies, therefore the very maintenance of domination implies its fragility (Bourdieu);[31] social competition does not involve factors of production but scarce goods that only bestow prestige if they are redistributed or destroyed in public ceremonies (Godelier).[32] This dynamic leads to limited standards of wealth and preservation of the means of production and subsistence on the part of the members of the community, which in turn prevents its internal differentiation.

---

27   Mauss 1954, pp. 37–41 and 72. Godelier 1999, pp. 56 ff., expounds and criticises Mauss's model. For the negotiation of social position through gift-exchange, see Miller 1986.

28   Bourdieu 1990, pp. 122–35.

29   Sahlins 1972, p. 133.

30   Sahlins 1974, and 1972, pp. 130–48. Runciman 1989, pp. 323–5, follows Sahlins's criterion: 'The practices which define the big-man's role do indeed impose the constraint – or contradiction – that the more he accumulates, the more he must give away and therefore the more he is at risk of alienating the followers on whom his power depends if he fails to do so ... [G]iven the constraints on the practices constitutive of big-man roles, no mutation or recombination could bring about and institutional change from within'.

31   Bourdieu 1990, p. 131.

32   Godelier 1972, p. 289.

The deployment of this functioning logic assumes the absence of an aristocracy (the case of Iceland is an example) or a weak social control on the part of the aristocracy and the state over peasant populations, since the relative autonomy of the latter is the condition of possibility of such logic. Thus, the emergence of the peasant mode in the early Middle Ages is associated with a historical process of impoverishment of the aristocracy and decline of the fiscal system which took place in Western Europe between the fifth and sixth centuries.

The historical conditions for the genesis of the peasant mode in Western Europe do not imply the total dissolution of the ancient forms of property, which correspond to various modes of labour exploitation (colonate, serfdom, taxation) directly or indirectly enabled by the structures of the fiscal state. It is rather a historical process of involution of the state and retrogression in the wealth levels of the aristocrats, who lost control over their possessions and the subjugated labour force. This process took place in different manners that altered the morphology of the aristocracy, giving rise to two variations: (1) the aristocracy becomes tribalised and its power is confined to leadership over free people (and to a very limited exploitation of the unfree); or (2) it narrows its area of influence, preserving effective rights of exploitation only over a minority of the peasantry.

The first case is the 'tribal' variation of the peasant mode, in which the members of the aristocracy are mostly chieftains similar to 'big men'; in this variation, exemplified in the proto-states of Northern Europe (England, Wales, Ireland, Denmark), property has not morphed into the right to claim rent. The free men owe their local leaders or their rulers military service and a small tribute which does not affect their economic autonomy and must be repaid; this bond becomes tangible in non-permanent clientelar relations in which the followers preserve the right to withdraw or change their loyalties. In this version, the aristocracy assimilates itself to the peasant mode; that is to say, it does not constitute a separate mode of production.[33]

In the second case, the extraction of surplus from dependent segments denotes the presence of relations of exploitation, and thereby of another mode of production that Wickham sums up in the concept of the feudal mode, which coexists with free spaces not dominated by the aristocracy where the peasant mode manifests itself. In this case, the independent peasants are in contact

---

33   Haldon observes that Wickham dismissed the difference in meaning between the terms 'aristocracy' and 'elite'; he suggests that the latter term would have been more appropriate (Haldon 2011, p. 52).

with feudal landowners with whom they maintain links that are more or less lax or sporadic. This is the more habitual form of existence of the peasant mode in Western Europe: integrated into a regional or micro-regional social whole in which feudal enclaves also exist.[34] Wickham's image of 'leopard spots' conveys this situation of coexistence of distinct modes of production within a social formation. Both modes (feudal and peasant) articulate in different ways, giving rise to an array of situations which basically express the pre-eminence of one mode or the other in the society in question. In a social formation dominated by the peasant mode, the position of the aristocracy, whose wealth and politicial influence are limited, will depend on the support of free people, which gives rise to practices of reciprocity, such as gift-giving, in exchange for loyalty. The relationship between the aristocracy and the free peasantry follows patterns similar to those observed in societies that have undergone a process of tribalisation. Thus, the rules arising from the internal logic of the peasant mode are rendered on the whole. The dominance of the peasant mode in the early medieval social formations is evidenced in the archaeological record, which generally reflects a simplified material culture.

Both forms of existence of the peasant mode (tribal or in combination with feudal enclaves) imply the subordination of the aristocracy to the logic of the gift, which inhibits the development of accumulation processes and constrains wealth levels to its limits; this dynamic leads to a principle thwarting the transformation of societies where the peasant mode is dominant. Nevertheless, from the point of view of the form of property, the peasant mode favours the emergence of inequalities and private accumulation, which arises predictably from the individual appropriation of the fruits of labour. Marx points to this aspect in the Germanic type of property, which reflects an emancipation from kinship and community, since the community exists only as a relationship between individual proprietors; the Germanic form of individual property does not depend on membership in a collective entity, nor does the collective intervene in its valorisation; the possibility of independent economic action is the source of dissolution of egalitarianism.[35] This feature of the Germanic mode has been emphasised by Alan Macfarlane with respect to the later appearance of capitalist relations.[36] According to Kosminsky, the peasant social differentiation in thirteenth-century England can be explained by the previous existence of

---

34   Banaji 2010, p. 218, criticises this, which he refers to as 'microregionality of modes of production'.

35   Marx 1964, pp. 75 ff., pp. 142–5 (Marx to Zasulich).

36   Macfarlane 2002.

individual private property, which underlies the formation of feudalism and its evolution.[37] Marx notes the undermining potential of private appropriation in his analysis of the nineteenth-century Russian agricultural commune, characterised by the predominance of divided petty cultivation; this enables private accumulation of movable goods susceptible to exchange, which stimulates internal differentiation.[38] On a similar note, Engels points out that individual exploitation accounts for the increasing inequality within the Russian peasantry and leads to its disintegration,[39] which was later confirmed by Lenin in his empirical analysis of the internal structure of this community.[40] The peasant mode is therefore based on an individualised form of appropriation of the conditions of production which favours the development of inequality. Thus, two opposing evolutionary tendencies are combined in the historical process.

As Wickham points out, the transition mechanism is the accumulation of land and the conversion of landowning peasants into tenants, which is in accordance with the historical evolution of the Germanic mode, whose tendency toward fragmentation leads to the development of feudal relations of exploitation – and later to capitalist relations. This process, which presents differentiated traits on a microregional level,[41] begins with the strengthening of the internal elites (tribal aristocracy) or the external ones (feudal aristocracy) and their distancing from the obligations of reciprocity. In the habitual form of existence of the peasant mode, whose dominance in the social formation depends on the entity of the feudal enclaves, the proximity of these enclaves exposes the independent peasant communities to seigneurial violence or the development of clientelar relations with outside aristocrats which generally involve village leaders; these bonds can lead to an enhanced social condition for those leaders, which tends to turn rank differences into class differences, or to the conversion of bonds of patronage into local relations of exploitation and domination.[42] The patronage of outside aristocrats would be a mechanism for the internalisation of the values of the feudal class and a factor neutral-

---

37   Kosminsky 1956, p. 207: 'The deep-seated causes of peasant differentiation probably lie as far back as the disintegration of the pre-feudal lands into the ownership of separate families. The formation of allodial holdings, and the development of land alienation, were bound to result in the creation of private states'.

38   Marx 1964, pp. 142–5 (Marx to Zasulich). For the complete second and third drafts, see Marx 1989, pp. 360–70.

39   Engels 1989.

40   Lenin 1964.

41   This process varied from village to village, Wickham 2005, pp. 432–3.

42   See the case of Malling, Wickham 2005, p. 432.

ising class struggle.[43] Here it is possible to suggest a certain parallel with Meil-lassoux's observations on the evolution of the domestic mode of production, which tends toward dissolution as a society of equal communities. According to Meillassoux, agricultural communites are vulnerable to external attack due to their stable location, their storage of goods, the presence of scattered producers, etc.; the need for protection leads to new organisational patterns (military alliances, etc.) which culminate in the establishment of class power; this domination, which is generally from outside the community, preserves the vocabulary of kinship or the appearance of reciprocity as an ideological under-pinning for exploitation.[44] For Bourdieu, this principle is already present in gift exchange, which tends to create asymmetrical bonds and engender rela-tions of dependence that take the guise of moral obligations; as the hierarchies become institutionalised, their reproduction will rest less on symbolic forms and will be carried out through less costly and more evident means.[45] In Gode-lier's scheme, the stabilisation of authority marks the first stage of the process by which social competition, which does not involve the access to the means of production and subsistence in primitive societies, shifts from the sphere of the distribution of products to the sphere of the distribution of factors of pro-duction.[46] In our case this shift is manifested in the expansion of tenancy.

In early medieval social formations, the advance of the relations of exploit-ation is evidenced in the development of craft specialisation, which reflects the demand of utilitarian goods on the part of the aristocracy in keeping with its increased political hierarchy and wealth. Notwithstanding, in the regions where the feudal mode of production predominated (for example, Northern France), the peasant mode preserved a relatively independent existence.[47] Considered as a whole, the process of transition to the full dominance of the feudal mode takes place in three stages:

> [F]irst, a steady strengthening of aristocratic status and wealth, inside the constraints of the peasant mode and/or in neighbouring areas; second, a catastrophe-flip from a peasant to a feudal economic logic; third, the steady reduction of areas of continuing peasant autonomy inside the overall dominance of the feudal mode.[48]

---

43 Wickham 2005, p. 440.
44 Meillassoux 1991, pp. 82–8.
45 Bourdieu 1990, pp. 122–35.
46 Godelier 1974b, pp. 34–5.
47 Wickham 2005, p. 547.
48 Wickham 2005, p. 588.

The aim of this theoretical proposition, as stated by Wickham in the first formulations of his concept, is to introduce 'more firmly' into the study of the early Middle Ages the functioning patterns that anthropologists have established for 'primitive' societies.[49] Other historians before him have applied these patterns to medieval Europe, but those patterns have not been converted into a comprehensive concept aimed at the understanding of the whole, or they have not been combined with the productive structure, limiting the analysis to the sphere of circulation.[50] On the other hand, the authors in the field of anthropology who have linked elements of the 'archaic' functioning with forms of production have based their schemes on societies where the development of individual private property is rare or non-existent.[51] From this perspective, the concept of peasant mode constitutes an undeniable contribution which could be considered in the framework of the analyses arising from the revision of the *Formen*, this time based on the property form of the Germanic mode.

It behooves us to note that this is not the author's view. In *Framing the Early Middle Ages*, Wickham does not mention the Germanic mode nor any other non-exploitative mode. In the author's opinion, the categorisation of non-exploitative modes is unsatisfactory;[52] consequently his proposition must also be considered an attempt in this direction growing out of the efforts at systematisation of classless societies undertaken by other authors (Sahlins, Meillassoux). Wickham wants to limit the inventory of modes of production to three basic forms of labour exploitation (slave, feudal and capitalist), unifying the ones that imply a control of the productive process by the direct producers. With the same criterion (simplifying the categorisation of modes of production), he suggests the addition of only one non-exploitative mode – the peasant mode – which would reflect 'the patterns of the peasant economy that can be found when landlords or the state do *not* take surplus in a systematic way'.[53] Given that the absence of relations of exploitation, as well as the extraction of surplus through extra-economic coercion, can be found in diverse forms of property (individual, communal), the universality of the peasant mode as

49   Wickham 1994d, p. 216.

50   For instance, Duby 1978, pp. 48–56, and Gurevich 1985, ch. 3. For further bibliography on the gift-exchange model and its application to early medieval societies, see Moreland 2000, p. 14, n. 62.

51   For instance, Meillassoux 1991, pp. 34–9; Sahlins 1972, pp. 92–4. According to Godelier 1974c, p. 87, private ownership is an exception when it comes to pre-capitalist modes of production.

52   Wickham 1994b, p. 45.

53   Wickham 2005, p. 261.

the mode of agrarian societies without aristocratic domination presents the same difficulties as the universality of the tributary mode ('feudal' in Wickham's terminology) as the mode of pre-capitalist class societies, a perspective that several authors have criticised.[54]

In 'The other transition', Wickham refers to the Germanic mode ('a definable mode inside Marx's inadequately analysed congeries of non-hierarchical systems that he called the "primitive communism" mode') and dismisses its presence in the early Middle Ages based on the existence of settlements of German peasants whom he identifies with structures 'focused on some communal property'.[55] Even though Marx, influenced by Maurer's work, hesitated over the features of the primitive Germanic community, his analysis underscores the individual component, which determines its potential for transformation. The degree of emancipation of the community is the criterion against which Marx compared the different forms and analysed what determines their specificity: the individual appropriation unmediated by the community is what distinguishes the Germanic mode from the ancient and the Asiatic modes;[56] this distinction squares with one of the main pillars of the *Formen*, namely the relationship between forms of property and the dynamism of societies.[57]

The shift in his perspective with regard to private property in primitive Germania is found in the drafts of the letter to Vera Zasulich, where Marx mulls over a period before private property around Tacitus's time ('agricultural community') in which the individuals own the house, its surroundings and have rights of possession on the arable, a formation that would later give way to

---

54   Banaji 2010, pp. 183–5 and 212–14; Anderson 1979, pp. 402 ff.; Manzano Moreno 1998; Astarita 1994, and 2003.

55   Wickham 1994a, pp. 29–30.

56   Marx states that '[i]ndividual landed property does not here appear as a contradictory form of communal landed property, nor as mediated by the community, but the other way round ... The community is neither the substance, on which the individual appears merely as the accident ... It is rather the common element in language, blood, etc., which is the premise of the individual proprietor; but on the other hand it has real being in its *actual assembly* for communal purposes; and, in so far as it has a separate economic existence, in the communally used hunting-grounds, pastures, etc., it is used thus by every individual proprietor as such, and not in his capacity as a representative of the state (as in Rome)' (Marx 1964, p. 80).

57   According to the *Formen*, '[t]he Asiatic form necessarily survives longest and most stubbornly. This is due to the fundamental principle on which it is based, that is, that the individual does not become independent of the community' (Marx 1964, p. 83).

the private property of the arable ('new community').[58] These hesitations have affected the characterisation of primitive Germania,[59] but not the type of property that Marx describes for the *Formen* which, in any case, following his last reflections, would be subject to a different chronology (the 'new community' would have developed at some moment between Tacitus and the migrations, and it features the free peasant still present in the Middle Ages). In conclusion, the Germanic mode of the *Formen* represents a specific form of property, regardless of whether it prevailed before or after Tacitus. In this respect, Dopsch has demolished the Mark theory through the philological analysis of Tacitus's *Germania*;[60] Boutruche also supports the existence of individual private property among primitive Germans.[61] Furthermore, the archaeological discovery of parcel limits confirms, for the society in question, a structure founded on private property as described in the *Formen*[62] (regardless of the specific form of settlement).

Wickham acknowledges the vitality of 'German and non-German' free peasant communities (given their former subjection to fiscal obligations, he deems them to be derived from the ancient mode) and their return to non-exploitative systems in the early Middle Ages.[63] These non-exploitative systems mostly reproduce the essence of the Germanic type, because they reproduce the allodial holding, the free heritable property.[64] Therefore, the concept of the peas-

---

58   Marx 1964, pp. 142–5 (Marx to Zasulich); also Marx 1989; Engels 1970, pp. 293–306; see Godelier 1977, pp. 83–99.

59   Anderson 1996, p. 108, considers that reallocation of arable land was still in use in Tacitus's times; according to Seccombe 1995, pp. 52–3, although private ownership was not unknown among the Germans, the extent of it depended on the development of agricultural techniques and agrarian practices allowing for the restoration of the soil so that it could be regularly cultivated by the same family. Boserup 1993, pp. 77–81, associates the emergence of individual property rights with agricultural intensification.

60   Dopsch 1951, pp. 58–74.

61   For a bibliography on this, see Boutruche 1959, p. 62, n. 5.

62   García Moreno 1992.

63   Wickham 1994a, p. 30.

64   Although initially associated with family possession, according to Bonnassie, '[t]ransporté dans l'Europe du Midi par les invasions germaniques, le mot "alleu" y change totalement de sens. Il vient s'y plaquer sur la vieille notion romaine de *proprietas*. Il cesse donc de désigner ici le patrimoine lignager pour s'appliquer à la propriété individuelle, divisible et aliénable sans aucune sorte d'entrave' (Bonnassie 1981, p. 18). See also Bonnassie 1975, p. 205. Gurevich 1992b, p. 204 ff., highlights the persistence of the original meaning of the *óðal* from which the word *allodium* would derive. This opinion is partially valid for Wickham 1994c, p. 166.

ant mode, which I would have called the 'allodial mode of production', does not imply a new form of property. Instead, it develops aspects related to the productive forces, the social relations of exchange and the laws of social functioning. These aspects are not foreign to the society on which the elaboration of the concept of Germanic mode is based, as evidenced in Tacitus's accounts of the low intensity of labour,[65] gift exchange as a form of social bonding,[66] the instability of chieftains,[67] and a differentiated nobility whose power over free men is limited and subordinated to the logic of the whole.[68]

Although Wickham does not develop the problem of property from a theoretical standpoint, he verifies the prevalence of independent landowning peasants in almost all the regions, and through his criticism of documents he demonstrates the real appropriation by free peasants of the productive resources and the product in the regions where they are referred to as tenants, as in the case of Anglo-Saxon England. Even though from the legal perspective one cannot assert the existence of peasant property in this case, the appropriation of the conditions of production and its results is not negated by the requirement of tribute, whose marginal character the author shows in his analysis of the composition of the payments owed to the rulers, which are generally informal contributions of hospitality; this is why he considers this land tenure system as 'tribal', and attributes the category of 'autonomous' rather than 'proprietors' to the free peasants who inhabit the large territorial units mentioned in Anglo Saxon charters (which maintain the lexicon of Roman law) as the exclusive property of lay or ecclesiastical entities.[69] As for the communal component (whose role is secondary in the Germanic mode of the *For-*

---

65   Tacito, *Germania*, 14: *Nec arare terram aut exspectare annum tam facile persuaseris quam vocare hostem et vulnera mereri. Pigrum quin immo et iners videtur sudore adquirere quod possis sanguine parare.*

66   Tacito, *Germania*, 15: *Mos est civitatibus ultro ac viritim conferre principibus vel armentorum vel frugum, quod pro honore acceptum etiam necessitatibus subvenit. Gaudent praecipue finitimarum gentium donis, quae non modo a singulis, sed et publice mittuntur*; ibid., 14: *[E]xigunt enim principis sui liberalitate illum bellatorem equum, illam cruentam victricemque frameam*; ibid., 21: *Convictibus et hospitiis non alia gens effusius indulget.*

67   Tacito, *Germania*, 11: *De minoribus rebus principes consultant; de maioribus, omnes ... Mox rex vel princeps, prout aetas cuique, prout nobilitas, prout decus bellorum, prout facundia est, audiuntur, auctoritate suadendi magis quam iubendi potestate.*

68   Tacito, *Germania*, 7: *Reges ex nobilitate, duces ex virtute sumunt. Nec regibus infinita aut libera potestas, et duces exemplo potius quam imperio, si prompti, si conspicui, si ante aciem agant, admiratione praesunt.*

69   Wickham 2005, pp. 314–26.

men), woodland, according to Wickham, 'for the most part it was accessible to anyone living in the area who wished to use it', regardless of its legal condition.[70]

Peasant autonomy is not attributable to a pattern of settlement. In societies of the early Middle Ages, the settlement in isolated farms proposed by Tacitus (and found in Iceland),[71] which Marx followed in his *Formen*, coexists with the grouping in villages; in turn, peasant property appears intermixed with aristocratic patrimony. The more concentrated peoplings favour cooperation in productive activities, and such cooperation breeds concerted action on the part of the members of the community, which reaffirms their autonomy. Due to the isolation of the productive units, in the Germanic mode the community is visualised as such when the proprietors meet in an assembly. In the peasant mode, the community is defined by the social action of its members, and it is conditioned by the form of existence of aristocratic patrimony (the more scattered, the better the chances of peasant protagonism). Peasant autonomy not only means that peasants can effectively dispose of the fruits of their labour; it also means that they are capable of action independent of the aristocracy, which in turn implies an inverse relation between peasant autonomy and the development of relations of patronage with magnates from outside the community.[72]

Finally, by virtue of the historical conditions of its emergence, the peasant mode (except in the paradigmatic case of Iceland and generally in the proto-states of Northern Europe) implies a coexistence with another mode of production, which brings the analysis to the sphere of social formation and the practices that reflect the articulation of the different modes and the subordination of ancient social forms to the dominant mode of production. With its stress on the logic of social functioning, Wickham's concept can be properly applied to the analysis of this problem.

---

70   Wickham 1994c, p. 188. The description of the communal elements of Malling is basically in accordance with the communal component of the Germanic mode of the *Formen*: 'Malling was not a legal entity, but it had a certain identity as a village. Villagers did not yet co-operate so much in economic tems ... but they did run livestock collectively, and also together took wood from the part of the woodland 10 km away that Malling had rights to ... The free men of Malling ... did however go together to the local legal assembly ... which was the meeting point of a dozen villages' (Wickham 2005, pp. 430–1).

71   Miller 1984, p. 99, n. 14. On dispersion and localisation of farms, see Callow 2006, p. 305.

72   On this point, see Knight 2011.

Peasant-Aristocrat Patronage Links: Transmutation of the Peasant Practice in a Feudalised Context

In the historical dynamic of the peasant mode, the development of clientelar links is a mechanism for the construction of power that goes hand in hand with the advance of feudal relations of exploitation. We will analyse a type of clientelar relation characteristic of Castile and León during the eleventh and twelfth centuries, which is also present in Galicia and Portugal, with the aim of establishing what this bond consists of and how we can document the transition to exploitative forms. In social formations dominated by the peasant mode, the aristocracy is subordinated to the logic of reciprocity; in our case, we will start from a social formation dominated by the feudal mode – a classic leopard-spot area, where the aristocracy coexists with autonomous peasants – and we will observe how this dominance subordinates surviving peasant practice by infusing it with new content. We will take up the criterion established by Meillassoux, Godelier and Bourdieu regarding the preservation of the appearance of reciprocity as a mechanism of justification or construction of relations of exploitation, and we will propose that this process undergoes intermediate stages where an ambivalence and gradual reformulation of the social practice can be observed.[73]

The clientelar bond we will analyse is manifested in a series of social practices: land endowment in exchange for military service, mediation and defense in judicial courts, fosterage, election of lords and hospitality. In peasant societies these practices reflect social relations based on the exchange of gifts; in the feudalised context we are analysing, however, these practices, though formally analogous, tend to place themselves at the service of the reproduction of the feudal class. The slow pace and the forms of this process conveying the expansion of feudalism are explained by the logic of the peasant mode, whose principles, even while undergoing a process of disintegration, still condition the behaviour of the aristocracy. The subordination of peasant practice happens in two stages:

(1) During the eleventh century, clientelar links in the area of Castile and León reflect an incomplete dominance of the feudal mode of production: the persons involved in these relationships (village notables, free peasants, humble knights) preserve a certain degree of autonomy and provide non-agrarian services except in the case of the servants and the unfree, with whom the aristo-

---

73   For an earlier period, see Astarita 2003–6, and 2011, p. 212.

cracy maintains ambivalent links. Clientelar relations are relatively unstable, although the ability to change loyalties tends to be reduced to a formulaic statement. Notwithstanding, this formulaic statement is used to express the client's condition as a free person or the promotion of the unfree, which indicates that non-aristocratic segments are still afforded a certain amount of protagonism; this circumstance is also manifested in the granting of lands in exchange for military support.

(2) In the early twelfth century, the process of subordination of autonomous peasants and their social forms has been accomplished: we witness the spread of collective links and the transformation of the service provided by clients into agrarian rent, as well as a crystallisation of the separation between *milites* and farm labourers by which the former are exempt from taxation and restrictions with regard to their political allegiance and are therefore able to join the feudal system as vassals, and the latter remain subjected to seigneurial lineages and taxation, that is to say, excluded from the category of free people from the point of view of their political capabilities and their ability to dispose of the fruits of labour. The transformation of clients into tenants is clearly visible from the early eleventh century in some pacts of the Galician-Portuguese area implying the loss of economic autonomy on the part of the clients, which reflects an earlier establishment of feudalism in that region.

The analysis of the bond between patrons and clients yields elements inherent to peasant practice that can promote this evolution. The change is also favoured by the structure of property which facilitates its transmission and disposition. This aspect has been highlighted by Reyna Pastor, who attributes seigneurial advance over village communities to the consolidation in the latter of individual property since the tenth century, within the framework of a system of property consistent with the Germanic form (combination of private and communal property, emancipation of the individual from the community); as stressed by Pierre Guichard, the disposition of individual property favours disposession and the fall into dependency, an evolution that is not observed in societies where the communal framework prevails, such as some Islamic societies.[74] In this regard, Miquel Barceló has analysed the stability of clan settlements in al-Andalus, and he believes this stability to be associated with the impossibility of trading in land, which hampers the formation of a feudal class

---

74   Pastor 1984. Pierre Guichard's comments appear in Pastor 1984, p. 116.

through absorption of patrimony.[75] Thus, this latter phenomenon encounters more favourable conditions in places with a predominance of communities emancipated from kinship.

What follows is an analysis of the transformation of clientelar bonds and their structural foundations stemming from the social functioning of the peasant mode. We will examine how the opposing evolutionary tendencies typical of this system combine (peasant dispossession/limitation of accumulation).

Gifts of Lands to Peasants

One of the features of the bond between patron and client is the granting of lands in exchange for services. Land endowments on the part of the patron abound in the eleventh-century records. They are charters of donation or sale which refer to the recipient's ability to choose a lord.[76] In almost every case, members of comital families cede land in order to obtain, maintain or repay a service, mainly military service, as can be deduced from the fact that the clients give or promise to give swords and horses in exchange for the gift.[77] The meaning of the phrase *bene facere* as a synonym of land endowment for military service can be traced to tenth-century laws which exempt from military service those knights who have not been granted material means of support, ordering them to seek a lord that will grant them.[78]

The endowments can be temporary, for life or hereditary. They are more likely loans of land subject to the duration of the bond. Notwithstanding, in some documents the ceded lands are equated with allodial holdings, which on principle is consistent with the form of property of the peasant mode: the recipients can donate the land, sell it, bequeath it, etc.[79] The grants include

---

75   Barceló 1990, pp. 105 ff. Guichard 1984, p. 131, has observed the existence of collective forms of appropriation and North African kinship structures that hamper land transfers in al-Andalus.

76   *Ut vadas ad qualem dominum volueris, pergas cum ipso solare ad qualemcumque dominum volueris, qui tibi bene fecerit*, etc. Herrero de la Fuente 1988a, and 1988b; Fernández Flórez 1991; Ruiz Asencio 1987, and 1990.

77   For instance, Herrero de la Fuente 1988b, doc. 826 (1086): *Ego Beliti Citiz a uobis Martino Flayniz, domino meo, dauo uobis una espata ualente xx solidos de argento.*

78   Muñoz y Romero 1847, p. 38, Fuero de Castrojeriz (974): *Caballero de castro, qui non tenuerit prestamo, non vadat in fonsado, nisi dederint ei espensam, et sarcano illo Merino et habeant segniorem, qui benefecerit illos.*

79   Herrero de la Fuente 1988a, doc. 566 (1054): *Aveas, vindeas, dones, commutes tu et filiis tuis quo tivi queris*; doc. 702 (1071): *abeasque licentiam facendi ex eo quod tua extiterit uoluntas*; Fernández Flórez 1991, doc. 1252 (1133): *et faciatis ex eo quicquid extiterit uestra*

the right to communal land as an accessory of the individual plot, precisely as found in the Germanic form.[80] A couple of cases note the client's prior condition as private proprietor: one of the recipients has previously sold some pieces of land acquired through purchase which are free and clear of any obligation.[81] Another case confirms the sale of lands that had been acquired as payment for non-agrarian service.[82]

It has been suggested that the terminology related to full ownership (*faciatis ex eo quicquid exiterit uestra uoluntas*, etc.) could reflect the constitution of a bond, which even if disposition of the property is possible, implies an obligation for the recipient.[83] As William Ian Miller observes in his study of family sagas, gifts of lands were avoided or feared in view of the implied relation of subordination to the giver derived from the fact that the debt could only be settled with another grant of lands.[84] The spread of this practice in eleventh-century Castile and León reflects the construction of power by means of gifts that can only be repaid with services, as well as the denaturation of allodial holdings, which tend to become tenancies subject to rent or conditioned property; the preservation of the lexicon of full ownership could result from the need to acknowledge the free condition of the land recipients, whom the law equates to (but does not confuse with) the aristocracy.[85]

In fact these procedures emulate the transactions between members of the aristocracy in which the gifts of lands are reciprocated with symbolic presents: the patrons receive horses, greyhounds, swords or mules from their clients as

---

uoluntas, uendere, donare; et habeatis ipsum solare confirmatum, uos et omnis posteritas uestra; doc. 1189 (1113): et quicquid tibi de illa placuerit facere, facias: uendere, dare, tua uoluntate complere, in uita siue post mortem, tu et ex omni progenie tua.

80   Herrero de la Fuente 1988a, doc. 634 (1063): *Facium tiui kartula de uno solare cum sua erea et cum suo orto et cum suo exitum ab intro et at foras.*

81   Herrero de la Fuente 1988a, doc. 624 (1063) and doc. 578 (1056): *Ut uinderem uobis ego Gundisaluo presbiter et germana mea Geluira una corte de mea comparacione ... ut de isto die de iuri nostro abstracto uestro sit tradito et faciatis de eo quod uestra extiterit uoluntas.*

82   Herrero de la Fuente 1988b, doc. 1086 (1102): *Et habui ego Citi Albariz ipso solare de incartacione de comite Pedro Ansuriz et de sua mulier, propter filios eorum que ego nutriui ... Facio tibi carta per tale foro quomodo ille comes michi fecit et vadas cum eo ubi volueris, tu et filius tuus et omnis progenie tua.*

83   Morsel 2008, p. 207.

84   Miller 1986, pp. 49 ff.

85   Pérez Prendez y Muñoz de Arraco 1988, Fuero de León (o), tit. x: *Praecipimus etiam ut nullus nobilis sive aliquis de benefactoria emat solare aut ortum alicuius junioris.*

counter-gifts.[86] The transfer of horses in exchange for protection and means of subsistence shows up in *Laxdæla saga*; Miller highlights the subordination of the economic content of the transaction, which is presented as a sale, to the social relationship established between the parties which precludes the disassociation of the goods from their bearers; he who acquires horses also acquires obligations toward their prior owner and his family, to whom he cedes lands.[87] In our case the clients probably did not part from the objects they offered as a symbolic closing of the transaction, since they used them to serve their patron and the objects symbolised that service. Their condition as knights was precarious: in a will dated between 1085 and 1115, the patron awards his client some land and the horse the latter was using, which shows that many knights did not own their horses, and that clients were provided with the equipment for military service.[88] In a covenant of 1073, the client is given land and a colt;[89] in another case, along with the land, the client receives a horse, a mule, three oxen, 22 sheep and seven pigs.[90] These goods are described as components of the productive unit, which permits an estimation of the amount of means of production at stake, equivalent to a domestic unit of modest proportions. It follows from this that our client is a peasant who is being granted basic means of subsistence and the essentials of military equipment with which he will be able to lend his support to various members of the aristocracy.[91]

The need to secure loyalties among the peasantry shows that the development of feudalism was incomplete in the area. Competition among lords is evidenced in material endowments aimed at gaining supporters. In 1063, Juliana Muñiz grants lands to Sesgudo Escámez in the locality of Santa Cruz; Sesgudo reciprocates with a horse.[92] The following year, Juliana rewards Sesgudo once more for his good service with a plot of land in another location,[93]

---

86   Herrero de la Fuente 1988a, doc. 634 (1063), 638 (1064), 702 (1071), 713 (1072), 719 (1073), 720 (1073); Herrero de la Fuente 1988b, doc. 826 (1086), 887 (1092), 795 (1081); Fernández Flórez 1991, doc. 1198 (1117).

87   Miller 1986, p. 48; *Laxdæla saga*, ch. 36.

88   Herrero de la Fuente 1988b, doc. 1173 (1085–1115): *Et tibi, Martino Munniz, dono uno solare, ubi tu volueris; et illum cauallum quem tenes de me, habeas solutum pro mea anima; pergasque cum ipso solare ad qualemcumque dominum uolueris.*

89   Herrero de la Fuente 1988a, doc. 721 (1073).

90   Ruiz Asencio 1990, doc. 1233 (1084).

91   Ruiz Asencio 1990, doc. 1233 (1084): *cum tale foro de mare ad mare, ad rei, ad conde, ad infancone, ad quale dono uoleris in ipso solare sedente medio die et media ora.*

92   Herrero de la Fuente 1988a, doc. 634 (1063).

93   Herrero de la Fuente 1988a, doc. 683 (1064).

which shows that Sesgudo's loyalty had to be renewed, and that land grants did not guarantee the sustained support of the clients. As for the clients, in some cases they appear as serving different patrons simultaneously: for example, in 1073 Rodrigo Miguélez is awarded lands belonging to Armentario Vélez; in exchange he offers a grey horse;[94] during the same year he receives another piece of land in the same village from Pedro Vermúdez and in full ownership, this time in exchange for a roan horse and a greyhound.[95] The dimensions of these properties (the amount that can be tilled with two oxen) correspond to a family holding,[96] which places our client among the peasantry of the village. At this level we witness competition in order to recruit supporters through gifts of lands, which must be equivalent to those of other lords in the same location; such is the case of Elvira, who in 1071 grants a client a piece of land in Santa Cruz 'of the same size as that of Sesgudo' (who had received lands from Juliana Muñiz).[97] The example also illustrates the coexistence of a variety of bonds within the same village, which in turn reflects peasant protagonism.

The individuals who take part in these relationships could resemble the *milites* of peasant origin detected by Bonnassie in eleventh-century Catalonia, less submissive villagers who served various lords at the same time without taking on relevant obligations with any of them and without becoming fully integrated into the system of feudal vassalage: the author distinguishes them from the *milites castri* committed to the defence of fortresses who would end up incorporated into the ranks of the aristocracy.[98] Historians have recognised the material endowments for a client's military service as a precedent of beneficial concessions[99] and they have also observed the direct transformation of clientelar bonds into feudo-vassalic relationships;[100] the incorporation of rural segments to the seigneurial armed retinue has been related to the reorganisation and adaptation of the aristocracy to the structural requirements of banal lordship.[101] In some cases, the relationship of *benefactoria* could be inscribed

---

94   Herrero de la Fuente 1988a, doc. 719 (1073).

95   Herrero de la Fuente 1988a, doc. 720 (1073): *Ut de isto die habeas licenciam faciendi de ipso solare et de ipsa hereditate quod tua extiterit uoluntas.*

96   Herrero de la Fuente 1988a, doc. 720 (1073): *cum suas terras, ut habeat uno iugo de boves ad duas folias in aratura quod laborent.*

97   Herrero de la Fuente 1988a, doc. 702 (1071): *Ut uinderemus tibi Steuano Ciluanez uno solare similiter tamanio quomodo est ille de Sesguto Examiz.*

98   Bonnassie 1975, II, pp. 800 ff.

99   Dopsch 1951, pp. 386 ff.; White 2003, p. 98.

100   Morsel 2008, p. 68.

101   Morsel 2008, pp. 149–50.

in this process of reformulation and expansion of the aristocracy involving the transformation of clients into vassals, which illustrates one of the avenues for the disintegration of peasant societies through the social promotion of their leaders; on the other hand, we will observe that the relatively undifferentiated group of clients tends to become split into *milites* and farm labourers over the course of the century; the former will likely become integrated into *féodalité*, whereas the latter become subject to feudal relations of exploitation.

Conflict Mediation and the Performance of Patrons in the Assembly

Patrons acted as conflict mediators and advocates for their clients in courts. These functions have been well documented in Galicia and Portugal. Let us review an example. In 1008, two siblings, Adosinda and Argerigo, sell a piece of land to the local priest in exchange for livestock and food. The reason for the transaction is that the priest has helped them by acting as mediator before Adosinda's husband, whom she has betrayed, and perhaps he also acted on their behalf before the higher authority to whom a fine for adultery is due, which the siblings apparently have only partially paid. The priest inter-cedes with Adosinda's husband on her behalf, he gathers representatives from both families in his own house, he counsels them and manages to recon-cile the parties. This performance is the essence of the covenant of '*bemfei-toria*'.[102]

Conflict resolution is the main manifestation of functional power in peasant mode societies.[103] Success in lawsuits depends to a large extent on the support marshalled for one cause, that is to say, on the number of men the leader can bring to the assembly in support of his suit, which is in direct relation with his reputation as a successful jurist. The role of local leaders as advocates, mediators and peacemakers has been highlighted by scholars of the Icelandic sagas.[104] The mediator's mission is to reconcile the parties in a manner that is

---

102   Portugaliae Monumenta Historica. Diplomata et chartae, CCII (1008), p. 124: *Quanto inde tenemus in nostro iure qum mater nostra goda ... nos tivi inde rovoramus medietate integra ... Et dedisti nobis adduc in pretio II boves et III modios de zivario et IIas cabras et uno carnario tanto nobis bene complacuit ... Et damus tibi ea pro occasione que abenit ad ipsa adosinda et in suo peccato devenit a tradictione et abuit pro me a dare CL solidos et dedit inde illos L ad uilifonso mumdinizi ... Et favolastis pro me ad meo marito virterla et dimisit mici illa merze et rezebit me pro sua muliere et consudunasti nos todos tres in tua kasa ad tua bemfeitoria.*

103   Wickham 2005, pp. 431–2, the advocacy for neighbours in court is the main role of Eahlmund and Ælfwine, Malling leaders. The reconstruction of Malling is based on the case of medieval Iceland.

104   Miller 1990, pp. 259–99, and 1984; Byock 2001, pp. 66 ff.

either complementary or an alternative to the judicial resolution of the case. As Bourdieu remarks, representation in courts and conflict mediation are typical forms of accumulation of symbolic capital.[105]

An episode of *Eyrbyggja saga* highlights one aspect of the intervention of third parties in disputes between households: land grants as repayment for representation services in courts. In this case the litigants do not wish to reconcile, but to win the case in the assembly.[106] Thorolf and Ulfar are feuding neighbours. Thorolf's son Arnkel, who is a renowned *goði*, always tries to compensate Ulfar for his father's hostile actions. Thorolf dispatches slaves to set fire to Ulfar's house; Arnkel seeks them out and kills them. Ulfar transfers his property to Arnkel (who favours his leadership over his kinship) in exchange for his protection. Thorolf demands compensation for his dead slaves; Arnkel refuses to pay it; Thorolf decides to bring his case to the courts, which requires that he find a specialist as renowned as Arnkel or even more so. Since Arnkel is one of the *goðar* of the district, Thorolf should appeal to Arnkel, but Thorolf makes use of his liberties to change allegiance and appeals to Snorri *goði* for him to present the case before the assembly. At first Snorri refuses, because the case is unpopular, but Thorolf secures his support by offering him lands. Thorolf transfers the lands but retains the usufruct; upon his death they will become Snorri's outright property.[107] There is rivalry between Snorri and Arnkel; Snorri has taken advantage of the opportunity to see Arnkel disinherited. Thorolf's interest in the matter, as Miller suggests, is not material, since the value of the land exceeds the compensation he could obtain for the slaves; by winning the case in the assembly, which is what he expects to do by means of Snorri's abilities, Thorolf enhances his reputation and reconstructs alliances predicated from his bond with a renowned chieftain. The gift of lands has served him to disinherit his son, from whom he is estranged, to intervene in a dispute between two chieftains competing to gain supporters, and to consolidate his own status through the success of his case in the assembly.

This example could illuminate some aspects of the clientelar relationship that concern us. In the adultery case reviewed above, the gift of land to the priest who brokered the reconciliation between both families does not appear disproportionate if one considers that the woman who cedes the land could

---

105   Bourdieu 1990, pp. 128–9.

106   *Eyrbyggja saga*, ch. 31. This episode has been analysed by Miller 1984, pp. 126–32, and 1990, pp. 289–94; Byock 1982, pp. 152–4, and 2001, pp. 99–117.

107   On the transfer of land in medieval Iceland, see Miller 1984, p. 126, n. 123, and 1986, p. 47, n. 106.

have been rejected by her husband and lost all chances of remarrying, which would have put her family, represented by her brother, in a grave predicament. In these circumstances, the siblings' bond with a prominent local character such as the priest is for them more valuable than the land, since it implies a certain position within the community and avoids a conflict between families. Just as in *Eyrbyggja saga*, the granting of lands – which is reciprocated with livestock and food – builds a social relationship which does not imply economic exploitation (there is no mention of tributes) but a political alliance between free people, even when the transaction contributes to the accrual of patrimony for one of the parties involved. It follows that this latter phenomenon, which in a general sense accompanies the expansion of feudal relations of exploitation, is rooted in precedents reflecting the social functioning of the peasant mode (the granting of land in return for mediation services), and whose condition of possibility is a property structure that objectively favours these transactions (the existence of individual private property). Byock characterises the property structure in Iceland as 'a system of allodial-type landownership' which protects the rights of the heirs, although the alienation of the property is eventually subject to the wishes or the weakness of the proprietors. Drawing from the episode of *Eyrbyggja saga* (mainly the transfer of lands from Ulfar to Arnkel) and other examples, Byock suggests that the intervention in conflicts is a tactic for the acquisition of land on the part of the chieftains, and that they resort to it depending on the balance of power they envision having if familial claims eventually arise.[108] The author offers examples in which *thingmenn* in trouble transfer lands to their chieftains in order to obtain protection or representation in court.[109] Thus, the potential for dissolution derived from the property form of the peasant mode is expressed in social practices rooted in status disputes, which in turn may suggest the existence of principles of change inherent to the logic of how peasant societies work.

The evolution of this tendency can be observed in some *benefactoria* covenants arising from the need of mediation or representation which lead to the loss of economic autonomy for the clients. These are agreements struck after a crime has been commmitted, which summon the patrons to one of the typical functions of political leaders in peasant mode societies: to help in court cases in which their clients are involved. (This phenomenon could derive from the relative prevalence of a primitive conception of honour, which explains the

---

108   Byock 1982, pp. 148 ff.

109   Byock 2001, pp. 275–81. Payments to chieftains during the support-gathering process were common practice; see Miller 1990, p. 242; also *Njal's saga*, ch. 49, 134, 138.

frequency of homicide among peasants and the resulting need for support in courts of law.)[110] In 1022, Gontoi and his wife cede half of their property to an individual linked to the monastery of Celanova in exchange for his help in a situation involving one of the couple's sons, who has committed adultery. Gontoi and his wife want to avoid the consequences of a lawsuit, and if things were to reach that instance, they want support in court; the document highlights this function of the patron: *abeamus de vobis defensionem et moderationem et in verbo et in facto et in concilio et in benefactoria.*[111]

The ability to convince and persuade with words, which is put to the test in the assembly, distinguishes the leaders in peasant societies and is one of the foundations of their authority. This attribute is associated with the figure of the patron in the cases quoted and originally it may have constituted one of the determining factors for the election of the lord. In the case of the priest who intervenes in a dispute between families, the capacity for persuasion is key to his performance (*et favolastis pro me*); in the other case, instead, the allusion to rhetorical abilities and performance in the assembly (*defensionem in verbo ... et in concilio*) seems to be a formulaic statement attached to the mention of the patron rather than an indication of his specific qualities, which reflects the subordination of the social practice to other contents, or their formal preservation, a prerequisite of their mutation; by acting as mediator (*abeamus de vobis moderationem*) the patron obtains the right to the appropriation of surpluses.[112]

In another case dating to 1012, a certain Daildo is accused of abduction by the king's local agents, count Rodrigo Ordóñez and the father of the victim.[113] Aloiti, the former abbot of Celanova, who has since been transferred to another monastery, shows up at the venue to pay the fine for abduction, perhaps because he had acted as Daildo's patron in prior occasions; in repayment, Daildo offers him two pieces of land, only one of which really belongs to him; the ruse is uncovered and Daildo is accused of calumny and ordered to cede two more pieces of land in replacement of the false one. After the intervention of some men (who, strictly speaking, fulfil the function of mediation), Aloiti takes pity on the man and forgives him with theatrical flair, which means

---

110   On the persistence of the feud culture, see Hyams 2001.

111   Andrade Cernadas 1995, doc. 547 (1022).

112   Andrade Cernadas 1995, doc. 547 (1022): *Et demus vobis per annis singulis ad area et at lagare medietate tam de pane et bibere quam etiam et de omnes fruges quod Dominus in ipsa villa dedit, medium vobis demus et medium remaneat pro nobis.*

113   Andrade Cernadas 1995, doc. 572 (1012).

Daildo ends up losing two properties instead of three.[114] The speech of the one who chairs the assembly, addressed to Aloiti the patron, demonstrates that in this case conflict mediation is perceived as an instrument of social disciplining: *Venistis ad ipsum monasterium ad corregendum, ad salvandum, ad moderandum, ad benefaciendum ad oves Dei que iam disperse erant*. Daildo will carry on cultivating both pieces of land and will give one third of the product to the monastery of Celanova.[115]

In contrast to the first case (the one of the local priest who manages to reconcile two families), in the two latter cases the assignees remain committed to rent payments, which indicates that the clientelar relationship no longer expresses an alliance between free people but the slip into dependency of one of the parties. Furthermore, while in the first case the patron mediated in a conflict between families, in the two latter ones the mediation is aimed at mitigating the effects of the administration of justice on the accused, which go beyond the settlement of the issue with a fine. This motivation, which arises when justice becomes a source of income and an instrument of subordination,[116] contributes to the spread of the practice of ceding lands to the mediators. This tendency illustrates the degradation of the peasant practice in a feudalised context: the gift of lands to compensate the service of prominent jurists, a tool for status negotiation in peasant societies, becomes in the new framework a regular mechanism for the absorption of property and the expansion of feudal relations of exploitation albeit preserving the appearance of the primitive practice, according to which the patrons are presented as capable figures able to successfully steer a cause in the assembly or negotiate an agreement.

The development of relations of exploitation in the area is also manifested in the dispute between fractions of the dominant class over those who have not yet been incorporated into the feudal system: the patrons attempt to protect their free clients from the seigneurial advance of rival powers. In

---

114   Andrade Cernadas 1995, doc. 572 (1012): *Et dum talia vidimus et aures audivimus et non habuimus unde omnia ipsa villa componere per lege, fabulauimus ad homines idoneos qui fabularunt vobis ad misericordia et pro vestra mercede vidistis et intellexistis lacrimis et suspiriis vestris et posuistis aurem ad audiendum, et cor ad intelligendum et dimistis nobis ipsam calumniam de ipsam villam quod abebamus ad duplare.*

115   Andrade Cernadas 1995, doc. 572 (1012): *ut demus vobis pannis singulis ad area et at lagare tercia integra, tam de pane quam de bibere.*

116   Andrade Cernadas 1995, doc. 572 (1012): *et eiecistis nos de illorum manuum et de sua ligamine.* On landownership formation through the exercise of justice see Sánchez Albornoz 1978, ch. 2, and Astarita 2007b, pp. 116 ff.

the following example we will examine the patron's actions in the assembly and outside of it as a result of a crime committed by one of his clients. The case is a homicide involving a client of count Sancho and the monastery of Celanova.[117] Tedón, a *maullatus* of count Sancho, has killed a man from the monastery of Celanova with his lance, for which he is chained and jailed. His wife offers a piece of land as bail and manages to have Tedón's chains removed until his situation is resolved. Once free, Tedón begins to whip up support: he turns to his patron, count Sancho, and tells him his own version of the events, according to which he has been wrongly accused. Infuriated by Tedon's account, the count sends a man to demand an explanation from the abbot;[118] the abbot maintains that Tedón is guilty and the envoy maintains his innocence, so the case is brought to the assembly, where the count, who chairs it, argues with the men of the monastery of Celanova and attempts to defend his client.[119] As a last recourse, the count decides to submit the case to arbitration, so that he can be exonerated; five persons give testimony, after which they proceed to the ordeal of hot water. This turns out a result favourable to the monastery of Celanova, which suggests that Tedón did not have the support of his own community.[120] Tedón and his wife leave the assembly in anguish, perhaps because they expected a different outcome as the count was their ally; in compensation for the homicide they have to cede one piece of land.[121]

The example illustrates the context surrounding the action of mediators, where the administration of justice is a mechanism for the accumulation of patrimony on the part of the accusers, which in this case is not in step with

---

117   Andrade Cernadas 1995, pp. 656–8, doc. 474 (1056). Sánchez Albornoz 1976a, pp. 89–90, has referred to this document, which in his opinion shows patron obligations in a relation of *benefactoria*.

118   Andrade Cernadas 1995, doc. 474 (1056): *Ille comite talia audiente causa non fuit illi placibile, sed exarsit nimis in forore et ira pro suo mallato, que absque veritate iudicaverant et tanta mala sustinuerat. Tunc suscitavit homine bono nomine Sandino ... et direxit ad ille abba pro qua causa talia egisset.*

119   Andrade Cernadas 1995, doc. 474 (1056): *baraliaverunt de ista actio non modica sed multa causa.*

120   For this understanding of the trial by ordeal, see Moore 1987, ch. 4.

121   Andrade Cernadas 1995, doc. 474 (1056): *Illos vero non habuerunt unde ista omnia adimplere, sed molestia detemti tulerunt se de concilio. At ubi iudex vidit talia prosequentes et ad concilio nullatenus venientes mandavit suo saione ut adsignasset ad ille abba et ad suos fratres hereditate de Mortaria sicut et fecit. Et teneant ea usque reddat ipse Tetone et sua mulier ipso omicidio sicut veritas docet.* The land cession to the monastery of Celanova in doc. 475.

the patron's sectoral interest. Quite to the contrary, the count does not wish his client, a free proprietor, to become subjected to a feudal contender, which is why he defends him before the assembly, recreating the political performance of primitive chieftains. Even though the count's intervention does not solve Tedon's predicament in view of the fact that Tedón has to cede a piece of land to the monastery of Celanova, the clientelar bond preserves the forms of peasant practice. The context, however, alters its essential content, since it shifts the patron's action from the sphere of status negotiation to the sphere of competition between fractions of the feudal class and puts at stake the economic autonomy of the client, who loses his condition of proprietor.

In one of the charters of Sahagún, the administration of justice in the locality is a requisite for being elected lord,[122] which indicates that the patron's intervention in his clients' disputes is still a typical practice, however much that practice, as we have observed in other areas, is now oriented to the absorption of properties or the defence of the clientelar base when the one absorbing the properties is a rival power. In turn, the obligation to accompany the patron to the assembly (one of the contents of the *goðar-bœndr* relationship) may have been a part of the service that clients had to render. This was an obligation for *milites* living in land that was not their own, who had to attend the assembly that the landowner attended.[123] There is some evidence of client attendance to assemblies: they show up as witnesses a short time after committing to a patron.[124] These sources point to the fact that the clients, whom we have identified as peasants, have not yet been totally removed from public courts, which confirms the dual character of the society in question.

---

122 Herrero de la Fuente 1988a, doc. 549 (1051): *uadat cum illo a quibus voluerit de heredes mei qui in ipsam villam iussionem habuerint.*

123 Pérez Prendes y Muñoz de Arraco 1988, Fuero de León (O), XXVI: *Si vero miles in Legione in solo alterius casam habuerit, bis in anno eat cum domino soli ad iunctam ... et habeat dominum qualemcumque voluerit.*

124 Herrero de la Fuente 1988a, doc. 549, 635; Herrero de la Fuente 1988b, doc. 826, 836, 887, 985, 818, 851, 1015 and 1031. Citi Pérez appears as a client in 1051 (doc. 549) and as a confirmer in 1063 (doc. 635); Velite Cítiz receives lands in 1086 (doc. 826) and appears in the witness-list one year later (doc. 836); Vela Velázquez acts as a confirmer (doc. 887) three years after receiving lands (doc. 985); Pedro Iústiz accepts lands in 1085 (doc. 818) and appears as a confirmer four years later (doc. 851); after litigation with the abbey, Pedro Cítiz agrees in court his condition of *homine de benefactoria* (doc. 1015); he appears as a confirmer the year after (doc. 1031).

Fosterage

In many cases, the covenants of *benefactoria* formalise fosterage bonds. They involve mostly clients bringing up the children of their patrons, a service for which the patron grants them lands, but we can also attest to bonds in the inverse direction; it can be stated broadly that both clients and patrons acted as fosterers.[125]

The Icelandic sagas offer numerous examples of the fosterage bond, which often seals agreements between families, matrimonial alliances or proposals for reconciliation. Hoskuld, one of the central characters of *Njal's saga*, has been brought up by Njal after his father Thrain was murdered by Skarp-Hedin, Njal's son (we will later address the motives of this murder).[126] After paying compensation for Thrain's death, Njal gifts Hoskuld with a ring and offers to take him home. Njal, a prominent Icelandic jurist, takes care of Hoskuld's education until he becomes a *goði*. In this case, the practice of fosterage complements the *wergeld* and consolidates the reconciliation of the families.

The fosterage bond, as opposed to adoption or *profiliatio*, does not imply heredity rights for the foster-children, although they are frequently endowed with lands; Njal buys lands for Hoskuld to settle in when he gets married. Notwithstanding, although foster-children do not enjoy the same privileges as biological children, they share with them the commitment to uphold the honour of the family that has raised them, which generally implies committing to blood vengeance.[127] In Hoskuld's case, the opportunity to act to redress his foster family's dishonour presents itself with the murder of Njal's natural son. Skarp-Hedin cannot conceive of a solution other than direct vengeance and he murders two of the participants, but a third one who manages to escape sues for reconciliation and obtains it through the intermediation of Hoskuld, who is by now the most renowned *goði* in the district. Skarp-Hedin will never forgive Hoskuld for having interceded in favour of an enemy of the family: this bad blood is behind the events that some time later lead to Skarp-Hedin's murder of the peaceful Hoskuld. Even though Hoskuld's death, unlike other deaths, is presented in the saga as a tragic event, it still reflects the social functioning: Hoskuld has failed to fulfil his duty toward the family that raised him.

Njal's saga also provides examples of members of high-ranking families being fostered by servants. Skarp-Hedin has been brought up by Thord, the son

---

125   *Multi eorum erant nutricii et alumpni militum ... et nutriebant filios et filias eorum,* cited by
        Alfonso 2002, p. 250.

126   *Njal's saga,* ch. 94.

127   Rose 1926. For references on fosterage in a variety of primitive societies, see Parkes 2003,
        pp. 741–82.

of a freedman. Thord becomes involved in one of Skarp-Hedin's disputes. When Thord's assassins (accompanied by Thrain, Hoskuld's father, who observes the scene) ambush him, they allude to the warlike qualities that Thord has passed on to Skarp-Hedin. Thord replies that those qualities will be put to the test because Skarp-Hedin will repay the gift he received by avenging the death of his foster-father.[128] In the dialogue between Thord and his assassins lies implicit the substance of gift-exchange according to Mauss, for whom the spiritual force attributed to the gift drives its return to the giver.[129] This is also implied in Hoskuld's acceptance of the ring and Njal's protection as gestures of the same nature; Hoskuld does not properly return the gift he accepted and therein lies the cause of his death. In the case of Skarp-Hedin and his foster-father Thord, even though Thord is a servant, his death causes Skarp-Hedin to become personally implicated, and despite having obtained compensation he fulfils the blood vengeance by slaying all the participants (including Thrain, whom he murders twenty years later);[130] thus, Skarp-Hedin upholds the rules of his society. The importance of Thord's death in the saga's narrative structure is a testimony to the hierarchy of the fosterage bond in peasant mode societies.

From the perspective of social competition, a principle of social imbalance is implicit in the circulation of individuals among households.[131] The foster-age bond of non-related persons is considered as a form of clientelar alliance between families of different rank, and a key political tool in the struggle between rival factions and clans.[132] In medieval Ireland, the delivery of children to subordinates is complemented with gifts of lands, in exchange for which the givers obtain the clients' political allegiance, military services and hospit-ality.[133]

---

128   *Njal's saga*, ch. 42:

    Sigmund said to him, 'Give yourself up, for now it is time for you to die'.

    'Certainly not', said Thord. 'Come and fight me in single combat'.

    'Certainly not', said Sigmund. 'We shall make use of our advantage in numbers. It's not surprising that Skarp-Hedin is so formidable, since the saying goes that one-fourth comes from the foster-father'.

    'You shall see the full force of that', said Thord, 'for Skarp-Hedin will avenge me'.

129   Mauss 1954, pp. 61–2. For criticisms, see Godelier 1999; Sahlins 1972, ch. 4; Wagner-Hasel 2003, among others. Mauss's explanation is valid for Gurevich 1985, ch. 2; see also Gurevich 1992a.

130   *Njal's saga*, ch. 92.

131   Miller 1990, pp. 122–4 and 171–4; Gurevich 1992a, pp. 187–8.

132   Parkes 2003, pp. 753 ff.

133   Parkes 2006, pp. 363.

The upbringing of the children of patrons is a characteristic practice of the *benefactoria* relationship. In 1102 an individual sells a piece of land he had obtained from count Pedro Ansúrez in compensation for having fostered his children.[134] Some authors have suggested that in this example the fosterage bond can be understood within the frame of vassalage, which would include the military instruction of the lord's children by his vassals.[135] However, as we shall explain, these are differentiated bonds involving distinct social segments.

In 1064, countess Mumadonna cedes lands to Velite Álvarez, a family servant, so that he may cultivate them.[136] Velite reciprocates the gift with a horse, a greyhound and a hound, suggesting that despite being a servant he holds a special position, which could be explained by the fact that he has fostered Mumadonna's son, count Pedro Muñoz. Four years later the count initiates proceedings to endow Velite with lands: he requests lands from Alfonso VI, a fact that could suggest a relative patrimonial weakness of the comital aristocracy while also demonstrating the importance they attributed to clientelar bonds, which comprised land donations for their servants. Alfonso VI gives the count, whom he calls *fideli meo*, the lands he had requested for Velite, *amo tuo* in the words of the king.[137] This indicates that the count has used his bond of vassalage with the king in order to build a relationship of *benefactoria* with his foster-father. Once the land is transferred to the count, he in turn grants it to Velite, who will be free to choose his lord. In both transactions, the one who receives the land (first the count and then Velite) repays the donation with horses, which places servants and aristocrats in the same plane. Finally, should Velite die without heirs the land will pass on to the monastery of Sahagún for the salvation of his soul, that of his patron and the king's, since the latter provided the land.[138] The bond of vassalage between the count and the king is not confused with the fosterage relationship; at most it could be argued that it conditions the relationship between the count and his foster-father: it allows the former to

---

134   Herrero de la Fuente 1988b, doc. 1086 (1102): *Et habui ego Citi Albariz ipso solare de incartacione de comite Pedro Ansuriz et de sua mulier, propter filios eorum que ego nutriui ... Facio tibi carta per tale foro quomodo ille comes michi fecit et vadas cum eo ubi volueris, tu et filius tuus et omnis progenie tua.*

135   Barton 1997, p. 47. Also Morsel 2008, pp. 83–4, suggests that fosterage was an aristocratic practice aimed at the consolidation of friendly relationships.

136   Herrero de la Fuente 1988a, doc. 638 (1064): *tibi criado nostro ... Et damus cum eos foro ... et ares quantum potueris.*

137   Herrero de la Fuente 1988a, doc. 675 (1068): *Do tibi ista corte quam michi petisti pro ad amo tuo Velliti Albaret.*

138   Herrero de la Fuente 1988a, doc. 675 and 676 (1068).

endow with lands and it imposes on the latter the obligation to transfer it *post mortem* to another sector of the aristocracy. This comes to fruition forty years later;[139] thus, a clientelar practice (land endowment to compensate fosterage services) contributes to the formation of church patrimony.

The participation of servants in the fosterage relationship and the special esteem in which they are held by their lords, as seen in *Njal's saga*, help us understand the gifts of land to dependents with whom aristocrats have established clientelar bonds. While in the first gift Velite is subject to providing labour services, in the second gift (the count's through Alfonso VI) no rents are mentioned, which allows for the interpretation of the covenant as a promotion compensating Velite for his fosterage of the count; indeed, Velite will be able to freely dispose of the lands he were to obtain through purchase or other methods,[140] which sets him apart from the servile condition.[141] The promotion of unfree persons who have acted as fosterers is a common occurrence: in 1155 countess Elvira Velázquiz grants freedom to the family who raised her, stipulating they can 'go wherever they want' and not pay tribute (*a nullo homine obsequium reddant*).[142] The donations granted to *collazos*, generally considered servile dependents, who reciprocate the gift of lands with swords,[143] can also be understood in similar terms; it has also been suggested that this word derives from *collacteus*, whose primitive sense is associated with artificial kinship.[144]

In these examples the covenant of *benefactoria* is a formula for the promotion of dependent individuals with whom the aristocracy maintains an ambivalent bond ranging from the demand for rents to the compensation for other types of services. In this sense, the predominance of the feudal mode of production is compatible with the persistence of archaic customs among members

---

139   Herrero de la Fuente 1988b, doc. 1155 (1107).

140   Herrero de la Fuente 1988a, doc. 675 (1068): *ut habeat ipsa corte cum omni hereditate que ad ipso solare pertinet; et quantum super hoc ganauerit uel plantauerit uel hedificauerit uel etiam comparauerit, liberam habeat possidendi potestatem.*

141   Pérez Prendes y Muñoz de Arraco 1988, Fuero de León (0), tit. x. On this norm, see Sánchez Albornoz 1976b, pp. 221–49.

142   Muñoz y Romero 1847, p. 162: *Et dedit mihi illa comitesa dona Gelvira de quam fuit criatione, facio vobis cartam ingenuitatis et libertatis, ut redeunde, vivendi, laremque fovendi vitam vestram ubi volueritis.*

143   Herrero de la Fuente 1988b, doc. 887 (1092).

144   According to Estepa Díez 2003, p. 52, those who gave this kind of gifts would actually be *milites*. This is hard to accept in the case of Velite Álvarez, to whom labour services were imposed.

of the aristocracy, who should not be viewed as external agents of the social practice they modify but rather as social actors who still partake in some of its contents which they partially negate.

In some cases, the land recipient has been brought up by the patron. In 1059, Diego Pátriz accepts lands from his foster-father, who is a member of a comital family. The text specifies that he will not be allowed to serve another lord as long as his patron is alive.[145] More than thirty years later, Diego Pátriz cedes the land to the monastery of Sahagún for the salvation of his soul and to free himself from all 'human service',[146] which means his sons, who retain usufruct, will be subject to seigneurial exploitation. Our client, who deems that the obligations often imposed by the abbot are very stringent – a perspective that sets him apart from the relation of serfdom – requests that his children be afforded some consideration when they are taxed, and that they be allowed to serve as knights if they have a horse.[147] It follows that this must have been the service he provided for his own patron, and that he has not been able to knight his sons, which leads us to deduce that he is of peasant origin. The example illustrates the precarious situation of some of the parties in these agreements (peasants eventually equipped with horses) and the loss of their economic autonomy over the course of two generations, a tendency that must be considered in conjunction with that of social advancement. The degradation of the political autonomy of the clients characteristic of the evolution of these bonds, is combined with mechanisms of accumulation specific to another sector of the aristocracy (the absorption of lands through grants *pro anima*), just as in the case of the count's foster-father examined above, which suggests that the evolution of clientelar relations has been subordinated to the global reproduction of the dominant class.

Fosterage bonds, as we have seen in *Njal's saga*, are binding. This content favours the consolidation of stable links and could explain the lasting quality of the covenants, an aspect that contradicts the theoretical ability to change allegiances. Witness the case examined above, where the client serves his

---

145   Herrero de la Fuente 1988a, doc. 606 (1059): *Facio cartulam donationis ... de hereditate mea propria quam habui ex patre meo comite Guttier Afonso ... Do et dono ipso solare tibi suprascripto Diaco propter creacionem quam sub Deo creaui te et propter seruicium bono ... Tantum in diebus nostris non permitto te seruire cum illo alio domno.*

146   Herrero de la Fuente 1988b, doc. 909 (1093): *non solum pro remedio anima mee, verum etiam et ut ego sim liber in omnia vita mea de omni servicio humano.*

147   Herrero de la Fuente 1988b, doc. 909 (1093): *Et filii mei non subiugati tam stricti sint in servicio sicut ceteri, sed ut tantummodo ponant XIIm dies in anno ad servicium domni abbatis; quos si habuerit kavallos serviant sicut kavallarii.*

patron and foster-father for life, not only by virtue of the land he is gifted but also by virtue of a bond of family loyalty obliging him to assume his patron's enmities and remain at his service. This double commitment is palpable in the services he calls 'human services' that he has provided for his foster-father for over thirty years, as distinguished from the tribute demanded by the abbot of Sahagún, which he considers a form of subjection (*et filii mei non subiugati tam stricti sint in servicio sicut ceteri*).

A privilege granted by Alfonso VI to the monastery of Samos prohibiting *milites* from having vassals *per amatiatum sive criandum* and punishing the locals who raised the children of *milites* confirms the spread of fosterage bonds during the eleventh century. This suggests that the inhabitants resorted to this bond to avoid their obligations toward the monastery,[148] and that it was habitual for *milites* and peasants to establish dealings of this kind, which the abbot suppresses in his attempt to impose his lordship over the place. From this we can deduce that the fosterage bond is distinguishable from a relation of exploitation, even when the child-giver and the feudal lord are designated with the same word (*qui se amo fecerit vel qui se in alium dominum transtulerit, ad dominum monasterii reducat*), which supports the notion that it is derived from practices of the peasant mode.

The type of relationship established between families linked by fosterage bonds also explains why clients become involved in their patrons' disputes. The twelfth-century regulations address this issue: a decree of Alfonso IX forbids lords from seizing property belonging to clients of other lords due to debts or enmities that the interested parties could hold against their patrons unless the clients were armed with lances.[149] It follows from this that military support was the norm among clients even if they were not fully equipped, and that they were vulnerable to the aggression of their patrons' enemies even if they did not participate in military activities. The fact that seigneurial behaviour toward someone else's clients is regulated points to a qualitative change, given that it transfers the problem from the sphere of conflict between families, which implicated clients in their patrons' disputes, to the sphere of the conflict between lords whose main bone of contention are the clients of rival lords and their possessions.

---

148 De Hinojosa 1919, p. 96: *Et si aliquis filius militis ibi nutritor vel aliquis ibi se posuit sub alio domino nisi sub domino samonensis, mando isti homini meo, quod filium militis, qui in cautos samonensis nutritor, foras de cautos eiciat.*

149 De Hinojosa 1919, p. 148: *quod nullus pignoret benefactoriam pro debito vel inimicitia domine benefactorie, nisi ipse beneficiatus fuerit lancearius.*

The link between the *benefactoria* and the practice of fosterage is confirmed in documents from the later Middle Ages related to *behetrías* (lordships derived from relations of *benefactoria*) which regulate aspects related to intra-lordly conflict: a fifteenth-century ordinance urges neighbours to defend the ruling lord from the interference of other powers; it stipulates that should a neighbour die in these circumstances, the local council shall raise his children.[150] This late example reflects the residual survival of peasant practices voided of substance, where the involvement of neighbours in their leaders' disputes no longer expresses a clientelar bond but the exercise of political rights on the part of the lord, which oblige the locals to fight in the ranks of the magnate whose lordship over the area is at stake.

The Power to Choose a Lord

Instability is a characteristic feature of the leaderships in peasant mode societies. In Iceland, each free man who is the head of a household must be attached to a *goði*, whom he can both choose and abandon. The *goði's* authority, regardless of the heritability of the position, depends on his ascendancy over the men attached to his leadership, who can withdraw their allegiance and attach themselves to another chieftain.[151] We have reviewed an example from *Eyrbyggja saga*, when Thorolf transfers his allegiance to Snorri *goði*. *Njal's saga* provides a paradigmatic case: Mord, who has inherited his position as *goði*, loses all his followers to Hoskuld (Njal's foster-son); the site where the assembly used to be held, normally equipped with makeshift structures, is in a state of neglect because when changing allegiances the men have shifted to the location where their chosen chieftain holds the assembly.[152] The community has real existence when the individual proprietors gather in an assembly;[153] concomitantly, the authority has real existence only when the leader enjoys the effective support of the individual proprietors: when losing his followers, Mord also loses the powers of the chieftaincy over which he holds hereditary rights.

The texts regulating *benefactoria* relations refer to the faculty to elect a lord for the subscribers of a covenant, the recipients of a *fuero* or those who accept

---

150   Oliva Herrer 2003, p. 201.
151   On chieftancies in medieval Iceland, see Chris Wickham's chapter in this book. See also Jón Viðar Sigurðsson 1995, p. 155; Helgui Þorláksson 2005, pp. 139–40; Byock 2001, pp. 119–20 and 126–8.
152   *Njal's saga*, ch. 107.
153   Marx 1964, p. 78.

gifts of land. This faculty is addressed in the legislation.[154] In general, the covenants of eleventh-century Castile and León do not contain restrictions regarding the clients' bonds: the typical expressions are *vadas cum eo ubi volueris*, or *ad unos aut alios domnos, qui tibi bene fecerit*, etc. These formulae reflect an acknowledgement of the land recipient's free condition (or his promotion to a free condition), seeing as one of the attributes of freedom is the ability to change allegiance.

In a majority of the charters, the subscriber of this type of covenant can in theory abandon the chosen lord and is free to lend his support to different members of the aristocracy.[155] He can choose, for example 'a king, a count, a bishop, an abbot, in Castile, in Galicia',[156] that is to say, he will pick his lord from the pool of the aristocracy and without geographical limits. In other charters the aristocratic spectrum is identified with the two main lineages, that of Banu Mirel and that of Alfonso Díaz.[157] Although this limitation restricts the number of potential patrons, in theory those who present certain qualities are eligible, as happens in peasant societies (in Iceland, for example, the men choose a chieftain from among a limited number of *goðar*), which acknowledeges that clients hold a certain political protagonism. This criterion undergoes a shift when patrons take the side of one of the two main lineages on referring to the election of a lord, thus constraining significantly the spectrum of possible political alliances for their clients.[158] Finally the election of a lord will be restricted to the patron's lineage.[159] In certain cases the patrons restrict their clients' bonds to specific persons of their family group: Urraca, a member of the lineage of Alfonso Díaz, stipulates that the individual to whom she

---

154   Pérez Prendes y Muñoz de Arraco 1988, Fuero de León (o), tit. XIII: *Praecipimus adhuc, ut homo qui est de benefactoria, cum omnibus bonis et haereditatibus suis eat liber quocumque voluerit.*

155   Herrero de la Fuente 1988a, doc. 566 (1054), 624 (1063), 634 (1063), 676 (1068), 702 (1071), 713 (1072), 719 (1973); Herrero de la Fuente 1988b, 737 (1074), 778 (1080), 788 (1080), 795 (1081), 818 (1085), 824 (1086), 825 (1086), 887 (1092), 1015 (1097), 1086 (1102), 1173 (1085); Fernández Flórez 1991, doc. 1189 (1113), 1198 (1117), 1252 (1133); Ruiz Asencio 1987, doc. 894 (1031); Ruiz Asencio 1990, doc. 1233 (1084).

156   Herrero de la Fuente 1988b, doc. 804 (1083).

157   Herrero de la Fuente 1988b, doc. 752 (1077).

158   Herrero de la Fuente 1988b, doc. 1077 (1101): *Vadatis cum illo inter filios et neptos de Vani Mirelliz*; doc. 811 (1084): *inter casata de Vani Mirel ad quale tibi melius fecerit*; Ruiz Asencio 1990, doc. 1192 (1073): *et vadeas cum eo medio die et media ora inter Vani Mirel qui tiui melior fecerit tu et filiis tuis et neptis tuis vel viisneptis.*

159   Herrero de la Fuente 1988b, doc. 1096 (1103), 1125 (1105), 826 (1086), 893 (1092), 959 (1095); Herrero de la Fuente 1988a, doc. 549 (1051).

has ceded lands, Rexendo, will be allowed to choose among the children and grandchildren of two of her brothers, the daughters of one sister, and the men of the monastery of Sahagún.[160] According to the data available on this family, Rexendo will be able to choose from among twenty people. This evolution tending to the limitation of the clients' allegiances is also evidenced when patrons secure services until their deaths.[161]

The imposition of serving one lord for life and remaining within the orbit of one family reflects the infusion of new meaning into the peasant practice, which tends to place itself at the service of feudal logic while preserving the vocabulary of liberty. The relative independence of the remaining free peasantry in a feudalised context accounts for the preservation of the formula regarding the election of the lord and also the successive curtailments it undergoes in practice, which are progressively incorporated into the texts. This process is enabled by some contents of the peasant practice. The fosterage bond, for example, facilitates the patron's tendency to restrict the circle of eligible lords to his family members. When the patron is both lord and child-giver, foster-son or foster-father, the essential content of the fosterage bond stimulates the formation of permanent clienteles and contributes to the degradation of the political autonomy of free proprietors. It follows that some aspects of the dynamics of the peasant mode can promote an evolution to more stable bonds, which contributes to the readaptation of social practice to the requisites of aristocratic dominance.

The tendency to restrict the election of the lord to members of the patron's own lineage is nascent during the eleventh century and dominant in the twelfth century, when *benefactoria* relationships no longer refer to individuals but to communities as a whole, which, for their part, have constituted themselves legally as such as inferred from the references to local authorities. The inhabitants of Andaluz, for instance, will choose a lord from among the kinsmen of the count who has granted them a set of norms.[162] The election of the lord has now become a collective practice: the community will have to choose

---

160 Herrero de la Fuente 1988a, doc. 620 (1062): *Et post mortem meam uadas inter filios et neptos de fratribus meis domno Monio et domno Gutier aut inter filias de domna Adosinda, soror mea, nominatas Goto et Monia, aut a domnos de Sancto Facundo, uel qui tibi melior fecerit.*

161 Herrero de la Fuente 1988a, 606 (1059), 620 (1062), 721 (1073); Herrero de la Fuente 1988b, doc. 952 and 953 (1095), 728 (1074).

162 Fuero de Andaluz: *hayan behetría entre mis fijos e mis nietos e en todo mi linaie*, cited by Sánchez-Albornoz 1976b, p. 209. This *fuero* is a translation from the original Latin version to Romance, available at: http://es.wikisource.org/wiki/Fuero_de_la_Comunidad _de_Villa_y_Tierra_de_Andaluz_de_1098.

the one preferred by the majority.[163] The higher powers' interest in disciplining the political bonds of the community is evidenced in the twelfth-century
legislation: in 1104, count García Ordóñez prohibits the coexistence of diverging alliances in Fresnillo, forcing the locals to choose from among one of his
descendants.[164] The same preoccupation is observed in the laws imposed on
the people of Escalona in 1130, which tend to standardise the allegiances of the
neighbours and restrict them to the family of the local *dominus*.[165] The *fuero* of
Belbimbre of 1187 attempts to suppress the establishment of multiple alliances
in the same village by stipulating that the locals should not submit to more
than one lord.[166] The same law allows *milites* to attach themselves to a lord of
their choosing,[167] which confirms that the ability to choose one's lord is associated with freedom, and that in the twelfth century this concept is becoming
exclusively identified with a privilege.

The Practice of Hospitality and the Requirement of Tribute
Contributing to the support of the itinerant court is a public burden, just as
military service and attendance to the assembly; it is likely that the supply of
victuals for the lord when he passed through a locality constituted an informal
service not expressly mentioned in the texts. This practice is consistent with
services rendered by the clients, which we have understood as derived from
the forms of reciprocal exchange typical of the peasant mode. In one of the
Sahagún documents, the gift of lands is repaid with bread, wine, clothes and
shoes,[168] which could have symbolised hospitality, in the same way that horses

---

163   Sánchez Albornoz 1976b, Fuero de Andaluz: *Et ser todos dun sennor et do fueren la mayor
      partida que vayan los otros.*

164   De Hinojosa 1919, p. 47, Fuero de Fresnillo, tit. 13: *Et non intretis in temptacione nec
      particione, sed abeatis benefectria cum vestras causas ad filiis nostris vel neptis seu ad
      qualem vobis placuerit aut meliore fecerit, ut ipsi serviatis.*

165   Muñoz y Romero 1847, p. 485: *Vos vero in diebus nostris non eritis divisi et post nostram
      mortem et filiis nostris cui volueritis et melior vobis fecerit, ipse servite cum omnia vestra
      bona.*

166   Martínez Díez 1982, p. 179, Fuero de Belbimbre y sus cuatro aldeas, year 1187, tit. 9: *Omnes
      habitatores ... unius tantum domini prestamerii adhereatis, et nulli liceat uos per partes
      diuidere, aud plurium dominorum dominatui subicere.*

167   Martínez Díez 1982, Fuero de Belbimbre y sus cuatro aldeas (1187), tit. 5: *Preterea omnibus
      uobis qui milites fueritis in Beneuiuere et in predictis quatuor barriis indulgeo et concedo
      quod nullam facenderam pectetis, et habeatis dominos quales habere uolueritis et domos
      uestras liberas possideatis.*

168   Herrero de la Fuente 1988b, doc. 824 (1086): *Accepimus de uobis in pretio, in pane et in vino
      et in vestire et in calcare, apreciatura in* CL *solidos.*

and swords symbolised military service. The possession of military tenancies carries the obligation to offer meals to the lord when he passes through the territory.[169] According to the literature on this subject, hospitality services are a part of the duties of those who take in foster-children and receive lands in exchange for their loyalty.[170] These are the services referred to in the documents on primitive *behetrías*, according to which the knights 'ate the victuals they found'.[171]

The transition from military obligations and voluntary contributions of food to the payment of agrarian rents has been considered in relation to the emergence of feudal relations of exploitation. Carlos Astarita has proposed that this transition is reflected in imprecise formulae in which the tribute is not yet conceived of as a regular exaction, nor has it acquired yet a stable composition; instead there is a prevalence of demands whose manner takes into account the will of the inhabitants (*quantum poterint ad comite*, etc.).[172] In the tribal societies of Northern Europe, the transition to the feudal mode is seen, according to Wickham, in the mutation of the 'tribal' tribute, a light contribution, into rents that are more complex, more onerous and susceptible to commercialisation; another expression of this transition to relations of exploitation is the demand for hospitality tributes by a growing number of persons.[173] In what concerns our analysis, the transformation of the services rendered by clients into agrarian rents represents the full incorporation of these individuals and their social forms into the dominant feudal dynamic of the area, which constitutes one aspect of the general process of expansion of feudalism over free spaces.

The demand for rents of a definite kind appears associated with the *benefactoria* in documents from the early twelfth century. In 1125, the norms imposed on the people of San Cebrián, who are allowed to choose their lord,[174] establish the amounts due as rent. The villagers are exempted from some taxes and the fine for homicide is cut in half; in exchange, they must hand over thirty loaves of bread, a certain amount of wine, and one side of bacon or one ram as long

---

169   García de Valdeavellano 1955 (Apéndice documental, doc. XII): *unum prandium semel in anno de debito in omnibus expensis, si contigerit me facere transitum per terram illam.*

170   Parkes 2006, p. 363.

171   López de Ayala 1991, p. 42 (Crónica de Don Pedro I, II, ch. XIV).

172   Astarita 2003–6, p. 34.

173   Wickham 2005, pp. 344–9.

174   De Hinojosa 1919, Fuero de San Cebrián, year 1125: *Do vobis benefetria ... ut tornetis ad qualem seniorem volueritis quem villa mandauerit.*

as they are able to obtain these products from their labour.[175] This condition could reflect a formative stage of the new social relations (the imposition of burdens on free people), in which the tribute, compulsory and defined as it is, preserves on paper its character as a more or less flexible supply of food. The delivery of agrarian surpluses is formally presented as a reciprocal exchange: the lord must treat the council to a meal.[176] It is noteworthy that although a tribute is being imposed on direct producers, hospitality is ostensibly an obligation of the lord, which allows for a transfer of surplus while preserving the formality of reciprocity. Just as in the case of previously examined practices, the dominant feudal logic of the area introduces new content while leaving intact the appearance of the custom, although in this case, in contrast to the early eleventh-century covenants, the archaic references are marginal, and the new contents reflect the full incorporation of these social forms into the feudal mode of production. In the locality of Andaluz, for instance, the rents that the locals will pay are established; the villagers can choose a lord from among the kinsmen of the count who has granted them a *fuero*; he who is chosen shall hold a feast for the community.[177] The continuance of food services on the part of the lord and the feasts he holds for the villagers who have chosen or accepted him as lord could have their precedent in the collective celebrations of peasant societies. In *Laxdœla saga* this practice is related to the need of legitimation: the feast that Olaf the Peacock, a renowned *goði*, holds for a large crowd of people in memory of his late father, who favoured Olaf in the distribution of the inheritance despite his being an illegitimate son, is aimed at Olaf's public validation as truly deserving his father's favour and the support the latter enjoyed.[178]

In the twelfth century these public feasts are replaced with money payments from the lord. The *fuero* of Lara of 1135, for example, obliges the people to deliver meat for the lord and his retinue when they visit the locality; the local authorities shall appraise the victuals and the lord shall pay for them, otherwise the villagers can deprive him of the food without being penalised.[179] Here we

---

175   De Hinojosa 1919, Fuero de San Cebrián, tit. 15: *Si colegerit de sua heriditate det istum forum, et si non colegerit non det … si habuerit porcos aut oves det, et si non habuerit non det.*

176   De Hinojosa 1919, Fuero de San Cebrián, tit. 12: *Et dominus det concilio … unum iantarem.*

177   Sánchez Albornoz 1976b, Fuero de Andaluz, 1.

178   *Laxdœla saga*, ch. 27.

179   Martínez Díez 1982, p. 141, Fuero de Lara, year 1135, tit. 38: *Quando uenerit dominus Lare in illam ciuitatem, accipiat ille iudex cum suo saione karne por espesa, et aprecient illam karnem homines de conceio, et det fidiatore* [in blank] *merino et pectet eum; nisi non dederit fidiatore illo merino, tollat eum et non habeat calumnia.*

observe on the one hand the conversion of feasts offered by the lord into money payments, and on the other hand the conversion of the spontaneous hospitality of the villagers into an obligation.

The reference to hospitality service in twelfth-century texts, which regulate the election of the lord or refer to this right, confirm that it was common practice to provide hospitality for the lord, and that it was beginning to be regulated during the period in question. This regulation sets limits pertaining to the group of service providers, which tend to be identified with peasant labourers: the 1135 *fuero* of Lara exempts those who own a horse and clergy from the obligation to provide shelter;[180] the *fuero* of Villadiego exempts knights and priests;[181] the set of norms imposed on the inhabitants of Villavicencio in 1156 frees knights from the obligation to house the lord.[182]

This legislation by which the obligation to provide shelter falls only on the farm labourers coexists with another in which the will of the latter is ambiguously contemplated, and at the same time it becomes apparent that hospitality services are being demanded by force. In the *fuero* of Escalona of 1130 we read: *posadas per forcia, non donent.*[183] In a study on the Latin vocabulary in Carolingian documents, Kuchenbuch suggests that the verb *donare*, which is rarely used and associated with *mansi ingenuiles*, could be an indicator of the higher status of the people from whom tribute is being demanded, and that its use could reflect new impositions.[184] According to this perspective, our example could reflect the tendency to impose hospitality services on people who had not previously been subjected to taxation. The inhabitants of Villavicencio must also 'donate' a certain amount of food and 'no more, unless they do so of their own accord'.[185] The ambivalent wording in the demands for this type of encumbrance from free people, which references both the will of the villagers and

180   Martínez Díez 1982, Fuero de Lara, year 1135, tit. 44: *Quando uenerit dominus Lare in illam ciuitatem, per mano de illo saione accipiant illos caualleros posadas, et non posent in casa de qui cauallo ouiere, necque in casa de uidua necque in casa de clerico, nisi fuerit clericus.*

181   Martínez Díez 1982, p. 137, Fuero de Villadiego, year 1134, tit. 13: *Et in casa de cauallero neque de clerigo neque de vidua non posset nullus homo.*

182   Muñoz y Romero 1847, p. 176, Fuero de Villavicencio: *Et qui pausare voluerit in illa villa, pauset in suis et postquam casas de suos homines fuerint plenas pausent per alios, set non in casa de caballero.*

183   Muñoz y Romero 1847, p. 487, Fuero de Escalona.

184   Kuchenbuch 2003, pp. 206–9.

185   Muñoz y Romero 1847, Fuero de Villavicencio, year 1156: *Donet pro suo foro decem panes, et media kanatellam de vino, et uno quarto de carnero, et duos lombos non magis, nisi sua sponte.*

seigneurial violence, is observed in the *fuero* of Belbimbre of 1187, which stipulates that the lord shall not break into the judge's house[186] and contemplates
the wishes of the host after three days of compulsory housing.[187]

The regulation of hospitality services involving the obligations of both lords
and peasants as well as lordly abuse is more fully developed in laws related to
lordships of *behetría* which spell out in detail the manner in which taxpayers
must provide food, clothing and accomodation to their lords and the payments
the latter must render for the victuals, which must be consumed *in situ*.[188] The
texts regulating these services allude to certain older legislation whose existence historians have verified and dated to the period between 1184 and 1185.[189]
This legislation, whose spirit is consistent with the laws of that period, may
be derived from the need to regulate the people's relations with the noblemen
among whom they picked a lord, probably members of the lineage with more
influence in the area, who attempt to formalise their condition as potential
lords and materialise in defined rents their right to be chosen as such.

During the twelfth century, the hospitality services, which everyone must
render on principle, tend to become concentrated in one social sector defined
by its exclusion from privilege and to be demanded by an increasing number
of persons; the regularity and composition of the service are established albeit
preserving the ceremonial aspect of reciprocity on the part of the lord, whose
prodigality is limited first to public feasts and later to money payments to the
service providers. This conventional generosity of the lord could be linked to his
symbolic legitimation as tax levier, which comes into being through practices
that are formally analogous to the ones that secured his leadership in the
pre-class society.

---

186   Martínez Díez 1982, Fuero de Belbimbre y sus cuatro aldeas (1187), tit. 17: *In domo iudicis
      nullus dominus uiolenter hospitetur.*

187   Martínez Díez 1982, Fuero de Belbimbre y sus cuatro aldeas (1187), tit. 10: *In quacumque
      domo prestamerum hospitali contingerit ... ultra trium dierum spacium contra uoluntatem
      hospitis sui prestamerus solo uno momento moram non faciat.*

188   *Códigos españoles concordados y anotados*: Fuero Viejo de Castilla and Ordenamiento
      de Alcalá de Henares de 1348 (hereafter FVC and OA). Lords must pay what they have
      consumed (FVC, I, VIII, 1); local inhabitants must report themselves, otherwise they will
      be punished (FVC, I, VIII, 2); lords will demand hospitality, foodstuff and clothing (FVC,
      I, VIII, 3); straw for their horses and wine (FVC, I, VIII, 1), firewood (FVC, I, VIII, 4), and
      vegetables (FVC, I, VIII, 5); the whole process shall be supervised by *boni homines* in order
      to prevent lordly abuse (OA, XXXII, XXVIII).

189   OA, XXXII; Barbero and Loring García 1991, pp. 27 ff.

Conclusions

In contrast to the criterion employed by Wickham to conceptualise exploitative modes of production by which they are reduced to forms of surplus extraction, his concept of the peasant mode accounts for the elements intervening in the productive process, for relations of production and property, for the logic of social functioning and the conditions for its genesis, reproduction and transformation. The elements deriving from the disposition of the product (low intensity of labour, reciprocity) are consistent with those of 'primitive' societies in different historical contexts. It follows that productive forces, and even relations of production, do not singularise a mode of production. A mode of production, according to the *Formen*, implies a form of property at its base. From this perspective, the peasant mode as it appears in Western Europe can be basically identified with the Germanic mode, which is why it could be conceived of as a re-elaboration of the latter devoted mainly to developing aspects of its functioning laws. These elements were assessed on the analytic level of the social formation, since they allow for the characterisation of the forms of articulation between the aristocracy and free communities, and in our case highlight the process of subordination of the latter to the feudal mode of production.

This process undergoes different stages characterised by the formal preservation of peasant mode practices and the progressive negation of its contents – or the subordination of the practice to already existing mechanisms of accumulation. Peasant practices, in turn, contain elements that favour the advance of the feudal logic. The gifts of lands in return for services of mediation and representation, a tool for status negotiation in peasant societies, become functional to the formation of aristocratic patrimony; the practice of fosterage, founded on reciprocity, contributes to the stabilisation of bonds. To the extent that this is achieved and political structure becomes less dependent on the conformity and support of peasant sectors (or, as Engels would put it, to the extent that social functions become independent from society), the aristocratic logic finds more space to deploy itself more openly. This is evidenced in the spread of oppressive practices on free people, which could explain the mutation of spontaneous contributions of victuals into hospitality rents that the lords seize by force in the period prior to their regulation. Thus, the condition of possiblity of seigneurial violence that historians associate with the rise of banal lordship would have been an earlier period of symbolic violence and reworking of the peasant practice during which stable bonds of subordination were consolidated.

The transformation of free clients into tenants subject to rent or feudal vassals is one of the forms of expansion of feudalism. Since in our case we begin with a social formation in which the aristocracy coexists with autonomous nuclei, the advance over these nuclei by means of the recruitment of vassals among the peasantry or the conversion of free clients into taxpayers reflects the dissolution of peasant societies and therefore the transition from one mode of production to another. This transition can be explained by the prevalence of individual private property susceptible to disposition and fragmentation which characterises the peasant mode at its base and underlies the social practices reflecting its social functioning. These social practices feature transactions involving land, which in turn implies the individual's emancipation from community and kin. Furthermore, the social functioning of the peasant mode, based on the logic of the gift, constrains the possibilities of accruing wealth and requires costly strategies on the part of those who attempt to build or maintain a position of power, which must rest on material concessions, respect for custom and mechanisms invoking the ideology of reciprocity. Even though in societies where feudalism has developed the peasant mode holds a subordinate position in the social formation, its principles condition the actions of the aristocracy. This delays the expansion of the new social relations and determines its modalities, which we have characterised as gradual and ambivalent.

Both the form of property and the social relations of the peasant mode carry evolutionary tendencies (to dispossession in the former, and to conservation or slow pace of accumulation in the latter) that combine in the historical process, as we have demonstrated in the empirical study of clientelar relations in Northern Spain, whose transformation into exploitative forms drags on for over a century and involves strategies of concession toward the free peasantry. These tendencies depict a dynamic proper to the peasant mode which is not contingent but derived from the structural traits of this mode of production: it is contained in the asymmetric substance of the gift and the potentialities of individual property, which undermine egalitarianism. This dynamic, as we have seen, can explain the structural transformations.

CHAPTER 6

Mode of Production, Social Action, and Historical Change: Some Questions and Issues

John Haldon

What is the heuristic value for the historian of the concept of a mode of production? At what level of analysis is it applicable and helpful in understanding historical social formations? There have been many attempts to restructure, redefine or reconstruct historical materialism and/or Marxism in recent years, largely, but not entirely, focusing on the issue of the relationship between means and relations of production; the relationship between 'base' and 'superstructure' and how these concepts are to be defined and employed; and the relationship between agency and structure (or the ways in which the latter is constituted by the former). Much of this effort has resulted from often quite justified critiques of some dogmatic or reductionist versions of a historical-materialist approach, and much of the response to such criticism has been founded on attempts to reinterpret what Marx may or may not be claimed to have said in his many and varied writings. Indeed, given the prevalence of relativistic social scientific and literary/cultural analysis, the possibility that there can be any sort of general explanatory concepts applicable to human social evolution across more than one cultural system or even across more than one set of discourses within a culture has been subject to serious criticism. Counter-challenges to such relativism have been mounted with some success, of course, and the potential for political action based on an informed understanding of historical processes has not been lost sight of. Trying to understand the past from a historical-materialist interpretative perspective is a choice based on a desire to find structure, shape, and the nature and sources of exploitation in human social praxis, on the one hand, and – crucially – to reveal causal relationships based in the material reproduction of social being, on the other. But this must include the causal associations between beliefs and social praxis. And I would argue that such an approach includes the possibility for cultural and literary analysis (for example) without conceding any ground to crude economism or determinism, and that the autonomy of cultural praxis can be respected within the broader framework of a realist and materialist approach to social being. My 'organic' or 'skeletal' model of the social relations of production, outlined below, is one way of representing the complex and dialectical relationships between belief and social action.[1]

My aim in this contribution is not to reproduce the broader debates mentioned above, but rather critically to assess the relationship between the ways in which we theorise mode of production, as exemplified through specific historical examples, and how we can relate this to our understanding of the material effect of belief systems on social praxis. This is an issue which has largely, and I think detrimentally, been left out of the picture in much empirical historical-materialist analysis of change, although it has not been absent from theoretical discussion; indeed the subject has generated a great deal of debate. In this respect I aim to steer a course between what has been termed 'analytical Marxism' as represented, for example, by Roemer and Elster, on the one hand, influenced by rational choice theories in sociology and economics as well as by methodological individualism;[2] and on the other hand, the structuralism of thinkers like Althusser, whose reduction of agency to structures does not help historical analysis.

The problems accompanying an individualist approach to the social sciences are relatively well known, but worth summarising – admittedly somewhat crudely – in order that this middle course can be clearly demarcated. Firstly, methodological individualist analysis assumes that society is simply an aggregate of individual behavioural traits or patterns motivated by personal disposition alone, so that social phenomena (such as group responses to stimuli or situations) become merely the net result of the activities of individuals pursuing a range of individual goals. While this is true in one sense, it ignores the potential for group identities and interests to overwhelm the individual's self-interest under certain conditions. Secondly, people are conceived of as actors who always behave in supposedly rational self-interest, which must not necessarily be the case; if individual material interests as observed in the data are assumed to reflect economic rationality, there is little or no space allowed for unintentional results or unobservable intentions, or indeed of the dialectic between actors; and the constraining/determining agency of social

---

1   See the sympathetic discussion and analysis in, for example, Lloyd 1993, which argues for a 'relational structuralism', broadly in sympathy with the sort of position argued here, but which sees the process of material reproductive praxis as having no more causal effect than that of cultural and social production, and thus wishes to move away from a historical *materialism* as such. I am grateful to Helmut Reimitz, Joe Ricci, Chris Wickham and especially Gregor McLennan for helpful comments on this chapter.

2   Roemer 1982; Elster 1985.

roles and structures is downplayed.[3] The result is often that any sort of explanation which admits group or individual social and psychological complexity becomes impossible, in spite of claims to the contrary.

In opposition to these approaches are those that may most usefully be represented by the work of Althusser, whose notion of a holistic social totality within which agency, actions and events are entirely structured and determined means that causal relationships are known only through relations of dominance and subjection. Such a closed system of structured agency means that there remains little or no space for individual agents to challenge the structures of which they are themselves an element, and societies thus change and social relationships are transformed only because of immanent structural contradictions.[4] Neither approach has been particularly successful when applied to historical analysis; indeed there has been virtually no such historical analysis except for discussions of more-or-less contemporary political and cultural developments – the ancient, medieval and pre-twentieth-century worlds remain untouched.

Given the amount of literature devoted to these debates over the last two or so decades in particular, it might be thought that these questions are settled, but that is far from the case, at least from the point of view of the practising historian. Alex Callinicos's work on this theme, for example, presents a well-theorised account of agency in structure, but does not – in my view – offer the historian a practical, empirical means – a methodology – for resolving the issues the discussion has raised, in particular of how to relate historical accounts of events, or other evidence for such events, analytically to the actors who made them what they were.[5] Of course, we should probably not overplay the opposition between structure on the one side, and agency on the other. 'Agency' itself always involves culturally determined meanings, practices, ideas, aspects of social being and self-realisation that all entail 'structures', with consequent emergent properties. Some time ago Jorge Larraín likewise offered a welcome 'reconstruction' of historical materialism in which human subjective agency within a structured context is central, and where economic determinism as well as overly structuralist interpretations are challenged;[6] and several

---

3 See, for example, Coleman 1974, 1979 and 1986; and the survey of Homans 1987. See the critical comments of Carling 1986, pp. 24–62; and the discussion in Callinicos 2004, pp. 69–84. Note also the discussion in Godelier 1972, esp. pp. 10–30.

4 For an older but still useful survey, see Benton 1984.

5 Callinicos 2004, especially the short discussion at pp. 85–102.

6 Larraín 1986.

others have argued in a similar vein.[7] Indeed, Larraín's approach is especially promising, arguing that a 'reconstructed' historical materialism takes account both of the structurally determined nature of social change and history, as well as the centrality of human agency and social praxis, the outcomes of which are not in any way preordained.[8] But the practising historian searches in vain for an empirically applicable approach to the issues, other than the methodology implicit in Marx's own classic essay on the events associated with the workers' uprisings in 1848, *The Eighteenth Brumaire of Louis Bonaparte*.[9] This short chapter is unlikely to resolve the problem, but it may at least raise the question and point to a possible way forward.[10] And at the outset I should make it clear that I am going to work around some of the major issues in accounts of the relationship between agency and structure, and more importantly between language as reportage and language as description, as problematised by sociolinguists in discussions of the interpretation of human intentionality and action.[11]

Mode of Production: Marx's Concept[12]

In order to prepare the ground for the discussion of agency and praxis that follows, I will sketch in some key precepts in relation to the overarching theoretical framework within which I want to think about these issues. I have argued elsewhere that mode of production really has a value only at a relatively high degree of abstraction, functioning as a means of differentiating at the level of political economy some very basic differences in the ways in which surplus wealth is generated and appropriated. Trying to formulate laws of motion beyond this level is, I suggest, misleading. In order to distinguish, for example, the late Roman world from that of its medieval successor, thus at a relatively high level of detail, mode of production does not help, no more than it does in attempting to differentiate between early nineteenth-century England and twenty-first-century Singapore, both capitalist social formations, yet utterly different in institutional detail and evolutionary trajectory. The concept of a given

---

7   See, for example, Godelier 1986.
8   See also McLennan 1989.
9   Marx 1968, pp. 94–179.
10   But see Gottlieb 1984.
11   Instead, I refer to the summary of some key discussions in Callinicos 2004, pp. 111–51, with the work of Bhaskar 1975; and Davidson 1984.
12   My comments here expand on discussion in Haldon 2014.

mode of production offers some very basic clues as to the potentials and evolutionary possibilities open to societies in which a particular mode of production is represented, but I do not think that it can be detailed in respect of organisational capacities and arrangements – for this we need to interrogate the sources and elucidate the dynamics of specific historical social formations, specific instantiations of a mode of production, within which different forms of labour organisation are found alongside different institutional arrangements for the appropriation of surplus.[13]

In the process of analysing capitalist relations of production, Marx inevitably had to think about social-economic relationships which were clearly of a non-capitalist nature, and it was in this way that his partial and often relatively uninformed (by modern standards) conceptualisations of the 'primitive communist', 'slave', 'ancient' and 'feudal' modes came into being.[14] Of course, Marx never devoted as much attention to theorising these modes as thoroughly as he did capitalism, which has opened the door to a great deal of discussion on just these issues. But he grounded his ideas on feudal relations in his studies of the late ancient and medieval history of Western and central Europe. He took the word 'feudal' as his descriptive term for the fundamental features of the set of economic relationships he found, because it was the dominant term current among historians at the time to describe the medieval societies they dealt with. It described in particular a set of juridical and institutional relationships which had come into existence over the period from the sixth/seventh to the tenth/eleventh centuries, based upon a particular organisation of labour power and surplus appropriation (dependant peasant tenants of varying degrees of social subordination paying rent in kind, services or cash to their landlords) within the structure of a particular system of political power relations (the feudal 'pyramid' of sub-infeudation and vassalage rooted in mutual military obligation). Marx's initial search was for that generalised system of surplus appropriation and distribution which preceded capitalism in England in particular, and out of which capitalist relations grew. Given the historical and geographical specificity of early capitalism, he was bound to look at the same region for its predecessor. But, just as capitalist relationships can be (and have been) universalised, it seemed to Marx that whatever he found as immediately pre-capitalist must also represent (a) a fundamentally different way

---

13   For a more detailed argument in this respect, see Haldon 2014.

14   These basic types are presented in Marx 1964 although, as is well known, he discussed them elsewhere as well, often adding or changing details of his argument as his views on the structure and dynamic of the capitalist mode evolved.

of organising the production of wealth and the appropriation of surplus, and therefore (b) a 'mode of production' – an 'epoch of production' as opposed to a labour process or set of techniques – which might similarly be universalised, regardless of the particular institutional characteristics differentiating Western European pre-capitalist social formations from those in other parts of the world. It was on this basis that he also set out both to locate other fundamental 'modes of production' upon which the societies and cultures of the past had been based, and to determine the key differentiating elements which distinguished one mode of production from another.

For Marx, therefore, mode of production referred quite straightforwardly to a model of a set of economic relationships, consisting of a specific combination of forces and relations of production. 'Forces of production' are taken to refer to both means of production and the technical levels or methods of production (including the labour process); 'relations of production' refers to the way in which the means of production (land, tools, livestock, etc.) are effectively controlled, and by whom; and the ways in which the direct producers are associated with those means of production and with their own labour power.[15] The two sets of criteria overlap; but it is the specific manner in which direct producers and means of production are combined which, in Marx's words, 'distinguishes the different economic epochs of the structure of society from one another', that is to say, which differentiates one mode of production from another.[16] The fundamental elements necessary to differentiate one mode from another are already clear from Marx's analysis of capitalism, although his discussion of non-capitalist modes is sketchy and incomplete. But the mode of appropriation of surplus and the ways in which the direct producers are combined with the means of production are crucial. Less explicit in Marx's analysis is the mode of distribution of surplus, and the fact that different modes of production place different constraints upon the possibilities for change. They also place different constraints upon the structures of political power, constraints that are particularly important for an understanding of the internal dynamic of a given historical social formation, that is to say, of a specific historical configuration of a particular mode of production.[17]

---

15   There is a concise exposition of Marx's notions in this respect in Therborn 1976, pp. 355 ff. Marx himself made a series of clear statements about these relationships: see, for example, Marx 1977a, vol. 3, p. 791.

16   Marx 1977a, vol. 2, pp. 36–7.

17   I take this formulation from Banaji 2010, pp. 22–3, who offers a valuable analytical account of the ways in which 'mode of production' is to be understood.

Marx's intentions in elaborating the concept of mode of production and applying it to the development of different types of human societies was, clearly, to employ it as a heuristic, as a means of asking questions about the basic structures which informed the ways in which a given social-economic system worked. Mode of production is an abstraction from known historical examples, representing no specific society, but rather one set of possible social relations of production from a limited number of such sets.[18] It is important to emphasise the *limited* here: across the vast terrain of human social-economic evolution, it is possible to reduce the almost infinite variety of *forms* of socio-economic organisation (i.e. culturally determined institutional arrangements) to a relatively small number of sets of basic economic relationships, modes of producing and extracting surplus. Distilled out into their most basic features, recent discussions would suggest that there may be at most five historical modes of producing, appropriating and distributing wealth and of combining labour power with the means of production – primitive/lineage/'peasant', tributary/feudal, ancient/slave (both of which remain problematic), capitalist;[19] and while each of these has as its corollary certain ecological and organisational conditions necessary to its reproduction, only the capitalist mode has ever received a detailed analysis by Marx, although Engels engaged with the issue of feudalism more intensively.

If a mode of production – a model of a set of socio-economic relations – has been adequately theorised (that is to say, if the relations between its constituent elements are coherent), it should serve as a heuristic device intended to suggest what questions should be asked of the evidence about a particular set of social and economic relationships, and how one can set about understanding the disparate and disjointed historical data as representative of a dynamic social totality. This was realised in Marx's presentation of exactly this type of analysis for capitalist relations of production as a general type, based on his painstaking researches on nineteenth-century British and European economies, and his elucidation of a series of 'laws' which govern the enormous complexity of capitalist production and exchange relations. Fundamental to the efficacy of his analysis and its social scientific value was the simple fact that he was able to demonstrate that, however different the various *forms* of capitalist economy actually were, they all operated on the same fundamental principles.

---

18   See Perlin 1985, pp. 90–2, 97–101, who categorises this approach as 'macrological'.
19   The 'peasant mode' is theorised as a separate mode from the primitive/lineage mode by Wickham 2005, pp. 536–40, and in this volume; for tributary, and problems with feudal, ancient and slave modes, see Haldon 1993, pp. 63–109.

'Capitalism' was thus, for Marx, a heuristic model of social-economic relations – a mode of production – while at the same time 'capitalist' was a descriptive term applied to all those actually existing social formations in which the set of production relations and forces of production described by that term were dominant.

Change, Transformation and Causation

Change, and the explanation of change, is at the very heart of any historical project – even where we want to find out more about how things worked in a given society at a given point in time, this is usually in order to understand both how that situation arose and how it then evolved. For those working within the broad reach of a historical-materialist approach, this raises some important questions, since the answer to such questions will also underpin both the research strategies (including what questions we want to ask) and the outcomes of an inquiry. However different their actual historical appearance, and however different the medium and institutional forms through which surplus is extracted, societies dominated by a particular mode of surplus appropriation have certain fundamental features in common, and are constrained in respect of their further development by these features – they thus subsume certain general laws of development, and Marx's original aim in looking at modes of production other than capitalism was precisely to contrast these elements across different modes and to try to reveal them. But as we have said, modes of production do not exist in any real form – they represent merely the theoretical exposition of specific sets of economic relations, so that in this respect *modes of production cannot develop*. On the contrary, it is social formations – the particular historical configurations of a mode of production – that change: mode of production provides a broad agenda, so to speak, delineating the essential nature of contradictions within production relations and the basic economic possibilities. Thus modes of production cannot *of themselves* give rise to a different mode of production, although of course the sets of relationships they represent can generate the conditions which may lead to their transformation. The latter is a possibility determined by the actual institutional forms of expression of the underlying economic relationships, which are subject to change or disruption at the level of class struggle and the political relations of power distribution.

It is essential to bear in mind that these institutional forms are, after all, the combination of sets of social practices, which local conditions have evolved to express fundamental relations of production and surplus appropriation. The universal laws of capitalist production are, in themselves, no more capable of dynamically transforming capitalist relations of production into something else, full of objective class antagonisms and contradictions in respect of forces and relations of production though they clearly are, than are tributary/feudal production relations.[20] Within both feudalism and capitalism, or any other mode of production, it is the *specific contexts* generated by *specific conjunctures* or configurations in time and place – in other words, particular moments at which structural disparities between forces and relations of production are realised in terms of social praxis – which lead to modal transformations. These are predictable only in the most general possible sense, delimited by the conditions of existence of given sets of relations of production and by the historically specific forms of their internal contradictions. Transformation is not therefore an *inevitable* consequence of process in time; but it is *always a possibility*, under specific sets of conditions.[21] It is the potential for shifts and transformations which general laws elucidate for each specific mode of production. So it is within a social formation that change actually occurs, where these contradictions work themselves out; and it is therefore at this level that the *explanation* for change must be sought. We need to examine and understand the shape, and the local and international context, of each social formation or set of related/interconnected social formations to see how transformative shifts in the dominance of particular sets of social relations of production are actually brought about.

Traditionally in historical-materialist debate, the motor for historical change, the 'prime mover', has been seen as the contradiction or tension between forces and relations of production, as embodied in the struggle between the various economic classes to assert their power over the means of production, including their own labour power – thus, in Rodney Hilton's definition in respect of feudal relations of production, the 'prime mover' consists in the class struggle between lords and serfs. In Marx's own formulation:

> In the social production of their existence, men inevitably enter into definite relations, which are independent of their will, namely relations

---

20   I will not belabour the point I have made elsewhere (Haldon 1993, pp. 75 ff.) that 'feudal' should be understood as a particular historical configuration of 'tributary', although I can see that some historians prefer to retain 'feudal' as the generic form. Chris Wickham has suggested that this is a minor semantic point that should not distract us from more important issues; Wickham 2008, see p. 5 and n. 5.

21   A point that has been effectively demonstrated empirically regarding feudal production relations by Wickham 2008.

of production appropriate to a given stage in the development of their material forces of production. The totality of these relations of production constitutes the economic structure of society ... At a certain stage of development, the material productive forces of society come into conflict with the existing relations of production or – this merely expresses the same thing in legal terms – with the property relations within the framework of which they have operated hitherto. From forms of development of the productive forces these relations turn into their fetters.[22]

As is widely recognised, this argument from economics has caused some major problems for Marxist historians, since in many cases it led to accusations, sometimes reasonably grounded, of economic essentialism or reductionism. But it depends on how we formulate 'economic', how we understand and whether we think Marx's notion of the tendency of the forces of production to grow is valid, and how we understand this contradiction between forces and relations of production.

Marx argued that the contradictions inherent in the situation brought about by the fettering of the productive forces by the social relations of production would lead to a period of revolutionary transformation of the latter, and hence the establishment of the dominance of a new mode of production. The idea is fundamental to Marx's notions of social-economic change, and has received accordingly a great deal of attention. It is possible to read it deterministically, of course, and some Marxists have therefore argued in favour of restricting the role of the forces of production as a determining element in the historical process.[23] Others have argued for a less teleological interpretation of the role of the forces of production in Marx's writings, arguing only that *if* the forces of production develop, *then* they will come into conflict with the relations of production (but only after a quantitative growth makes a qualitative shift possible).[24] The form that any 'fettering' can take will be determined by the mode of production in question (in respect of the structural limitations and possibilities it permits). Those socio-economic interests that perceive themselves as threatened by the potential shifts in the relations of production will

---

22   Marx 1977b, pp. 20–1.
23   See, for example, McMurtry 1978; Shaw 1978, both of whom consider that the forces of production are relevant only to recent (or capitalist) history.
24   For example, Levine 1984, pp. 164 ff.; Levine and Olin Wright 1980; and especially Callinicos 2004, pp. 54 ff., who presents a detailed account of the arguments surrounding Cohen's attempt to reintroduce the forces as a central and causal element in Marxist explanation (see Cohen 1978).

hence feel compelled to address the issue directly and take action to inhibit such shifts and the transformation in social and political structures they entail. The economically dominant class may well succeed in instituting political and economic measures sufficient to stabilise the situation to their own advantage, of course, but it is precisely this that gives the political and economic struggle between contradictory class interests a particular centrality in respect of the outcome. At the same time, the 'organic' crisis may represent a long-term state of affairs, in turn promoting a situation in which first one, then another, antagonistic set of production relations is dominant.

In historical terms, this may take several forms. It may give rise to a situation in which new relations of production come to dominate in one social formation but not its neighbours, so that external competition for resources as a result of the internal shifts in the political relations of distribution of surplus wealth creates the conditions for conflict and war. The divergent interests of the nascent nation-states in Europe from the seventeenth century in particular until the triumph of industrial capitalism in the middle of the nineteenth century provides a good example. Similarly, the tension between historical configurations of slavery, which dominated productive organisation in Italy in the first century BCE and CE (and thus indirectly the rest of the Roman empire, through the fact of the dominance of the Italian elite at the heart of the empire), for example, and the tributary mode which was characteristic of production relations throughout the rest of that empire, provides another example. In such contexts the way is open for a third factor, namely the state, to impose a degree of equilibrium between the conflicting interests. While the state is an emergent element, a product of the social relations which prevail, it can remain relatively autonomous given the appropriate circumstances. Either way, the relationship between the productive forces and the social relations of production, in the context of the structural capacities of the human agents whose praxis constitutes those social relationships, is one of explanatory significance for historical materialism. It means, in effect, that the conditions which might promote crisis in a particular historical manifestation of a given mode can be specified in broad terms, just as the structural possibilities within which the social relations of production can respond to such contradictions can be broadly sketched in. But this involves no substantive predictive capacity: it is merely to assert that, *where* certain sets of conditions are met, *then* certain types of transformation may follow, dependent upon the outcome of the struggle for control of the means of production between antagonistic classes. The actual form such changes take, and the configuration of the social relations of production which evolve out of them, must depend upon empirical analysis for further elucidation.

A good demonstration of this can be found in the example of European economic development in the period between the second or third century and the thirteenth or fourteenth century: given what we now know about commerce, the degree of monetisation of economies, levels of production and consumption, and technological developments between roughly 100 CE and 1200 CE, I see no evidence whatsoever of a situation anywhere in the Western Eurasian world where forces of production expanded qualitatively to the extent that they were either fettered or challenged by the fundamental set of production relations characteristic of the tributary mode, certainly not to the extent that, from a Marxist perspective, we might identify a modal change. There are, of course, developments in the technology of the windmill and water mill, in the processing of iron ore, in traction-harness for beasts of burden, in the breeding of heavier draught- and warhorses, in military architecture and artillery. But with few exceptions these were already rooted in the late ancient world, and more importantly affected the overall economic and productive capacity of society only extremely slowly as they were transmitted from region to region.[25] Only from the twelfth century at the earliest did they have a qualitative as well as a quantitative impact on economic relationships on a large scale, and in the context of aristocratic and state reaction to a rapidly changing world economy.[26] By the same token, trade and commerce flourished in the later ancient world from the Atlantic across to the Indian Ocean, and while production and demand declined on a macro-regional basis for a period between the later sixth/seventh century and the later ninth/tenth century, recovering strongly thereafter, once again it is impossible to see the quantitative and qualitative transformation in the forces of production that promoted the sort of modal shift required by the classic understanding of the concept 'mode of production'.[27] There were changes, shifts, sometimes dramatic transformations across the period, often highly regionally nuanced; none of them qualifies as a modal transformation.

Against Determinism: What Do (or Should) Historical Materialists Mean by 'The Economic'?

For Marx, the notion of 'base' or 'basis' referred to the fundamental sets of economic relationships characteristic of each mode of production in the sense of an abstract, idealised system. It meant that *all* societies which functioned on

---

25   For a useful summary, with further literature, see Le Goff 1988, pp. 200–29.

26   Again, see Wickham 2008, esp. pp. 13–18.

27   See, for example, albeit from a very different perspective, Abu-Lughod 1989.

the basis of the same pattern of structured relationships could be reasonably described as belonging to the same mode of production, and thus subject to the same general laws of development. However different their actual historical appearance, and however different the medium through which surplus is extracted, societies dominated by a particular mode of surplus appropriation have certain fundamental features in common, and are constrained in respect of their further development by these features; they can thus be said to subsume certain general laws of development, which can, however, only be determined by empirical research, and it is the potential for shifts and transformations which general laws elucidate for each specific mode of production. The point is precisely to enable the historian to look behind phenomenal forms, the infinite range of culturally determined social praxis (what Marx referred to as the superstructure) through which these fundamental relationships were expressed; and hence to locate the causal relationships which explained the direction, speed and degree of socio-economic change.

The traditional metaphor of base and superstructure is now rarely invoked, not simply because it led to simplistic and deterministic interpretations by Marxist historians themselves, nor because it (often justifiably) led to accusations of such reductionism, and therefore the dismissal of Marxist interpretations by non- or anti-Marxist writers, but rather because it is clearly inadequate as an explanatory concept. Marx and Engels were constrained by the base/superstructure model because it was designed specifically to highlight the inadequacies of classical political economic ideas about how societies work from an economic perspective, on the one hand, and traditional ideas about the nature of the state, ideology and so on, on the other. It was unfortunate, but perhaps inevitable, that unhappy formulations such as 'secondary structures' were misleading. And in fact both writers understood the inadequacies of this particular heuristic for a wider-ranging analysis, and tried to escape from its apparent determinism by comments such as: 'We have all neglected (this aspect) more than it deserves. It is the old story: form is always neglected at first for content'.[28] And it is understandable that this spatial model of base and superstructure which, while being more than just a metaphor, was never intended to provide more than a general guide to the way in which economic and social relationships could be thought, has been frequently both misused and misunderstood. So much is implicit in Marx's comment on the relationship between the owners of the means of production and those whose labour power they exploit: 'The specific economic form, in which unpaid surplus labour is pumped out of

---

28   See Engels 1968a, pp. 690–1.

direct producers, determines the relationship of rulers and ruled, as it grows directly out of production itself *and, in turn, reacts upon it as a determining element*. Upon this, however, is founded the entire formation of the economic community which grows up out of the production relations themselves, *thereby simultaneously its specific political form'*.[29]

In order to retain, justify and illustrate the notion of the totality of social relations of production (the economic) as being fundamental to the ways in which any given social formation can function – as being determinant in the sense that they frame the possibilities of institutional and cultural forms, set limits to the exploitation of social power, yet facilitate the possibility for human practice to transcend those structures – I want to emphasise two aspects.

To begin with, those dimensions of the social structure which appear to dominate very many non-capitalist societies, but which are equally, in appearance, non-economic dimensions, regulate nevertheless the reproduction of specific sets of social relations.[30] As examples, what Marx sometimes refers to as the 'dominance' of religion in many social formations (in medieval Europe, for example), although I will prefer the term 'penetration' (see below), or of kinship structures in Australian Aboriginal societies, or yet again of politics and religion in the classical Greek world, have all been used as rods with which to beat Marxist approaches for their ostensible economic reductionism. But as Marx himself stressed, these supposedly entirely non-economic 'superstructural' dimensions also fulfilled the *function* of relations of production; for all societies consist of structures which function to maintain and reproduce the sets of social relations of production of which they are composed.[31] This does not, of course, reduce all reality to economics: such structures are always multifunctional or, better, multi-effectual; but they remain autonomous institutionally and structurally integral to the reproduction of the social relations of production. Descent, marriage and inheritance are regulated in all societies

29   Marx 1977a, p. 791.

30   See especially Godelier 1978a. The idea has been taken up by several writers dealing with pre-capitalist social formations, generally of the segmentary lineage or the sectional type: see again, with examples, Godelier 1984, pp. 3–27, esp. 13 ff. In what follows I have found Miller 1984, and Sayer 1987, especially stimulating.

31   'The middle ages could not live on Catholicism, nor the ancient world on politics' (Marx 1977a, vol. 1, p. 85 and n. 2). Engels employed the notion of 'ultimate determination' by the economy as a way of attempting to illustrate the ways in which social relations of production provide the framework within which other aspects of social life are inscribed, but through which 'secondary structures' also determine the form and development of economic relations (Engels 1968b, pp. 682–3).

by kinship (whether or not this is represented through a particular set of religious and ideological institutions); and in all societies the relationship between human beings and the divine or non-human (supernatural) is regulated and explicated by religion of a greater or lesser degree of theoretical sophistication, whether we are talking of the sophisticated soteriology of either Islam or Christianity, or the complex animism of the nomadic cultures of the central Asian steppe. Yet not all societies are dominated by either kinship or religious systems; and the explicit function of these regulatory systems alone, where they represent the dominant mode of public and private discourse, cannot in itself explain this pre-eminence: another function must also be in play. And this function must be that of a social relation (or set of relations) of production. By the same token, Marx clearly envisaged the forces of production themselves as a relation of production, since they entail both the means of production and the ways in which production is carried on. These are clearly 'economic' relationships, yet in the great majority of traditional societies this process – the labour process – is assured and reproduced precisely through sets of practices and social-institutional arrangements which have no such transparently 'economic' appearance: kinship arrangements, family structures and a gendered division of labour, caste and lineage attributions, age-sets, or legal statuses, all representing particular forms of political organisation, all forms of social praxis through which a particular set of social relations of production operates or is given effect.

It is the historian's task to locate the nature of the dominance of a particular dimension, and to find out how it has evolved also as the representative form of the relations of production. The fundamental point to bear in mind is how sets of institutions and social practices such as politics, kinship and religion express relations of production, and what their effect is in the totality of social relationships. The contingent effects of social reproductive practice in general amounts (amongst other emergent consequences and practices) to the maintenance of particular structures, chiefly relations of production. In this sense, we may speak of the *function* of a particular combination of practices insofar as their combination has certain *effects*. It is because the intentions of human agents are constrained within the cultural possibilities opened to them by the totality of practices in their society, that their unintentional effects causally contribute to the reproduction of those culturally limiting or delimiting sets of relationships and practices. Where major transformations or shifts in relationships occur, we can expect also to find breakdowns in the effectiveness of cultural constraints on the relevant practices; and the site of such ruptures is likely also to be the site of contradictory relations of production.

A second point is that, the better to understand the dialectical nature of these relationships, as well as their multi-functionality, we might rather conceive of the economic as part of an organism as the basis upon which other functions are founded, rather than spatially. My preferred metaphor here is to see economic relationships as a skeleton, articulated in such a way as to determine both the limits and the basic configuration of the body – a social formation – of which it is an essential element, but where all the other elements – the organs and soft tissue, as it were – superficial or not, are vital to the particular appearance and evolution of a society in a specific form.[32] None of the elements stands or can stand on its own, including the skeleton; but there is, nevertheless, a sense in which certain practices – the skeleton – establish a pattern for the ways in which all the other forms actually operate. Just as the different primates have different skeletons, differently articulated but with bodies constructed from the same basic set of corresponding organs and tissues, so different social and economic formations represent different specific historical articulations of a particular mode of production, their differently articulated relations of production determining the general possibilities and limits of the social practices from which they are constituted. Like the skeleton, therefore, relations of production do not *cause* a social formation; but they do have a determining influence on its physical forms, its capacities to deal with external influences, its potential to evolve in one direction or another, and its limitations in respect of production, consumption and expenditure of energy. Like a skeleton (which grows and changes over time), social relations are also dynamic and constantly in a state of flux, open to change and transformation – contradictions, stresses and incompatibilities evolve as the elements from which they are constituted act back upon them. Shifts and changes in the capacities of the soft tissue and articulations of a body can be compared with beliefs, perceptions, interests and their corresponding practices, as well as external/environmental and ecological pressures, and so forth. This seems to me a more useful and helpful way to conceptualise the totality of social relations of production and relate their different elements dialectically, without using the base-superstructure metaphor, which is so liable to distortion or misunderstanding. Such an analogy makes it possible at least to see the determining nature of economic relationships, without at the same time suggesting that they are either causally prior or that they are not themselves determined in their mode of expression by other factors.[33]

---

32   The general approach is not entirely original; see Simmel 1992.

33   Here I would part company from Sayer 1987, pp. 91–2, who argues for the base-super-

A Problem for Historical Materialism? Social Action and the Materiality of Belief Systems

As a historian of the medieval world, and particularly as a historian of the medieval eastern Roman, or Byzantine, empire, it has often struck me that far too little attention is paid to the material impact on day-to-day social praxis of what people believed about their society and their role in it. This is not to suggest that not enough attention is paid to beliefs, religion, cultural values and ideas, as such – on the contrary, a bibliography of any period or region of medieval history would quickly show that the situation is quite the opposite. But analyses of the ways in which these aspects of social being affect the wider social world are largely absent. Such an impact on the actual institutional forms and potentialities of the social relations of production inhabited by social actors must in consequence directly affect the way a given social formation – a particular historical configuration of a mode of production, to repeat the point – works and evolves. What people believe structures how they act; and how they act is directly relevant to our understanding of how a society works. As W.G. Runciman has expressed it, patterns of 'representations, beliefs and attitudes ... are transmitted from mind to mind by imitation or learning', similarly to 'social evolution, in which selected rule-governing practices define institutional roles which are occupied and performed by successive individual incumbents who work in a similar path-dependent but open-ended way'. Such 'memes', as Runciman terms them, directly impact on social agency – religious belief (for example), therefore, possesses itself a structuring role in social relationships, and cannot be left out of the picture as a merely 'superstructural' element. Another way of expressing this is, in Runciman's words, through the difference between 'culture' and 'structure', between the substance of social institutions and roles on the one hand, and the patterns of social relationships they form in social praxis on the other.[34]

This has become especially evident in recent debates following the publication of Chris Wickham's magisterial *Framing the early Middle Ages*, less because

---

structure metaphor as expressive of a relationship between social being and social consciousness. While he is surely correct to argue that Marx's model was not intended to represent the relationship between a set of discrete instances or practices, he is surely incorrect in suggesting that neither did Marx intend the relationship to reflect no causal association at all. On the contrary, as suggested here, it was the causal relationship which concerned Marx, especially insofar as the impact of economic structures on social praxis and cultural logic was concerned.

34   See Runciman 2011, p. 100; and 1989b, pp. 8–9.

of what he does not do in that book and more because of some of the critical issues others have raised, in particular the question of beliefs and 'the church'.[35] The issue is important, it seems to me, because of the points made in the preceding section regarding the way in which sets of institutions and social practices such as politics, kinship and religion can express relations of production. We reasonably assume, and build into our explanations of social change, the combined effects of human social praxis in the maintenance or transformation of social relations of production. Yet people are not simply agents of the structures they inhabit, one of the much criticised results of a strongly structuralist approach to agency and praxis – they are agents, but they are also themselves constitutive of those structures.[36] There is a dialectical relationship between being and doing, and if we take this seriously then it means we need to seek out the connections between what people believe about their world and their place in it, at a variety of different levels of their social existence, and how they 'do' being the person they think they are. So while the relationship between consciousness and practice must be understood as a dialectic through which individuals receive their subjective awareness of self and personal environment, it also provides them with the conceptual apparatus through which they can in turn express what they know about the world, and act back upon it. At the same time, that relationship sets limits to what they can know and how they can know, limits within which what we might call 'the culturally possible' can be thought.

Contingently, the symbolic universe (the totality of cultural knowledge and practice in a social formation, within which and through which regular everyday life is carried on) is itself a product of social practice, through which it is continuously reproduced. The activities carried on by individuals actively engaged in socially reproducing themselves, and hence in reproducing the social relations of production and reproduction of their particular cultural system, along with its roles and social institutions, have the material cultural effect of reproducing the structural forms within which the same individuals are inscribed. This is for me a more useful way of thinking about the ways in which beliefs 'interpellate' individuals in Althusser's sense, because it retains a stronger emphasis on the individual's constitutive function in a social-cultural

---

35   An issue I raised in passing myself: see my review of Wickham, in Haldon 2011, pp. 67–8, as did others: see Costambeys 2006, pp. 417–19; and Moreland 2011, pp. 184–5, 188–9.

36   See above, and Benton 1984; on agency, and from two very different perspectives, see the discussions in Secord 1982, and Callinicos 2004, esp. pp. 38 ff. The point is made clearly in the work of Miller, Larraín, Sayer and Godelier, already cited.

context.[37] Historical data cannot, of course, offer the same types of answer as those available to sociology and psychology, but nevertheless general theories of mind and of cognition derived from these disciplines can be applied to the product of past human consciousness, as preserved in historical documents, for example, whether written sources or other types of artefact. The context may have changed, but the essentially cultural nature of human cognitive activity remains. The corollary to this is that in describing short- or long-term change in the way a social formation works, the way a state develops, or the ways in which – for example – kinship relations affect political structure, we do not penetrate beyond the level of plausible hypothesis unless we motivate the social actors, whether individuals or groups, in respect of the ideas and beliefs informing their practice. In many cases this is not possible, because there is no evidence for this aspect of social being. But where there is – where we do possess histories, letters, conciliar documents, laws, poetry, hagiography and a host of other forms of evidence for how people thought their world – we run the risk of a reductionist argument unless we take the cultural discourse of the society into account as well as the sets of economic and political relations which are visible in the same evidence. For the historian of more recent times, or for sociologists, this issue is barely a problem – it is quite rightly taken for granted, first, that ideas directly impact on behaviour and more especially on public politics, and secondly, that the relationship between ideas and practice is more or less transparent, because the observer can trace the relationships much more clearly through the relevant sources.[38] For the historian of pre-modern cultures, the former may not be doubted, but it is rarely taken into direct consideration, and where it is, the methodology for linking the two arenas of social being is generally intuitive and rooted in a highly individualised reading of the relevant texts or other sources.[39]

---

37   I borrow 'symbolic universe' from Berger and Luckmann 1967, esp. pp. 110 ff. (deriving in turn from Durkheim) and Schütz 1960. The phenomenology of Schütz, and Berger and Luckmann, and the symbolic interactionism of G.H. Mead, seem to me to make good partners in the generation of a realist materialist theorisation of the relationship between consciousness and practice (see Goff 1980).

38   See, for example, Dan Rodgers's account of late twentieth-century political ideas and popular and intellectual debate in the US (Rodgers 2011). For a useful sociological survey and discussion of the interface and interaction between beliefs, identities and social action, see Akerlof and Kranton 2010.

39   An outstanding exception is Brown 2012, who shows how Christian concepts and negotiations of wealth and property in respect of their practical significance and function, as well as conceptual value for the community, generated forms of social praxis, hence social

One way of approaching the ways in which ideology acts upon social praxis so as to affect the workings of the social relations of production is to look for the degree to which the process called by anthropologists 'ritual penetration'[40] plays a role in the distribution of surplus wealth and in the potential of the social relations of production to reproduce themselves. It would not be unreasonable to argue that the 'ritual penetration' of a society in respect of specific sets of belief-based social practices, which are themselves the expression of the structure of social relations of production, is common to all social formations. One need only consider the ways in which Christianity and Islam, amongst other systems, have inflected the daily practices of believers and the communities that they constitute.[41] But it is not necessarily these particular practices which have come to be the dominant expression of relations of production in all societies, since, as we have already noted, each social-cultural formation represents these economic relations in different forms, the location and origins of which must be the subject of specific empirical analysis. Thus, as noted already, patterns of investment of wealth directly reflect what people believe about their world. This is the case whether they invest in civic infrastructure and amenities, as in the Hellenistic and Roman world up to the third century; whether they invest in church- or temple-building or the endowment of religious foundations, artwork and decoration, or charity; or whether they invest in court offices, tax-farms or commercial ventures, or a combination of all of these. They all reflect prevailing values and assumptions about what is important in their world. Religious belief and/or cultural value-systems do not float free of the socio-economic relationships of which they are themselves a constitutive element, clearly. They can be seen directly to affect patterns of wealth investment and, in consequence, the ways in which elites, for example, appropriate and consume wealth, as well as the ways in which political regimes are

---

and political structures, that directly impacted upon longer-term implications for Europe and the West into and beyond the medieval period.

40   A process through which an ideological system, such as Hinduism, Islam or Christianity, also sets the normative rules for parts or all of the legal, social and economic relationships within a culture – in other words, where 'ritual' and observance are embodied in social praxis, not just in ideas or attitudes. They are thus constitutive of (as well as reproduced by) the social relations of production, to a greater or lesser degree, depending on the particular historical configuration at issue. For the following, see also Haldon 2012, pp. 1111–47; and see Heitzman 1991, pp. 23–54; and see Mann 1986, p. 361. On the ways in which surplus distribution can be mediated through the control of centres of religious devotion and the deities associated with them, see especially the discussion of Friedman 1975, pp. 170 ff.

41   As exemplified – to take just one case – in late ancient and early medieval Christianity, for example; see Brown 2003, esp. pp. 25–34; and Brown's work in note 36 above.

able to maintain themselves, or not. They express and articulate also the ways in which individuals and groups can 'think' themselves, how they generate, maintain or change identities, and how such conceptual frameworks appear in, for example, written sources or other forms of historical document such as inscriptions. And they thus express also, as the forms of social practice through which social and economic relationships are given shape and effect, the relations of production of their society. If we want to understand, causally, changes in such phenomena, we need to take beliefs and the framework they set seriously into consideration as one key element in the notion of change, otherwise we end up merely describing them and seeing them as epiphenomena with no causal value. Indeed, since beliefs must directly motivate – for example – political action, and thus relations of production, it seems obvious that if we want to understand the processes of change, we need to build beliefs and their contingent social effects into our model of causal relationships.

Some of the clearest examples of 'ritual incorporation/penetration' can be found in India and pre-Columbian America. In the case of South Indian cultures and their dominant symbolic universe, it was the particular combination of a specific ecological context, kinship structure and religious configuration which promoted the unique importance and centrality of a set of ritual, transactional networks. The ideological structures of Hindu society were a central pillar of the existence of the Vijayanagara Empire from the fourteenth through into the seventeenth century, for example. Temples and monastery-like seminaries had a high moral standing, and local sentiment and devotion was totally bound into the religious narratives and symbolic universe of Hinduism. Since deities could select as well as defend those whom they wished to worship them, the acceptance by monasteries and temples of Vijayanagara overlordship (in return for donations and grants of wealth in various forms) was a crucial step in the consolidation and maintenance of Vijayanagara power. The function of ritual incorporation within a common symbolic universe – or, to express it differently, the perception of divine acceptance and promotion of a specific political leadership, and the implications this had for the social praxis of elites in particular – took on an especial significance.[42] The empire itself was structured as a series of concentric zones, focused around a political core. This central region was the source of immediate state or royal income, while the areas furthest away from the centre of military and political coercion were attached primarily through occasional military expeditions and by connections of a

---

42   For the origins of the Vijayanagar Empire, see Stein 1989, pp. 18 ff.; and for the importance
       of ritual incorporation, pp. 102–5 with literature.

ritual nature. Royal rituals were based in key religious foci, through whose authority the rulers reinforced their legitimacy and claims to overlordship, and in return for which they undertook to support such institutions through a variety of endowments, regular gifts in cash and in kind, grants of labour services, and so on. Through involvement in such rituals, members of dominant social groups were incorporated within a network of royal and spiritual patronage. By so doing, they also legitimated their own local authority and power, so that the system as a whole served to legitimate a particular set of political institutions and power relations, and a set of social-economic relations: both the mode of surplus appropriation, in the general sense and, particularly, the mode of surplus distribution. None of this is to suggest that rulers were unaware of the process of religious-political manipulation necessary to the maintenance of their power, and especially of the need to maintain control over resources in order to invest in this ritual system on a grand scale in order to continually legitimate their position. Power relationships were expressed indirectly and through the mediation of a ritualised concept of *dharma* or 'righteousness', through which both divine support and earthly political legitimation, and therefore supremacy were secured. It was the loss of the 'dharmic' authority which encouraged the relocation of ritual ties, a diminution in resources, and a consequent loss of political-military coercive power – a concept similar to key beliefs embodied within Sasanian Persian imperial ideology, rooted in part in the idea of sacred kingship but with the Avestan/Zoroastrian idea of kingly 'glory', *xwarrah*, which would protect the king as long as he provided order and prosperity. The key point is, however, that the concepts embedded and initially generated, historically, within social praxis react back upon it and, in Althusser's terms, overdetermine it, so that a system of beliefs can be seen to have a direct material impact on forms of social action which constitute an element in the relations of production. Political authority, and the potential to extract resources in the Vijayanagar Empire, depended on a combination of military/political coercion and connections of a ritual nature. Rulers certainly understood the process of religious-political manipulation necessary to the maintenance of their power, and in particular the need to maintain control over resources in order to invest in this ritual system in order to legitimate their position. Close parallels can be found in the 'segmentary' states of South and Central America, where temple-centred redistribution of surplus and tribute was a crucial means through which surplus appropriation and political authority were maintained.[43]

---

43   For the function of ritual 'enclosure' in pre-Columbian South American cultures, for example, see Marcus 1976, and esp. 1984.

Both Islamic and Christian rulers in the East and the West legitimated the extraction and distribution of surplus – which is to say, in effect, the continued existence of their respective states – through political/theological systems of thought which highlighted the necessary duty of the state and its rulers to defend the faith and to promote the variety of associated activities which this entailed. At the same time, they had to be seen to reinforce and reaffirm their particular symbolic universe through ritualised expressions of faith and the redistribution of considerable amounts of surplus wealth to religious foundations of various types, or through certain ideologically legitimating ritual actions. Such systems evolved only gradually, for the most part. As they penetrated throughout society, inflecting daily life in myriad ways, the production of surplus wealth and the forms and purposes of its distribution were likewise affected. The extraction of tithes in the medieval West and of alms or *zakat* in the Islamic world directly affected the ways in which states and elites could exploit the labour of the producers, both in terms of the rate of exploitation of labour as well as control over the distribution of surplus. As another example we might point to the settlement of parts of the former Roman provinces of Gaul in the fifth and early sixth century. The conquests and extension of Merovingian royal power, together with the institutional and administrative means of exacting wealth which the first Merovingian kings adopted, generated a new class of warrior magnate families partly derived from older clan elites and leaders. The members of this nascent elite invested some of their wealth in secular property and in warfare; but they also invested in the Church: bishoprics and the ecclesiastical lands to which they thereby had access, and monastic foundations. This institutional Christianisation of society and its 'ritual penetration' by the Church and by Christian observance and morality directly affected how labour was exploited and how surpluses were appropriated and consumed.

In the Byzantine world, the complex ceremonial of the imperial palace, the detailed hierarchy of ranks and offices, and the daily acting-out of rituals designed expressly to recall and to imitate the harmony and peace of the heavenly order, were all fundamental expressions of the symbolic order. The close relationship between the emperor (with the state) and the Church, and the supervision by the Church of popular beliefs and kinship structures, for example, created an equally impressive ideological and symbolic system of legitimation. Yet, in this particular historical formation, and in contrast to the South Indian examples, it did not itself express also, or serve as, a key institution of surplus distribution necessary to the economic survival of the state institution. Similar networks can be seen in the Islamic world, in Western Christendom, and in the Chinese Empire. And in the case of both Christianity

and Islam, ritual incorporation (that is to say, conversion) served as a fundamental tool of political integration and domination.

Social Action and Ritual Incorporation: Christianity in Byzantium

The extraction and distribution of surplus is universally legitimated through
systems of belief, ideologies in which the 'necessary' duty of individuals, states
and communities to defend their beliefs, values and identities, and to promote
the variety of associated activities, are represented in particular ideas and concepts. Thus similar forms of ritual penetration can be seen in the Islamic world,
in Western Christendom, and in China. And in the case of both Christianity and
Islam, one aspect of ritual incorporation – that is to say, conversion – served
as a fundamental tool of political integration and domination, while the religious systems established both the framework for social praxis as well as the
thought-world within which it was conceived and apprehended. At one level,
the observance of specific modes of behaviour in human social intercourse
determined the degree to which an individual was identified as a member of
a community or group, or not. At another level, for example, medieval Christian and Muslim rulers had to be seen to reinforce and reaffirm their particular
symbolic universe through ritualised expressions of faith and the redistribution
of considerable amounts of surplus wealth to religious foundations of various
types, or through certain ideologically legitimating ritual actions. There are
many examples of states evolving a closely-integrated ritual and ideological
identity with specific religious structures, a mutual identity of interests which
benefited both parties by legitimating the secular authority in the eyes of the
mass of believers and through which the spiritual authority usually received
considerable advantages in respect of land, income from gifts and endowments, and so on. The Byzantine state provides an excellent example, where
rulers and their relatives, as well as members of all social classes, bestowed
enormous amounts of wealth in a variety of forms upon – for example – monastic foundations; although similar points might be made, yet with very different implications for both social and institutional structures, for the medieval
West.

   It is apparent, however, that while such ritual and incorporative networks
functioned as an element in the relations of production in the south Indian
case, determining at times the rate of exploitation of producers as well as
the mode of distribution of surplus, this was not the case in the Christian or
Islamic worlds of Western Eurasia. Yet religious ideology directly affected relations between individuals and official religious organisations or priesthoods,

for example, as well as between the latter and rulers. A key strand in Byzantine imperial ideology was that of imperial universalism, embodied in its Christian form from the later fourth century CE as a universalising ideology, marked by both exclusivism and intolerance towards competing belief systems. This imperialism identified the *imperium Romanum* with 'orthodox' Christianity, equated with the civilised, God-protected Empire of the Christian, orthodox Romans. Imperialism through territorial expansion was accompanied by a growing emphasis on imperialism as the spiritual conquest of the world through mission, conversion, and the establishment of an orthodox Christian *oikoumene* under imperial leadership.[44] The Church represented one of the most powerful ideological and economic institutions of the late Roman and Byzantine world. It was responsible for a vast transactional network stretching across the Mediterranean. By the early seventh century, Christianity of one variety or another was without doubt the majority belief system of the Roman world, although isolated pockets of pre-Christian traditions and cults survived in some areas. In philosophical terms, it represented a theology which claimed universal validity and a system of belief based on faith in a messianic saviour, and during its first four hundred years of existence it had evolved a sophisticated and highly developed theological armoury. In practical terms, it incorporated a plurality of ways of interpreting the world, influenced by the inherited patterns of belief from the cultural traditions in which it developed and upon which it had been imposed. Through its formal teaching and theology, it was presented by the clergy and the literate and learned minority as the single correct form of belief – orthodoxy – even though its first centuries were marked by a series of intellectual and political clashes over the definitions at issue.[45]

A fundamental feature of the East Roman Church was the close political-ideological relationship it held with the secular power, embodied by the emperor. The development in the fourth century of an imperial Christian ideological system rooted in both Romano-Hellenistic political concepts and Christian theology established an unbreakable association, which was thereafter to set limits to, and yet also to legitimise, the actions of emperor and patriarch. In its most abstract form, it was understood as a relationship of mutual dependence, but the duty of the secular ruler was both to defend 'correct belief' (*orthodoxia*) as well as to protect the interests of the Church – in the form of the honour and respect accorded the priestly office – which catered

---

44   Dagron 1993; Ivanov 2008.

45   On Christianity and the evolution of Orthodoxy, see Winkelmann 1980; Dagron 1993; Hussey 1986; Dvornik 1966, 2, pp. 614–15, 652–3.

for the spiritual needs of the Christian flock. Accordingly, it was understood that the health of the state was assured only when the traditions of orthodox belief (as derived from the Apostles and the Fathers of the Church) were faithfully practised and handed down. This utopian expression of harmony and order – which the earthly kingdom was meant to strive to achieve, in imitation of Heaven – was reflected in imperial religious and secular politics and in the ways in which the emperors understood their practical role in respect of the Church, especially with regard to the convening of ecclesiastical councils and the incorporation of the principles embodied in these ideas in imperial legislation.[46] Heresy and heterodoxy were two of the constant issues which the Church, and the emperors, had to confront. The geographical and cultural variety of the Byzantine world meant that in many regions traditional, pre- or non-Christian practices could linger on unobserved for centuries, albeit in isolated and relatively limited groups. By the same token, heterodox beliefs could evolve which might, and did in some cases, evolve into major challenges to the imperial authority. Heresy was equated with political treason, conflating the religious-spiritual with the secular ideological spheres of political thought, and directly involving the imperial government in the eradication or conversion of those who believed differently, who were not right-believing, 'orthodox'. The local and ecumenical councils tried to grapple with some of the causes for heresy, namely the lack of clerical discipline or supervision in far-flung regions, the ignorance of some of the lower clergy as well as of the ordinary populace, or the arrival of immigrant population groups with different views or a different understanding of the basic elements of Christianity. Thus the Church was constantly active in this respect, often on a very low-key basis.

Now, of course, it must be apparent that this system of beliefs, in all the various modes through which it existed within the different sectors of Byzantine society and across the different geographical regions of the empire (with their very varied local cultural traditions), and the official and unofficial structures which maintained and supported it, was not itself a relation of production in any way. But it did represent the totality of values and beliefs, or symbolic universe, which people inhabited culturally, and thus determined the cultural logic through which the world, and what went on in it, could be apprehended, made sense of and acted upon. And this is the key point. Kinship relationships, the transmission of property, indeed the Roman legal inheritance as such, were all

---

46   On imperial ideology and the role of the emperor, see Dvornik 1966; Hussey 1986, pp. 297–
      310.

understood through the prism of a Christian moral universe. At the level of the state, in respect of the legitimisation of imperial power and authority; in terms of the ways through which the various groups and individuals who made up the elite secured and legitimated their own position in the social order; and at the level of the producing population, in respect of the rate of exploitation of labour power and the ways through which surplus wealth was expropriated, the ritual penetration of Byzantine society by Christian values and culturally determined practice is evident.

So far, therefore, we have identified a problem in historical materialism as it is traditionally conceived and used, and we have also seen that one way of bridging the gap between the economic and the cultural/ideological is to look at the degree of ritual penetration of a society or culture by a dominant ideological system. A useful, explicit example of the way these social mechanisms function may be sought in the ways in which Byzantine culture responded to the economic challenge presented by Italian mercantile and commercial enterprise in the eleventh and twelfth centuries.[47] The methods through which fiscal resources were assessed, collected and distributed within the territories controlled by the Byzantine state generated over the centuries a particular set of administrative-bureaucratic procedures, so that a whole institutional-managerial apparatus evolved, socially and ideologically legitimated and realised in the imperial system of precedence. The close relationship between fiscal apparatus and military organisation, especially in respect of the mechanisms through which troops and state officials in general could be supported, is the dominant feature.[48] Little room remained for reinvestment in commercial activity or enterprise at the level of production and distribution of wealth. Even when the state farmed fiscal contracts, the opportunities for private entrepreneurial activity were limited less by state intervention than by social convention: what one did with newly acquired wealth was to invest not in independent commercial enterprise, but rather in the state apparatus.[49] Titles, imperial sinecures or actual offices, and court positions were first on the list of priorities. And although land and the rent accruing from landed property (in addition to the ideologically positive realisation of self-sufficiency) were important considerations, it is clear that imperial titles and pensions were just as fundamental to the economic position of the power elite. Investment in commerce certainly took place, but however substantial it might have been, it was ideologically margin-

---

47   See also the summary in Haldon 2013.
48   See in particular Haldon 1999, esp. pp. 139–48.
49   Lemerle 1967.

alised, in terms of cultural rewards and symbolic value.[50] There is no reason to doubt the existence of a flourishing and successful commercial sector in the Byzantine empire during much of the ninth, tenth and eleventh centuries, for example, but little is known about it, and there is no evidence that it actively colonised trade routes and markets outside the limits of the immediate political influence of the empire, except possibly in the brief period from the 1030s to 1080s when, under emperors who needed to build up a metropolitan political base, merchants and commerce attained a slightly higher status than had been usual.[51] Merchants were an active and important element in urban economies by the eleventh century, but occupied a relatively subordinate – indeed almost invisible – position in the process of wealth redistribution as a whole; they possessed no status or value within the value-system of the average Byzantine. And this is not a question of Byzantines refusing to engage with commerce on the grounds that it was in some way dishonourable, an attitude (inherited from Classical attitudes and values) to be found in some texts, and a view found in the older literature, based on a simple repetition of the expression of their identity and values by a small number of literate members of the Byzantine cultural elite. This view undoubtedly was applicable to a few people, or at least to the professed views of a few individuals; but there is good evidence that successful merchant activity and commerce were held in some esteem. Indeed, both wealthy and less wealthy Byzantines were interested in the profits from trade and commerce or from the industrial production of, for example, silks (as in the area around Thebes in Greece in the eleventh and twelfth centuries, for example, where there evolved a flourishing silk industry). And by the same token, the government would hardly have invested in the maintenance of a system of customs posts at key ports had the income from trade been negligible.[52]

The archaeological evidence for trade within the empire as well as between imperial territories and outside, both in terms of artifacts and ceramics traded, as well as shipwrecks of the types of vessel used in such trade, is substantial. As previously noted, despite being an important part of urban economies by

---

50   For detailed analysis of the issue of Byzantine investment in commercial activity, see Haldon 2009, esp. pp. 181–2, 193–204, with sources and literature; Magdalino 1989. For the lack of commercial interest on the part of the dominant elite, see Hendy 1985, pp. 567–9; with Laiou 1991, pp. 266–85, and 2002a.

51   See Harvey 1989, pp. 235–6 on fairs and markets; Hendy 1985, pp. 570–90; and the surveys in Laiou 2002b, pp. 697–770, and 2002c.

52   For customs income, see also Oikonomides 1993, see 652–4; Hendy 1985, pp. 157 ff., esp. pp. 174–5 and 598 ff.; and on customs organisation, see Antoniadis-Bibicou 1963.

the eleventh century (and probably before), merchants were relatively sub-ordinated in the process of wealth redistribution as a whole, possessing no status within the value-system of the members of the social, economic and cultural establishment, especially at Constantinople. The relationship between the state, its political structures and the dominant social-economic elite thus rendered commerce marginal in ideological terms, so that wealth generated through trade appears to have been consumed directly by those engaged in such activities, or invested in the system of honours and precedence, titles and sinecures, centred on the capital and the imperial palace. That the state derived profits, in the form of the 10 percent *kommerkion* or customs tax imposed on goods at a range of important coastal or frontier collection points is clear, and we possess both textual references to the officials responsible, as well as many of their lead seals, used to conduct official business. Even at the height of the period of economic expansion during the middle and later twelfth century, the total revenue for the state from the non-agricultural sector was little more than a fifth of that from the agrarian sector. So the relative income from such sources was, until after the Fourth Crusade in 1204 and the consequent dramatic shrinkage of the empire territorially, quite small in comparison with the income from land and related taxes and dues. Only then, as the ratio of landed income to commercial income was radically altered, did trade become a significant element in the state's economy as well as in its awareness.[53]

Thus the relationship between the state, its political structures and the dominant social-economic elite in the Byzantine world rendered commerce marginal in both practical economic and ideological terms. This is fundamentally different from the situation that evolved in the Italian maritime merchant cities with which the Byzantines did business in the later eleventh and twelfth centuries, especially Venice, Genoa and Pisa. While they possessed agricultural hinterlands which generated some elite revenues, the cities were dominated by businessmen whose wealth and political power was generally dependent as much, if not more so, on commerce as on rents.[54] This was true of Venice as well as several other trading cities, which evolved a vested interest in the maintenance and promotion of as lucrative and advantageous a commerce as possible, so that the economic and political interests of the leading and middling elements were identical with the interests of the city, its political identity and its

53   See Laiou 2002c for a survey of this material, emphasising also the rise in importance of
       trade and commerce after the ninth century.
54   See López 1937.

independence from outside interference.[55] While the Byzantine government tried constantly to minimise the concessions it had to grant the Venetians (and later the Genoese and Pisans) in return for their political support, it played,[56] in contrast to the Italian maritime cities, no role at all in promoting indigenous enterprise (as far as can be ascertained), whether for political or economic reasons, and viewed commerce as simply another (minor) source of state income: commercial activity was both seen as, and was in reality, quite marginal to the society, political system and *Weltanschauung* in which it was rooted.

No dynamic merchant elite that could play a role at court, in politics or government, evolved in Byzantium. But this is not because they were outnumbered by Italians;[57] nor is it due to a purely ideological distaste for, or lack of interest in, such activity; nor is it merely the failure of an archaic and statist political-economic system to respond to new conditions. Rather it was the effect of the relationship between the political and ideological structure of the central imperial state on the one hand, and the perceptions and vested interests of the dominant social-economic elite on the other, for whose economic and political advancement an interest in commerce appeared to be both economically and politically quite irrelevant. Though there was certainly considerable interest in trade and commerce, it was neither socially nor culturally esteemed, so that for those who were involved in trade it brought no social advancement. One result was that where it did bring great wealth, those who had achieved it chose to invest in the established patterns of social status and imperial title and office. And because Italian commerce during the period from the ninth to the middle of the twelfth century was on a relatively modest scale, regarded as unimportant to the economic priorities of both state and aristocracy in Byzantium, it was enabled to prosper, perceived as neither potential challenge nor threat. Demographic expansion in Italy from the eleventh century stimulated the demand for Byzantine grain and other agrarian produce, which meant that Venetian and other traders slowly built up an established network of routes, ports and market bases, originally based on carrying Byzantine bulk as well as luxury goods and Italian or western imports to Constantinople, later expanding to a longer-distance commerce to meet the needs of an expanding Italian market. By the middle of the twelfth century, the Venetians, Genoese and Pisans had, to

---

55   For general discussion, see Hyde 1973; Abulafia 1987; Postan and Rich 1952, pp. 327–36, 345–6; Martin 1988.

56   See Lilie 1984, pp. 103–15.

57   See Lilie 1984, pp. 290–302.

a greater or lesser extent, and with different emphases in different regions, been able to entrench themselves in both the commercial and the political worlds of the eastern Mediterranean, Aegean and Black seas and thus set up a substantial challenge to the established political and economic relationships of those regions.[58]

The point here is not that Byzantines were culturally averse to commerce, but rather that those aspects of social praxis which represented the means to fulfil elite social and economic aspirations and identities generated, and were reinforced by, particular sets of ideas about the world in which trade and commerce played a marginal role. While in themselves produced and reproduced within a given set of economic relationships – the social relations of production of the Byzantine world – such ideas acted back upon these relationships. When the conditions which gave rise to those modes of social practice changed, but the order of the various elements of the symbolic universe did not, when ideas about the world did not adjust in step with such changes, then the value-system of society, or key elements thereof, could and did affect the social praxis of members of the elite to the detriment of their longer term economic and thus political interests. Byzantine ideas about how the world worked, their ability to think outside the cultural norms of their symbolic universe, were limited by those very norms. They made choices in accordance with their own cultural logic and rationales. These normative perceptions of their world determined their actions, thus mutually reinforcing patterns of social praxis which, in the event, failed to represent what we, from our historians' standpoint, can see were their vested interests, both politically and economically, from the point of view of a rationalist economic logic. This offers, in fact, a good example of the ways in which certain modes of social praxis were competitively selected (i.e. they survived better in their context) because they had the effect, in a specific historical and cultural situation, of meeting the particular demands of social structural reproduction. When the broader context shifts, when the conditions of existence within which such praxis is embedded transform or alter, social praxis must respond accordingly if the social groups or social and economic institutions and relationships these practices represent are to survive. But beliefs about the world often lag behind changes in their conditions of existence. Where such beliefs fail to respond appropriately, constraining social praxis rather than enabling it, they have a negative impact on the interests of the social-economic group which carried them. We are thus presented with

---

58   See Postan and Rich 1952, pp. 327–8, and Lilie 1984, p. 290; and especially the discussion of Martin 1988.

an example of the ways in which social relations effectively hinder the evolution of productive forces – if commerce is understood in the latter sense. This
particular conjuncture in Byzantine history offers one example of this causal
relationship, but one could draw from any social-cultural system for parallel examples. Byzantine beliefs about the world and how to act upon it were
sufficiently reinforced by the dominant concepts of their symbolic universe
in respect of status acquisition, the sources of wealth, and the maintenance
of socio-economic position, such that neither modes of social action nor the
ideas framed by such 'ways of doing' could be adjusted sufficiently to avoid the
economic and political disasters which befell the Byzantine state in the later
twelfth century.[59]

I have spent some time moving from the level of mode of production, through
social formation and the nature of the economic, to the ways in which historical change is located, and identifiably so, in the actions of individuals and
groups. In other words, I have attempted to sketch out how I envisage the
broader framework within which we motivate causal explanation (mode of
production) is linked, via the social relations of production inhering within
a given cultural system, with the social praxis of the agents, both individuals
and groups, who constitute those relationships. The explanatory connection
between belief, praxis and change offers a way of defining the causal impact
of how people think about their world. Historians who do not identify themselves with historical-materialist perspectives have been far more successful
in pulling the *affective* power of beliefs into their understanding of social and
political change, even if this is under-theorised or, alternatively, attributed
with a degree of autonomy which a historical-materialist perspective would be
unwilling to concede.[60] And where avowedly Marxist or historical-materialist
historians have built such relationships into their explanations of historical
change (for example, Christopher Hill, Eric Hobsbawm or Barrington Moore),
they have often been assumed to be moving away from historical-materialist
explanatory models because they are not economically reductionist! Marxist
historians, for the reasons noted above, generally approach their work from the

---

59   Runciman 1989a; for a useful review and discussion, see Wickham 1991, pp. 188–203.
60   For the former, almost any historical analysis of social change will exemplify the point;
     for the latter, we might cite the work of Michael Mann, for example: Mann 1986, vol. 1,
     whose construct of 'ideological power' offers an appropriately useful heuristic. For a
     medievalist perspective, see also some of the essays in Reuter 2006. My point is, simply,
     that too few historians do other than merely see beliefs as reflections of or built upon more
     'fundamental' economic relations.

perspective of social and economic structures and the transformations they undergo, and it is time to recognise that this cannot be a successful enterprise until more than lip-service is paid to the notion that human social agents are themselves the embodiment and the carriers, as well as the product, of social institutions, and build their beliefs and their concomitant social practices into explanations of the processes of change. Whether, in the process of constructing such an approach, we find ourselves moving away from 'Marxism' – whatever that now means, given the enormous range of 'marxisms' on offer – or historical materialism, to a more complex pluralist causal model, is a different question. By adopting the 'organic/skeletal' model of social relations of production outlined above, I think we retain a heuristically effective and still causally materialist explanatory system.

CHAPTER 7

Simple Commodity Production and Value Theory in Late Feudalism

Octavio Colombo

The object of this study is to analyse the conditions of existence for peasant simple commodity production in late feudalism. This issue is closely linked to the problems related to the functioning of the theory of value in a pre-capitalist context, which shall be examined in particular detail. Although the argument is a general one, we shall support it with historical references from village documents dating to the later Middle Ages in Castile.

The structure of the peasantry in the Castilian central plateau bounded by the Duero and Tajo rivers presents unique general features that define the structural limits of the phenomena to be analysed. Such elements are: the predominance of agrarian production; the predominance of small units of production – normally family-owned ones – geared to consumption; the social organisation of these independent units within a framework of community structures (the so-called *concejos*). All of the above implies the non-separation of the producers from the means of production, and therefore a commodification process that is partial and focused mostly on the local markets. Finally, producers find themselves subject to feudal forms of surplus extraction, mainly in the form of money.

We will present our argument in the following order. Firstly, we shall discuss two different conceptions with regard to the functioning of the theory of value in pre-capitalist contexts which can be traced to the works of Marx and Engels (section I). Then we will explore the more general content of the Marxist theory of value, especially in relation to the concept of simple commodity production (section II). This will be followed by an examination of some general features of simple commodity production in a feudal context (sections III to V): the unpredictability of production, the influence of extra-economic elements on the determination of prices, and the effects derived from different forms of pre-capitalist surplus appropriation. Some general conclusions are summarised in the last section.

I

Due to its widespread circulation, influence and intellectual authority, the 'Supplement' written by Engels in 1895 for Volume III of *Capital* is without a doubt the most significant text analysing the functioning of the theory of value.[1]

In his polemic with Werner Sombart and Conrad Schmidt, who had expressed objections to the historical and analytical centrality of the law of value, Engels developed the problem that came to be known as the 'historic' transformation of values into prices of production. In defence of the Marxian law, he held that labour time as the sole regulator of the exchanges had been valid throughout the whole period of commodity production, from its remotest origins up to the emergence of the developed forms of capitalist production. The sheer simplicity of the productive operations and the consequent transparency of the labour time employed, coupled with haggling – a common practice in non-developed markets – would have allowed for the direct commensurability of different concrete labours as well as the close adaptation between values and prices.

Engels's position has an epistemological root, which he had put forward many years before when he stated that the logical development of the economic categories is 'nothing but the historical method, only stripped of the historical form and diverting chance occurrences'.[2] Therefore, since political economy begins with the study of the commodity, and consequently with the law of value, Engels considered that this law was the first and simplest relationship existing in history, a methodological discussion that will be addressed later on.

It is not difficult to find a similar idea in the work of Marx. Strictly speaking, all Engels did in his 'Supplement' was to develop the logical possibilities contained in a brief statement by Marx.[3] For value to govern the exchanges, Marx posits succinctly that:

> nothing more is necessary than 1) for the exchange of the various commodities to cease being purely accidental or only occasional; 2) so far as direct exchange of commodities is concerned, for these commodit-

---

1 Engels 1966, esp. pp. 895 ff.
2 Engels 1971a, p. 225. Another reference to the parallelism between the logical and historical development in his 'Preface' of 1894 to Volume III of *Capital* (Marx 1966, p. 14).
3 Marx states that 'it is quite appropriate to regard the values of commodities as not only theoretically but also historically *prius* to the price of production' (Marx 1966, p. 177).

ies to be produced on both sides in approximately sufficient quantities to meet mutual requirements, something learned from mutual experience in trading and therefore a natural outgrowth of continued trading; and 3) so far as selling is concerned, for no natural or artificial monopoly to enable either of the contracting sides to sell commodities above their value or to compel them to undersell. By accidental monopoly we mean a monopoly which a buyer or seller acquires through an accidental state of supply and demand.[4]

These conditions would be applicable both to landowning peasants and to craftsmen, 'in the ancient as well as in the modern world'.[5]

Let us defer the analysis of these conditions for the time being in order to examine a different perspective on this problem, according to which a tendential exchange of equivalents is not verified in pre-capitalist situations because the conditions for a full operation of the law of value do not exist. Even Engels, in previous works, had contributed evidence that undermined the sweeping statements made in the 'Supplement'. By the mid-1840s, in his seminal research on *The Condition of the Working Class in England*, he was able to clearly show that the violation of the equivalence in the exchanges was a method recurrently used to the detriment of the working class, be it in the wage contract or when workers appeared in the market as consumers.[6] Furthermore, when he re-edited this work almost half a century later, Engels made it clear that those methods of appropriation tended to disappear with the deployment of the capitalist market. In the Preface written in 1892, he considers as 'a law of modern political economy that the larger the scale on which capitalistic production is carried on, the less can it support the petty devices of swindling and pilfering which characterise its early stages'.[7] Those forms of exploitation through trade lose importance and functionality with the consolidation of large industry and the forms of surplus value extraction linked to it, revealing that the cause of the exploitation and misery of the working class is not to be found in those fraudulent extortions, but in the capitalist system itself. In this comment, made only three years before the 'Supplement' to *Capital*, the operation of the law of value appears as an inseparable element from the capitalist mode of production as a developed whole, and not as a preceding premise.

---

4 Marx 1966, p. 178.
5 Marx 1966, p. 177.
6 Engels 1971b, esp. pp. 80–7. Also see Rule 1986, ch. 2.
7 Engels 1971b, p. 360.

Marx also hints at this idea. His best-known statements on this subject refer to the profit of pre-capitalist trade, a clear-cut example of appropriation through circulation, where commodities exist as values only in a qualitative sense, allowing for the commensurability of different use values, 'but they are not values of equal magnitude'.[8] Merchant capital can perform in the extent to which it acts as an intermediary between autonomous economic entities geared to the production of use values, for whom, therefore, the traded part of the surplus is of a relatively secondary importance.

Although in the aforementioned analysis Marx refers to the exchange among communities, nothing seems to preclude the application of these conclusions to the case of exchanges among independent producers (or domestic economies) geared to the production of use values. Indeed, this is what he does in his reflections on the peasant smallholding devoted to direct subsistence, a structure of production that allows the market price to be placed much below the value. The peasant can forgo the returns he is entitled to as a small capitalist and the rent he is entitled to as a small landowner 'so long as the price of the product covers these wages, he will cultivate his land, and often at wages down to a physical minimum'.[9] Under these conditions, peasant surplus labour time is given to society for free. This is a case in which the disparity between value and price derives not from the action of merchant capital, but from a noncapitalist structure of production, where the low price in relation to the value will not lead to a decrease in production (that is, abandonment of the crops).

But it is in the *Grundrisse* where Marx more clearly states this thesis. He writes:

> Prices are old; exchange also; but the increasing dominance of the former by costs of production, as well as the increasing dominance of the latter over all relations of production, only develop fully, and continue to develop ever more completely, in bourgeois society, the society of free competition.[10]

These two aspects are mutually dependent: prices come to reflect labour time, and because of this they can rule the distribution of social work, whereas, conversely, the predominance of exchange relations among producers assures

---

8   Marx 1966, p. 329.

9   Marx 1966, pp. 805–6. Marx considers that this is why the price of cereal is lower in countries where landed property is small than in those where the capitalist mode of production has developed.

10   Marx 1973, p. 156.

the tendential adaptation of the labour time invested to the socially necessary labour time, understanding the latter in two senses: (a) that the average
technology be used; and (b) that the product satisfy social needs. Marx uses
this conclusion to contrast it with the ahistorical naturalisation of commercial
relations typical of Classical Political Economy: '[w]hat Adam Smith, in true
eighteenth-century manner, puts in the prehistoric period, the period preceding history, is rather a product of history'.[11]

The reference to Smith is less contingent than it seems: it can undoubtedly
be considered as the most important precedent pertaining to the problem we
are analysing. In effect, in a well-known chapter of *The Wealth of Nations* Smith
claims that labour is the 'real measure' of the exchange value of all goods, what
he calls 'real price' in contrast to the 'nominal price' or in money.[12] According to
Smith, this was valid for primitive exchanges and only for them, since as soon
as the accumulation of capital and private property of land appear, benefit and
rent, together with labour, constitute the elements of value.[13] Later on, Ricardo
would counter this substitution of the labour theory of value for a theory of the
'sum' of the elements of value, arguing that labour is the cause of value also in
capitalist society.[14]

Therefore, what the foremost exponents of the classical theory were debat-
ing was whether labour time remained the sole component of value even in
the presence of benefit and rent. However, there was no controversy regarding the fact that, according to Smith, in the 'early and rude state of society ...
the only circumstance which can afford any rule for exchanging' is embodied
labour.[15] How do prices adjust to this pattern? Smith was aware of the difficulty
in estimating the equivalence among different labour types, but he considered
that a rough equality was achieved 'by the haggling and bargaining of the market', which, while not exact, was reasonably approximate.[16] The resemblance
between Smith's reasoning and that of Engels in the 'Supplement' of 1895 is hard
to miss: once again, we come across the idea that labour is the only input of production in primitive situations, and hence the only possible standard of meas-

---

11   Marx 1973, p. 156.
12   Smith 1910, pp. 26 ff. Smith hesitated, however, between the amount of labour embodied in
      a certain commodity and the amount of labour that can be acquired with it in the market
      as measure of value, a confusion already pointed out by Ricardo 1971, pp. 57–8; see Roll
      1956, pp. 154–60.
13   Smith 1910, pp. 41–4; Dobb 1973, pp. 43 ff.
14   Ricardo 1971, ch. 1, Section iii, pp. 65 ff.
15   Smith 1910, p. 41.
16   Smith 1910, p. 27.

urement, and that haggling works as a mechanism of equalisation between value and price. To put it in a polemical way, Marx's statement that Smith put as preceding history what in fact was a product of history (that is to say, that Smith presented as a chronological antecedent what in fact is the fundamental law of the development of the capitalist economy), can undoubtedly be applied to Ricardo and, to a good extent, to this argument of Engels. Indeed, it can even be applied to the concise Marxian statements about value as a historical antecedent of production prices.

In order to be entirely fair to Engels's 'Supplement', however, it is necessary to highlight two aspects which we consider to be of the utmost relevance, although the author presents them as subordinate statements. Engels admits, in the first place, that with the appearance of money, 'the determination of value by labour time was no longer visible upon the surface of commodity exchange'.[17] This statement is of great importance, not only because the appearance of a general equivalent is both a very early phenomenon and one that is historically widespread given the limitations of direct barter, but above all because the awareness that what is being exchanged is human labour, together with the possibility to calculate the labour time embodied in the different commodities (given the elementary nature of the labour process), was, according to Engels, a crucial argument to explain the equivalence in the exchange. If, with the appearance of money, the content of the commercial transactions is no longer as transparent as before, the mechanism by which a correspondence between value and price was established through haggling loses ground.

Secondly, Engels points out that with the introduction of money, the adaptation of prices to the law of value 'grows more pronounced on the one hand, while on the other it is already interrupted by the interference of usurers' capital and fleecing by taxation'.[18] We are again confronted with a statement that surely cannot be considered incidental, since it is a reflection that can be applied to all pre-capitalist situations with forms of money capital – which acquire value from the exchange of non-equivalents – and forms of political appropriation of surplus – that is, mechanisms of exploitation typical of all pre-capitalist class societies, which determine the main forms of distribution of social product. Further on we will have the opportunity to analyse these distorting factors in detail.

We have presented two essentially diverging conceptions of the problem. The first one posits that the law of value has been fully and immediately valid,

---

17   Engels 1966, p. 899.
18   Engels 1966, p. 898.

that is, that prices have been directly proportional to labour time throughout the pre-capitalist commodity production period and the early capitalist period, up until the appearance of significant differences in the organic composition of capital among the different branches of production, which causes direct proportionality to be mediated by the equalisation of the profit rate.[19] The second one, on the contrary, posits that it is the development of the capitalist market that tendentially guarantees the exchange of equivalents – be it in terms of price value or production prices – whereas in pre-capitalist commodity exchanges the law of value works in an incomplete or imperfect way. Hints of both conceptions can be found in Marx as well as in Engels, and those references have been picked up in the fruitful discussions on the issue that arose later: we are confronted with an ambivalence that will have to be explained in terms of the contradictory nature of the problem analysed.[20]

Before doing so, however, it is convenient to complete the picture of the approaches mentioned by exploring in depth the analysis of some aspects related to the Marxist theory of value and to the concept of simple commodity production.

II

The idea that the law of value is valid in pre-capitalist conditions seems to find strong support in the concept of simple commodity production that is commonly understood to underlie the reasoning in the first section of Volume I of *Capital*. This concept is not an arbitrary theoretical construct, a 'model' of social structure created by Marx, nor is it a pretended historical reference to a period before capitalist development.[21] Rather, it appears as the result of an abstraction: since the analysis must begin with the simplest and most general form in bourgeois society – the commodity – the abstraction of all other,

---

19 Since it is evident that the issue of production prices is not germane to pre-capitalist economies, from now on we shall refer generically to the (proportional) adaptation of prices to values.

20 Especially: Meek 1956; Morishima and Catephores 1975; Meek 1976; Morishima and Catephores 1976. The topic was dealt with in a more tangential way in Fine 1986a; questioned by Catephores 1986; the reply of Ben Fine in Fine 1986b; these three contributions in Fine 1986c.

21 Recent studies on Marxist dialectics have thoroughly documented this issue; here we generally follow those interpretations. An excellent presentation of the issue can be found in Arthur 2004.

and more developed, categories implies the concept of simple commodity production, as that is the simplest form that commodity production can take. In other words, the commodity considered as the simplest concrete element implies simple commodity production (that is to say, private property, division of labour and production for exchange), just because it excludes the capitalist nature of production, that is to say, because for the time being the analysis dispenses with the more developed categories of bourgeois society, which can only be understood later on.

Therefore, simple commodity production is neither an arbitrary supposition, nor an antecedent in a historical-temporal sense. The latter is confirmed by the first statement in *Capital*, where Marx holds that the analysis must begin with the commodity because the commodity is the elementary form in which the wealth 'of those societies in which the capitalist mode of production prevails' presents itself.[22] Modern bourgeois society is not presented as coming *after* but *simultaneously* (although implicitly at the beginning) with its own 'elementary form', and the deployment of its potentialities, especially the concept of value contained in it, implies the capitalist mode of production as the context.

But scientific knowledge can only proceed by analysing the concurrent determinants one after the other in order to create a reasoned representation of the whole. That is why the ordering of categories from the simplest to the more complex is not determined by the order of their appearance in history, but 'by their mutual relation in modern bourgeois society'.[23] In other words, the commodity as the 'elementary form' with which the analysis must begin presupposes a capitalist society whose 'elementary form' it *is*, while as an abstraction the concept of commodity excludes capitalist society because it is *only* its 'elementary form'.

The capitalist mode of production, therefore, appears as presupposed from the beginning, and the development of the analysis will only make explicit this implicit idea, in such a way that in the end it will appear as a concrete whole in place.[24] But if at the beginning there is a presupposed context and this

---

22 Marx 1965, p. 35. In the same way, Marx points out that his starting point is 'the simplest social form in which the labour product is represented in contemporary society' (Marx 1972).

23 Marx 1971, p. 210.

24 '[A]t the beginning of the entire movement of investigation the commodity already presupposes social production (capital) of which it is only an "aspect", or determination, but it is not yet posited as such an aspect' (Banaji 1979, pp. 28–9).

context is only really known at the end, this implies that the beginning, at the beginning itself – being an immediate and an abstract – does not yet have a true foundation and is therefore not really known. This is why Hegel claims that scientific knowledge has the form of a circle.[25] Thinking of the method of *Capital* from this perspective, the commodity in its developed form, and therefore the full operation of the law of value, cannot be understood as 'something given', determined from the beginning, to which the concepts of capital, wage labour, etc. are then added. On the contrary, the commodity that initially appears as the starting point, appears again at the end as the result of the capitalist production process, as the product of capital, and it is this double nature, of being at the same time both the starting point and the end point, premise and result, which defines it as such.[26] The first section of *Capital*, therefore, cannot be considered as sufficient grounds for the thesis of validity of the law of value in pre-capitalist societies.

It could be reasonably argued, however, that the commodity as such is, undoubtedly, a historical premise of capital (although as a necessary and general form it can only be its result). The unilateral affirmation of this truth is at the root of the arguments that claim the existence of a close parallelism between the methods of logic and historical evolution. The controversy lies, then, on whether the forms of pre-capitalist commodity production, which imply a necessarily partial commodification of the products of labour, can be considered sufficient requisites (and not only necessary historical premises) for a full operation of the law of value, or whether, on the contrary, the law of value can only work when the commodity form becomes necessary and general, which only occurs as a result of the global dynamics of the capitalist mode of production – in which case the commodity forms in pre-capitalist societies should be considered embryonic, incomplete forms that only allow for a distorted operation of the law of value.

These comments on Marx's method do not, however, encompass the full meaning of the concept of simple commodity production. As the simplest form that the production of commodities can adopt, it is not only a result of the abstraction necessary to begin the study of the capitalist mode of production, but a form in existence in several historically determined societies, past and present, and the same can be said, naturally, of its typical logic, c–

---

25   See Stace 1955, pp. 110 ff.

26   'If the structure of *Capital* is indeed scientific, then it is based on a *system* of concepts, interlocked and interdependent, and one cannot simply sample individual concepts as one might recipes in a cookbook' (Shaikh 1981, p. 267; Marx 1976a, part III).

M–C.[27] However, simple commodity production only exists historically as a subordinate form within the context of different dominant modes of production.[28] This is understandable: it would be a clear contradiction to envision an entirely egalitarian society in which all producers are private owners of the means of production with a highly developed division of labour and markets, but whose logic is one of the production of use values. The argument has been expressed by some authors[29] and it can be considered valid in a general sense as a critique of the potential existence of an allegedly 'pure' or dominant form of simple commodity production. For our purposes, however, what matters is not the negation of the concept as such, but the necessity to analyse such forms in certain historical and structural contexts. As Milonakis points out, simple commodity production is a 'form of production' whose general conditions of existence are given by the dominant mode of production within which it exists.[30] Thus, the dominant mode of production becomes a fundamental determinant of its functioning. If, as an abstraction, it was necessary and sufficient to deploy the contradictions inherent to the commodity form, this level of analysis does not suffice when it comes to understanding the characteristics of simple commodity production within pre-capitalist societies: the abstract-universal concept must now be specified. As we will attempt to show in due course, the social and technical determinants that frame, at least in a general sense, such societies constitute elements that must necessarily be taken into account for the study of the forms in which the law of value operates in such contexts.

The previous considerations are reinforced by inquiring into the conditions of possibility for the operation of the law of value. The question demands that we go beyond the unilateral approach of the quantitative aspect of commodity exchange, by relating it to the problem of the distribution of social labour. In his well-known letter to Kugelmann dated 11 July 1868, Marx clearly explained that the law of value is the form in which the proportional distribution of labour operates to satisfy the different needs 'in a state of society where the interconnection of social labour is manifested in the *private exchange* of the individual products of labour'.[31] In the absence of a conscientious and planned

---

27   Chevalier 1983, pp. 153–86; Friedmann 1978, pp. 71–100. For the feudal system, see Hilton 1985a, pp. 3–23.

28   Friedmann 1980, pp. 158–84; Scott 1986.

29   Especially by those who adhere to the most extreme versions of the 'value form', for example, Itoh 1988, p. 78.

30   Milonakis 1995, pp. 327–55.

31   Marx and Engels 1941, p. 246.

regulation of production, the exchange at values establishes this distribution of the social labour in specific proportions of concrete labour; in other words, the permanent difference between value and price, which is a consequence of the anarchic nature of production, induces this distribution, as a tendency to an 'equilibrium' that otherwise never happens, or that happens only by accident. The quantitative aspect of the relation between value and price can only be justly appreciated from this perspective, that is to say, insofar as the convergence takes place through a continuous differentiation that stimulates a permanent reallocation of private resources for the satisfaction of social needs. This is why Marx objected to the project of a 'money-labour', which attempted to eliminate 'the real difference and contradiction between price and value' by eliminating the nominal diversity.[32]

But the essential condition for this movement to take place is the existence of a reasonable level of competition in the market: this is the far from negligible role that the oscillations of supply and demand play in the Marxist theory.[33] In the capitalist system, the law of value imposes itself through the inter-capitalist competition that, guided by the search for greater profits, spurs the adoption of new technologies and capital mobility between branches. The logic of capital as self-valorising value causes this perpetual movement in the production sphere. In its quest for larger profits, capital objectively tends to adapt prices to the socially necessary labour time, understanding the latter by the double determinant of average labour time and social need for the product. The mechanism is known: the difference between prices and values is expressed as the difference between the profit rate of each company or branch and the average profit rate, allowing for the adoption of new technologies or the migration of capital between branches. Thus, the organic relationship between production for markets and the circulation of commodities is established: each concrete labour becomes a mere incarnation of abstract labour, the latter is distributed between the different sectors of production from decisions which are guided by the movement of prices (which affects the profit rate), and lastly, such movement is determined by the socially necessary labour time for the production of each use value.

---

32   Marx 1973, p. 138.

33   'For a commodity to be sold at its market-value, i.e., proportionally to the necessary social labour contained in it, the total quantity of social labour used in producing the total mass of this commodity must correspond to the quantity of the social want for it, i.e., the effective social want. Competition, the fluctuations of market-prices which correspond to the fluctuations of demand and supply, tend continually to reduce to this scale the total quantity of labour devoted to each kind of commodity' (Marx 1966, p. 192).

In simple commodity production, the tendential adaptation of prices to values through the reallocation of resources in the production sphere can only take place through labour mobility, which would imply the same indifference to concrete labour and the same influence of price movements on production decisions that are verified in the capitalist society. This can only be considered credible in the case of a tendentially complete commodification of the labour products, and even so it would not be a fully efficient mechanism because production is geared toward subsistence: the comparison between the commodity that begins the circuit c–m–c and the one that closes it, as qualitatively different use values, can never have the same level of quantitative precision that the comparison between m and m' allows in the capital circuit. The differences between value and price, which in the capitalist economy appear in an indirect but efficient way as variations in the profit rate, are here relatively obscured by the logic of the production system. The scope of this statement and its relation to the general features of the pre-capitalist peasant markets are examined in the next sections.

In summary, the argument so far only develops the Marxian idea that in developed mercantile societies, the law of value 'forcibly asserts itself like an over-riding law of Nature'.[34] That is to say, the law of value imposes itself not because producers demand an equivalent in terms of labour for the commodities they take to the market, but as an objective result of the decisions they make from the movement of prices. The fact that when exchanging things they are exchanging portions of social labour is a later discovery of scientific analysis. 'We are not aware of this, nevertheless we do it', says Marx.[35] The exchange at values is not grounded, as Smith and Engels believe for pre-capitalist situations, on the fact that producers measure the goods in labour time, but on the existence of economic mechanisms which, independently of any other relative level of awareness, establish an organic bond between production and circulation; which logically includes a certain property structure and, as we shall see, a certain level of development of the productive forces.

III

The reflections presented so far have a high level of abstraction, which could explain the relative stagnation affecting the debates on the issue. A more concrete approach to the phenomena under study is needed in order to overcome

---

34   Marx 1965, p. 75.
35   Marx 1965, p. 74.

this situation, including the fundamental determinants that characterise them, since those determinants, as we shall try to show, condition the pre-capitalist forms of commodity circulation.

We can begin by considering some characteristics of pre-capitalist markets that would support the thesis of the full validity of the law of value; indeed, such elements are in no way irrelevant. Perhaps the most apparent one is the simplicity of the production processes, an aspect that Engels mentioned in his 'Supplement'. In his argument, this kind of technological transparency would have allowed the peasant to know with a certain degree of precision the labour time invested in the goods he obtained through the market, which allowed him to estimate the equivalence in the terms of exchange. Besides, the relative slowness of technical innovation that characterises pre-capitalist economies would contribute to keep such labour time constant for long periods, facilitating the adaptation of prices to values due to the stability of the latter. A determinant derived from these conditions of production completes the picture: the relative invariability of social needs in general, and in particular of those which are satisfied through the market. A situation like the one described above, therefore, would not demand abrupt and significant movements of resource reallocation in the production sphere. The 'point of equilibrium' for the satisfaction of the different social needs with the available productive resources would be achieved in a relatively smooth way, as a natural consequence of experience, and the stability in production and consumption conditions would mean that such an equilibrium could be sustained for long periods without resorting to adjustments other than marginal socially imperceptible ones.

The concurrence of other factors helps support this reasoning. The marginal reallocation of resources would be facilitated by the inexistence of production branches as such. In the villages, as Xenophon points out in reference to the peasants of Antiquity, the same craftsman made beds, doors, ploughs, tables, and even houses: the reduced dimensions of the market made it impossible for him to survive otherwise.[36] This lack of rigidity in the productive specialisation would facilitate the correction of excessive distortions in the structure of prices, at least when they have their origin in the difference between the magnitude of the supply of a certain use value and the social demand for it. Besides, as a rule the craftsmen were not completely separated from agrarian production, and cultivated small pieces of land. Hence, the possibility that producers with direct access to the means of production had to fall back onto self-consumption in case of a deep deterioration of the terms of exchange worked as an added

---

36   *Cyropaedeia*, VIII, 2, 5.

resource reinforcing this state of affairs. The defensive isolation in the 'natural economy' would work, in this way, as a form of indirect competition, since it constitutes an alternative to an unfavourable movement of prices.[37]

A very important historical concept that would confirm this analysis is the notion of 'just price' which, at least in European medieval tradition, constitutes the touchstone not only of theological reflections on exchange, but also, and most importantly, of the particular social practices developed by the peasants who participated in the markets. Indeed, the village documents from the later Middle Ages are filled with references to the justice of the exchanges: peasants complain that the prices of certain goods are 'unjust', the local authorities establish that it is 'just' that certain goods should cost so much, etc. A revealing example from 1502 is a case in point: in the Castilian village of Cáceres, the wine producers and merchants demanded an increase in prices, arguing that labour productivity in the local vineyards was low in comparison to that of other regions.[38] All this can undoubtedly be considered as empirical grounds supporting the thesis of the transparent nature of pre-capitalist value relations: the concept of justice applied to the quantitative aspect of the transactions is inseparable from some notion of equivalence, as well as from some capacity for its perception and evaluation. Therefore, it would be a proper manifestation of the social conditions that allow a close adaptation between values and prices.

The picture presented above includes the essential determinants that support the thesis of a full validity of the law of value whose importance cannot be ignored. It can, however, be objected that such determinants have been selected in a relatively arbitrary and unilateral way, without relating them to equally important structural characteristics that modify the meaning of the analysis and contradict that thesis. The considerations below attempt to correct this shortcoming by taking into account some characteristics inherent to the production and commercialisation conditions of pre-capitalist peasant economies. Our object is to arrive at a conceptual reconstruction that, without losing its general nature, allows us to express in concrete terms the commercial phenomena under study insofar as they are immersed in social wholes that condition them.

The fluctuating nature of the agrarian product, which is by far and under any criterion the most important aspect of total production in pre-capitalist societies, is one element ignored by the previous analysis whose repercussions

---

37   Milonakis 1995, p. 335.

38   García Oliva 1988, doc. 209, 14/9/1502, p. 408: *las vinnas que se plantasen en la dicha villa de Cáçeres serían muy costosas de labrar e llevavan poco fruto.*

cannot be minimised. In agriculture there are 'infinite accidents that man's calculation cannot foresee',[39] hence the emphasis that ancient thought placed on the idea that the success of labour depended on the favour of the divine forces. Medieval documents abound in references to shortages due to climate and their destructive impact on trade relations.[40] It is interesting to note that feudal powers took advantage of these price fluctuations in order to carry out various abusive practices in the collection of taxes in kind, demanding that the product be relinquished at the time of the shortage and higher prices, which resulted in increased extraction and aggravated the producers' circumstance.[41]

The unpredictable variability of labour productivity, a consequence of the relatively small control of man over nature, constitutes an inherent feature of pre-capitalist societies;[42] and the same can be said of the lack of efficient means of transportation that would have allowed for the relative equalisation of the local or regional imbalances. This situation, by itself, negates to a large extent the stable nature of production that, as we have seen, would derive from the slowness of technological innovation. In consequence, it affects the absolute and relative structure of the solvent demand, since the latter is a function of the producers' income.

Even in the favourable hypothesis that on principle the variations in agrarian prices were inversely proportionate to production volume, one bad harvest would substantially affect the food supply, because the marketable surplus of the agrarian producers would decrease more than proportionately with respect to global volume. The combination of the fluctuating nature of labour productivity with a structure of small producers geared to subsistence amplifies the disruptive effect on market conditions. Even with better prices, most of the producers would have nothing to sell once their needs of self-consumption had been met, and they could even be forced to cover these through the market. Given this reduction in the peasants' income, the demand of non-agrarian

---

39 Xenophon, *Oeconomicus*, v, 18.

40 The documents attribute the variations in productivity to the 'weather', the 'year' and to the epidemics that struck livestock. There are innumerable references of this sort both in the chronicles of the period and in the *Cortes* documents. Here are a few examples taken from the meetings of the council of the village of Madrid in Millares Carlo and Artiles Rodríguez 1932; I, 17/7/1483 (p. 251); 9/6/1484 (p. 337); II, 14/4/1489 (p. 137); 24/4/1489 (p. 140), 14/4/1492 (p. 334).

41 Real Academia de la Historia 1866, pet. 13 (year 1433); Hernández Pierna 1995, doc. 85, 28/7/1495; Monsalvo Antón 1995, doc. 18, 7/5/1498; García Pérez 1996, doc. 44, 6/7/1499; García Oliva 1988, doc. 206, 30/6/1502.

42 Vilar 1974, pp. 37–58.

products (whose prices would go down even though labour times were not modified) would decrease, and those who offer those non-agrarian products must also acquire their means of subsistence at a higher price. The crisis of agrarian sub-production, then, leads to a crisis of sub-consumption in the secondary sector, a confluence that is manifested at the level of the social whole as a demographic crisis.[43] Under these conditions, the bankruptcy of the market implies the bankruptcy of the peasants' economy of subsistence, but it does not imply a form of unconscious and anarchist social regulation (but regulation after all) of the production.

This situation, which is typical of partially commodified agrarian economies, only reflects, in the form of chronic imbalances between supply and demand, the low development of the productive forces, which is understood as the impossibility to guarantee that needs will be met with the available social resources, even when both resources and needs remain stable. If we take into consideration the three conditions that Marx had established for exchange at values to take place, it becomes apparent that the production of different commodities in proportions adequate to the needs (2nd condition) is not a simple result of the continuous development of the exchanges (1st condition), but it also requires a certain degree of control over nature that is not found in pre-capitalist societies.

This situation allows us to understand the high degree of rationality in the behaviour of peasants, who do not make production decisions based on price movements. Indeed, no producer in those circumstances would reduce the cultivated area after an abundant harvest season and low prices; neither would he have the possibility of increasing it in the inverse scenario. Given the secondary nature of the marketable surplus, and given that the evolution of prices – agrarian and non-agrarian – does not reflect the need to reallocate productive resources but the unpredictable nature of the output, the non-indifference of the producer with respect to concrete labour constitutes a reassurance to guarantee the social reproduction in spite of the relatively undetermined nature of labour productivity. Therefore, even when, as we have supposed, agrarian prices should evolve in all cases in an inversely proportional manner with regard to productivity, it cannot be stated in any substantive sense that the law of value should be operating in full force as a mechanism of distribution of social labour among private producers, that is, as a regulatory law of production. It would only be valid for agrarian commodities, and in an exclusively quantitative sense, that is, in relation to the magnitude of the value but not as

---

43   A phenomenon that was especially studied by Labrousse 1933.

a social form regulating relations between producers.[44] Such a notion could fit the definition of value proposed by Classical Political Economy, but not that of Marxist theory.[45]

The relative impermeability between production and circulation in partially commodified societies, as seen in the late medieval world, is therefore due to profound material and social reasons, not to miscalculation on the part of pre-capitalist producers, to the weight of tradition on them or to their psychic incapacity, as has sometimes been suggested.

IV

Having said that, we must now question the assumption that prices evolve following closely the fluctuations in labour productivity. If the law of value does not work in a qualitative sense, it is really hard to believe that it would work in its quantitative aspect; that is, that without determining the distribution of social labour, it does determine the proportions of the exchanges.[46] In fact, it can be shown that this is not the case. We only need to consider that the oscillations in agrarian production imply that only accidentally does the production correspond with the needs (the supply with the demand), a *sine qua non* condition for prices to be proportional to values. Of course, this also occurs in the capitalist market, but the difference in degree becomes qualitative in this case. In capitalism, the oscillations of supply and demand trigger compensatory mechanisms that allow for both magnitudes to coincide on average in the middle term, and therefore for the prices to coincide on average with values.[47] On the contrary, in pre-capitalist markets these oscillations cannot be corrected because, as we have seen, they derive from the non-developed nature of the

---

44 And this only in the very ample sense of labour time invested in the production of a certain use value.

45 Marx criticised Smith and Ricardo for having considered only the analysis of the magnitude of value, ignoring the specific nature of the value form as a historically determined social relation (Marx 1965, pp. 80–1, n. 2).

46 This is what Milonakis erroneously seems to believe (Milonakis 1995, pp. 335–6).

47 Marx 1966, p. 190. It is this coincidence that justifies the need for the theory of value, as Marx explains some lines above: 'If supply equals demand, they cease to act, and for this very reason commodities are sold at their market-values ... If supply and demand balance one another, they cease to explain anything, do not affect market-values, and therefore leave us so much more in the dark about the reasons why the market-value is expressed in just this sum of money and no other' (Marx 1966, p. 189).

productive forces. And to this we must add the secondary and residual nature of the marketable surplus, which implies that fluctuations in the latter have much greater amplitude than the ones of the total volume of production, and therefore they are not proportional to the variations in productivity.

The situation thus presented implies that in a bad harvest the increase of labour time required for the production of one unit of agrarian product (due to the decrease in productivity) corresponds to a reduction in the global labour time destined to production for exchange (due to the more than proportional decrease of the marketable surplus), a phenomenon that compounds the effect of the sub-production crisis on prices. Furthermore, this is an exactly inverse movement to the one registered in the capitalist economy, where a price increase over the value, inasmuch as it manifests itself as an increase in the profit rate, leads to the allocation of more (not less) social labour to the commodified production of that use value.

It can be postulated, then, that the social and technical characteristics of peasant production imply that production does not necessarily correspond with the social needs in a tendential manner, and that market supply does not proportionally correspond with the volume of production. In these conditions, the magnitude of the difference between price and value comes to be determined by reasons which are external to the production sphere, and even external to the economic relation in a narrow sense. It must be remembered, in this respect, that the socially necessary labour time as a foundation for value, is assessed in terms of *present* labour needed for production and reproduction of a specific use value. Indeed, the exorbitant prices achieved by the means of subsistence in moments of serious shortage reflect the temporary unrepeatable nature of such goods. We are confronted, in fact, with the chronic generation of monopoly scenarios arising from an 'accidental state of supply and demand' that Marx mentions in his third condition as an obstacle for exchange at values to take place. In addition, as we have already seen, the variations in agrarian prices determine the demand for non-agrarian commodities, and thus their prices are also affected not only in relative terms but also as absolute magnitudes.

Given these structural conditions of indetermination and unpredictability that surround the formation of prices, it is not at all surprising that market conditions in peasant communities were not left to the capricious interplay of purely economic forces.[48] Indeed, we have plenty and varied historical inform-

---

48   Which is, strictly speaking, nothing more than a particular aspect of the inexistence of the economic sphere as an autonomous sphere within the social whole.

ation showing that the determination of prices is mediated by extra-economic elements.[49] In some cases, the political authority fixes prices unilaterally. The general rules promoted by the European feudal powers in the context of the prolonged late medieval crisis, which unified prices and wages in their extensive domains regardless of the varying economic conditions in each place, reflect this subordination of the market to political regulations.[50]

The less rigid exchange systems require a more extensive comment, because the understanding of their nature is ultimately at the centre of the controversy. Let us consider again the problematic of the 'just price'. We have already reviewed the argument, which connotes implicitly a degree of conscious perception of equivalence, and where the relative undifferentiation of different concrete labours allows this equivalence to regulate the exchanges through labour mobility. Let us examine the problem in detail. Can it be postulated that the labour invested is the subjective standard of reference in the determination of prices? Although it is really difficult to solve this problem in a clear-cut manner, several elements allow us to doubt this reasoning's apparent simplicity.

In pre-capitalist societies, labour is often not even perceived as an action directed to the transformation of nature, that is to say, as an activity that creates the product.[51] This idea is especially valid for agriculture, the activity of the overwhelming majority of the population, in which the result of the production process is objectively mediated by the intervention of natural forces beyond human control. In this regard, the temporal and technical distance blurs the role of human activity, which appears as effort and punishment, as a tribute to divinity rather than a productive action. The worship of nature and magical practices meant to manipulate supernatural powers to one's own advantage reflect the limitations that producers face on a daily basis in barely developed agrarian societies.[52]

---

49   In extreme circumstances, we find fixed prices entirely determined by cultural traditions, although this situation is more common in intercommunity commerce, a case that exceeds the limits we have established; see Herskovits 1952, ch. IX. The most evident example is when a tribe exchanges with others the same commodity at different fixed rates depending on the nature of the relations linked to each buyer; see Godelier 1973a, pp. 259–93.

50   Romero 1980, pp. 60 ff. In the case of the Castilian Crown, the most important price regulations correspond to the years 1268, 1351 and 1369. For the English case, see Seabourne 2003.

51   A global vision of the medieval period can be found in Fossier 2000. As regards Ancient Greece, see Vernant 1965, esp. ch. IV.

52   Gurevich 1990, pp. 81 ff.

Proposing generalisations with regard to craft labour is more challenging.[53] The craftsman's activity underwent a significant revaluation during the medieval period, especially in the context of the development of the division of labour which was characteristic of the central Middle Ages.[54] But this progress, which was reflected in Christian ideology and achieved its maximum expression in the semi-artistic nature of luxury manufactures, was not linked to a rehabilitation of labour in its strict economic sense, but as a form to guarantee a decent livelihood (that is to say, in accordance with the place of the producer in the social hierarchy).[55] The direct, unmediated relationship between producer and product warrants the social appreciation of the skilled occupation and gives the subject moral satisfaction, but precisely because of this it is unlikely that labour time as an economic magnitude devoid of any other consideration should be considered the subjectively evident standard of measurement by which to establish the exchange terms among different commodities.

Although it exceeds the limits of this work, it should be noted that the thesis according to which producers calculate the price according to the labour invested is also questionable in at least some contemporary scenarios. Cook's study on Mexican *metateros* provides us with a very useful example. In defence of Engels's thesis, the author states that producers 'count the total number of labour-days spent in producing a *metate* and convert this to a money equivalent by referring to the going wage for a day laborer'.[56] The case is illuminating because, in fact, the equivalence of the embodied labour time with respect to valid wages negates the thesis of the correspondence between value and price, for the simple reason that wages suppose unpaid labour time (and of course it ignores the wear of the labour tools). The producers, immersed in a capitalist economy, have at their disposal a monetary parameter to know

---

53   In slave societies, where, according to Marx, the producer is assimilated to the inorganic conditions of production, the craftsman is also affected by that dominant social conception. According to Aristotle, production works in the same way as nature: as the plant comes from the plant through the seed, the house comes from the house through the craftsman: *Metaphysics*, z, 9. The object is not the result of the producer's labour, but of an external form to which the person must submit.

54   Le Goff 1977. And this even when the ideology of the feudal lord continued considering the popular handcraft skilled occupations as *low and vile*; Real Academia de la Historia 1866, *Cortes* of Valladolid of 1447, p. 542.

55   Gurevich 1985.

56   Cook 1982, p. 280. The *metate* is a manual windmill made of stone used in the domestic processing of grains.

the 'value of their labour': the value paid in the market for labour power. The subjective comparison between 'invested labour – valid wages – price' means that the product is sold below its value as a consequence of the social conditions in which this form of commodity production geared to subsistence develops. We bring up this case here because it confirms that the conditions of reproduction of simple commodity production are determined by the dominant social relations, which in this particular case is the salary relationship.

Let us move on to the other aspect, complementary to the previous one, which is implicit in Engels's thesis: the assumption that limited specialisation, in a context of low technological development, makes self-evident the qualitative commensurability of the different concrete labours and enables the labour mobility that guarantees the equivalence.

The problem refers in part to the considerations already mentioned: the non-recognition of labour as a productive activity in general implies its non-recognition as abstract, directly interchangeable labour. The equalisation of the different concrete labours is not solved at a technical level, but at a social one. It is a matter not of subjective consciousness, but of social structure. No matter how elementary they are, a weaver's labour is qualitatively different from that of a tailor, and twenty yards of linen can only equal a coat as long as an abstraction of those specific qualities is made through a social trade relation, even though producers are not aware of it. Here there seems to be some confusion between the reduction of complex labour to simple labour, which can indeed be facilitated by low technical development, and the transformation of concrete labour into abstract labour, a problem of a radically different nature. Specifically, Ricardo's conception (but not the Marxist one) makes the mistake of ignoring the difference between concrete and abstract labour, which leads to identifying the substance of value with the labour immediately invested in production and not with the abstract socially necessary labour time.[57] It is not the simplicity of the productive process, but the alienation of the producer from the product as a result of the generalised production of commodities, which allows for the conversion of each singular and concrete labour into mere manifestation of universal and abstract human labour.

Lastly, we must address the problem of labour mobility, since it could be argued that even without the intervention of the subjective element we have just analysed (that is to say, without the subjective existence of the qualitative equality of labour in general and therefore its quantitative equivalence in the

---

57   Gerstein 1986.

exchange), an elementary technological production structure with low development of specialisation would allow by itself the necessary labour mobility to guarantee the adaptation of prices to values.

Again, the problem is not technical but social. As we have explained above, peasants do not make their productive decisions based on prices, and this behaviour is consistent with the essential features of partially commodified agrarian economies. Besides, the relations of production – especially the pre-capitalist relations of exploitation – bind the peasant to farming: thus, the producer's social form of existence becomes partially identified with a particular form of the productive process. Also, it is likely that craftsmen, as Xenophon says, could conceivably produce an array of related goods. This implies, undoubtedly, labour mobility within the loosely defined skilled occupations, or, in other words, of 'families' of related skilled occupations, but nothing else beyond that. A carpenter could produce from beds to houses, but not shoes; a shoemaker could not produce nails, or a blacksmith clothes, etc. The fifteenth-century price regulations in the Castilian kingdom normally mention about two hundred hand-made products corresponding to several dozen skilled occupations, and even this we know to be an incomplete listing. Furthermore, in late medieval villages, the production or commercialisation of many key goods is carried out through a system of 'obligados': only those who obtain a licence from the local authorities are permitted to trade, and this authorisation implies in turn an obligation to provide certain commodities.[58]

But even in the cases in which labour mobility is a verifiable phenomenon, the logic guiding it does not necessarily tend to guarantee the adaptation of prices to values. The semi-peasant and semi-craftsman producer's behaviour, on the contrary, can have the undesired effect of making matters worse. According to the abovementioned study by Cook, the production of metates increases in bad harvest seasons, because the agrarian production is insufficient to assure the subsistence of the domestic units, so some parts of the domestic unit become occasional producers of manufactures.[59] As a result, in a situation in which the demand of hand-made products is lower and the price cheaper, the producers, finding themselves unable to gear their efforts towards the production of goods which are effectively insufficient, direct their energies towards the sectors in which there is an oversupply.

---

58   This is the system that normally applies to butchers, innkeepers, bakers, etc. For example, in the Castilian village of Piedrahíta, bakers must register on an official list and they are obliged to work as such the whole year; Luis López 1987, doc. 89, 6/9/1511.

59   Cook 1982, p. 312.

Finally, the reversion to the natural economy, which has been presented as a possible response mechanism in the face of excessive price distortions, also has its limits. As soon as the tax obligations in money appear, the participation of the producer in the market stops being an 'alternative' and instead becomes an imposition.[60] It can also be suggested that the division of labour imposes an inescapable recourse to the markets, albeit one that is less coercive in the beginning: peasants can defer their purchases in a particularly unfavourable juncture, but it is highly unlikely that they could commit for a continued or prolonged period to an autarchy that not even the classic ideal of the *oikos* regarded as feasible.[61] There is historical evidence to confirm this argument: the most recent research on the late medieval period highlights that trade relations tend to grow even in the context of sudden fluctuations in price and in the value of money.[62]

All this does not negate the existence of some kind of perception of equivalence; as we have already said, it is implicit in the notion itself of 'just price'. What ought to raise doubts, however, is firstly whether this general criterion of justice had a clear correspondence with the cost of production measured in labour time.[63] On the other hand, if we assume a mediated or distorted perception of non-equivalence in terms of 'abusive' prices – which we believe to be a more acceptable notion – it can be doubted that this should give rise, in the concrete conditions in which production develops, to an adjustment in the distribution of social labour that should guarantee the re-establishment of the correspondence of prices with values. Indeed, in the event of a disproportionate increase in the prices of certain goods, the private decision to apply resources to their production is only one of the possible alternatives. Another alternative, which is consistent with our reasoning and duly documented, is to resort to non-economic mechanisms to counteract what is considered an 'unjust price'. This is the reason why the more or less rigid mechanisms of price

---

60   Wood 1999 has emphasised the coercive nature of the involvement in the market.

61   That is why Aristotle says that the commerce destined to obtain use values for consumption is an inseparable activity from the art of domestic administration, and as such is not to be condemned; *Politics*, 1257 a. For Plato, the impossibility to be self-sufficient is the proper ground of the state; *Republic*, 369 b.

62   Dyer 2005. The classical study on the subject is Britnell 1993.

63   It has been stated, more reasonably, that this criterion of justice has as a reference the reproduction of the social form of existence of the producer, a mechanism that explains, for example, that the craftsman who makes sumptuary goods should systematically sell below the value, thus allowing, at least partly, for the valuation of the commercial capital; see Astarita 1992. See also Gurevich 1985.

fixing are so widespread in village communities, a feature that by itself ratifies that placing the dictates of the social and political imperatives above those of the market is the only socially viable alternative. When peasants demand that the authorities price the commodities, they are ratifying that prices do not work for them as indicators for production, and that, therefore, there is no objective economic mechanism that guarantees their tendential adaptation to values. The obsessive preoccupation with the justness of prices, which will only disappear with the development of capitalist social relations and of a market that does not need to be 'perfect' in order to be autonomous, makes this plainly visible. Otherwise, the relative awareness of the non-equivalence can only operate from outside the productive structure, as a political or moral imperative that tries to impose itself in an authoritative way over a commodified economy that it does not control (because it is based on private production), but which does not have internal mechanisms that guarantee its self-regulation either.

As is to be expected, normally the price set by the authorities is not arbitrary, but it has some relation to the economic variables.[64] In medieval Castilian villages, the agricultural products and their by-products, like wine, are usually priced annually; a mechanism that partially contemplates the harvest yields and at the same time prevents seasonal variations that favour speculation. Even in other cases, like those of fish, meat and water, the moment of the year, quality and availability are taken into account when setting the price. Local merchants are allowed to add a profit percentage which is legally fixed over the price they paid when they bought their commodities.[65] But this process of price formation can in no way be considered exclusively or mainly determined by labour time, and even less by the circumstantial conditions of supply and demand.[66] We must bear in mind, in this sense, that price fixing is only an aspect of a much broader policy of regulation, which includes, depending on the cases, prohibition of exports or imports, obligation to sell in the marketplace, priority of purchase for consumers over resellers, coercion to work in the 'obligatory' skilled occupations, fixed percentages of profit for merchants, etc. Sometimes they even cancel any other way of alternative commercialisation, as shown in an example from a medieval village: neighbours can only sell their leather to tanners and shoemakers of the village, at the price fixed by the council.[67]

---

64   By the end of the Middle Ages, the theory of 'just price' admits a degree of elasticity that it did not have before; Tawney 1961, ch. 1.

65   There are plenty of references to these cases in Colombo 2008.

66   As stated by the classic liberal conception; see De Roover 1958.

67   Luis López 1993, Sotillo de La Adrada, 27/9/1500, ch. CXXIIII.

The issue of 'just price' as a social practice, therefore, cannot be understood if one abstracts from this context, reducing the issue to the analysis of scholastic reflections on the topic. The quantitative determination of prices is the result of a complex process, and as a result it is conditioned by it. It bears reiterating that this is valid even when the objective economic conditions were not completely ignored by these political decisions, and even when these norms were less omnipotent than they aspired to be, since in moments of severe crisis and imbalances they are incapable of solving the objective problems of social reproduction. But it is true, as Luis de Molina stated in the sixteenth century, that the instance of political-institutional decision comes between the production conditions and the commercialisation conditions, following the 'criterion of the prudent', a criterion that does not limit itself to sanctioning the circumstantial situation of the economic factors.[68] Witness this particular case in which we know the difference between 'just price' and 'free price': in the Castilian village of Piedrahíta, the price of a couple of partridges – traditionally 16 *maravedíes* – had increased to 40 during the first decades of the sixteenth century. The authorities dictate a maximum price of 20 *maravedíes*, and at the same time they prohibit their export.[69] The intention in cases like this one is to introduce a principle of stability in order to protect the reproduction of small producers in their relation to a market that, by not reflecting the production conditions, cannot operate by itself as an instance of social articulation, and cannot guarantee the tendential equivalence of the exchanges. Let's make the meaning of the statement clear: this does not reflect the intervention of a 'moral economy of the crowd' over a market that otherwise would be governed by autonomous economic mechanisms, but the presence of a socio-political regulatory framework which is indispensable due to the indetermination and accidental nature that characterise markets where the law of value does not fully function. In such structural conditions, interventionism is in fact an inseparable aspect of commercial relations, since it responds to an objective social need derived from the non-developed conditions of production and of the market.

Excluding the cases of more rigid prices, in which there is no room for any type of negotiation, it behooves us to address the issue of haggling, a practice deemed to be responsible for guaranteeing equivalence at the circulation level, even when labour distribution is not governed by the law of value.[70] It can

---

68   De Molina 1981, Disputa 348; as regards the difference between 'just price' and 'free price' in modern economic theory, see the extensive 'Introducción' by Francisco Camacho, pp. 9–105.

69   Luis López 1987, doc. 97, 8/1/1513.

70   A general analysis of haggling can be found in Uchendu 1967, pp. 37–50.

indeed be assumed that when production corresponds with the social need, haggling, or even a flexible fixing of the 'just price', establishes an approximate equivalence. In our opinion, this ought to be interpreted as an *occasional* or *accidental* exchange of equivalents, since it does not reflect the full operation of the law of value as a mechanism that guarantees equivalence in a *tendential* way. Excluding this situation, price haggling comes to be determined by the relative power of those involved. What is more, the power of the parties in the negotiation is obviously influenced by other factors: the peasant may be forced to accept a disadvantageous deal due to the absence of opportunity costs,[71] because he needs to sell in order to pay taxes or debts, etc. (see below). Haggling, as any other social practice, can only be understood in a specific context. All that can be said in a general sense is that the mere existence of haggling as a generalised practice indicates that, in any specific moment considered, there is not a unique price for each commodity, but 'particular prices' for each transaction, determined by the relative powers of negotiation of the intervening subjects.[72] When the peasant appears as seller in the market, the normative level of the 'just price' is compatible with the undervalued sale by the peasant, since the 'just price' is always a maximum price, which is consistent with the protection of the buyer that typifies this 'economy of consumption'. And when the economic imbalances worsen beyond a certain limit, be it due to an objective shortage or to practices of stockpiling and speculation – which we shall address shortly – all commercial legislation turns out to be ineffective and the negotiation of prices openly becomes an aspect of the class struggle for the appropriation of the product.

In this scenario, the price may be placed somewhere within a broad range surrounding the equivalent price, a range in which the transaction would imply transference of value, but without necessarily affecting the minimum reproduction of the disadvantaged producer. Ideally, this occurs when producers satisfy all of their needs through direct consumption, commercialising only the surplus in a strict sense, a situation in which the breadth in the range of possible prices that fulfil the stated purpose does not have, in theory, any kind of limit. Contrarily, when commodification includes part of the subsistence, tax obligations or production costs, the deterioration in the terms of exchange affects the reproduction possibilities of the producer in the short- or mid-term – an impact

---

71   This factor has been considered essential in the so-called 'rural industry', as a mechanism that allows the sub-valuation of domestic labour power in favour of merchant capital; see Kriedte, Medick and Schlumbohm 1981.

72   Gallego Martínez 1992, p. 11.

whose concrete incidence is a function derived from the degree of commodi-fication and from the magnitude of the difference between price and value.[73]

The degree to which a certain historical situation is closer to one case or another must be grounded in the analysis of concrete cases. The general statement only serves as a means to clarify a double phenomenon that is apparently contradictory. In effect, it allows us to explain that even when the exchange is not equivalent, the whole social structure is able to reproduce itself over time. But it also explains, on the other hand, that this very reproduction can carry the conditions of the transformation, insofar as in certain historical contexts some social subjects are able to direct the indeterminate nature of the terms of exchange to their benefit, which gives rise to processes of differential accumulation that, in turn, tendentially affect the part of the product that corresponds to the producer's subsistence. We shall briefly develop this point in the next section.

V

The political-institutional intervention of community powers in the determin-ation of prices and the general conditions of commercialisation is not the only extra-economic element that shapes the dynamic of the exchanges. Also at this level, feudal extractions play a major role. Normally, moreover, the amounts of these impositions do not have a close relation with the variable productive yields: on the contrary, they are either constant or they are determined by the political situation, as is the case of the 'extraordinary' taxes.[74] In the feudal sys-tem, although there is a tendency to stabilisation demanded by the nascent development of a centralised bureaucracy and carried out through the leases of rents, the amounts effectively collected depend ultimately on the classes' rel-ative positions of strength. Lastly, from the point of view of their actual impact

---

73   This is the key aspect of the critique of the statement of Witold Kula made by Patnaik 1988.

74   Labour rents would be an exception. Nevertheless, the tithe or any other form of rent in kind calculated as a percentage of the gross production (including seeds) turns out to be a regressive imposition that affects more than proportionately the poorer domestic units, and whose percentage encumbrance is greater in bad harvest seasons. Lastly, at least in the feudal system, the taxes on circulation tend to become fixed impositions on the community from their inception: see, for example, the 'reparto de alcabala' made by the council of Pinares among all its neighbours, in Del Ser Quijano 1987, doc. 69–74, December of 1488. The impact of rents on peasant reproduction has been correctly analysed by Roseberry 1976.

over peasant reproduction, it must be pointed out that in a generic sense feudal extractions also include the monetary devaluations, the chronic abuses in rent collections and the no less frequent effects of seigneurial banditry.[75]

The consequences of these forms of surplus extraction on the operating conditions of peasant markets are notorious. When taxes materialise into money, the producer finds himself periodically under the obligation to sell his surplus in order to make the payment; what is more, the sale is not followed by a purchase, but this money is withdrawn from commercial circulation and goes into the extra-economic circuits of distribution of the product among classes. This phenomenon of 'forced commercialisation' forces the peasant, due to considerations which are external to his material reproduction in a strict sense,[76] to sell 'at any price'. Commercialisation conditions worsen if, as is often the case, the tax is collected immediately after the harvest, at the moment when the supply is greater.

The existence of extractions that are not proportional to income, and can become arbitrary in situations of political upheaval, introduces a new accidental element in the markets. This only expresses, at the circulation level, the nature of the social relations that characterise the pre-capitalist societies of classes. Since producers are not full owners of the means of production, but holders subject to extra-economic coercion, the implicit idea in simple commodity production that one's own labour is the only entitlement for appropriation is not fulfilled. Inevitably, pre-capitalist relations of property condition the operation of the law of value. Only by converting the exploited classes of the past into communities of free private proprietors can anything different be formulated.

The contradictions of these forms of exploitation facilitate the development of peasants' indebtedness. Specifically, this is about a much larger problem, already documented in the Old Testament, whose conditions of possibility derive from the annual fluctuations and the seasonal nature of peasant production in a context of partial commodification. In addition, when the domestic units find themselves under the obligation to periodically comply with the rent payment, or are subject to arbitrary extractions by the dominant class, the fragility of their everyday reproduction is compounded. In the face of impositions

75   On devaluations, see Spufford 1988. On seigneurial banditry in Castile, see Moreta 1978; complaints on the abuses of tax collectors are recurrent in the *Cortes de los Antiguos Reinos de León y de Castilla* (Real Academia de la Historia 1866). As is known, the first attempt at scientific rationalisation of the tax system in relation to a global analysis of the productive structure corresponds to physiocracy.

76   That is to say, for reasons related to his social reproduction as exploited.

that do not have a strict correlation with the volume of production, they must get into debt in order to pay. An eloquent example: in 1477, none other than the Catholic Monarchs, ignoring the unanimous ecclesiastical condemnation of usury, ordered the council of Ávila to allow peasants to take interest-bearing loans so that they could pay the tax.[77] Later on, the servicing of debts and their increased interest rates recreate and compound the conditions of 'forced commercialisation', and the successive recourse to debt tends to become an integral part of the reproduction conditions of the producer.[78] Other mechanisms of usurious exploitation, like the advance sale of product at a low price,[79] or the purchase of subsistence goods on credit at exorbitant prices,[80] constitute morphed manifestations of these types of unequal exchange. The historical documentation ratifies the significance of these obstacles to the operation of the law of value which, as stated above, Engels pertinently pointed out.

It is therefore confirmed that the third and last condition that Marx stipulated for exchange at values to take place is substantially called into question: the conditions that force producers to sell 'at any price' have a great incidence in peasant pre-capitalist markets. And this is not only due to the specific interference of class powers from outside the village. Even the community structure, which carries within itself the contradictions that characterise privately developed social production, internalises and reproduces the phenomena of appropriation through circulation, thus distorting the operation of the law of value. Indeed, medieval peasantry, especially in communities with partial but relatively high commodification indexes, presents internal social differentiations, which, combined with the commercial phenomena analysed, enable accumulation on the part of better-off peasants. When the mid-size and poor peasants are forced to sell at a low price in order to pay the rent, the situation is advantageous for the wealthier peasants who have monetary reserves (and for whom the taxes tend to be proportionately lower).[81] These sectors stockpile subsistence goods, and they may even create artificial shortages of food, so as

---

77   Casado Quintanilla 1994, doc. 22, 9/3/1477.
78   Roseberry 1978, pp. 3–18. As late as 1947, the neighbours of the village of Pinares are involved in legal actions for the renewal of obligations that originated in loans taken out to pay taxes twenty years before; Del Ser Quijano 1987, doc. 85, 3/1/1497.
79   In Castile, peasants who are short of money are forced to pre-sell their production at such low prices that they later become trapped in a vicious cycle of indebtedness; Real Academia de la Historia 1866, pet. 34 (year 1433), p. 180.
80   Some complaints regarding sales on credit at exorbitant prices in Luis López 1987, doc. 113, 18/3/1525, p. 235; Monsalvo Antón 1995, vol. XIV, doc. 24, 18/3/1498, p. 59.
81   Da Graca 2003.

to resell it at higher prices later on, probably to the producers who had previously been forced to undersell their surplus.[82] The mechanisms of valuation deployed by these sectors include not only stockpiling and speculation, but also fraud with false weights and measures, and the adulteration of the quality of products.[83] Therefore, in certain historical circumstances, the obstacles to the operation of the law of value enable the emergence of a village capital that valorises itself through unequal exchange, and which in its development tends to deploy practices of accumulation that compound the non-adaptation of prices to values.

VI

We have attempted to show that non-developed forms of commodification are far from being characterised by their simplicity and immediacy – that is to say, by the transparent operation of the law of value unmediated by the equalisation of the profit rates. Quite to the contrary, they are notable for their relative indetermination, for material reasons as well as for social ones. This does not effectively preclude the existence of exchanges that do respect the equivalence, just as the operation of the law of value in developed capitalist economies does not preclude the existence of unequal exchanges. To put it in an axiomatic way, the full operation of the law of value is not only compatible with, but also presupposes the existence of exchanges that do not respect the equivalence, since it rules the exchange only in a tendential manner. Correspondingly, the existence of equivalent exchanges is compatible with an incomplete operation of the law of value, inasmuch as such exchanges can accidentally occur without the existence of a mechanism that guarantees their tendential equivalence.

At the same time, this leads to an emphasis on the integral relation between the 'quantitative' and 'qualitative' aspects of value, which the debates on the issue have tended to split apart in a unilateral and abstract way.[84] Thus, the supporters of the 'embodied labour' approach believe in the full validity of the law of value in pre-capitalist contexts, whereas those who uphold a qualitative approach to value as 'form' have denied the importance of labour time even in

---

82   This situation is denounced in Real Academia de la Historia 1866, pet. 34 (year 1425), p. 73.

83   Kula 1986. A detailed description of commercial frauds based on the manipulation of weights and measures was presented to Juan II by municipal public prosecutors in the *Cortes* of Toledo of 1436 (Real Academia de la Historia 1866, p. 251 ff.). Different examples of these forms of appropriation are in Colombo 2011.

84   With regard to this, see Likitkijsomboon 1995.

developed capitalist economies. To the contrary, in the preceding analysis we have tried to show that value as a social relation can only function when prices reflect the production conditions, and this occurs only when the relations of production are governed by the law of value. In consequence, a general formulation of the concept of simple commodity production cannot be immediately applied to the study of the medieval peasant economy; first it must determine through historical analysis the manner in which the latter is shaped by the dominant mode of production.[85]

---

85   Here we depart from the manner of approaching the issue presented in Diquattro 2007, which employs purely analytical forms in its theoretical aspects, and subjective forms in the historical aspects, in order to deny the operation of the law of value in the North American colonies of the eighteenth century, which he characterises as 'a kind of moral economy' (p. 464) in which producers 'did not want to sacrifice their economic independence ... neither did they aspire to be capitalists' (p. 460).

References

Abulafia, David 1987, *Italy, Sicily and the Mediterranean, 1100–1400*, London: Variorum Reprints.

Abu-Lughod, Janet 1989, *Before European Hegemony: The World System A.D. 1250–1350*, Oxford/New York: Oxford University Press.

Ahmad, Aijaz 1992, 'Marx on India: A Clarification', in *Theory: Classes, Nations, Literatures*, London: Verso.

Akerlof, George A. and Rachel E. Kranton 2010, *Identity Economics: How Our Identities Shape Our Work, Wages and Well-Being*, Princeton/Oxford: Princeton University Press.

Alfonso, Isabel 2002, 'Conflictos en las behetrías', in *Los señoríos de behetría*, edited by Carlos Estepa Díez and Cristina Jular Pérez-Alfaro, Madrid: Consejo Superior de Investigaciones Científicas.

Allam, Schafik 1973, *Hieratische Ostraka und Papyri aus der Ramessidenzeit*, Urkunden zum Rechtsleben im alten Ägypten, 1, Tübingen: Selbstverlag des Herausgebers.

———— 1989, 'Some Remarks on the Trial of Mose', *Journal of Egyptian Archaeology*, 75: 103–12.

———— 1990, 'A New Look at the Adoption Papyrus (Reconsidered)', *Journal of Egyptian Archaeology*, 76: 189–91.

———— 2004, 'Une classe ouvrière: les merit', in *La dépendance rurale dans l'Antiquité égyptienne et proche-orientale*, edited by Bernadette Menu, Cairo: Institut Français d'Archéologie Orientale.

Allen, James P. 2002, *The Heqanakht Papyri*, New York: Metropolitan Museum of Art.

Allen, Robert C. 1992, *Enclosure and the Yeoman: the Agricultural Development of the South Midlands, 1450–1850*, Oxford: Clarendon Press.

Althusser, Louis and Étienne Balibar 1970 [1968], *Reading Capital*, London: New Left Books.

Amin, Samir 1976 [1973], *Unequal Development: An Essay on the Social Formations of Peripheral Capitalism*, Sussex: The Harvester Press.

Anderson, Perry 1979 [1974], *Lineages of the Absolutist State*, London: Verso.

———— 1996 [1974], *Passages from Antiquity to Feudalism*, London: Verso.

Andersson, Theodore M. 1964, *The Problem of Icelandic Saga Origins*, New Haven, CT: Yale University Press.

Andrade Cernadas, José Miguel (ed.) 1995, *O Tombo de Celanova*, II, Santiago de Compostela: Consello da cultura galega.

Andreau, Jean 2001, *Banque et affaires dans le monde romain. IVe siècle av. J.-C.–IIIe siècle ap. J.-C.*, Paris: Seuil.

Andreu, Guillemette 1991, 'Deux stèles de commissaires de police (jmy-r šnt) de la Première Période Intermédiaire', *Cahiers de Recherches de l'Institut de Papyrologie et d'Égyptologie de Lille*, 13: 17–23.

Anrup, Roland and María Eugenia Chaves 2005, 'La plebe en una sociedad de todos los colores. La construcción de un imaginario social y político en la colonia tardía en Cartagena y Guayaquil', *Caravelle Cahiers du Monde Hispanique et Luso-Brésilien*, 84: 93–128.

Antoniadis-Bibicou, Hélène 1963, *Recherches sur les douanes à Byzance, l'"octava", le "kommerkion" et les commerciaires*, Paris: Cahiers des Annales.

Arndt, Wilhelmus and Bruno Krusch (eds.) 1885, *Gregorii episcopi Turonensis, Historia Francorum, Monumenta Germaniae Historica, Scriptores rerum Merovingicarum*, I, 1, Hannover: Hahn.

Árni Daníel Júlíusson 2010, 'Signs of power', *Viking and Medieval Scandinavia*, 6: 1–29.

Arthur, Christopher 2004, *The New Dialectic and Marx's Capital*, Leiden/Boston: Brill.

Assmann, Jan 1999, 'Cultural and Literary Texts', in *Definitely: Egyptian Literature*, Lingua Aegyptia, Studia Monographica 2, edited by Gerald Moers, Göttingen: Seminar für Ägyptologie und Koptologie.

———— 2005 [1996], *Egipto: Historia de un Sentido*, Madrid: Abada.

Astarita, Carlos 1992, *Desarrollo desigual en los orígenes del capitalismo*, Buenos Aires: Tesis XI.

———— 1994, 'La discutida universalidad del sistema tributario', *Studia Historica. Historia Medieval*, 12: 191–201.

———— 2000a, 'Historia y ciencias sociales. Préstamos y reconstrucción de categorías analíticas', *Sociohistórica*, 8: 13–43.

———— 2000b, 'La primera de las mutaciones feudales', *Anales de Historia Antigua, Medieval y Moderna*, 33: 75–106.

———— 2003, 'El factor político en los modos feudal y tributario. Génesis y estructura en perspectiva comparada', in *El modo de producción tributario*, edited by Carlos García Mac Gaw and John Haldon, monographic issue of *Anales de Historia Antigua, Medieval y Moderna*, 35–6: 133–74.

———— 2003–6, 'Prácticas del conde y formación del feudalismo. Siglos VIII al XI', *Anales de la Universidad de Alicante. Historia Medieval*, 14: 21–52.

———— 2005, *Del feudalismo al capitalismo. Cambio social y político en Castilla y Europa Occidental, 1250–1520*, Valencia: Publications de la Universitat de València/Universidad de Granada.

———— 2007a, 'Construcción histórica y construcción historiográfica de la temprana Edad Media', *Studia Historica. Historia Medieval*, 25: 247–69.

———— 2007b, 'Tesis sobre un origen gentilicio patrimonial del feudalismo en el noroeste de España. Revisión crítica', *Anales de Historia Antigua, Medieval y Moderna*, 39: 99–127.

———— 2011, 'Peasant-Based Societies in Chris Wickham's Thought', *Historical Materi-alism*, 19(1): 194–220.

Aston, Trevor Henry and Charles H.E. Philpin (eds.) 1985, *The Brenner Debate*, Cambridge: Cambridge University Press.

Azzara, Claudio and Pierandrea Moro 1998, *I capitolari italici. Storia e diritto della dominazione carolingia in Italia*, Rome/Milan: Viella/Editrice La Storia.

Azzara, Claudio and Stefano Gasparri 2004, *Le leggi dei longobardi. Storia, memoria e diritto di un popolo germanico*, Rome: Viella/Editrice La Storia.

Baer, Klaus 1962, 'The Low Price of Land in Ancient Egypt', *Journal of the American Research Center in Egypt*, 1: 25–45.

———— 1963, 'An Eleventh Dynasty Farmer's Letters to His Family', *Journal of the American Oriental Society*, 83, 1: 1–19.

Bagge, Sverre 1991, *Society and Politics in Snorri Sturluson's Heimskringla*, Berkeley: University of California Press.

———— 2010, *From Viking Stronghold to Christian Kingdom*, Copenhagen: Museum Tusculanum.

Bailey, Anne M. and Joseph R. Llobera 1981, *The Asiatic Mode of Production: Science and Politics*, London: Routledge & Kegan Paul.

Baines, John 1996, 'Contextualizing Egyptian Representations of Society and Ethnicity', in *The Study of the Ancient Near East in the 21st Century*, edited by Jerrold S. Cooper and Glenn M. Schwartz, Indiana: Eisenbrauns.

Banaji, Jairus 1979, 'From the Commodity to Capital: Hegel's Dialectic in Marx's *Capital*', in *Value: The Representation of Labour in Capitalism*, edited by Diane Elson, London: CSE Books.

———— 2010, *Theory as History: Essays on Modes of Production and Exploitation*, Leiden/Boston: Brill.

———— 2011, 'Late Antiquity to the Early Middle Ages', *Historical Materialism*, 19(1): 109–44.

Bang, Peter F. 2008, *The Roman Bazaar*, Cambridge: Cambridge University Press.

Barbero, Abilio and María Isabel Loring García 1991, '"Del palacio a la cocina": estudio sobre el conducho en el Fuero Viejo', *En la España Medieval*, 14: 19–44.

Barceló, Miquel 1990, 'Vísperas de feudales. La sociedad de *Sharq* al-Andalus justo antes de la conquista catalana', in *España. Al-Andalus. Sefarad: síntesis y nuevas perspectivas*, edited by Felipe Maíllo Salgado, Salamanca: Ediciones Universidad de Salamanca.

———— 1994, '¿Qué antropología para al-Andalus?', in *Los orígenes del feudalismo en el mundo mediterráneo*, edited by Pierre Toubert and Chris Wickham, Valencia: Universidad de Granada.

Bard, Kathryn A. 2000, 'The Emergence of the Egyptian State', in *The Oxford History of Ancient Egypt*, edited by Ian Shaw, Oxford: Oxford University Press.

Barton, Simon 1997, *The Aristocracy in Twelfth-Century León and Castile*, Cambridge: Cambridge University Press.

Bartra, Roger 1975, *Marxismo y sociedades antiguas. El modo de producción asiático y el México prehispánico*, Mexico D.F.: Grijalbo.

——— (ed.) 1983 [1969], *El modo de producción asiático. Antología de textos sobre problemas de la historia de los países coloniales*, Mexico D.F.: Era.

Baud, Michel 1999, *Famille royale et pouvoir sous l'Ancien Empire égyptien*, Cairo: Institut Français d'Archéologie Orientale.

Benton, Ted 1984, *The Rise and Fall of Structural Marxism*, London: Macmillan.

Berger, Peter and Thomas Luckmann 1967, *The Social Construction of Reality*, Harmondsworth: Penguin Books.

Bermejo Barosoain, Africa 1988, 'La estratificación social a la vista de los contratos de aprendizaje artístico. Pamplona en la segunda mitad del siglo XVI', *Actas del II Congreso Mundial Vasco*, Vol. 3, *Economía, sociedad y cultura durante el Antiguo Régimen*, San Sebastián: Editorial Txertoa Argitaldaria.

Bernstein, Henry and Terence Byres 2001, 'From Peasant Studies to Agrarian Change', *Journal of Agrarian Change*, 1(1): 1–56.

Beyerle, Franz and Rudolf Buchner (eds.) 1954, *Lex Ribuaria, Monumenta Germaniae Historica, Leges nationum Germanicarum*, III, 2, Hannover: Hahn.

Bhaskar, Roy 1978 [1975], *A Realist Theory of Science*, Hassocks: Harvester Press.

Biezunska-Malowist, Iza and Marian Malowist 1989, 'L'esclavage antique et moderne. Les possibilités de recherches comparées', in *Mélanges Pierre Lévêque 2. Anthropologie et société*, edited by Marie Madeleine Mactoux and Evelyne Geny, Paris: Annales Littéraires de l'Université de Besançon.

Bjørkvik, Hallvard 1970, 'Nyare forskning i norsk seinmellomalder', in *Nytt fra norsk middelalder*, II, Oslo: Norsk lektorlag.

Blackburn, Robin 1996, 'Slave Exploitation and the Elementary Structures of Enslavement', in *Serfdom and Slavery: Studies in Legal Bondage*, edited by Michael L. Bush, London/New York: Longman.

Blackledge, Paul 2006, *Reflections on the Marxist Theory of History*, Manchester: Manchester University Press.

Blackman, Aylward M. and Thomas E. Peet, 1925, 'Papyrus Lansing: A Translation with Notes', *Journal of Egyptian Archaeology*, 11: 284–98.

Bloch, Marc, Moses Finley et al. (eds.) 1975, *La transición del esclavismo al feudalismo*, Madrid: Akal.

Bloch, Maurice 1991, 'Language, Anthropology and Cognitive Science', *Man*, New Series, 26(2): 183–98.

——— 2004 [1983], *Marxism and Anthropology*, London: Routledge.

Bois, Guy 1984 [1976], *The Crisis of Feudalism: Economy and Society in Eastern Normandy c. 1300–1550*, Cambridge: Cambridge University Press.

———— 1989, *La mutation de l'an mil: Lournand, village mâconnais de l'Antiquité au féodalisme*, Paris: Fayard.

Bonnassie, Pierre 1975, *La Catalogne du milieu du xe à la fin du xie siècle: croissance et mutations d'une société*, 2 Vols., Toulouse: Association des Publications de l'Université de Toulouse-Le Mirail.

———— 1981, *Les cinquante mots clefs de l'histoire médiévale*, Toulouse: Éditions Privat.

———— 1985, 'Survie et extinction du régime esclavagiste dans l'Occident du haut Moyen Âge (ive–xie s.)', *Cahiers de Civilisation médiévale*, 28: 307–43.

Bonnaz, Yves 1987, *Chroniques asturiennes. Fin ixe siècle*, Paris: Éditions du Centre National de la Recherche Scientifique.

Boretius, Alfredus (ed.) 1883, *Capitularia regum Francorum, Monumenta Germaniae Historica*, I, 3, Hannover: Hahn.

Boserup, Ester 1993 [1965], *The Conditions of Agricultural Growth*, London: Earthscan Publications Ltd.

Bosticco, Sergio 1959, *Le Stele egiziane dall'Antico al Nuovo Regno*, Rome: Museo Archeologico di Firenze.

Bourdieu, Pierre 1990 [1980], *The Logic of Practice*, Stanford: Stanford University Press.

Bourriau, Janine 2000, 'The Second Intermediate Period (c. 1650–1550 BC)', in *The Oxford History of Ancient Egypt*, edited by Ian Shaw, Oxford: Oxford University Press.

Boutruche, Robert 1959, *Seigneurie et féodalité*, I: *Le premier âge des liens d'homme à homme*, Paris: Aubier.

Bradley, Keith R. 1998, *Slavery and Rebellion in the Roman World: 140 BC–70 BC*, Bloomington, IN: Indiana University Press.

Brenner, Robert 1976, 'Agrarian Class Structure and Economic Development in Pre-Industrial Europe', *Past and Present*, 70: 30–75.

———— 2000, 'The Low Countries in the Transition to Capitalism', *Journal of Agrarian Change*, 1(2): 169–241.

Brennu-Njáls saga, 1954, *Íslenzk fornrit*, 12, edited by Einar Ó. Sveinsson, Reykjavík: Hið íslenzka bókmenntafélag.

Britnell, Richard H. 1993, *The Commercialisation of English Society 1000–1500*, Cambridge: Cambridge University Press.

———— 2001, 'Specialization of Work in England, 1100–1300', *The Economic History Review*, 54(1): 1–16.

Brown, Peter 2003 [1996], *The Rise of Western Christendom*, Oxford: Blackwell Publishers.

———— 2012, *Through the Eye of a Needle: Wealth, the Fall of Rome and the Making of Christianity in the West, 350–550 AD*, Princeton, NJ: Princeton University Press.

Brundage, James 1987, *Law, Sex, and Christian Society in Medieval Europe*, Chicago/London: University of Chicago Press.

Butzer, Karl W. 1976, *Early Hydraulic Civilization in Egypt: A Study in Cultural Ecology*, Chicago: University of Chicago Press.

Byock, Jesse 1982, *Feud in the Icelandic Saga*, Berkeley/Los Angeles/London: University of California Press.

———— 2001, *Viking Age Iceland*, London: Penguin.

Byres, Terence J. and Harbans Mukhia (eds.) 1986, *Feudalism and Non-European Societies*, London: Frank Cass.

Cahen, Claude 1963, 'Réflexions sur l'usage du mot féodalité', in *Recherches Internationales à la lumière du marxisme*, 37: 203–14.

Calleja Puerta, Miguel 2001, *El conde Suero Vermudez, su parentela y su entorno social. La aristocracia asturleonesa en los siglos XI y XII*, Oviedo: KRK ediciones.

Callender, Gae 2000, 'The Middle Kingdom Renaissance (c. 2055–1650 BC)', in *The Oxford History of Ancient Egypt*, edited by Ian Shaw, Oxford: Oxford University Press.

Callinicos, Alex 2004, *Making History: Agency, Structure and Change in Social Theory*, Leiden/Boston: Brill.

Callow, Chris 2001, *Landscape, Tradition and Power in a Region of Medieval Iceland*, Birmingham University PhD thesis.

———— 2006, 'Reconstructing the Past in Medieval Iceland', *Early Medieval Europe*, 14(3): 297–324.

Campagno, Marcelo 2003, 'El modo de producción tributario y el Antiguo Egipto. Reconsiderando las tesis de Samir Amin', in *El modo de producción tributario*, edited by Carlos García Mac Gaw and John Haldon, monographic issue of *Anales de Historia Antigua, Medieval y Moderna*, 35–6: 61–80.

Campbell, Colin 1912, *The Miraculous Birth of King Amon-Hotep III. And Other Egyptian Studies*, Edinburgh: Oliver and Boyd.

Campos, Julio and Ismael Roca Meliá 1971, *Reglas monásticas de la España visigoda*, Madrid: La Editorial Católica.

Capogrossi Colognesi, Luigi 1982, 'Grandi Proprietari, contadini e coloni nell'Italia romana (I–III D.C.)', in *Società Romana e Impero Tardoantico*, edited by Andrea Giardina, Rome: Laterza.

Carandini, Andrea 1985, 'Schiavitù antica e moderna a confronto', in *Settefinestre. Una villa schiavistica nell'Etruria romana*, edited by Andrea Carandini, Modena: Ed. Panini.

Cardoso, Ciro 1973, 'El modo de producción esclavista colonial en América', in *Modos de producción en América Latina*, edited by Carlos Sempat Assadourian et al., Mexico: Cuadernos de Pasado y Presente 40.

———— 1982, *Egito antigo*, São Paulo: Brasiliense.

———— 1986, 'Les communautés villageoises dans l'Égypte ancienne', *Dialogues d'Histoire Ancienne*, 12: 9–31.

———— 1988, *Sociedades do Antigo Oriente Próximo*, São Paulo: Ática.

———— 1990, *Modo de Produção Asiático. Nova Visita a um Velho Conceito*, Rio de Janeiro: Editora Campus.

———— 1993, *Hekanakht: pujança passageira do privado no Egito antigo*, Niterói: Universidad Federal Fluminense.

———— 2009, 'Las unidades domésticas en el Egipto antiguo', in *Parentesco, patronazgo y Estado en las sociedades antiguas*, edited by Marcelo Campagno, Buenos Aires: Facultad de Filosofía y Letras.

Carling, Alan 1986, 'Rational Choice Marxism', *New Left Review*, 160: 24–62.

Carr, Karen E. 2002, *Vandals to Visigoths: Rural Settlement Patterns in Early Medieval Spain*, Ann Arbor, MI: University of Michigan Press.

Carrington, Roger C. 1931, 'Studies in the Campanian *Villae Rusticae*', *Journal of Roman Studies*, 21: 110–30.

Casado Quintanilla, Blas 1994, *Documentación Real del Archivo del Concejo abulense (1475–1499)*, Ávila: Institución 'Gran Duque de Alba'.

Catephores, George 1986, 'The Historical Transformation Problem. A Reply', in *The Value Dimension: Marx versus Ricardo and Sraffa*, edited by Ben Fine, London/New York: Routledge & Kegan Paul.

Centre d'Études et de Recherches Marxistes 1972, *Sur le féodalisme*, Paris: Editions Sociales.

Černý, Jaroslav 1945, 'The Will of Naunakhte and the Related Documents', *Journal of Egyptian Archaeology*, 31: 29–53.

Černý, Jaroslav and Alan Gardiner 1957, *Hieratic Ostraca*, Vol. 1, Oxford: Griffith Institute at the University Press.

Cervelló Autuori, Josep 1996, *Egipto y África. Origen de la civilización y la monarquía faraónicas en su contexto africano*, Barcelona: Ausa.

Chalmeta, Pedro 1973, 'Le problème de la féodalité hors de l'Europe chrétienne: le cas de l'Espagne musulmane', *Actas del II Coloquio Hispano-Tunecino de Estudios Históricos*, Madrid: Insituto hispano-árabe de cultura.

Chavarría Arnau, Alexandra 2004, 'Interpreting the Transformation of Late Roman *villas*: the Case of Hispania', in *Landscape of Change: Rural Evolutions in Late Antiquity and the Early Middle Ages*, edited by Neil Christie, Aldershot: Ashgate.

Chesneaux, Jean 1964, 'Le mode de production asiatique: quelques perspectives de recherche', *La Pensée*, 114: 33–55.

———— 1983 [1969], 'Perspectivas de investigación', in *El modo de producción asiático. Antología de textos sobre problemas de la historia de los países coloniales*, Mexico D.F.: Era.

Chevalier, Jacques 1983, 'There is Nothing Simple about Simple Commodity Production', *Journal of Peasant Studies*, 10(4): 153–86.

Childe, Gordon Vere 1936, *Man Makes Himself*, London: Watts.

———— 1942, *What Happened in History*, Harmondsworth: Penguin Books.

Clover, Carol J. 1982, *The Medieval Saga*, Ithaca, NY: Cornell University Press.

Códigos españoles concordados y anotados, 1872, Vol. 1, Madrid: Antonio de San Martín, Editor.

Cohen, Gerald 1978, *Karl Marx's Theory of History: A Defence*, Oxford: Clarendon Press.

Coleman, James 1974, *Power and the Structure of Society*, New York: W.W. Norton.

———— 1979, 'Rational Actors in Macrosociological Analysis', in *Rational Action: Studies in Philosophy and Social Science*, edited by Ross Harrison, Cambridge: Cambridge University Press.

———— 1986, *Individual Interests and Collective Action*, Cambridge: Cambridge University Press.

Collantes de Terán Sánchez, Antonio 1983, 'El artesanado sevillano a través de los protocolos notariales', *Annales de la Faculté des Lettres et Sciences Humaines de Nice (Les Espagnes médiévales. Aspects économiques et sociaux)*, 46: 165–74.

Colombo, Octavio 2008, 'Crecimiento mercantil y regulación política (Castilla, siglos XIV–XV)', *Studia Historica. Historia Medieval*, 26: 153–75.

———— 2011, 'El intercambio desigual en los mercados locales. Formas de explotación comercial del campesinado en la Castilla del siglo XV', *Edad Media. Revista de Historia*, 12: 215–42.

Comninel, George 2000, 'English Feudalism and the Origins of Capitalism', *Journal of Peasant Studies*, 27(4): 1–53.

Cook, Scott 1982, *Zapotec Stoneworkers: The Dynamics of Rural Simple Commodity Production in Modern Mexican Capitalism*, Lanham: University Press of America.

Cooney, Kathlyn M. 2006, 'An Informal Workshop: Textual Evidence for Private Funerary Art Production in the Ramesside Period', in *Living and Writing in Deir el-Medine. Socio-historical Embodiment of Deir el-Medine Texts*, edited by Andreas Dorn and Tobias Hofmann, Basel: Schwabe.

———— 2007, *The Cost of Death: The Social and Economic Value of Ancient Egyptian Funerary Art in the Ramesside Period*, Egyptologische Uitgaven series 22, Leiden: Netherlands Institute of the Near East.

Córdoba de la Llave, Ricardo 1984, 'Notas para el estudio de los aprendices en Córdoba a finales del siglo XV', *Ifigea*, 1: 49–56.

Costambeys, Marios 2006, 'Review of *Framing the Early Middle Ages*, by Chris Wickham', *The Economic History Review*, 59: 417–19.

Cruz-Uribe, Eugene 1988, 'A New Look at the Adoption Papyrus', *Journal of Egyptian Archaeology*, 74: 220–3.

Da Graca, Laura 2003, 'Feudal Dynamics and Runciman's Competitive Selection of Practices in Late Medieval Castile: An Essay on Differing Processes of Social Differentiation in a Pre-Capitalist Context', *Journal of Agrarian Change*, 3(3): 333–66.

———— 2008, 'Reflexiones metodológicas sobre el estudio comparativo de Chris Wickham', *Edad Media. Revista de Historia*, 9: 265–97.

——— 2009, *Poder político y dinámica feudal. Procesos de diferenciación social en distintas formas señoriales (siglos XIV–XVI)*, Valladolid: Universidad de Valladolid/Secretariado de Publicaciones e Intercambio Editorial.

Dagron, Gilbert 1993, 'Le Christianisme byzantin du VIIe au milieu du XIe siècle', in *Histoire du Christianisme IV: évêques, moines et empereurs (610–1054)*, edited by Gilbert Dagron, Pierre Riché et al., Paris: Desclée.

Dal Lago, Enrico and Constantina Katsari 2008, 'The Study of Ancient and Modern Slave Systems', in *Slave Systems: Ancient and Modern*, edited by Enrico Dal Lago and Constantina Katsari, Cambridge: Cambridge University Press.

David, Arlette 2011, 'The nmH and the Paradox of the Voiceless of the Eloquent Peasant', *Journal of Egyptian Archaeology*, 97: 73–85.

Davidson, Donald 1984, *Inquiries into Truth and Interpretation*, Oxford: Clarendon Press.

Davidson, Neil 2011, 'Centuries of Transition', *Historical Materialism*, 19(1): 73–97.

Davies, Wendy 1996, 'On Servile Status in the Early Middle Ages', in *Serfdom and Slavery: Studies in Legal Bondage*, edited by Michael Bush, London/New York: Longman.

Davis, David B. 2000, 'Looking at Slavery from Broader Perspectives', *American Historical Review*, 105(2): 452–66.

De Ayala Martínez, Carlos 1994, 'Relaciones de propiedad y estructura económica del reino de León: los marcos de producción agraria y el trabajo campesino (850–1230)', in *El reino de León en la alta Edad Media*, VI, *Fuentes y estudios de historia leonesa*, 53, León: Archivo Histórico Diocesano.

De Hinojosa, Eduardo (ed.) 1919, *Documentos para la historia de las instituciones de León y Castilla (siglos X–XV)*, Madrid: Centro de Estudios Históricos.

De Ligt, Luuk 2000, 'Studies in Legal and Agrarian History II: Tenancy under the Republic', *Athenaeum*, 88: 377–91.

De Melo Tunes, Cássio M. 1990, 'O Modo de Produção Asiático e o Egito Antigo', in *Modo de Produção Asiático. Nova Visita a um Velho Conceito*, Rio de Janeiro: Editora Campus.

De Molina, Luis 1981 [1597], *La teoría del justo precio*, Madrid: Editora Nacional.

De Neeve, Pieter W. 1984a, *Peasants in Peril. Location and Economy in Italy in the Second Century BC*, Amsterdam: Gieben.

——— 1984b, *Colonus*, Amsterdam: Gieben.

De Roover, Raymond 1958, 'The Concept of the Just Price: Theory and Economic Policy', *The Journal of Economic History*, 18(4): 418–34.

De Salis, Ludovicus Rudolfus (ed.) 1892, *Leges Burgundionum, Monumenta Germaniae Historica, Leges nationum Germanicarum*, Hannover: Hahn.

Del Álamo, Juan (ed.) 1950, *Colección diplomática de San Salvador de Oña (822–1284)*, I, Madrid: Consejo Superior de Investigaciones Científicas. Escuela de Estudios Medievales.

Del Ser Quijano, Gregorio (ed.) 1981, *Documentación de la catedral de León (siglos IX–X)*, Salamanca: Ediciones Universidad de Salamanca.

———— 1987, *Documentación medieval del archivo municipal de San Bartolomé de Pinares (Ávila)*, Ávila: Institución 'Gran Duque de Alba'.

———— 1994, *Colección diplomática de Santa María de Otero de las Dueñas (León)*, *(854–1037)*, Salamanca: Ediciones Universidad de Salamanca.

Dhoquois, Guy 1971, *Pour l'histoire*, Paris: Anthropos.

———— 1973, 'La formación económico-social como combinación de modos de producción', in *El concepto de formación económico-social*, edited by Cesare Luporini and Emilio Sereni, Mexico: Cuadernos de Pasado y Presente 39.

Diakonoff, Igor M. 1974, *Structure of Society and State in Early Dynastic Sumer*, Monographs of the Ancient Near East 1/3, Los Angeles: Undena Publications.

Díaz Canseco, Laureano 1924, 'Sobre los fueros del valle de Fenar, Castrocalbón y Pajares: notas para el estudio del fuero de León', *Anuario de Historia del Derecho Español*, 1: 337–81.

Diego Espinel, Andrés 2011, 'El Reino Medio', in *El Antiguo Egipto: Sociedad, Economía y Política*, edited by José Miguel Parra Ortiz, Madrid: Marcial Pons.

Diquattro, Arthur 2007, 'The Labor Theory of Value and Simple Commodity Production', *Science & Society*, 71(4): 455–83.

Dobb, Maurice 1946, *Studies in the Development of Capitalism*, London: Routledge & Kegan Paul.

———— 1973, *Theories of Value and Distribution since Adam Smith: Ideology and Economic Theory*, Cambridge: Cambridge University Press.

Dockés, Pierre 1982 [1979], *Medieval Slavery and Liberation*, Chicago: University of Chicago Press.

Dopsch, Alfons 1951 [1918], *Fundamentos económicos y sociales de la cultura europea (de César a Carlomagno)*, Buenos Aires: Fondo de Cultura Económica.

Duby, Georges 1978 [1973], *The Early Growth of the European Economy: Warriors and Peasants from the Seventh to the Twelfth Century*, New York: Cornell University Press.

Dunn, Stephen 1982, *The Fall and Rise of the Asiatic Mode of Production*, London: Routledge & Kegan Paul.

Dvornik, Francis 1966, *Early Christian and Byzantine Political Philosophy*, 2, Washington D.C.: Dumbarton Oaks Studies Nine.

Dyer, Christopher 1994 [1991], 'Were There Any Capitalists in Fifteenth-Century England?', in *Everyday Life in Medieval England*, Hambledon/London: Cambridge University Press.

———— 2005, *An Age of Transition? Economy and Society in England in the Later Middle Ages*, Oxford: Clarendon Press.

Dyson, Stephen L. 2003, *The Roman Countryside*, London: Duckworth.

Edgerton, William F. 1951, 'The Strikes in Ramses III's Twenty-Ninth Year', *Journal of Near Eastern Studies*, 10(3): 137–45.

Elster, John 1985, *Making Sense of Marx*, Cambridge: Cambridge University Press.

Endrei, Walter 1971, 'Changements dans la productivité de l'industrie lainière au Moyen Âge', *Annales. Economies, Sociétés, Civilisations*, 26, 6: 1291–9.

Engels, Frederick 1966 [1895], 'Supplement to *Capital*, Volume III', in Karl Marx, *Capital*, Volume III, Moscow: Progress Publishers.

————— 1968a [1893], 'Letter to F. Mehring', in Karl Marx and Frederick Engels, *Selected Works in One Volume*, London: Lawrence and Wishart.

————— 1968b [1890], 'Letter to J. Bloch', in Karl Marx and Frederick Engels, *Selected Works in One Volume*, London: Lawrence and Wishart.

————— 1970 [1884], *The Origins of the Family, Private Property and the State*, in *Marx and Engels Selected Works*, Vol. 3, Moscow: Progress Publishers.

————— 1971a [1845], *The Condition of the Working Class in England*, Oxford: Basil Blackwell.

————— 1971b, 'Karl Marx. A Contribution to the Critique of Political Economy', in Karl Marx, *A Contribution to the Critique of Political Economy*, London: Lawrence and Wishart.

————— 1983 [1853] 'Letter to Marx 6 June 1853', in *Marx and Engels Collected Works*, Vol. 39, Moscow: Progress Publishers.

————— 1987 [1878], *Anti-Dühring*, in *Marx and Engels Collected Works*, Vol. 25, Moscow: Progress Publishers.

————— 1989 [1875], *On Social Relations in Russia*, in *Marx and Engels Collected Works*, Vol. 24, Moscow: Progress Publishers.

Engemann, Carlos 2006, *De Laços e de Nós: constituição e dinâmica de comunidades escravas em grandes plantéis do sudeste brasileiro do Oitocentos*, Rio de Janeiro, PhD Thesis, available from: http://teses.ufrj.br/IFCS_D/CarlosEngemann.pdf.

Engerman, Stanley 1973, 'Some Considerations Relating to Property Rights in Man', *The Journal of Economic History*, 33(1), The Tasks of Economic History: 43–65.

Engerman, Stanley and Eugene Genovese 1983, 'Comments on "Slavery in a Nonexport Economy" III', *The Hispanic American Historical Review*, 63(3): 585–90.

Epstein, Stephan R. 1998, 'Craft, Guilds, Apprenticeship, and Technological Change in Preindustrial Europe', *The Journal of Economic History*, 58(3): 684–713.

Erman, Adolf 1894, *Life in Ancient Egypt*, London: Macmillan.

España Sagrada 1782, Vol. 13, Madrid: Oficina de Pedro Marín.

————— 1786, Vol. 14, Madrid: Oficina de Pedro Marín.

————— 1789, Vol. 17, Madrid: Oficina de la Viuda e Hijo de Marín.

————— 1792, Vol. 19, Madrid: Oficina de la Viuda e Hijo de Marín.

Estepa Díez, Carlos 2003, *Las behetrías castellanas*, I, Valladolid: Junta de Castilla y León.

Evans, John K. 1980, 'Plebs Rustica', *American Journal of Ancient History*, 5: 19–47.

Eyrbyggja saga, 1935, *Íslenzk fornrit*, 4, edited by Einar Ó. Sveinsson and Matthías Thórðarson, Reykjavík: Hið íslenzka bókmenntafélag.

Eyrbyggja saga, 1959, edited by Paul Schach and Lee M. Hollander, Nebraska: University of Nebraska Press.

Eyre, Christopher J. 1979, 'A "Strike" Text from the Theban Necropolis', in *Glimpses of Ancient Egypt: Studies Fairman*, edited by John Ruffle et al., Warminster: Aris & Phillips.

——— 1992, 'The Adoption Papyrus in Social Context', *Journal of Egyptian Archaeology*, 78: 207–21.

——— 1994, 'Feudal Tenure and Absentee Landlords', in *Grund und Boden in Altägypten (rechtliche und sozio-ökonomische Verhältnisse): Akten des internationalen Symposions, Tübingen 18–20 Juni 1990*, edited by Schafik Allam, Untersuchungen zum Rechtsleben im alten Ägypten, 2, Tübingen: Selbstverlag des Herausgebers.

——— 1999, 'The Village Economy in Pharaonic Egypt', in *Agriculture in Egypt from Pharaonic to Modern Times*, edited by Alan K. Bowman and Eugene Rogan, Proceedings of the British Academy 96, Oxford: Oxford University Press.

——— 2004, 'How Relevant was Personal Status to the Functioning of the Rural Economy in Pharaonic Egypt?', in *La dépendance rurale dans l'Antiquité égyptienne et proche-orientale*, edited by Bernadette Menu, Bibliothèque d'Étude 140, Cairo: Institut Français d'Archéologie Orientale.

——— 2010, 'The Economy: Pharaonic', in *A Companion to Ancient Egypt*, edited by Alan B. Lloyd, Oxford: Wiley-Blackwell.

Fagrskinna, 1985, *Íslenzk fornrit*, 29, edited by Bjarni Einarsson, Reykjavík: Hið íslenzka bókmenntafélag.

Faulkner, Raymond 1991, *A Concise Dictionary of Middle Egyptian*, Oxford: Griffith Institute.

Fenoaltea, Stefano 1984, 'Slavery and Supervision in Comparative Perspective: A Model', *The Journal of Economic History*, 44(3): 635–68.

Fernández Catón, José María et al. (eds.) 1999, *Colección diplomática del monasterio de Sahagún*, Vol. 6, *Índices: antropónimos, topónimos, cargos, oficios e instituciones, fuentes y bibliografía citadas, innovaciones monogramáticas y verbales, citas bíblicas y jurídicas de los tomos I y de la Colección diplomática del monasterio de Sahagún (857–1230)*, Colección de Fuentes y Estudios de Historia Leonesa, León: Archivo Histórico Diocesano.

Fernández del Pozo, José María 1984, 'Alfonso V, rey de León. Estudio histórico documental', in *León y su historia. Miscelánea Histórica. Fuentes y estudios de historia leonesa*, León: Archivo Histórico Diocesano.

Fernández Flórez, José Antonio (ed.) 1991, *Colección diplomática del monasterio de*

Sahagún, IV (1110–1199), *Colección de Fuentes y Estudios de Historia Leonesa*, León: Archivo Histórico Diocesano.

———— 1994, *Colección diplomática del monasterio de Sahagún (857–1230)*, Vol. 5, (*1200–1300*), *Colección de Fuentes y Estudios de Historia Leonesa*, León: Archivo Histórico Diocesano.

Findlay, Ronald 1975, 'Slavery, Incentives, and Manumission: A Theoretical Model', *Journal of Political Economy*, 83(5): 923–33.

Fine, Ben 1986a, 'On Marx's Theory of Agricultural Rent', in *The Value Dimension: Marx versus Ricardo and Sraffa*, edited by Ben Fine, London/New York: Routledge & Kegan Paul.

———— 1986b, 'On the Historical Transformation Problem', in *The Value Dimension: Marx versus Ricardo and Sraffa*, edited by Ben Fine, London/New York: Routledge & Kegan Paul.

———— (ed.) 1986c, *The Value Dimension: Marx versus Ricardo and Sraffa*, London/New York: Routledge & Kegan Paul.

Finley, Moses I. 1976, 'Private Farm Tenancy in Italy Before Diocletian', in *Studies in Roman Property*, edited by Moses Finley, Cambridge: Cambridge University Press.

———— 1981, 'Debt-Bondage and the Problem of Slavery', in *Economy and Society in Ancient Greece*, edited by Brent D. Shaw and Richard P. Saller, London: Chatto & Windus.

———— 1998 [1980], *Ancient Slavery and Modern Ideology*, edited by Brent D. Shaw, Princeton, NJ: Markus Wiener Publishers.

Florentino, Manolo and José R. Goes 1997, *A paz das senzalas. Famílias escravas e tráfico atlântico. Rio de Janeiro, c. 1790–c. 1850*, Rio de Janeiro: Civilização Brasileira.

Floriano, Antonio C. 1949–1951, *Diplomática española del período astur. Estudio de las fuentes documentales del reino de Asturias (718–910)*, I, Oviedo: Instituto de Estudios Asturianos.

Fogel, Robert W. and Stanley L. Engerman 1989 [1974], *Time on the Cross: The Economics of American Negro Slavery*, New York/London: W.W. Norton and Company.

Fossier, Robert 2000, *Le travail au Moyen Âge*, Paris: Hachette Littératures.

Fourquin, Guy 1975, 'Le premier Moyen Âge', in *Histoire de la France rurale*, collective work under the directorship of Georges Duby and Armand Wallon, 1, Paris: Éditions du Seuil.

Frandsen, Paul J. 1990, 'Editing Reality: The Turin Strike Papyrus', in *Studies in Egyptology Presented to Miriam Lichtheim*, edited by Sarah Israelit-Groll, Jerusalem: Magnes Press, Hebrew University.

Frank, Tenney 1975 [1933], *An Economic Survey of Ancient Rome*, I, New York: Octagon Books.

Franke, Detlef 1983, *Altägyptische verwandtschaftsbezeichnungen im Mittleren Reich*, Hamburger Ägyptologische Studien 3, Hamburg: Verlag Borg.

—————— 1991, 'The Career of Khnumhotep III. Of Beni Hasan and the so-called "Decline of the Nomarchs"', in *Middle Kingdom Studies*, edited by Stephen Quirke, New Malden: SIA Publishing.

—————— 2000, 'First Intermediate Period', in *The Oxford Encyclopedia of Ancient Egypt*, edited by Donald Redford, Oxford: Oxford University Press.

Frederiksen, Martin 1984, *Campania*, edited with additions by Nicholas Purcell, London: British School of Rome.

Freund, Bill 1985, 'The Modes of Production Debate in African Studies', *Canadian Journal of African Studies*, 19(1): 23–9.

Friedman, Jonathan 1975, 'Tribes, States and Transformations', in *Marxist Analyses and Social Anthropology*, edited by Maurice Bloch, London: Malaby.

Friedmann, Harriet 1978, 'Simple Commodity Production and Wage Labour in the American Plains', *Journal of Peasant Studies*, 6(1): 71–100.

—————— 1980, 'Household Production and the National Economy: Concepts for the Analysis of Agrarian Formations', *Journal of Peasant Studies*, 7(2): 158–84.

Gaballa, Ali Gaballa 1977, *The Memphite Tomb-Chapel of Mose*, Warminster: Aris & Phillips.

Gallego Martínez, Domingo 1992, 'Precios y circulación del excedente en las economías rurales: una aproximación analítica', *Noticiario de Historia Agraria*, 3: 7–31.

García de Valdeavellano, Luis 1952, *Historia de España*, Vol. 1, Madrid: Alianza.

—————— 1955, 'El prestimonio. Contribución al estudio de las manifestaciones de feudalismo en los reinos de León y Castilla durante la Edad Media', *Anuario de Historia del Derecho Español*, XXV: 5–122.

—————— 1969, *Orígenes de la burguesía en la España medieval*, Madrid: Espasa-Calpe.

García Mac Gaw, Carlos 2006, 'La transición del esclavismo al feudalismo y la *villa esclavista*', *Dialogues d'Histoire Ancienne*, 32(2): 27–41.

—————— 2007, 'La ciudad-estado y las relaciones de producción esclavistas en el Imperio Romano', in *La ciudad en el Mediterráneo Antiguo*, edited by Julián Gallego and Carlos García Mac Gaw, Buenos Aires: Ed. del Signo.

—————— 2008, 'La ciudad antigua: aspectos económicos e historiográficos', *Studia historica. Historia antigua*, 26: 237–69.

García Moreno, Luis 1992, *Las claves de los pueblos germánicos*, Barcelona: Planeta.

García Oliva, María Dolores 1988, *Documentación histórica del Archivo municipal de Cáceres (1475–1504)*, Cáceres: Institución Cultural 'El Brocense', Diputación Provincial.

García Pérez, Juan 1996, *Documentación medieval abulense en el Registro General del Sello*, Vol. XV (18-I-1499 a 24-XII-1499), Ávila: Institución 'Gran Duque de Alba'.

Gardiner, Alan H. 1905, 'The Inscription of Mes: A Contribution to the Study of Egyptian Judicial Procedure', in *Untersuchungen zur Geschichte und Altertumskunde Ägyptens*, Vol. IV, edited by Kurt Sethe, Leipzig: J.C. Hinrischs.

———— 1906, 'Four Papyri of the Eighteenth Dynasty from Kahun', *Zeitschrift für Ägyptische Sprache und Altertumskunde*, 43: 27–47.

———— 1940, 'Adoption Extraordinary', *Journal of Egyptian Archaeology*, 26: 23–9.

———— 1941, 'Ramesside Texts Relating to the Taxation and Transport of Corn', *Journal of Egyptian Archaeology*, 27: 19–73.

———— 1941–52, *The Wilbour Papyrus*, London: Oxford University Press.

———— 1947, *Ancient Egyptian Onomastica*, Vol. II, London: Oxford University Press.

———— 1948, *Ramesside Administrative Documents*, Oxford: Griffith Institute.

Garnsey, Peter 1998a [1976], 'Peasants in Ancient Roman Society', in *Cities, Peasants and Food in Classical Antiquity*, edited by Peter Garnsey and Walter Scheidel, with addenda by Walter Scheidel, Cambridge: Cambridge University Press.

———— 1998b [1976], 'Non-Slave Labour in the Roman World', in *Cities, Peasants and Food in Classical Antiquity*, edited by Peter Garnsey and Walter Scheidel, with addenda by Walter Scheidel, Cambridge: Cambridge University Press.

Gebran, Philomena (ed.) 1978, *Conceito de modo de produção*, Rio de Janeiro: Paz e Terra.

Gerstein, Ira 1986, 'Production, Circulation and Value: The Significance of the "Transformation Problem" in Marx's Critique of Political Economy', in *The Value Dimension: Marx versus Ricardo and Sraffa*, edited by Ben Fine, London/New York: Routledge & Kegan Paul.

Geschiere, Peter 1985, 'Applications of the Lineage Mode of Production in African Studies', *Canadian Journal of African Studies*, 19(1): 80–90.

Ghosh, Shami 2011, *Kings' Sagas and Norwegian History*, Leiden: Brill.

Giardina, Andrea and Aldo Schiavone (eds.) 1981, *Società romana e produzione schiavistica*; Vol. I: *L'Italia: Insediamenti e forme economiche*; Vol. II: *Merci, mercati e scambi nel Mediterraneo*; Vol. III: *Modelli etici, diritto e trasformazione sociali*, Rome/Bari: Laterza.

Giliberti, Giuseppe 1988, *Servus quasi colonus. Forme non tradizionali di organizzazione del lavoro nella società romana*, Naples: E. Jovene.

Giordano, Oronzo 1983 [1979], *Religiosidad popular en la alta Edad Media*, Madrid: Gredos.

Glucksmann, Christine 1973, 'Modo de producción, formación económico-social, teoría de la transición a propósito de Lenin', in *El concepto de formación económico-social*, edited by Cesare Luporini and Emilio Sereni, Mexico: Cuadernos de Pasado y Presente 39.

Godelier, Maurice 1964, *La notion de mode de production asiatique et les schémas marxistes d'évolution des sociétés*, Paris: Centre d' études et de recherches marxistes.

———— 1970, *Sur les sociétés précapitalistes*, Paris: Editions Sociales.

———— 1971 [1970], *Sobre el modo de producción asiático*, Buenos Aires: Quintaria.

———— 1972 [1966], *Rationality and Irrationality in Economics*, New York/London: Monthly Review Press.

————— 1973a, '"Monnaie de Sel" et Circulation des Marchandises chez les Baruya de Nouvelle-Guinée', in *Horizon, trajets marxistes en anthropologie*, Paris: François Maspero.

————— 1973b, 'Le concept de formation économique et sociale, l'exemple des Incas', in *Horizon, trajets marxistes et anthropologie*, Paris: François Maspero.

————— 1974a, 'Une anthropologie économique est-elle possible?', in *Un domaine contesté: l'anthropologie économique*, edited by Maurice Godelier, Paris: Mouton.

————— 1974b [1970], 'El pensamiento de Marx y Engels sobre las sociedades primitivas: intento de balance crítico', in *Economía, fetichismo y religión en las sociedades primitivas*, Madrid: Siglo XXI.

————— 1974c, 'La antropología económica', in *Economía, fetichismo y religión en las sociedades primitivas*, Madrid: Siglo XXI.

————— 1977 [1970], *Teoría marxista de las sociedades precapitalistas*, Barcelona: Laia.

————— 1978a, 'Infrastructures, Societies and History', *Current Anthropology*, 19(4): 763–71.

————— 1978b, 'The Concept of the "Asiatic Mode of Production" and Marxist Models of Social Evolution', in *Relations of Production: Marxist Approaches to Economic Anthropology*, edited by David Seddon, London: Frank Cass.

————— 1981 [1980], *Instituciones económicas*, Barcelona: Editorial Anagrama.

————— 1984 [1975], 'Modes of Production, Kinship and Demographic Structures', in *Marxist Analyses and Social Anthropology*, edited by Maurice Bloch, London: Tavistock Publications.

————— 1986 [1984], *The Mental and the Material*, London: Verso.

————— 1989 [1984], *Lo ideal y lo material*, Madrid: Taurus.

————— 1999 [1996], *The Enigma of the Gift*, Chicago: University of Chicago Press.

Goedicke, Hans 1970, *Die Privaten Rechtsinschriften aus dem Alten Reich*, Vienna: Notring.

————— 1984, *Studies in the Hekanakhte Papers*, Baltimore, MD: Halgo.

Goff, Tom W. 1980, *Marx and Mead: Contribution to a Sociology of Knowledge*, London: Routledge & Kegan Paul.

Gonzalès, Antonio 2003, *Pline le Jeune. Esclaves et affranchis à Rome*, Besançon: Presses universitaires de Franche-Comté.

Goodman, David E. 1977, 'Rural Structure, Surplus Mobilisation and Modes of Production in a Peripheral Region: The Brazilian North-East', *Journal of Peasant Studies*, 5: 3–32.

Goody, Jack 1996, *The East in the West*, Cambridge: Cambridge University Press.

Gottlieb, Roger 1984, 'Feudalism and Historical Materialism: A Critique and Synthesis', *Science and Society*, 48(1): 1–37.

Grandet, Pierre 1994, *Le Papyrus Harris I: BM 9999*, Bibliothèque d'Étude 109, Cairo: Institut Français d'Archéologie Orientale.

Grajetzki, Wolfram 2009, *Court Officials of the Egyptian Middle Kingdom*, London: Duckworth Egyptology.

Griffith, Francis Llewellyn 1889, *The Inscription of Siût and Dêr Rîfeh*, London: Trübner.

———— 1898, *Hieratic Papyri from Kahun and Gurob*, London: Bernard Quaritch.

Guenther, Rigobert and Gerhard Schrot 1953, 'Problèmes théoriques de la société esclavagiste', *Recherches internationales à la lumière du marxisme*, 2: 7–30.

Guichard, Pierre 1976 [1973], *Al-Andalus. Estructura antropológica de una sociedad islámica en Occidente*, Barcelona: Barral Editores.

———— 1984, 'El problema de la existencia de estructuras de tipo "feudal" en la sociedad de al-Andalus (el ejemplo de la región valenciana)', in *Estructuras feudales y feudalismo en el mundo mediterráneo*, edited by Pierre Bonnassie et al., Barcelona: Crítica.

Gunnar Karlsson 1972, 'Goðar og bændur', *Saga*, 10: 5–57.

———— 2000, *Iceland's 1100 Years*, London: C. Hurst & Co.

———— 2004, *Goðamennung*, Reykjavík: Heimskringla.

Gurevich, Aaron 1972, 'Representations et attitudes à l'egard de la propriété pendant le haut Moyen Âge', *Annales Économies, Sociétés, Civilisations*, 27(3): 523–47.

———— 1982 [1969], *Le origini del feudalesimo*, Rome: Laterza.

———— 1985 [1972], *Categories of Medieval Culture*, London: Routledge & Kegan Paul.

———— 1990 [1981], *Medieval Popular Culture: Problems of Belief and Perception*, New York: Cambridge University Press.

———— 1992a [1968], 'Wealth and Gift-Bestowal among the Ancient Scandinavians', in *Historical Anthropology of the Middle Ages*, Cambridge: Polity Press.

———— 1992b [1987], 'Semantics of the Medieval Community: "Farmstead", "Land", "World"', in *Historical Anthropology of the Middle Ages*, Cambridge: Polity Press.

Gutiérrez Lloret, Sonia 1998, 'Eastern Spain in the Sixth Century in the Light of Archeology', in *The Sixth Century: Production, Distribution and Demand*, edited by Richard Hodges and William Bowden, Leiden: Brill.

Habachi, Labib 1985, *The Sanctuary of Heqaib*, Elephantine 4, Mainz am Rhein: Philipp von Zabern.

Haldon, John 1993, *The State and the Tributary Mode of Production*, London/New York: Verso.

———— 1995, 'The Feudalism Debate Once More: The Case of Byzantium', in *State, Army and Society in Byzantium*, Norfolk: Galliard.

———— 1999, *Warfare, State and Society in the Byzantine World, 565–1204*, London: UCL Press.

———— 2009, 'Social Élites, Wealth and Power', in *The Social History of Byzantium*, edited by John Haldon, Oxford: Blackwell Publishers.

———— 2011, 'Framing the Early Middle Ages', *Historical Materialism*, 19(1): 47–72.

———— 2012, 'Comparative State Formation: The Later Roman Empire in the Wider

World', in *The Oxford Handbook of Late Antiquity*, edited by Scott Johnson, Oxford/ New York: Oxford University Press.

—— 2013a, 'The Byzantine Successor State ca. 600–1453', in *The Oxford Handbook of the Ancient State: Near East and Mediterranean*, edited by Peter Bang and Walter Scheidel, Oxford: Oxford University Press.

—— 2013b, 'Theories of Practice: Marxist History-Writing and Complexity', *Historical Materialism*, 21(4): 36–70.

Haldon, John and Carlos García Mac Gaw (eds.) 2003, *El modo de producción tributario*, monographic issue of *Anales de Historia Antigua, Medieval y Moderna*, 35–6.

Haldon, John et al. 1998, *El modo de producción tributario: una discusión interdisciplinaria*, special issue of *Hispania* 58(3): 200.

Hall, Harry R. 1924, 'The Middle Kingdom and the Hyksos Conquest', in *The Cambridge Ancient History*, Vol. I, edited by John Bury et al., Cambridge: Cambridge University Press.

Haring, Ben J. 1997, *Divine Households: Administrative and Economic Aspects of the New Kingdom Royal Memorial Temples in Western Thebes*, Egyptologische Uitgaven 12. Leiden: Nederlands Instituut voor het Nabije Oosten.

Harman, Chris 2011, 'Chris Wickham's *Framing the Early Middle Ages*', *Historical Materialism*, 19(1): 98–108.

Harries, Patrick 1985, 'Modes of Production and Modes of Analysis: The South African Case', *Canadian Journal of African Studies* 19(1): 30–7.

Harris, David R. 1994, *The Archaeology of V. Gordon Childe*, Chicago: University of Chicago Press.

Harris, William V. 1971, *Rome in Etruria and Umbria*, Oxford: The Clarendon Press.

Harrison, Mark 1977, 'The Peasant Mode of Production in the Work of A.V. Chayanov', *Journal of Peasant Studies*, 4(4): 232–5.

Harvey, Alan 1989, *Economic Expansion in the Byzantine Empire (900–1200)*, Cambridge: Cambridge University Press.

Hayes, William C. 1961, 'The Middle Kingdom in Egypt', in *The Cambridge Ancient History*, Vol. I, edited by Iorwerth E.S. Edwards et al., Cambridge: Cambridge University Press.

Heitzman, James 1991, 'Ritual Polity and Economy: The Transactional Network of an Imperial Temple in Medieval South India', *Journal of the Economic and Social History of the Orient*, 34(1): 23–54.

Helck, Wolfgang 1963, 'Der Papyrus Berlin P. 3047', *Journal of the American Research Center in Egypt*, 2: 65–73.

—— 1971, *Die Beziehungen Ägyptens zu Vorderasien im 3. und 2. Jahrtausend v. Chr.*, Ägyptologische Abhandlungen 5, Wiesbaden: Harrassowitz.

—— 1977, *Die Lehre für König Merikare: kleine ägyptische Texte*, Wiesbaden: Harrassowitz.

Helgui Þorláksson 2005, 'Historical Background: Iceland 870–1400', in *A Companion to Old Norse-Icelandic Literature*, edited by Rory McTurck, London: Blackwell.

Hendy, Michael F. 1985, *Studies in the Byzantine Monetary Economy, ca. 300–1500*, Cambridge: Cambridge University Press.

Henning, Joachim 2007, 'Early European Towns: The Development of the Economy in the Frankish Realm Between Dynamism and Deceleration. AD 500–1100', in *Post-Roman Towns, Trade and Settlement in Europe and Byzantium*, edited by Joachim Henning, Vol. 1, *The Heirs of the Roman West*, Berlin/New York: Walter de Gruyter.

Hernández Pierna, Juan 1995, *Documentación medieval abulense en el Registro General del Sello*, Vol. XI (3-I-1495 a 13-XII-1495), Ávila: Institución 'Gran Duque de Alba'.

Herrero de la Fuente, Marta (ed.) 1988a, *Colección diplomática del monasterio de Sahagún (857–1230)*, Vol. II (1000–1073), *Colección de Fuentes y Estudios de Historia Leonesa*, León: Archivo Histórico Diocesano.

———— 1988b, *Colección diplomática del monasterio de Sahagún (857–1230)*, Vol. III (1074–1109), *Colección de Fuentes y Estudios de Historia Leonesa*, León: Archivo Histórico Diocesano.

Herskovits, Melville 1952, *Economic Anthropology: A Study in Comparative Economics*, New York: A. Knopf.

Herzog, Pierre 1973, 'El punto de vista de un economista', in *El concepto de formación económico-social*, edited by Cesare Luporini and Emilio Sereni, Mexico: Cuadernos de Pasado y Presente 39.

Hilton, Rodney 1947, *The Economic Development of Some Leicestershire Estates in the 14th and 15th Centuries*, Oxford: Oxford University Press.

———— 1985a, 'Medieval Market Towns and Simple Commodity Production', *Past and Present*, 109: 3–23.

———— 1985b, *Class Conflict and the Crisis of Feudalism*, London: Hambledon Press.

Hindess, Barry and Paul Hirst 1975, *Pre-Capitalist Modes of Production*, London: Routledge & Kegan Paul.

———— 1977, *Mode of Production and Social Formation*, London/New York: Macmillan.

Hoffman, Michael A. 1979, *Egypt Before the Pharaohs*, London: Knopf.

Hoffman, Philip T. 1996, *Growth in a Traditional Society: The French Countryside 1450–1815*, Princeton, NJ: Princeton University Press.

Holton, Robert J. 1981, 'Marxist Theories of Social Change and the Transition from Feudalism to Capitalism', *Theory and Society*, 10(6): 833–67.

Homans, George 1987, 'Behaviourism and After', in *Social Theory Today*, edited by Anthony Giddens and Jonathan H. Turner, Cambridge: Polity Press.

Hopkins, Keith 1978, *Conquerors and Slaves*, Cambridge: Cambridge University Press.

———— 1980, 'Taxes and Trade in the Roman Empire, 200 BC–AD 400', *Journal of Roman Studies*, 70: 101–25.

———— 2002, 'Rome, Taxes, Rents and Trade', in *The Ancient Economy*, edited by Walter Scheidel and Sitta Von Reden, New York: Routledge.

Howgego, Christopher 1994, 'Coin Circulation and the Integration of the Roman Economy', *Journal of Roman Archaelogy*, 7: 5–21.

Hoyle, Richard W. 1990, 'Tenure and the Land Market in Early Modern England: Or a Late Contribution to the Brenner Debate', *Economic History Review*, 43(1): 1–20.

Hussey, Joan M. 1986, *The Orthodox Church in the Byzantine Empire*, Oxford: Clarendon Press.

Hyams, Paul 2001, 'Feud and the State in Late Anglo-Saxon England', *The Journal of British Studies*, 40(1): 1–43.

Hyde, John Kenneth 1973, *Society and Politics in Medieval Italy: The Evolution of the Civic Life 1000–1350*, London: Macmillan.

Itoh, Makoto 1988, *The Basic Theory of Capitalism: The Forms and Substance of the Capitalist Economy*, Totowa, NJ: Barnes & Noble.

Ivanov, Sergei 2008, 'Religious Missions', in *The Cambridge History of the Byzantine Empire, c. 500–1492*, edited by Jonathan Shepard, Cambridge: Cambridge University Press.

James, Thomas G.H. 1962, *The Hekanakhte Papers and other Early Middle Kingdom Documents*, New York: Publications of the Metropolitan Museum of Art Egyptian Expedition.

Jameson, Michael H. 1977–8, 'Agriculture and Slavery in Classical Athens', *Classical Journal* 73: 122–45.

Janssen, Jac J. 1975, *Commodity Prices from the Ramessid Period*, Leiden: Brill.

———— 1979a, 'Background Information on the Strikes of Year 29 of Ramesses III', *Oriens Antiquus*, 18: 301–8.

———— 1979b, 'The Role of the Temple in the Egyptian Economy During the New Kingdom', in *State and Temple Economy in the Ancient Near East*, edited by Edward Lipinski, *Proceedings of the International Conference organised by the Katholieke Universiteit Leuven from the 10th to the 14th of April 1978*, OLA 6, Vol. II, Leuven: Departement Oriëntalistiek.

———— 1986, 'Agrarian Administration in Egypt during the Twentieth Dynasty', *Bibliotheca Orientalis*, 43: 351–66.

———— 1992, 'The Year of the Strikes', *Bulletin de la Société d'Égyptologie de Genève*, 16: 41–9.

Jón Viðar Sigurðsson 1995, 'The Icelandic Aristocracy after the Fall of the Free State', *Scandinavian Journal of History*, 20(3): 153–66.

———— 1999, *Chieftains and Power in the Icelandic Commonwealth*, Odense: Odense University Press.

Jones, Richard 1852, *Textbook of Lectures on the Political Economy of Nations*, Hertford: Stephen Austin.

Karras, Ruth Mazo 1988, *Slavery and Society in Medieval Scandinavia*, New Haven, CT: Yale University Press.

Katary, Sally L.D. 1989, *Land Tenure in the Ramesside Period*, London: Kegan Paul International.

Kautsky, Karl 1970 [1899], *La cuestión agraria. Estudio de las tendencias de la agricultura moderna y de la política agraria de la socialdemocracia*, Paris: Ruedo Ibérico.

Kaye, Harvey J. 1984, *The British Marxist Historians*, Cambridge: Polity.

Kehoe, Dennis 1997, *Investment, Profit and Tenancy: The Jurists and the Roman Agrarian Economy*, Ann Arbor, MI: University of Michigan Press.

——— 2007, 'The Early Roman Empire: Production', in *The Cambridge Economic History of the Greco-Roman World*, edited by Walter Scheidel, Ian Morris and Richard Saller, Cambridge: Cambridge University Press.

Kemp, Barry 1972, 'Temple and Town in Ancient Egypt', in *Man, Settlement and Urbanism*, edited by Peter J. Ucko et al., London: Duckworth.

——— 2006 [1989], *Ancient Egypt: Anatomy of a Civilization*, New York: Routledge.

Khazanov, Anatoly Michailovich 1994 [1983], *Nomads and the Outside World*, Madison, WI: University of Wisconsin Press.

Kitchen, Kenneth A. 1979, *Ramesside Inscriptions, Historical and Biographical*, II, Oxford: Blackwell.

——— 1981, *Ramesside Inscriptions: Historical and Biographical*, IV, Oxford: Blackwell.

——— 1983, *Ramesside Inscriptions: Historical and Biographical*, VI, Oxford: Blackwell.

Knight, Kelvin 2011, 'Agency and Ethics, Past and Present', *Historical Materialism*, 19(1): 145–74.

Kolendo, Jerzy 1991 [1989], 'El campesino', in *El hombre romano*, edited by Andrea Giardina, Madrid: Alianza.

Konstan, David 1975, 'Marxism and Roman Slavery', in *Marxism and the Classics*, special issue of *Arethusa*, 8: 145–69.

Kosminsky, Eugene A. 1956, *Studies in the Agrarian History of England in the Thirteenth Century*, Oxford: Basil Blackwell.

Krader, Lawrence 1972, *The Ethnological Notebooks of Karl Marx: (Studies of Morgan, Phear, Maine, Lubbock)*, Assen, The Netherlands: Van Gorcum & comp. b.v.

——— 1975, *The Asiatic Mode of Production: Sources, Development and Critique in the Writings of Karl Marx*, Assen, The Netherlands: Van Gorcum & comp. b.v.

Kriedte, Peter, Hans Medick and Jürgen Schlumbohm 1981, *Industrialization Before Industrialization: Rural Industry in the Genesis of Capitalism*, Cambridge: Cambridge University Press.

Kuchenbuch, Ludolf 2003, '*Porcus donativus*: Language Use and Gifting in Seigneurial Records Between the Eighth and the Twelfth Centuries', in *Negotiating the Gift: Pre-modern Figurations of Exchange*, edited by Gadi Algazi, Valentin Groebner et al., Göttingen: Vandenhoeck & Ruprecht.

Kuchenbuch, Ludolf and Bernd Michael 1977, 'Zur Struktur und Dynamik der "feuda-
len" Produktionsweise im vorindustriellen Europa', in *Feudalismus: Materialen zur
Theorie und Geschichte*, edited by Ludolf Kuchenbuch and Bernd Michael, Frankfurt: Ullstein.

Kula, Witold 1986, *Measures and Men*, Princeton, NJ: Princeton University Press.

Labica, Georges 1973, 'Cuatro observaciones sobre los conceptos de modo de producción y de formación económica de la sociedad', in *El concepto de formación
económico-social*, edited by Cesare Luporini and Emilio Sereni, Mexico: Cuadernos
de Pasado y Presente 39.

Labrousse, Ernest 1933, *Esquisse du mouvement des prix et des revenues en France au
XVIII siècle*, Paris: Dalloz.

Lacau, Pierre 1926, *Stèles du Nouvel Empire. Catalogue général des Antiquités Égyp-
tiennes du Musée du Cairo*, Cairo: Institut Français d'Archéologie Orientale.

Laclau, Ernesto 1973, 'Feudalismo y capitalismo en América Latina', in *Los modos de
producción en América Latina*, edited by Carlos Sempat Assadourian et al., Mexico:
Cuadernos de Pasado y Presente 40.

Laiou, Angeliki 1991, 'God and Mammon: Credit, Trade, Profit and the Canonists', in
Byzantium in the Twelfth Century, edited by Nicolas Oikonomides, Athens: Hetaireia
Vyzantinōn kai Metavyzantinōn Meletōn.

———— 2002a, 'Economic Thought and Ideology', in *The Economic History of Byzantium from the Seventh through the Fifteenth Century*, edited by Angeliki Laiou et al.,
Washington D.C.: Dumbarton Oaks.

———— 2002b, 'Exchange and Trade, Seventh-Twelfth Centuries', in *The Economic History of Byzantium from the Seventh through the Fifteenth century*, edited by Angeliki
Laiou et al., Washington, DC: Dumbarton Oaks.

———— 2002c, 'The Byzantine Economy: An Overview', in *The Economic History of
Byzantium from the Seventh through the Fifteenth Century*, edited by Angeliki Laiou
et al., Washington, DC: Dumbarton Oaks.

Larraín, Jorge 1986, *A Reconstruction of Historical Materialism*, London: Allen & Unwin.

Laslett, Peter 1965, *The World We Have Lost: Further Explored*, London: Methuen & Co.
Ltd.

Laxdæla saga, 1934, *Íslenzk fornrit*, 5, edited by Einar Ó. Sveinsson, Reykjavík: Hið
íslenzka bókmenntafélag.

Laxdæla saga, 1969, edited by Magnus Magnusson and Hermann Palsson, London:
Penguin.

Le Goff, Jacques 1977, 'Travail, techniques et artisans dans les systèmes de valeur
du haut Moyen Âge (v^e-xe siècle)', in *Pour un autre Moyen Âge*, Paris: Éditions
Gallimard.

———— 1988, *Medieval Civilization*, Oxford: Basil Blackwell.

Leal, Bernardo 2003, 'Los esclavos en el Chocó, vistos a través de documentos judiciales del siglo XVIII', in *VI Cátedra Anual de Historia Ernesto Restrepo Tirado, 150 años de la abolición de la esclavitud en Colombia. Desde la marginalidad a la construcción de la nación*, Bogota: Editorial Aguilar, Altea, Taurus, Alfaguara S.A.

Lekas, Padelis 1988, *Marx on Classical Antiquity: Problems of Historical Methodology*, Brighton: Wheatsheaf Books.

Lemerle, Paul 1967, 'Roga et rente d'état aux Xe–XIe siècles', *Revue des Études Byzantines*, 25: 77–100.

Lenin, Vladimir I. 1963 [1894], *What the 'Friends of the People' Are and How They Fight the Social-Democrats*, in *Collected Works*, Vol. 1, Moscow: Progress Publishers.

——— 1964 [1899], *The Development of Capitalism in Russia: The Process of the Formation of a Home Market for Large-Scale Industry*, Moscow: Progress Publishers.

Lesko, Leonard H. 1994, *Pharaoh's Workers: The Villagers of Deir el-Medina*, Ithaca and London: Cornell University Press.

Levine, Andrew 1984, *Arguing for Socialism*, London: Routledge & Kegan Paul.

Levine, Andrew and Erik Olin Wright 1980, 'Rationality and Class Struggle', *New Left Review*, 123: 47–68.

Lichtheim, George 1963, 'Marx and the "Asiatic Mode of Production"', *St. Anthony's Papers*, 14: 86–112.

Lichtheim, Miriam 1975, *Ancient Egyptian Literature – AEL –*, Vol. 1, Berkeley: University of California Press.

——— 1976, *Ancient Egyptian Literature – AEL –*, Vol. 2, Berkeley: University of California Press.

——— 1988, *Ancient Egyptian Autobiographies Chiefly of the Middle Kingdom: A Study and an Anthology*, Orbis Biblicus et Orientalis 84, Göttingen: Vandenhoeck & Ruprecht.

Likitkijsomboon, Pichit 1995, 'Marxian Theories of Value-Form', *Review of Radical Political Economics*, 27(2): 73–105.

Lilie, Ralph-Johannes 1984, *Handel und Politik zwischen dem byzantinischen Reich und den italienischen Kommunen Venedig, Pisa und Genua in der Epoche der Komnenen und der Angeloi (1081–1204)*, Amsterdam: Adolf M. Hakkert.

Liverani, Mario 1975, 'Communautés de village et palais royal dans la Syrie du IIème millénaire', *Journal of the Economic and Social History of the Orient*, 18: 146–64.

——— 1976, 'Il modo di produzione', in *L'alba della civiltà*, edited by Sabatino Moscati, Turin: UTET.

Liverani, Paolo 1984, 'L'ager veientanus in età repubblicana', *Papers of the British School at Rome*, 52: 37–48.

Lloyd, Christopher 1993, *The Structures of History*, Oxford: Blackwell.

Loone, Eero 1995, 'O'Leary, Marx and Asia', *Studia Philosophica*, 2(38): 88–95.

López de Ayala, Pedro 1991, *Crónicas*, edited by Jose Luis Martín, Barcelona: Planeta.

López Ferreiro, Antonio 1898, *Historia de la Santa A.M. iglesia de Santiago de Com-*

postela, 1, Apéndice, Santiago de Compostela: Imp. y Enc. del Seminario Conciliar Central.

López, Roberto Sabatino 1937, 'Aux origines du capitalisme génois', *Annales d'histoire économique et sociale*, 9: 429–54.

Loprieno, Antonio 1988, *Topos und Mimesis: Zum Ausländer in der ägyptischen Literatur*, Wiesbaden: Harrassowitz.

Loret, Victor 1901, 'La grande inscription de Mes a Saqqarah', *Zeitschrift für Ägyptische Sprache und Altertumskunde*, 29: 1–10.

Loscertales de García de Valdeavellano, Pilar (ed.) 1976, *Tumbo del monasterio de Sobrado de los Monjes*, 2 Vols., Madrid: Publicaciones Diputación Provincial de la Coruña.

Luis López, Carmelo 1987, *Colección documental del archivo municipal de Piedrahíta (1372–1549)*, Ávila: Institución 'Gran Duque de Alba'.

———— 1993, *Documentación medieval de los archivos municipales de La Adrada, Candeleda, Higuera de las Dueñas y Sotillo de La Adrada*, Ávila: Institución 'Gran Duque de Alba'.

Lukács, Georg 1967 [1923], 'Class consciousness', in *History and Class Consciousness*, London: Jonathan Cape.

———— 2004 [1986], *Ontología del ser social: el trabajo*, edited by Antonino Infranca and Miguel Vedda, Buenos Aires: Herramienta.

Lupo, Silvia 2007, *Territorial Appropriation During the Old Kingdom, XXVIIIth–XXIIIrd Centuries BC: The Royal Necropolises and the Pyramid Towns in Egypt*, Oxford: Archaeopress.

———— 2011, 'El papel de los hijos reales en la consolidación del estado egipcio durante el Reino Antiguo: una alternativa de análisis', *Cuadernos del Sur-Historia*, 39: 109–22.

Luporini, Cesare 1973a, 'Dialéctica marxista e historicismo', in *El concepto de formación económico-social*, edited by Cesare Luporini and Emilio Sereni, Mexico: Cuadernos de Pasado y Presente 39.

———— 1973b, 'Marx según Marx', in *El concepto de formación económico-social*, edited by Cesare Luporini and Emilio Sereni, Mexico: Cuadernos de Pasado y Presente 39.

———— 1981, 'Crítica de la política y crítica de la economía política de Marx', in *Teoría marxista de la política*, edited by Giacomo Marramao et al., Mexico: Cuadernos de Pasado y Presente 89.

Macfarlane, Alan 2002, 'Karl Marx and the Origins of Capitalism', Cambridge: King's College, available from: http://www.alanmacfarlane.com/TEXTS/MARX.pdf

Magdalino, Paul 1989, 'Honour among Romaioi: The Framework of Social Values in the World of Digenes Akrites and Kekaumenos', *Byzantine and Modern Greek Studies*, 13: 183–218.

Mandel, Ernest 1971, *The Formation of the Economic Thought of Karl Marx*, New York: Monthly Review Press.

Mann, Michael 1986, *The Sources of Social Power*, 1: *A History of Power from the Beginnings to A.D. 1760*, Cambridge: Cambridge University Press.

Manzano Moreno, Eduardo 1998, 'Relaciones sociales en sociedades precapitalistas: una crítica al concepto de "modo de producción tributario"', *Hispania*, 58(200): 881–913.

Marcus, Joyce 1976, *Emblem and State in the Classic Maya Lowlands*, Washington D.C.: Dumbarton Oaks.

——— 1984, 'Lowland Maya Archaeology at the Crossroads', *American Antiquity*, 48: 454–88.

Martín, José Luis 2005, 'El azogue viejo. La fundación del sistema urbano salmantino', in *La Plaza Mayor de Salamanca*, 1, *Antecedentes medievales y modernos*, edited by Alberto Estella Goytre, Salamanca: Caja Duero.

Martin, Michael 1988, 'The Venetians in the Byzantine Empire Before 1204', *Byzantinische Forschungen*, 13: 201–14.

Martin, René 1974, '"Familia rustica": Les esclaves chez les agronomes latins', in *Actes du Colloque 1972 sur l'Esclavage, Annales Littéraires de l'Université de Besançon*, 163, Paris: Belles Lettres.

Martínez Díez, Gonzalo (ed.) 1982, *Fueros locales en el territorio de la provincia de Burgos*, Burgos: Caja de Ahorros Municipal de Burgos.

——— 1988, 'Los fueros leoneses, 1017–1336', in *El reino de León en la Alta Edad Media*, 1, *Cortes, concilios y fueros. Colección de Fuentes y Estudios de Historia Leonesa*, 48, León: Archivo Histórico Diocesano.

Martínez García, Luis 2008, 'Jurisdicción, propiedad y señorío en el espacio castellano del Camino de Santiago (ss. XI y XII)', *Hispania*, LXVIII(228): 11–36.

Martínez Sopena, Pascual 1987, 'Parentesco y poder en León durante el siglo XI. La "casata" de Alfonso Díaz', *Studia Historica. Historia Medieval*, 5: 33–87.

Marx, Karl 1964, *Pre-Capitalist Economic Formations*, edited by Eric Hobsbawm, New York: International Publishers.

——— 1965 [1867], *Capital*, Volume I, Moscow: Progress Publishers.

——— 1966 [1894], *Capital*, Volume III, Moscow: Progress Publishers.

——— 1968 [1852], *The Eighteenth Brumaire of Louis Bonaparte*, in Karl Marx and Frederick Engels, *Selected Works*, London: Lawrence and Wishart.

——— 1971 [1859], *A Contribution to the Critique of Political Economy*, London: Lawrence and Wishart.

——— 1972 [1881], 'Marginal Notes on Adolph Wagner's "Lehrbuch der politischen Ökonomie"', *Theoretical Practice*, Issue 5.

——— 1973 [1857–8], *Grundrisse. Foundations of the Critique of Political Economy (Rough Draft)*, London: Penguin Books/New Left Review.

——— 1976a [1864], *Results of the Immediate Process of Production*, Appendix to *Capital*, Volume I, London: Penguin Books.

———— 1976b, *Das Kapital. Kritik der politischen Ökonomie*, 1, Frankfurt: Verlag Marxistische Blätter.

———— 1977a, *Capital*, 3 Vols., Moscow/London: Progress Publishers.

———— 1977b [1859], 'Introduction', in *A Contribution to the Critique of Political Economy*, edited by Maurice Dobb, Moscow: Progress Publishers.

———— 1979 [1853], 'The British Rule in India', in *Marx and Engels Collected Works*, Vol. 12, Moscow: Progress Publishers.

———— 1983 [1853] 'Letter to Engels 2 June 1853', in *Marx and Engels Collected Works*, Vol. 39, Moscow: Progress Publishers.

———— 1989 [1881], 'Drafts of the Letter to Vera Zasulich', in *Marx and Engels Collected Works*, Vol. 24, Moscow: Progress Publishers.

Marx, Karl and Frederick Engels 1941, *Selected Correspondence, 1846–1895*, London: Lawrence and Wishart.

———— 1965 [1845–6], *The German Ideology*, London: Lawrence and Wishart.

———— 1969 [1845–6], 'Die deutsche Ideologie', *Werke*, Vol. 3, Berlin/DDR: Dietz Verlag.

Mauss, Marcel 1954 [1925], *The Gift: Forms and Functions of Exchange in Archaic Societies*, Glencoe, IL: The Free Press.

Mazar, Amihai 1990, *Archaeology of the Land of the Bible 10000–586 BCE*, New York: Doubleday.

McDowell, Andrea 1993, *Hieratic Ostraca in the Hunterian Museum Glasgow (The Colin Campbell Ostraca)*, Oxford: Griffith Institute.

———— 1999, *Village Life in Ancient Egypt*, Oxford: Oxford University Press.

Mckeown, Niall 2007, *The Invention of Ancient Slavery?*, London: Duckworth.

McLennan, Gregor 1989, *Marxism, Pluralism and Beyond: Classic Debates and New Departures*, Cambridge: Polity Press.

Mcmurtry, John 1978, *The Structure of Marx's World View*, Princeton, NJ: Princeton University Press.

Meek, Ronald 1956, 'Some Notes on the "Transformation Problem"', *The Economic Journal*, 66(261): 94–107.

———— 1976, 'Is There an "Historical Transformation Problem"?: A Comment', *The Economic Journal*, 86(342): 342–7.

Meeks, Dimitri 1979, 'Les donations aux temples dans l' Égypte du Ier millénaire avant J.C.', in *State and Temple Economy in the Ancient Near East*, Vol. II, edited by Edward Lipinski, Leuven: Departement Oriëntalistiek.

Meillassoux, Claude 1991 [1975], *Maidens, Meal and Money: Capitalism and the Domestic Community*, Cambridge: Cambridge University Press.

———— 1992 [1988], *The Anthropology of Slavery*, Chicago: University of Chicago Press.

Melotti, Umberto 1977, *Marx and the Third World*, London: Macmillan Press.

Menu, Bernadette 1970, *Le régime juridique des terres et du personnel attaché à la terre dans le Papyrus Wilbour*, 17, Publications de la faculté des lettres et sciences humaines 1, Institut de papyrologie et d'égyptologie, Lille: Faculté des lettres et sciences humaines.

———— 1982, 'Le régime juridique des terres en Égypte pharaonique', in *Recherches sur l'histoire juridique, économique et sociale de l'ancienne Égypte*, Versailles: w/p.

———— 1998, *Recherches sur l'histoire juridique, économique et sociale de l'ancienne Égypte*, II, BdE 122, Cairo: Institut Français d'Archéologie Orientale.

———— 2004, *Égypte pharaonique. Nouvelles recherches sur l'histoire juridique, économique et sociale de l'ancienne Égypte*, Paris: L'Harmattan.

Menu, Bernadette and Ibrahim Harari 1974, 'La notion de propriété privée dans l'Ancien Empire égyptien', *Cahier de recherches de l'Institut de papyrologie et d'égyptologie de Lille*, 2: 125–54.

Migne, Jacques-Paul 1854, 'Historia Compostellana', *Patrologia Latina*, Vol. 170, Paris: D'Amboise.

Millares Carlo, Agustín and Jerano Artiles Rodríguez 1932, *Ayuntamiento de Madrid. Archivo de Villa: Libro de acuerdos del concejo madrileño, 1464–1600*, 2 Vols., Madrid: Artes Gráficas Municipales.

Miller, Richard 1984, *Analyzing Marx: Morality, Power and History*, Princeton, NJ: Princeton University Press.

Miller, William Ian 1984, 'Avoiding Legal Judgment: The Submission of Disputes to Arbitration in Medieval Iceland', *The American Journal of Legal History*, 28(2): 95–134.

———— 1986, 'Gift, Sale, Payment, Raid: Case Studies in the Negotiation and Classification of Exchange in Medieval Iceland', *Speculum*, 61(1): 18–50.

———— 1990, *Bloodtaking and Peacemaking: Feud, Law and Society in Saga Iceland*, Chicago/London: University of Chicago Press.

Milonakis, Dimitris 1995, 'Commodity Production and Price Formation Before Capitalism; A Value Theoretic Approach', *Journal of Peasant Studies*, 22(2): 327–55.

Mínguez Fernández, José María (ed.) 1976, *Colección diplomática del monasterio de Sahagún (siglos IX–X)*, Vol. I, León: Archivo Histórico Diocesano.

Miranda Rocha, Cristiany 2004, *Histórias de famílias escravas. Campinas, século XIX*, São Paulo: Ed. da Unicamp.

Monsalvo Antón, José María 1986, 'Poder político y aparatos de estado en la Castilla bajomedieval. Consideraciones sobre su problemática', *Studia Historica. Historia Medieval*, IV(2): 101–67.

———— (ed.) 1995, *Documentación medieval abulense en el Registro General del Sello*, Vol. XIV (2-I-1498 a 21-XII-1498), Ávila: Institución 'Gran Duque de Alba'.

Moore, Robert Ian 1987, *The Formation of a Persecuting Society: Authority and Deviance in Western Europe 950–1250*, Oxford/New York: Basil Blackwell.

Morel, Jean-Paul 1989, 'The Transformation of Italy, 300–133 BC: The Evidence of Archaeology', in *Cambridge Ancient History*, Second Edition, Vol. 8, Cambridge: Cambridge University Press.

Moreland, John 2000, 'Concepts of the Early Medieval Economy', in *The Long Eighth Century: Production, Distribution and Demand*, edited by Inge Lyse Hansen and Chris Wickham, Leiden/Boston: Brill.

———— 2011, 'Land and Power from Roman Britain to Anglo-Saxon England?', *Historical Materialism*, 19(1): 175–93.

Moreno García, Juan Carlos 1994, '*Hwt* y la retribución de los funcionarios provinciales en el Imperio Antiguo: el caso de Jbj de Deir el-Gebrawi (*Urk.* I 144:3–145:3)', *Aula Orientalis*, 12: 29–50.

———— 1996, 'Hwt et le milieu rural égyptien du IIIe millénaire', *Zeitschrift für Ägyptische Sprache und Altertumskunde*, 123: 116–38.

———— 1998, 'La population mrt: Une approche du problème de la servitude dans l'Égypte du IIIe millénaire (I)', *Journal of Egyptian Archaeology*, 84: 71–83.

———— 2001, 'L'organisation sociale de l'agriculture dans l'Égypte pharaonique pendant l'ancien empire (2650–2150 avant J.-C.)', *Journal of the Economic and Social History of the Orient*, 44(4): 411–50.

———— 2004a, *Egipto en el Imperio Antiguo [2650–2150 antes de Cristo]*, Barcelona: Bellaterra.

———— 2004b, 'Elites y Agricultura Institucional: el papel de los templos provinciales egipcios durante el Imperio Antiguo', *Huelva Arqueológica*, 19: 27–55.

———— 2008, 'La dépendance rurale en Égypte ancienne', *Journal of the Economic and Social History of the Orient*, 51: 99–150.

———— 2011a, 'El Primer Período Intermedio' in *El Antiguo Egipto: Sociedad, Economía y Política*, edited by José Miguel Parra Ortiz, Madrid: Marcial Pons.

———— 2011b, 'Les mnhw: société et transformations agraires en Égypte entre la fin du IIe et le début du Ier millénaire', *Revue d'Égyptologie*, 62: 105–14.

Moret, Alexandre 1901, 'Un procès de famille sous la XIXe dynastie', *Zeitschrift für Ägyptische Sprache und Altertumskunde*, 39: 11–39.

Moreta, Salustiano 1978, *Malhechores feudales. Violencia, antagonismo y alianzas de clases en Castilla, siglos XIII–XIV*, Madrid: Cátedra.

Morgan, Lewis H. 1877, *Ancient Society*, London: Macmillan and Company.

Morishima, Michio and George Catephores 1975, 'Is There an "Historical Transformation Problem"?', *The Economic Journal*, 85(338): 309–28.

———— 1976, 'The "Historical Transformation Problem": A Reply', *The Economic Journal*, 86(342): 348–52.

Morsel, Joseph 2008 [2004], *La aristocracia medieval. El dominio social en Occidente (siglos V–XV)*, Valencia: Publicacions de la Universitat de València.

Moseley, Katherine P. and Immanuel Wallerstein 1978, 'Pre-Capitalist Social Structures', *Annual Review of Sociology*, 4: 259–90.

Muñoz y Romero, Tomás (ed.) 1847, *Colección de fueros municipales y cartas-pueblas de Castilla, León, Corona de Aragón y Navarra*, Madrid: Imprenta de Don José María Alonso, editor.

Myking, John Ragnar and Carsten Porskrog Rasmussen 2010, 'Scandinavia, 1000–1750', in *Social Relations: Property and Power*, edited by Bas van Bavel and Richard Hoyle, Turnhout: Brepols.

Namboodiripad, Elamkulam M.S. 1952, *The National Question in Kerala*, Bombay: Peoples Publishing House.

———— 2010, 'Marx, the Asiatic Mode and the Study of Indian History', in *History, Society and Land Relations*, New Delhi: Left Word Books.

Navailles, Robert and François Neveu 1989, 'Qu'entendait-on par 'journée d'esclave' au Nouvel Empire? (hrw m hm(t), hrw n b3k)', *Revue d'Égyptologie*, 40: 113–23.

Naville, Edouard 1896, *The Temple of Deir el Bahari*, II, London: Egypt Exploration Fund.

Nippel, Wilfried 2005, 'Marx, Weber, and Classical Slavery', *Classics Ireland*, 12: 31–59.

Njal's saga, 1960, edited by Magnus Magnusson and Hermann Palsson, London: Penguin.

Nordal, Sigurður 1957, *The Historical Element in the Icelandic Family Sagas*, Glasgow: Jackson, Son and Co.

Norges gamle lov indtil 1387, I, 1846, edited by Rudolf Keyser and Peter Andreas Munch, Christiania: Chr. Gröndahl.

O'Connor, David 1972, 'The Geography of settlement in Ancient Egypt', in *Man, Settlement and Urbanism*, edited by Peter Ucko et al., London: Duckworth.

O'Donoghue, Heather 2005, *Skaldic Verse and the Poetics of Saga Narrative*, Oxford: Oxford University Press.

O'Leary, Brendan (ed.) 1989, 'Marx and Engels on the Asiatic Mode of Production and India', in *The Asiatic Mode of Production: Oriental Despotism, Historical Materialism, and Indian History*, Oxford and New York: Basil Blackwell.

Oikonomides, Nicolas 1993, 'Le marchand byzantin des provinces (IXe–XIe s.)', in *Mercati e mercanti nell'alto medioevo. Settimane di studio sull'alto medioevo*, 40, Spoleto: Centro Italiano di Studi sull'alto medioevo.

Oliva Herrer, Hipólito Rafael (ed.) 2003, *Ordenanzas de Becerril de Campos (circa 1492). Transcripción y estudio*, Diputación de Palencia: Institución Tello Téllez de Meneses, CECEL-CESIC.

Orning, Hans Jacob 2008, *Unpredictability and Presence*, Leiden: Brill.

Orri Vésteinsson 2000, *The Christianization of Iceland*, Oxford: Oxford University Press.

———— 2007, 'A Divided Society', *Viking and Medieval Scandinavia*, 3: 117–39.

Ostrogorsky, Georg et al. 1974, *Féodalisme à Byzance*, monographic issue of *Recherches internationales à la lumière du marxisme*, 79, Paris: Editions de la Nouvelle Critique.

Padgug, Robert 1975, 'Classes and Society in Classical Greece', in *Marxism and the Classics*, special issue of *Arethusa*, 8: 85–117.

Papazian, Hratch 1999, *The 'Per Shena': From Palace Estate to Sacred Storehouse. The Structure and Evolution of an Ancient Egyptian Economic Institution*, A Dissertation

Proposal Presented to the Department of Near Eastern Languages and Civilizations, Chicago: University of Chicago.

Parain, Charles 1963, 'Les caracteres spécifiques de la lutte de classes dans l'antiquité classique', *La Pensée*, 108: 3–25.

Parain, Charles et al. 1975, *Formes d'exploitation du travail et rapports sociaux dans l'Antiquité classique*, monographic issue of *Recherches internationales à la lumière du marxisme* 84, Paris: Critique.

Parkes, Peter 2003, 'Fostering Fealty: A Comparative Analysis of Tributary Allegiances of Adoptive Kinship', *Comparative Studies in Society and History*, 45(4): 741–82.

────── 2006, 'Celtic Fosterage. Adoptive Kinship and Clientage in Northwest Europe', *Society for Comparative Study of Society and History*: 359–95.

Parkinson, Richard 2002, *Poetry and Culture in Middle Kingdom Egypt: A Dark Side to Perfection*, London: Continuum.

Parra Ortiz, José Miguel 2009, 'El Reino Antiguo', in *El Antiguo Egipto: Sociedad, Economía y Política*, edited by José Miguel Parra Ortiz, Madrid: Marcial Pons.

Pastor, Reyna 1984, 'Sobre la articulación de las formaciones económico-sociales: comunidades de aldea y señoríos en el norte de la Península Ibérica (siglos X–XIII)', in *Estructuras feudales y feudalismo*, edited by Pierre Bonnassie et al., Barcelona: Crítica.

Patnaik, Utsa 1988, 'Peasants and Prices: Some Theoretical Aspects', *Social Scientist*, 16(9): 46–64.

Patterson, Orlando 1979, 'On Slavery and Slave Formations', *New Left Review*, 117: 31–67.

────── 1982, *Slavery and Social Death: A Comparative Study*, Cambridge, MA: Harvard University Press.

Pérez Prendes y Muñoz de Arraco, José Manuel (ed.) 1988, 'La potestad legislativa en el reino de León. Notas sobre el fuero de León, el concilio de Coyanza y las Cortes de León de 1188', in *El reino de León en la Alta Edad Media*, 1, *Cortes, concilios y fueros. Fuentes y estudios de historia leonesa*, N° 48, León: Archivo Histórico Diocesano.

Perlin, Frank 1985, 'Concepts of Order and Comparison, with a Diversion on Counter Ideologies and Corporate Institutions in Late Pre-Colonial India', *Journal of Peasant Studies*, 12: 87–165.

Perotti, Elena 1974, 'Esclaves ΧΩΡΙΣ ΟΙΚΟΥΝΤΕΣ', in *Actes du Colloque 1972 sur l'esclavage, Annales Littéraires de l'Université de Besançon*, 163, Paris: Les Belles Lettres.

Petit, Paul 1972, 'L'esclavage antique dans l'historiographie soviétique', in *Actes du Colloque d'histoire sociale*, Paris: Les Belles Lettres.

Petrie, William M. 1925, *Tombs of the Courtiers and Oxyrhynkhos*, London: British School of Archaeology in Egypt.

Phillips, William D. Jr. 1985, *Slavery from Roman Times to the Early Transatlantic Trade*, Minneapolis: University of Minnesota Press.

Piacentini, Patrizia 1994, 'On the Titles of the *HqAw Hwt*', in *Grund und Boden in Altägypten: Rechtliche und sozio-ökonomische Verhältnisse*, edited by Schafik Allam, Tübingen: Selbstverlag des Herausgebers.

Pietri, Luce 1986, 'L'ordine senatorio in Gallia dal 476 alla fine del VI secolo', in *Società romana e imperio tardoantico*, I, *Istituzioni, ceti, economie*, edited by Andrea Giardina, Rome/Bari: Laterza.

Pirenne, Henri 1978, *Economic and Social History of Medieval Europe*, London: Routledge & Kegan Paul.

Pita Pico, Roger 2003, 'Negros y mulatos libres en las provincias de Girón, Socorro y Vélez durante los siglos XVII y XVIII: Nuevas formas de dependencia más allá de la libertad', *Boletín de Historia y Antigüedades*, XC, 823: 753–84.

Pleyte, Willem and Francesco Rossi 1869–76, *Papyrus de Turin*, 2 Vols. London: S. Birch.

Polanyi, Karl et al. 1957, *Trade and Market in the Early Empires: Economies in History and Theory*, Glencoe, IL: The Free Press.

Poly, Jean-Pierre 1998, 'La crise, la paysannerie libre et la féodalité', in *Les féodalités*, edited by Éric Bournazel and Jean-Pierre Poly, Paris: Presses Universitaires de France.

Portugaliae Monumenta Historica, Vol. I, *Diplomata et chartae*, 1868, Lisbon: Academia das Ciências.

Posener, Georges 1956, *Littérature et politique dans l'Égypte de la XIIe dynastie*, Bibliothèque de l' Ecole des Hautes Etudes 307, Paris: Champion.

Posener-Kriéger, Paule 1975, 'Les papyrus de Gébélein. Remarques Préliminaires', *Revue d'Égyptologie*, 27: 211–21.

Postan, Michael and Edwin Rich 1952, *The Cambridge Economic History of Europe*, II: *Trade and Industry in the Middle Ages*, Cambridge: Cambridge University Press.

Potter, Timothy 1987, *Roman Italy*, Berkeley/Los Angeles: University of California Press.

Poulantzas, Nicos 1973, *Political Power and Social Classes*, London: New Left Book.

———— 1975, *Classes in Contemporary Capitalism*, London: Verso.

Prieto, Alberto et al. 1986, *El modo de producción esclavista*, Madrid: Akal.

Puyol y Alonso, Julio (ed.) 1920, 'Crónicas Anónimas de Sahagún', *Boletín de la Real Academia de la Historia*, 76: 7–26, 111–26, 242–57, 339–56, 395–419, 512–19; 77: 51–9, 162–92.

Rathbone, Dominique W. 1981, 'The Development of the Agriculture in the *ager Cosanus* During the Roman Republic: Problems of Evidence and Interpretation', *Journal of Roman Studies*, 71: 10–23.

Rawson, Elizabeth 1976, 'The Ciceronian Aristocracy and its Properties', in *Studies in Roman Property*, edited by Moses I. Finley, Cambridge: Cambridge University Press.

Real Academia de la Historia 1863, *Cortes de los antiguos reinos de León y Castilla*, Vol. 2, Madrid: Imprenta y Estereotipia de M. Rivadeneyra.

————— 1866, *Cortes de los antiguos reinos de León y Castilla*, Vol. 3, Madrid: Imprenta y Estereotipia de M. Rivadeneyra.

Redford, Donald B. 1993, *Egypt, Canaan and Israel in Ancient Times*, Cairo: The American University in Cairo Press.

Represa, Amando 1973, 'Génesis y evolución urbana de la Zamora medieval', *Hispania*, 122: 525–46.

Reuter, Timothy 2006, *Medieval Polities and Modern Mentalities*, edited by Janet Nelson, Cambridge: Cambridge University Press.

Ricardo, David 1971 [1817], *On the Principles of Political Economy and Taxation*, London: Penguin Books.

Richards, Janet 2005, *Society and Death in Ancient Egypt: Mortuary Landscapes of the Middle Kingdom*, Cambridge: Cambridge University Press.

Rigby, Stephen H. 1995, *English Society in the Later Middle Ages: Class, Status and Gender*, London: Macmillan.

Rodgers, Daniel 2011, *Age of Fracture*, Cambridge, MA: Belknap Press.

Rodinson, Maxime 1978 [1966], *Islam and Capitalism*, Austin, TX: University of Texas Press.

Rodríguez Fernández, Justiniano (ed.) 1984, *Los fueros del reino de León*, Vol. 2, Madrid: Ediciones leonesas.

Roeder, Günther 1913, *Aegyptische Inschriften aus den königlichen Museen zu Berlin*, Leipzig: J.C. Hinrichs.

Roemer, John 1982, *A General Theory of Exploitation and Class*, Cambridge, MA: Harvard University Press.

Roll, Eric 1956, *A History of Economic Thought*, Englewood Cliffs, NJ: Prentice Hall.

Römer, Malte 1994, *Gottes- und Priesterherrschaft in Ägypten am Ende des Neuen Reiches: Ein religionsgeschichtliches Phänomen und seine sozialen Grundlagen*, Wiesbaden: Harrassowitz.

Romero, José Luis 1980, *Crisis y orden en el mundo feudoburgués*, Mexico: Siglo XXI.

Rosafio, Pasquale 1993, 'The Emergence of Tenancy and the *Precarium*', in *De Agricultura: In Memoriam Pieter Willem de Neeve*, edited by Heleen Sancisi-Weerdenburg et al., Amsterdam: Gieben.

Rose, Horace Arthur 1926, 'Fosterage in Brittany and Iceland', *Folklore*, 37(4): 398–9.

Roseberry, William 1976, 'Rent, Differentiation, and the Development of Capitalism among Peasants', *American Anthropologist*, 78(1): 45–58.

————— 1978, 'Peasants as Proletarians', *Critique of Anthropology*, 3(11): 3–18.

Rostovtzeff, Miguel 1962, *Historia social y económica del imperio romano*, Vol. 1, Madrid: Espasa-Calpe.

Roth, Ann Macy 1991, *Egyptian Phyles in the Old Kingdom: The Evolution of a System of Social Organization*, Chicago: The Oriental Institute of the University of Chicago.

Ruiz Asencio, José Manuel (ed.) 1987, *Colección documental del Archivo de la Catedral de León (775–1230)*, Vol. III (986–1031), *Colección de Fuentes y Estudios de Historia Leonesa*, León: Archivo Histórico Diocesano.

———— 1990, *Colección documental del Archivo Catedral de León (775–1230)*, Vol. IV (1032–1109), *Colección de Fuentes y Estudios de Historia Leonesa*, León: Archivo Histórico Diocesano.

Ruiz Rodríguez, Arturo et al. 1979, *Primeras sociedades de clase y modo de producción asiático*, Madrid: Akal.

Ruiz Tejado, María José 1988, 'Aprendices gremiales en Vitoria (1550–1575)', *Actas del II Congreso Mundial Vasco*, Vol. 3, *Economía, sociedad y cultura durante el Antiguo Régimen*, San Sebastián: Editorial Txertoa Argitaldaria.

Rule, John 1986, *The Labouring Classes in Early Industrial England, 1750–1850*, London: Longman Group.

Runciman, Walter G. 1989a, *A Treatise on Social Theory*, I: *The Methodology of Social Theory*, Cambridge: Cambridge University Press.

———— 1989b, *A Treatise on Social Theory*, II: *Substantive Social Theory*, Cambridge: Cambridge University Press.

———— 2011, 'Empire as a Topic in Comparative Sociology', in *Tributary Empires in Global History*, edited by Peter F. Bang and Christopher Bayly, Basingstoke/New York: Palgrave Macmillan.

Ryholt, Kim 1997, *The Political Situation in Egypt during the Second Intermediate Period c. 1800–1550 BC*, Carsten Niebuhr Institute Publications 20, Copenhagen: Museum Tuscalanum Press.

Sahlins, Marshall 1972, *Stone Age Economics*, Chicago/New York: Aldine Atherton.

———— 1974, 'L'économie tribale', in *Un domaine contesté: l'anthropologie économique*, edited by Maurice Godelier, Paris: Mouton.

Said, Edward W. 1977, *Orientalism*, London: Penguin.

Salrach, Josep Ma. 1997, 'Orígens i transformacions de la senyoria a Catalunya (segles IX–XIII)', *Revista d'Història Medieval*, 8: 25–55.

Sánchez Albornoz, Claudio 1969, *Orígenes de la burguesía en la España medieval*, Madrid: Espasa-Calpe.

———— 1976a [1924], 'Las behetrías', in *Viejos y nuevos estudios sobre las instituciones medievales españolas*, Vol. I, Madrid: Espasa-Calpe.

———— 1976b [1927], 'Muchas páginas más sobre las behetrías', in *Viejos y nuevos estudios sobre las instituciones medievales españolas*, Vol. I, Madrid: Espasa-Calpe.

———— 1977, 'Los siervos en el noroeste hispano hacia un milenio', *Cuadernos de Historia de España*, 61–2: 6–95.

———— 1978, *El régimen de la tierra en el reino asturleonés hace mil años*, Buenos Aires: Universidad de Buenos Aires/Instituto de Historia de España.

Saunders, Tom 1995, 'Trade, Towns and States', *Norwegian Archaeological Review*, 28: 31–53.

Sawer, Marian 1977, *Marxism and the Question of the Asiatic Mode of Production*, The Hague: Martinus Nijhoff.

Sayer, Derek 1987, *The Violence of Abstraction: The Analytic Foundations of Historical Materialism*, Oxford: Blackwell.

Scheidel, Walter 2005, 'Human Mobility in Roman Italy, ii: The Slave Population', *Journal of Roman Studies*, 95: 64–79.

—— 2008, 'The Comparative Economics of Slavery in the Greco-Roman World', in *Slave Systems: Ancient and Modern*, edited by Enrico Dal Lago and Constantina Katsari, Cambridge: Cambridge University Press.

Schiavone, Aldo 2000, *The End of the Past: Ancient Rome and the Modern West*, Cambridge, MA: Harvard University Press.

Schulman, Alan R. 1964, *Military Rank, Title and Organization in the Egyptian New Kingdom*, Berlin: Hessling.

—— 1988, *Ceremonial Execution and Public Rewards: Some Historical Scenes on New Kingdom Private Stelae*, Orbis biblicus et orientalis, 75, Göttingen: Vandenhoeck and Ruprecht.

Schütz, Alfred 1960, *Der sinnhafte Aufbau der sozialen Welt*, Vienna: Springer.

Scott, Alison 1986 (ed.), *Rethinking Petty Commodity Production*, Special Issue Series, *Social Analysis*, 20.

Scott, Christopher David 1976, 'Peasants, Proletarianisation and the Articulation of Modes of Production: The Case of Sugar-Cane Cutters in Northern Peru, 1940–1969', *Journal of Peasant Studies*, 3: 321–42.

Seabourne, Gwen 2003, *Royal Regulation of Loans and Sales in Medieval England*, Woodbridge: Boydell.

Seccombe, Wally 1995, *A Millenium of Family Change: Feudalism to Capitalism in Northwestern Europe*, London/New York: Verso.

Secord, Paul F. 1982, *Explaining Human Behavior: Consciousness, Human Action and Social Structure*, Beverley Hills, CA: Sage Publications.

Seidl, Erwin 1939, *Einführung in die ägyptische Rechtsgeschichte bis zum Ende des neuen Reiches*, Ägyptologische Forschungen 10, Glückstadt: Augustin.

Seidlmayer, Stephan 1990, *Gräberfelder aus dem Übergang vom Alten zum Mittleren Reich*, SAGA 1, Heidelberg: Studien zur Archäologie der Ersten Zwischenzeit.

—— 2000, 'The First Intermediate Period', in *The Oxford History of Ancient Egypt*, edited by Ian Shaw, Oxford: Oxford University Press.

Sempat Assadourian, Carlos et al. (eds.) 1973, *Modos de producción en América Latina*, Mexico: Cuadernos de Pasado y Presente 40.

Sereni, Emilio 1973a, 'La categoría de formación económico-social', in *El concepto de formación económico-social*, edited by Cesare Luporini and Emilio Sereni, Mexico: Cuadernos de Pasado y Presente 39.

———— 1973b, 'La formazione economico-sociale schiavistica', *Studi Storici*, 4: 731–59.

Serrano Delgado, José Miguel 1993, *Textos para la Historia antigua de Egipto*, Madrid: Cátedra.

Serrano, Luciano (ed.) 1906a, *Fuentes para la historia de Castilla por los PP benedictinos de Silos*, I, *Colección diplomática de San Salvador de El Moral*, Valladolid: Cuesta, editor.

———— 1906b, *Fuentes para la historia de Castilla por los PP benedictinos de Silos*, I, *Cartulario del infantado de Covarrubias*, Valladolid: Cuesta, editor.

———— 1910, *Fuentes para la historia de Castilla por los PP benedictinos de Silos*, III, *Becerro gótico de Cardeña*, Valladolid: Cuesta, editor.

———— 1930, *Cartulario de San Millán de la Cogolla*, Madrid: Junta para Ampliación de Estudios e Investigaciones Científicas.

Shaikh, Anwar 1981, 'The Poverty of Algebra', in *The Value Controversy*, edited by Ian Steedman, London: Verso.

Shapiro, Michael 1962, 'Stages of Social Development', *Marxism Today*, September 6: 282–4.

Shaw, William 1978, *Marx's Theory of History*, London: Hutchinson.

Simmel, Georg 1992 [1908], *Soziologie: Untersuchungen über die Formen der Vergesellschaftung*, edited by Otthein Rammstedt, Frankfurt: Suhrkamp.

Sirago, Vito 1971, *L'agricoltura italiana nel II sec. a.c.*, Naples: Liguori Editore.

Sivéry, Gérard 1990, *Terroirs et communautés rurales dans l'Europe Occidentale au Moyen Âge*, Lille: Presses Universitaires de Lille.

Smith, Adam 1910 [1776], *The Wealth of Nations* (with an Introduction by Prof. Edwin R.A. Seligman), Vol. I, London/New York: J.M. Dent & Sons Ltd./E.P. Duton & Co.

Smither, Paul C. 1948, 'The Report Concerning the Slave-Girl Senbet', *Journal of Egyptian Archaeology*, 34: 31–4.

Snorri Sturluson 1941–51, *Heimskringla*, ed. Bjarni Aðalbjarnarson, 3 vols., *Íslenzk fornrit*, 26–8, Reykjavík.

Sofri, Gianni 1969, *Il modo di produzione asiatico. Storia di una controversia marxista*, Turin: Einaudi.

Soiffer, Stephen and Gary Howe 1982, 'Patrons, Clients and the Articulation of Modes of Production: An Examination of the Penetration of Capitalism into Peripheral Agriculture in Northeastern Brazil', *Journal of Peasant Studies*, 9: 176–206.

Sombart, Werner 1919, *Der moderne Kapitalismus*, I, Munich/Leipzig: Duncker and Humblot.

Soriano Llopis, I. 2007, *La formación del Estado en el Valle Medio del Río Amarillo. Un acercamiento teórico y práctico a los inicios de la Edad del Bronce en China*, Barcelona: RECERCAT Dipòsit de la recerca de Catalunya. Available from: http://www.recercat .net/bitstream/handle/2072/4056/Treball%20de%20Recerca%201.pdf?sequence=1

Spalinger, Anthony 1984, 'The Will of Senimose', in *Studien zu Sprache und Religion Ägyptens Zu Ehren von Wolfhart Westendorf überreicht von seinen Freunden und Schülern*, Vol. 1, edited by Friedrich Junge, Göttingen: Hubert.

Spiegelberg, Wilhelm 1897, 'The Inscriptions', in *Six Temples at Thebes*, edited by William M.F. Petrie, London: Quaritch.

——— 1904, 'Varia. LXXVII: Zu whj-t "Stamm, Ansiedelung"', *Recueil de Travaux*, 26: 143–54.

Spike, Tamara, Lindsey Harrington et al. 2007, 'Si todo el mundo fuera Inglaterra: la teoría de Peter Laslett sobre la composición de los grupos domésticos vs. la realidad tapatía, 1821–1822', *Estudios Sociales Nueva Época*, 2: 25–37.

Spufford, Peter 1988, *Money and its Use in Medieval Europe*, Cambridge: Cambridge University Press.

Stace, Walter 1955 [1924], *The Philosophy of Hegel: A Systematic Exposition*, New York: Dover Publications.

Staerman, Elena M. 1957 [1952], 'La chute du régime esclavagiste', *Recherches internationales à la lumière du marxisme*, 2: 113–58.

Stampp, Kenneth 1956, *The Peculiar Institution: Slavery in the Ante-Bellum South*, New York: Alfred A. Knopf.

Starcenbaum, Marcelo 2011, 'El marxismo incómodo: Althusser en la experiencia de *Pasado y Presente*', Revista www.izquierdas.cl, 11: 35–53.

Starr, Chester 1958, 'An Overdose of Slavery', *The Journal of Economic History*, 18(1): 17–32.

Ste. Croix, Geoffrey E.M. de 1981, *The Class Struggle in the Ancient Greek World: From the Archaic Age to the Arab Conquests*, London: Duckworth.

Steblin-Kamenskij, Mikhail Ivanovich 1973, *The Saga Mind*, Odense: Odense University Press.

Stein, Burton 1989, *Vijayanagara*, Cambridge: Cambridge University Press.

Steindorff, Georg 1935, *Aniba: Mission archéologique de Nubie*, II, Hamburg: Druck von J.J. Augustin.

Strudwick, Nigel C. 2005, *Texts from the Pyramid Age*, Atlanta, GA: Society of Biblical Literature.

Sturlunga saga, 1946, 2 Vols., edited by Jón Johannesson et al., Reykjavík: Sturlunguútgáfan.

Suret-Canale Jean 1961, *L'Afrique Noire*, Paris: Éditions Sociales.

——— 1964, 'Les sociétés traditionnelles en Afrique noire et le concept du mode de production asiatique', *La Pensée*, 177: 19–22.

Sweezy, Paul 1976, 'A Critique', in *The Transition from Feudalism to Capitalism*, edited by Rodney Hilton, London: New Left Books.

Tacito, Cornelio 1945, *Germania. De origine situ moribus ac populis Germanorum. Liber*, edited by Angelo C. Firmani, revised by Luigi Castiglioni, Torino: Paravia.

Tan, Joseph B. 2000, *Marx, Historical Materialism and the Asiatic mode of Production*,

Master's thesis, School of Communication, Vancouver: Simon Fraser University, available from: http://www.collectionscanada.gc.ca/obj/s4/f2/dsk2/ftp01/MQ61502 .pdf

Tawney, Richard H. 1912, *The Agrarian Problem in the Sixteenth Century*, London: Longmans, Green and Co.

———— 1961 [1926], *Religion and the Rise of Capitalism*, New York: The New American Library.

Terradas i Saborit, Ignasi 1980, 'Els orígens de la institució de l'hereu a Catalunya: vers una interpretació contextual', *Quaderns de l'ICA*, 1: 64–97.

Théodoridès, Aristide 1965, 'Le Papyrus des Adoptions', *Revue Internationale des Droits de l'Antiquité*, 12: 79–142.

———— 1966, 'Le "testament" de Naunakhte', *Revue Internationale des Droits de l'Antiquité*, 13: 31–70.

———— 1968, 'Procès relatif à une vente qui devait être acquittée par la livraison d'un travail servile (Papyrus Berlin 9785)', *Revue Internationale des Droits de l'Antiquité*, 15: 39–104.

———— 1970, 'Le testament dans l'Égypte ancienne (essentiellement d'aprés le papyrus Kahoun VII; la Stéle de Senimose et le Papyrus Turin 2021)', *Revue Internationale des Droits de l'Antiquité*, 17: 117–216.

Therborn, Göran 1976, *Science, Class and Society*, London: Verso.

To Figueras, Lluís 1993, 'Señorío y familia: los orígenes del "hereu" catalán (siglos X–XII)', *Studia Historica. Historia Medieval*, 11: 57–79.

Toubert, Pierre 1990, 'La part du grand domaine dans le décollage économique de l'Occident (VIIIe–Xe siècles)', in *La Croissance agricole du Haut Moyen Âge. Chronologie, modalités, géographie*. Actes du Xe Colloque de Flaran, 1988.

———— 2006, *Europa en su primer crecimiento. De Carlomagno al año mil*, Valencia: Universitat de València.

Troy, Lana 2002 [1998], 'Resource Management and Ideological Manifestation: The Towns and Cities of Ancient Egypt', in *Development of Urbanism from a Global Perspective*, Uppsala: Uppsala Universiteit. Available from: http://www.arkeologi.uu .se/afr/projects/BOOK/Troy/troy.htm.

Turley, David 2000, *Slavery*, Oxford: Blackwell.

Turnau, Irena 1988, 'The Organization of the European Textile Industry from the Thirteenth to the Eighteenth Century', *Journal of European Economic History*, 17(3): 583–602.

Ubieto Arteta, Antonio (ed.) 1961, *Colección diplomática de Cuéllar*, Segovia: Publicaciones Históricas de la Excma. Diputación de Segovia.

Uchendu, Victor 1967, 'Some Principles of Haggling in Peasant Markets', *Economic Development and Cultural Change*, 16(1): 37–50.

Urk. I, Sethe, Kurt H. 1933, *Urkunden des Alten Reichs*, Leipzig: J.C. Hinrichs.

Urk. IV, Sethe, Kurt H. 1906–9, *Urkunden der 18. Dynastie, Urkunden des ägyptischen Altertums*, Leipzig: J.C. Hinrichs.

Vandier, Jacques 1950, *Mo'alla: La tombe d'Ankhtifi et la tombe de Sebekhotep*, Bibliothèque d'Étude, 18, Cairo: Institut Français d'Archéologie Orientale.

Varille, Alexandre 1935–8, *La Stèle de Sa-Mentou-ouser*, Mélanges Maspero Vol. 1/2, Cairo: Mémoires d'l' Institut Français d'Archéologie Orientale 66.

Vera, Domenico 1989, 'Del servus al servus quasi colonus: una altra transició', *L'Avenç*, 131: 32–7.

———— 1992–3, 'Schiavitù rurale e colonato nell'Italia imperiale', *Scienze dell'Antichità. Storia, archeologia, antropologia*, 6–7: 291–339.

Verhulst, Adriaan 1989, 'The Origins of Towns in the Low Countries and the Pirenne Thesis', *Past and Present*, 122: 3–35.

———— 1991, 'The Decline of Slavery and the Economic Expansion of the Early Middle Ages', *Past and Present*, 133: 195–203.

Verlinden, Charles 1955, *L'esclavage dans l'Europe médiévale*, 1, Bruges: Publications de la Faculté des Lettres de l' Université de Gand.

Vernant, Jean-Pierre 1965, *Mythe et pensée chez les grecs*, Paris: Maspero.

Veyne, Paul 1981, 'Le dossier des esclaves colons romains', *Revue Historique*, 265(1): 3–25.

Vidal-Naquet, Pierre 1964, 'Histoire et idéologie: Karl Wittfogel et le concept de "mode de production asiatique"', *Annales. Économies, Sociétés, Civilisations*, 19e année, 3: 531–49.

Víga-Glúms saga, 1956, *Íslenzk fornrit*, 9, edited by Jónas Kristjánsson, Reykjavík: Hið íslenzka bókmenntafélag.

Vilar, Pierre 1974, 'Réflexions sur la "crise de l'ancien type". "Inégalité des récoltes" et "sous-développement"', in *Conjoncture économique, structures sociales. Hommage à Ernest Labrousse*, Paris/The Hague: Mouton Éditeur.

Visacovsky, Sergio E. and Enrique Garguin 2009, 'Introducción', in *Moralidades, economías e identidades de clase media*, Buenos Aires: Antropofagia.

Vittinghoff, Friedrich 1960, 'Die Theorie des historischen Materialismus über den antiken Sklavenhalterstaat', *Saeculum*, 11: 89–131.

Von Beckerath, Jürgen 1965, *Untersuchungen zur politischen Geschichte der zweiten Zwischenzeit in Ägypten*, Ägyptologische Forschungen 23, Glückstadt: J.J. Augustin.

Wagner-Hasel, Beate 2003, 'Egoistic Exchange and Altruistic Gift: On the Roots of Marcel Mauss's Theory of the Gift', in *Negotiating the Gift: Pre-Modern Figurations of Exchange*, edited by Gadi Algazi, Valentin Groebner et al., Göttingen: Vandenhoeck & Ruprecht.

Wb. Erman, Adolf and Hermann Grapow 1971, *Wörterbuch der ägyptischen Sprache*, Berlin: Akademie-Verlag.

Wente, Edward F. 1990, *Letters from Ancient Egypt*, Atlanta, GA: Scholars Press.

West, Robert C. 1972, *La minería de aluvión en Colombia durante el período colonial*, Bogota: Dirección de Divulgación Cultural, Universidad Nacional de Colombia.

White, Kenneth D. 1970, *Roman Farming*, London: Thames and Hudson.

White, Stephen. 2003, 'Service for Fiefs or Fiefs for Service: The Politics of Reciprocity', in *Negotiating the Gift: Pre-Modern Figurations of Exchange*, edited by Gadi Algazi, Valentin Groebner et al., Göttingen: Vandenhoeck & Ruprecht.

Whittaker, Charles R. 1987, 'Circe's Pigs: From Slavery to Serfdom in the Later Roman World', in *Classical Slavery*, edited by Moses I. Finley, London: Frank Cass & Co.

—————— (ed.) 1993, *Land, City and Trade in the Roman Empire*, Aldershot: Ashgate Variorum Reprints.

Whittle, Jane 2000, *The Development of Agrarian Capitalism: Land and Labour in Norfolk 1440–1580*, Oxford: Clarendon Press.

Wickham, Chris 1983, 'Pastoralism and Underdevelopment in the Early Middle Ages', *Settimane di Studio dei Centro Italiano di Studi Sull'Alto Medioevo*, 31: 401–51.

—————— 1988, 'Marx, Sherlock Holmes, and Late Roman Commerce', *Journal of Roman Studies*, 78: 183–93.

—————— 1991, 'Systactic Structures: Social Theory for Historians', *Past and Present*, 132: 188–203.

—————— 1994a [1984], 'The Other Transition: From the Ancient World to Feudalism', in *Land and Power: Studies in Italian and European Social History, 400–1200*, London: British School at Rome.

—————— 1994b [1985], 'The Uniqueness of the East', in *Land and Power: Studies in Italian and European Social History, 400–1200*, London: British School at Rome.

—————— 1994c [1989], 'European Forests in the Early Middle Ages: Landscape and Land Clearance', in *Land and Power: Studies in Italian and European Social History, 400–1200*, London: British School at Rome.

—————— 1994d [1992], 'Problems of Comparing Rural Societies in Early Medieval Western Europe', in *Land and Power: Studies in Italian and European Social History, 400–1200*, London: British School at Rome.

—————— 1999, 'Poesia, prosa e memoria', in *Storiografia e poesia nella cultura medioevale*, Rome: Istituto storico italiano per il medio evo.

—————— 2005, *Framing the Early Middle Ages: Europe and the Mediterranean 400–800*, Oxford: Oxford University Press.

—————— 2008, 'Productive Forces and the Economic Logic of the Feudal Mode of Production', *Historical Materialism*, 16: 3–22.

Willems, Harco 2010, 'The First Intermediate Period and the Middle Kingdom', in *A Companion to Ancient Egypt*, edited by Alan B. Lloyd, Oxford: Wiley-Blackwell.

Wilson, John 1951, *The Burden of Egypt*, Chicago: University of Chicago Press.

Winkelmann, Friedhelm 1980, *Die östlichen Kirchen in der Epoche der christologischen Auseinandersetzungen (5.–7. Jahrhundert)*, Kirchengeschichte in Einzeldarstellungen I/6, Berlin: Evang. Verlagsants.

Winlock, Herbert E. 1922, 'Excavations at Thebes', in *The Metropolitan Museum of Art Bulletin*, Part 2: The Egyptian Expedition, MCMXXI–MCMXXII, 17(12): 19–49.

Witcher, Robert 2006, 'Settlement and Society in Early Imperial Etruria', *Journal of Roman Studies*, 96: 88–123.

Wittfogel, Karl 1981 [1957], *Oriental Despotism: A Comparative Study of Total Power*, New York: Vintage Books.

Wolpe, Harold (ed.) 1980, *The Articulation of Modes of Production: Essays from 'Economy and Society'*, London: Routledge & Kegan Paul.

Wood, Ellen Meiksins 1988, *Peasant-Citizen and Slave: The Foundations of the Athenian Democracy*, London: Verso.

———— 1999, *The Origin of Capitalism*, New York: Monthly Review Press.

Zaccagnini, Carlo 1989, 'Asiatic Mode of Production and Ancient Near East: Notes Towards a Discussion', in *Production and Consumption*, edited by Carlo Zaccagnini, Budapest: University of Budapest.

Zamora, Juan Ángel 1997, *Sobre el "modo de producción asiático" en Ugarit*, Madrid and Zaragoza: Consejo Superior de Investigaciones Científicas e Institución 'Fernando el Católico'.

Zeumer, Karolus (ed.) 1902, *Leges Visigothorum, Monumenta Germaniae Historica, Leges nationum Germanicarum*, I, Hannover: Hahn.

Zingarelli, Andrea P. 2010a, 'Introducción. Dossier: Mito, literatura y política en el Egipto antiguo', *Trabajos y Comunicaciones*, 36: 207–30.

———— 2010b, *Trade and Market in New Kingdom Egypt: Internal Socio-Economic Processes and Transformations*, Oxford: Archaeopress.

Zivie, Christiane 1976, *Giza au deuxième millénaire*, Bibliothèque d'Étude 70, Cairo: Institut Français d'Archéologie Orientale.

Index